Laurent B

Silverlight

UNLEASHED

SAMS | 800 East 96th Street, Indianapolis, Indiana 46240 USA

Silverlight 2 Unleashed

ISBN-13: 978-0-672-33014-8
ISBN-10: 0-672-330148

Library of Congress Cataloging-in-Publication Data

Bugnion, Laurent.

Silverlight 2.0 unleashed / Laurent Bugnion. – 1st ed.

p. cm.

ISBN 978-0-672-33014-8

1. Silverlight (Electronic resource) 2. Multimedia systems. 3. User interfaces (Computer systems) 4. Application software–Development. I. Title.

QA76.575.B84 2008

006.7–dc22

2008040836

Printed in the United States of America

First Printing October 2008

Trademarks

Warning and Disclaimer

Bulk Sales

Sams Publishing offers excellent discounts on this book when ordered in quantity for bulk purchases or special sales. For more information, please contact

U.S. Corporate and Government Sales

1-800-382-3419

corpsales@pearsontechgroup.com

For sales outside of the U.S., please contact

International Sales

international@pearson.com

Editor-in-Chief
Karen Gettman

Executive Editor
Neil Rowe

Development Editor
Mark Renfrow

Managing Editor
Patrick Kanouse

Project Editor
Mandie Frank

Copy Editor
Geneil Breeze

Indexers
Tim Wright
Brad Herriman

Proofreader
Deborah Williams

Technical Editors
J. Boyd Nolan
Martha Rotter

Publishing Coordinator
Cindy Teeters

Designer
Gary Adair

Compositor
Bronkella Publishing, LLC

Contents at a Glance

Table of Contents

Foreword

There are two undeniable trends in the software development world. The first is toward web style deployment of applications. The web is quickly maturing as an application delivery platform, and increasingly, web applications are seen as the right solution for many styles of applications. The second is toward richness of applications. User experience is becoming increasingly important; consumer-facing applications attracting and retaining users has never been harder and even small usability improvements often make the difference. In business applications, CIOs are realizing that if they can save even a few seconds on every transaction by making employees more effective they can save millions of dollars.

Not surprisingly, Silverlight 2 sits squarely in this sweetspot.

Silverlight 2 is a web application technology. The Silverlight runtime itself is smaller than the average Britney Spears song and is seamless to install on *any* browser (Internet Explorer, Firefox, Safari, and so on) and on *any* platform (Windows, Mac, Linux). Silverlight applications are small and fast to deploy and have zero impact on the client machine. There is no install or uninstall step for Silverlight applications, and all these applications run in a sandbox that ensure they cannot harm user machines or other applications.

Silverlight 2 enables building great user experiences. Through the power of the convergence around video, vector graphics and a powerful developer framework, Silverlight is the ideal platform for UX. Developers have full expressiveness with the power of the CLR under the hood in Silverlight. The C# and VB languages allow developers to be productive today without learning new languages and development tools. The XAML markup allows designers to use Expression and other design tools to build great transitions and animations so that applications look and feel great. All of this together enables Silverlight applications to deliver more productive experiences to end users helping them get their jobs done faster.

This book unleashes Silverlight for you. Laurent not only has a deep understanding of Silverlight, where it is now and where it is going, but he also deeply understands real world programming concerns. This book will make learning Silverlight fun.

I can't wait to see what you build with it.

Brad Abrams
Product Unit Manager
Microsoft Corporation
http://blogs.msdn.com/brada

September 2008

About the Author

Laurent Bugnion works as a senior software developer and architect in Switzerland, where he lives with his wife, Chi Meei, and his two daughters, Alise (2001) and Laeticia (2004). Originally an electronics engineer from the Engineering School of Yverdon (Switzerland), his interests quickly moved to software, and he achieved a post-graduate degree in software engineering in 1999 in the Engineering School of Rapperswil (Switzerland).

Currently, his interests are very much set on WPF, Silverlight, and other .NET 3.5 technologies, which he helped introduce, teach, and coach at Siemens for the past three years. Prior to that, he first wrote embedded C/C++, and then moved to desktop computers in Java, JavaScript, and eventually .NET (WinForms and ASP.NET). After more than 12 years spent developing various software products at Siemens, Laurent is employed since December 2008 by IdentityMine, one of the world's leading firms in WPF and Silverlight development and design.

Privately, Laurent has also been active, developing websites and web applications in HTML, JavaScript, CSS, ASP, and currently ASP.NET. He has done his best to contribute to various developers communities, first in the JavaScript newsgroups, and then in Microsoft's forums related to ASP.NET, C#, WPF, and Silverlight. He blogs regularly on http://blog.galasoft.ch and publishes articles, prototypes, and demos related to the mentioned technologies.

Laurent became a Microsoft Most Valuable Professional (MVP) in 2007 for ASP.NET and then in 2008 for Client Application Development. In 2008, he also earned an MCTS for Windows Presentation Foundation.

Dedication

How to write this book without your never-ending, ever patient support, Chi Meei… This was once again a crazy project, and I couldn't have done it without your approval and your help. By your constant support and the energy and dedication you put into shielding me from the small worries of life, you made this book possible. I love you.

To Alise and Laeticia, my two princesses. Before you appeared in my life, I thought I was happy. Now I know something big was missing. I love you both so much.

Un jour sans danser est un jour perdu
Maurice Béjart

Je ne sais pas ce qui est beau, mais je sais ce que j'aime et je trouve ça amplement suffisant.
Boris Vian

Le Poète est semblable au prince des nuées
Qui hante la tempête et se rit de l'archer;
Exilé sur le sol au milieu des huées,
Ses ailes de géant l'empêchent de marcher.
Baudelaire – L'Albatros

Acknowledgments

A book about a to-be-released technology cannot be written without strong support from the community, both within Microsoft and outside it. Making a complete list of all the people who encouraged me and helped me in this daunting task is impossible, but I want to mention and thank some people (and for some of them, friends) explicitly (and in no particular order):

- ▶ At Microsoft: Scott Guthrie, Tim Sneath, Ian Ellison-Taylor, Brad Abrams, Rob Relyea, Tim Heuer, Adam Kinney, Peter Blois, Unni Ravindranathan, Joe Stegman, Mike Harsh, Karen Corby, Kathy Kam, Corrina Barber, Beatriz Costa, James Clarke, John Gossmann, Karsten Januszewski, Adam Nathan, Christian Schormann, Mark Feinholz, Ted Hu, Jeff Wilcox, Justin Angel, and many others from the Dev Div, for building the stuff my dreams are made of (and for writing about it!). I've seen the "new Microsoft" at work, and I like it!

- ▶ In the Silverlight and WPF community: Josh Smith, Jonathan Russ, Brennon Williams, Karl Shifflett, Marlon Grech, Corrado Cavalli, Grant Hinkson, Nathan Dunlap, Josh Wagoner, Robby Ingebretsen, Kevin Moore, Shawn Wildermuth, Dave Campbell, Jon Galloway, Grant Hinkson, John Papa, and all the WPF Disciples for teaching me all I know (or so it feels).

- ▶ The team at Sams and especially Neil Rowe, Mark Renfrow, Mandie Frank, and Geneil Breeze for their patience and support for this first-time author.

- ▶ The whole MVP community and especially the Client Application Development members, for welcoming me and making me feel worth it.

- ▶ All my friends, online and offline, who had to bear with me being either working on the book or talking about the book or thinking about the book or, you know, sleeping (and probably dreaming about the book).

A *very special thanks* to Brennon Williams who gave me such invaluable comments and advice; to J. Boyd Nolan for reviewing and editing, and for converting this book's examples from C# in VB.NET; to Adam Nathan who advised me about the book's outline before I even started writing it; to Shawn Wildermuth for pulling me out of many a technical hole; to Peter Blois for listening patiently to my bug reports and proposing solutions; to Tim Heuer and Adam Kinney, for clearly showing that Silverlight is more than just a job to them; to all the Silverlight Insiders for the always interesting and often life-saving discussions.

Software engineering is a passion. To all of you whom I learn from everyday, and to whom I try to teach a little through my blog, my site, or in conferences, thank you for making this more than a job: a way of life.

We Want to Hear from You!

As the reader of this book, *you* are our most important critic and commentator. We value your opinion and want to know what we're doing right, what we could do better, what areas you'd like to see us publish in, and any other words of wisdom you're willing to pass our way.

You can email or write me directly to let me know what you did or didn't like about this book—as well as what we can do to make our books stronger.

Please note that I cannot help you with technical problems related to the topic of this book, and that due to the high volume of mail I receive, I might not be able to reply to every message.

When you write, please be sure to include this book's title and author as well as your name and phone or email address. I will carefully review your comments and share them with the author and editors who worked on the book.

E-mail: webdev@samspublishing.com

Mail: Neil Rowe
        Executive Editor
        Sams Publishing
        800 East 96th Street
        Indianapolis, IN 46240 USA

Reader Services

Visit our website and register this book at www.informit.com/title/9780672330148 for convenient access to any updates, downloads, or errata that might be available for this book.

Introduction

With the release of Windows Presentation Foundation (a new graphical user interface framework for Windows desktop applications) in 2006 and of Silverlight in 2008, client application development took a turn for the best. Microsoft boldly decided to abandon some concepts and technologies that had been used since the first release of Windows and to do something new and better. While it sometimes seems difficult to keep up with the pace of change imposed on software developers, this one is really worth it. Microsoft's bet on Silverlight and WPF is huge, and it cannot fail. These technologies represent the future of client application development.

Because it runs on multiple platforms in a web browser plug-in that will soon be available on most of the rich clients accessing the Internet, because it can be deployed as easily as any web content and be served from any web server without additional infrastructure, and because of the rich graphic interfaces it allows to be built and the amazingly easy connectivity to remote services that it offers, Silverlight will be a major player in the world of *rich interactive applications* (*RIA*). Silverlight is also a gateway to Windows Presentation Foundation, the client application technology that represents the future of Microsoft Windows programming for desktop computers.

In a World Wide Web where Adobe Flash currently has a leading edge, Silverlight represents much more than just an alternative: It is the .NET way! Every .NET programmer will feel at home with Silverlight, because the libraries, the programming languages (C#, VB.NET, Ruby, Python), and the development environment (Visual Studio, Expression Studio) are the same. In addition, new concepts developed and refined in Windows Presentation Foundation are made available to Silverlight programmers, such as data binding, separation of behavior and looks, lookless controls that can be styled and templated at will in powerful design tools such as Expression Blend, a rich animation system, media integration, and so on. XAML, the new XML-based Application Markup Language developed by Microsoft, can be leveraged as a bridge between developers and designers to enable new workflows.

This book is not and was never intended to be a complete reference of the Silverlight platform. Honestly, I am not even sure that you need a book for this: The Internet is at your disposal and has a better, more complete, and more actual reference base than any book can ever offer. No, this book is here to help you discover why programming is fun and why Silverlight is even more fun, and to contaminate you with the Silverlight virus. Complex concepts are explained in simple terms, with many hands-on demos and figures so that beginners as well as advanced developers quickly will feel at home.

About Code in This Book

We tried to keep formatting as consistent as possible throughout the book and to make the code look like it does in Visual Studio. The code is color coded to help you work faster and recognize key concepts in XAML, C#, JavaScript, and HTML in Studio and in Expression Blend.

The source code lines are only numbered where it is relevant, for example, when the text makes explicit reference to a line number.

The whole source code for this book is available online at www.galasoft.ch/SL2U/Code. For C# code, a translation in VB.NET is also available, courtesy of this book's technical editor, J. Boyd Nolan.

One Year Older

I started working on this book in September 2007, and I am now exactly one year older. Professionally speaking, it has been the most interesting year of my life. Since I started working as a developer in 1996, I have worked with many client technologies and programming languages, including C, VB, Java, HTML, CSS, JavaScript, ASP.NET, Windows Forms and finally Windows Presentation Foundation and Silverlight. In all these years, I have never been as excited about a new programming platform. Writing a book is hard, and it's a lot of work. But it was also fun and so interesting that I always felt right doing it. If I had to do it again, I would sign without hesitation. And now that it's going to be published, I can't wait to see what you, the reader, will create in Silverlight. Software has much to do with art, and Silverlight is the richest palette you can imagine. So grab the book and your computer, start coding and designing, and show the world what you can do. I will be waiting.

Happy coding!

Laurent

CHAPTER 1

Introducing Silverlight

It all started when Microsoft presented its revolutionary user interface (UI) framework, *Windows Presentation Foundation*, to an enthusiastic crowd of graphics designers, software developers, and businessmen in March 2006 at the new MIX conference in Las Vegas. Microsoft also added one session about a lesser-known technology with the rather barbarian name *Windows Presentation Foundation Everywhere, or WPF/E*. There was nothing much to see yet, but the abstract was enticing: "With WPF/E you'll be able to build rich, interactive experiences that run in major Web browsers on major platforms as well as on mobile devices."

A little more than a year later, at the second edition of the same MIX conference, Scott Guthrie (general manager at Microsoft, responsible for most of the .NET teams) climbed on stage and gave the crowd an amazing software demonstration. The barbarian WPF/E was gone; in its place was Silverlight (see Figure 1.1).

A bright new logo revolved on the screens. Gradients and animations were all over the place. Planes flew over the web browser's window, connecting US cities while Scott was planning his next trips; a chess application let the browser's JavaScript engine play against .NET, demonstrating without any doubt the superior power of the compiled .NET application over JavaScript's interpreted code. Yes, the browser was running .NET!—not only in Internet Explorer but also on Firefox! And yes, even on a Macintosh computer.

It was an intense hour! Later that day, more demos of the new Expression Encoder were presented, which allows users to produce movies and run them in the web browser, after having copied them to a streaming (or to a nonstreaming) web server. Even better, with the Expression Encoder you can now change the look and feel of the video player completely, basing your work on predefined templates, but also changing everything from colors to shapes in Expression Blend.

FIGURE 1.1   Microsoft Silverlight logo

NOTE

All the sessions presented at MIX 2006, 2007 and 2008 can be viewed online at http://sessions.visitmix.com.

These first demos were only the start of an amazing three days packed with Silverlight content. In a little less than a year, Silverlight had made it from little-known side attraction to major technology with a huge potential.

Where Does Silverlight Come From?

A little history can be interesting to understand where Silverlight came from, and how it is positioned among the many UI technologies available today. Depending on your past experience, you may be well aware of the facts presented in the next sections. In that case, feel free to skip ahead (the next interesting section for you will probably be "Running on Multiple Platforms"). If you don't want to skip ahead, or if you feel like refreshing your memory, keep reading as this section and the next few sections fast forward from the antiquity of the World Wide Web to the magic of today.

Web pages have been around for a long time. In fact, HTML was presented to the world as early as 1992. (You know the old line about dog years being equal to seven human years? Well, 1992 in computer years is, like, Middle Age for humans!) Of course, HTML was limited in the beginning. Web pages were simple, composed mostly of text and hypertext (the most revolutionary idea of HTML, and the origin of the name *Hypertext Markup Language*).

Very quickly, however, the inventors of HTML saw the need for richer content to be made available in web pages. The first step in that direction was the invention of the IMG tag, allowing images to be placed inline. The basis for richer content was there, and the first popular web browser, Mosaic, displayed these pages.

Automating Web Pages with JavaScript

The next big step forward in the quest for rich content was the addition of a JavaScript engine running in the web browser.

This programming language (added in 1995 to the Netscape web browser, and then in 1996 in Microsoft Internet Explorer) enabled a much richer interaction with the user. Earlier, the only possible user action was through a *postback* to the web server, meaning that any data entered by the user had to be sent back to the server for handling, and the result was returned as a *response*. Obviously, this model was slow, especially at the time of dial-up connections.

With JavaScript, it was possible to provide a basic treatment of data on the client directly, without postback. A first

> **NOTE**
>
> There are many names for this scripting language, from Netscape's JavaScript to Microsoft's JScript to the standard ECMAScript. In this book, the term "JavaScript" will be used without distinction.

> **WARNING**
>
> Client-side validation can easily be side tracked, and it is *always* necessary to validate data on the server too!

obvious use for this client-side technology was a prevalidation of data, making sure that the user was not sending useless information to the server, wasting bandwidth and valuable server time. With JavaScript enabled, errors could be caught early, and faulty data would never leave the client. Of course, as soon as a web server interaction was needed, for example, to retrieve data, for complex calculations, to authenticate users, and so on, a postback was needed. This model still prevails in many websites even today.

Cascading Style Sheets

Another big step forward in the creation of rich web content has been the creation of *Cascading Style Sheets (CSS)*. Finally a separation of content and layout was made possible. The look and feel of a web page could be extracted from the page itself and governed by the use of rules placed in external files. This model has many advantages:

▶ The responsibilities can easily be shared by various teams, depending on their skills. Graphics designers can be in charge of the look, developers of the functionality, while marketing is in charge of the content.

▶ In smaller projects, the developer can concentrate on the page's structure and functionality first, and create the look later, after the content is fully known. This way of working is much more efficient than doing everything at the same time.

▶ The page's look can be changed easily without touching the page itself.

▶ Same styles can be reused over and over again without having to rewrite the code. Classes can be located in a central location and *referenced* anywhere. In fact, it's even possible to have styles on a central server and be used on other web servers, related or not.

As CSS became more and more sophisticated, the pages became more and more beautiful, to a point where the aspect of the pages, in some cases, becomes as important as the content itself. One can argue endlessly whether that's a good thing (after all, content is what users are really looking for, isn't it?), but if you can choose between boring content and beautiful content, surely the beauty will make the experience more pleasurable.

> **WARNING**
>
> Although CSS allows creating beautiful pages, it also allows creating ugly looks. Unfortunately, the technology has no taste; only the developer/designer has some (or hasn't any). That's true for Silverlight (and any UI technology) as well.

Progressing to DHTML

As the JavaScript and CSS engines became more advanced, some interaction was made possible between them. *DHTML (Dynamic HTML)* was born. Actually, DHTML is not a technology; it's a combination of JavaScript and CSS used in the context of HTML.

Using JavaScript as a programming language, it is possible to access elements of the page itself (content and style), and to modify them. Since this is client-side technology, no interaction with the server is required for this kind of effect.

Because CSS allows the setting of an element's opacity, it is possible to create fade-in/ fade-out effects. With the possibility to set an element's position in an absolute manner, JavaScript allows you to move an element across the screen. In addition to "just" adding some kind of intelligence and good looks to the web pages, the interaction between CSS and JavaScript enabled the creation of richer, smoother web pages.

Although this all sounds nice, DHTML is rather limited:

▶ Opacity is not supported in all browsers, and the ones that support it don't use a standard syntax, making it kind of a maintenance nightmare.

▶ Moving elements across the screen can only be done at limited speed and is not as smooth as you would want.

▶ It is impossible to rotate elements. If you want to show a rotated button, you need to simulate this using multiple images, and the effect will not be smooth.

▶ Text (such as a title, in a logo, etc...) can only be rotated by using images. In that case, the localization becomes a nightmare, because you need to translate each image in each language you want to support.

▶ The "hit test area" for any element is always square. In other words, even if you have an image of a round button with a transparent background, you may activate the action even if you click outside the round area. The mouse cursor will turn to a hand even though the mouse is still on the transparent area.

Thankfully, Silverlight corrects all these shortcomings, and since it can be "blended" among HTML elements, it offers a real possibility to graphically enrich a web page.

Communicating in a Richer Way with AJAX

In addition to enabling DHTML, JavaScript brought a huge improvement to client-server communication, and to creating a smoother user experience: *Asynchronous JavaScript And XML (AJAX)*, a cumbersome name for a great technology. In short, AJAX allows JavaScript to send a request to the web server, and to get the response without the web page being refreshed. Instead of using the normal postback mechanism, the whole communication occurs in the background, and the user doesn't notice it.

> **TIP**
>
> AJAX is not very easy to program. Like you will see later, Silverlight 2 offers a great deal of improvement in this area too and makes background communication much easier.

With this technology, the user can get additional information from the server without losing the context he is working in. The user experience is also much smoother, because new information gets loaded without the "traumatic" reloading of the page and the temporary white screen caused by it.

Using Third-Party Plug-Ins

With the limitations of DHTML, various third-party additions to the web browser have been created with the explicit intent to enhance the user experience. The most notorious technologies are probably Java applets, ActiveX controls, and Flash applications. This section reviews the advantages and shortcomings of these technologies to understand better how Silverlight compares.

> **NOTE**
>
> An annoying shortcoming of all the technologies described in this section is that it is impossible to place HTML content in front of a third-party plug-in. The Java applet, ActiveX control, or Flash application will always be in the top level. Silverlight corrects this problem and makes it possible to have HTML content blending with Silverlight content.
>
> Also, the HTML–JavaScript–Silverlight interaction is better than with any of these older technologies. The boundaries are thinner than ever.

Using Java Applets

Java applets were extraordinarily popular for a short time and then became unpopular. While some web pages still use the Java technology, their number is decreasing. The main problem with Java is that the runtime is very slow to start. When you load a page with a Java applet on it, the initial loading time makes it a painful experience.

On the plus side, Java is a great programming language. It paved the way for .NET, and many of the best features of C# are greatly inspired by the Java language. It also enables advanced graphical effects, such as the famous ripple effect.

Limited Java-to-JavaScript and JavaScript-to-Java communication is possible. However, the interface used for this communication is not supported by all the web browsers that Java runs into. Also, the syntax is not easy to learn, and communication is awkward.

Java makes it possible to open alternative communication ways to the web
server. For example, it enables the server
to "talk" directly to the client, which is
impossible with classic web communication. While this can be a huge techno-
logical advantage in certain scenarios, it

> **NOTE**
>
> Every book about web technology should make one thing clear: Java and JavaScript have strictly no relationship. When you program JavaScript, you do *not* program Java.

can also, under certain circumstances, represent a security threat. Because of this, the
acceptance of Java applets by big, security-sensitive corporations has been slow and has
pretty much "killed" Java in the web browser.

Using ActiveX Controls

When Microsoft introduced the COM technology in 1993, it also made it possible to
create so-called ActiveX controls, "packing" pieces of software and communicating with
the external world using the COM interfaces. With this, it is possible to develop controls
using classic Windows technology (including fast C++ code), and to place it in a web
browser. It is even possible to have some limited interaction with JavaScript and through
this to the web page.

The major shortcoming of ActiveX is that it uses an obsolete, almost 15-year-old technology. Also, ActiveX controls can only be used in Internet Explorer on Windows.

Using Flash Applications

Adobe Flash is probably the most
popular third-party plug-in currently
available. On the plus side, it allows
advanced graphical effects, and it's not
rare to find websites programmed
entirely in Flash. While Flash content is
often called "Flash movies," it's probably
fairer to call them "applications."

> **WARNING**
>
> Programming a website entirely in Flash (or in Silverlight) is not a good idea. Many platforms (especially mobile phones, PDAs, and so on) do not allow accessing such sites (or only in a limited manner). This type of technology should only be used to enhance the content of a website, not to replace it completely.

Flash's major shortcoming is that it is
difficult to program. A (commercial)
editor is needed to create the front-end
user interface. Additionally, the code-
behind can only be programmed in a
language called ActionScript, which is a
subset of JavaScript. The fact that Flash
has been created primarily for graphics
designers makes it difficult for software
developers to use the tools and to create
compelling content and functionality.

> **NOTE**
>
> Microsoft doesn't advertise Silverlight as a Flash "killer." This strategy would probably be doomed anyway, considering how many Flash designers there are, and how much Flash content is available online. Since both technologies can run safely side-by-side, there is really no need to start a religion war about which is the best!

A limited interaction between the Flash application and the containing HTML page is possible through JavaScript. Some interaction between the Flash application and the containing HTML page is possible through JavaScript.

Running on Multiple Platforms

One important factor when you develop a third-party web technology is to run it on as many platforms as possible. The Web is, by definition, ubiquitous, and it is not rare to find Internet-enabled devices of every shape and power. Adobe Flash is a good example of this: The plug-in is available for a great number of browsers on a great number of operating systems. This makes Flash a powerful platform, and Microsoft understands the need for Silverlight to run in multiple browsers too.

As said earlier, at the time of this writing, the Silverlight runtime is available for Internet Explorer and Firefox on Windows, and for Firefox and Safari on Macintosh. A version for Linux is in preparation. The real challenge is to offer consistent interfaces on all the

> **NOTE**
>
> In order to run Silverlight on many platforms in a consistent way, Microsoft is also collaborating with Novell and the makers of the open source .NET framework "Mono."

platforms on which Silverlight runs. So far, this goal has been very successful, and is a great achievement in the quest for a unified web environment.

Some prototypes of Silverlight for smartphones have also been presented, but not much is known about what will be supported on these limited devices. A first version of Silverlight for mobile phone (running on Windows Mobile and also on Nokia mobile phones) should be released by the end of 2008. This should support Silverlight 1 applications, including video.

Because Silverlight runs on so many platforms, some limitations in the functionality (compared to the full .NET platform) are unavoidable. Many factors must be considered:

- The goal is to keep the runtime small, so that it can easily be installed over Internet connections. The goal in the foreseeable future is to keep it under (or equal to) 5MB. When you compare to the size of the full .NET runtime (and even if you remove all the server-side bits), it's obvious that not everything can be implemented.

- Features requiring a lot of hardware acceleration (especially 3D animations) will probably be too hard to implement consistently on multiple platforms (not even mentioning small limited mobile devices).

> **TIP**
>
> Hardware acceleration is the process through which some of the complex calculations are executed by hardware processors specializing in graphics (as opposed to software). Hardware graphic processors are much faster than anything that software can calculate.

- Various platforms use various underlying graphic technologies, and some of these technologies may not allow all the desired effects. It's already pretty amazing to see how consistent the implementation is on both Windows and Macintosh. For Silverlight to be viable, it is imperative that it remain totally compatible on all supported platforms and browsers.

All these reasons create a lot of intense discussions to decide what will make it to Silverlight and what won't. It will be interesting to observe the development of the platform!

> **TIP**
>
> Microsoft is listening to you! Don't hesitate to contact evangelists and other Silverlight developers, either through the Silverlight forums (http://silverlight.net/forums), or through their blogs (check the section titled "Reading Silverlight-related blogs" in Chapter 24, "Silverlight: Continuing the Journey"). Let them know what you do with the technology, and what your expectations are. Just like third-party developers influenced the way WPF is growing, the same process is true for Silverlight! Let them hear your voice!

Making the Web Application Secure

Security in web applications is a huge challenge. Even though Microsoft has more often than any other company been the target of virulent criticisms because some of their applications or operating systems were not secure enough, it's fair to say that any popular web technology is exposed and has had security issues (Java, Firefox, the Linux operating system, the new Google Chrome web browser and many others have all been the target of attacks).

Microsoft is taking the security of Silverlight-based applications very seriously. Silverlight applications run in a "sandbox" that limits the functionality of the application and protects the computer it runs on against attacks. Every time a feature is allowed by the sandbox, it is carefully tested to make sure that the change doesn't present a hole for a potential attack.

If humanity was intrinsically good, programming would be easier, but of course, security is not just a matter of attackers, it also has a lot to do with bad code, memory corruptions, and so on. Thankfully, the .NET programming platform (the so-called "managed code") is a secure way of programming. Unlike older unmanaged C++ code, many bugs are eliminated already at the source by the much safer managed programming languages. Memory corruption is almost impossible; memory is automatically freed by the *Garbage collector* when it is not used anymore, making memory leaks much more infrequent.

Obviously it would be naive to believe that Silverlight will never be attacked, or that Silverlight applications will never crash. However, thanks to the experience gathered by the .NET teams, thanks to the managed programming languages, and thanks to the extra attention invested by Microsoft into that matter, Silverlight should provide a very safe environment.

Introducing Silverlight.net

The community website http://silverlight.net contains a collection of valuable information about Silverlight, including quickstarts, samples, tutorials, and so on. Maybe the most interesting section is the gallery, available at http://silverlight.net/community/communitygallery.aspx.

Here you will find a lot of samples, made by Microsoft and third-party developers. This is a good starting point to get an idea of what Silverlight is capable of. Currently, the gallery is divided into two subsections: Silverlight 1.0 (with JavaScript) and Silverlight 2 (with .NET). However, if you install Silverlight 2 (as we recommend), you can still execute older applications.

What Do You Need to Run Silverlight?

Silverlight is an add-on to the web browser. It gets installed separately and adds functionality to your web pages. It is currently available for Internet Explorer and Firefox on the Windows XP and Vista operating systems; it is also available for Firefox and Safari on the Macintosh. At the time of this writing, a version for Linux is in preparation, following a historical agreement between Microsoft and Novell.

To run Silverlight applications, you need a compatible web browser. When you point a Silverlight-capable web browser to a web page with Silverlight content, you get a small Install Microsoft Silverlight icon, as shown in Figure 1.2, instead of the Silverlight content.

FIGURE 1.2   The Install Microsoft Silverlight icon

- ▶ Click on the icon to be taken to a Microsoft web page where you can download and install the Silverlight runtime on your PC.

- ▶ After installing Silverlight in Internet Explorer, you don't even need to restart your web browser. In Firefox, you might have to, but it's not that big a deal.

Alternatively, you can install Silverlight 2 from http://silverlight.net/GetStarted.

WARNING

If you worked with Silverlight before and you already installed a version older than the one required by the current application, you will also see the "Install Microsoft Silverlight" button.

You can check the Silverlight version by right-clicking on any Silverlight application, choosing the Silverlight Configuration menu, and selecting the About tab.

Updating Your Runtime—Automatically

Once the runtime is installed, the Silverlight content will automatically be started. Also, a version check will happen when Silverlight is started; if a newer version is available, you can choose to install it automatically. This can be set up in the Silverlight configuration dialog by following these steps:

> **NOTE**
>
> Silverlight gets installed only once, and then runs in Firefox or IE (on the Mac, on Safari and Firefox) with the same runtime. If you change the options in Firefox, it will be valid in the other browser installed on the same PC too!

1. Navigate to http://silverlight.net/samples/1.0/Page-Turn/default.html. This starts one of the earlier Silverlight demos created by Microsoft: The PageTurn sample application.

> **TIP**
>
> You can turn pages by clicking and dragging your mouse on the bottom-right corner of the photo album. If you click on the small open book icon on the bottom right, you see a list of thumbnails.

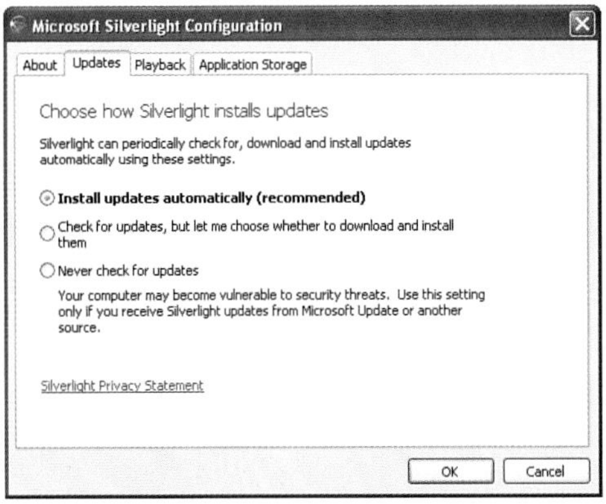

2. Right-click on the Silverlight application and choose Silverlight Configuration.

3. Click on the Updates tab.

4. Choose the options you want (see Figure 1.3).

FIGURE 1.3   Silverlight configuration

Trying Silverlight Demos

The cool thing with Silverlight is that it's so easy to deploy: Simply put the files on a web server, and anyone in the world with a Silverlight-capable browser can see the applications.

The applications developed by Microsoft for demo purposes are also available online. Additionally, third-party developers can also publish their own sample applications to the Silverlight.net website. As mentioned previously Microsoft used two demo applications when they first introduced Silverlight to the public: the Chess application and the Silverlight Airline sample.

Playing Chess Against Silverlight

At the time of writing, the Chess demo (see Figure 1.4) is not available yet for Silverlight 2. You can, however, see a video illustrating this application at http://on10.net/blog/tina/ Microsoft-Silverlight-Chess. Also, keep checking the Silverlight.net gallery where the demo and its source code should be posted soon.

FIGURE 1.4   Chess application

In this application, you get a chance to play against the machine: The Human button is selected on the bottom. On the top, you can choose to play against another human (boooooring), against JavaScript (remember, JScript is Microsoft's name for its implementation of the technology) or against .NET.

The implementation for the chess engine is exactly the same in JavaScript and in .NET. So the most interesting thing to do in that application is to let JavaScript play against .NET:

1. On top, make sure that the .NET button is selected.

2. On the bottom, select the JScript button.

3. Observe how both engines are playing against each other. The most interesting data is the number of nodes per second calculated by each engine. This is an indication of how fast each engine can process data. Typically, .NET calculates approximately 1,000 times faster than JavaScript!

Running this application always leads to the same result: .NET wins over JavaScript, because it is just so much faster. This is a good proof (if it was needed) of some of the advantages we will encounter when we use .NET for advanced calculations instead of the JavaScript engine.

Planning Your Trips with the Airline Application

The airline application shown in Figure 1.5 was also shown on stage at MIX07 and presents what could be an airline reservation system in the (near) future. Here too, the demo is not yet available for Silverlight 2 at the time of writing but should be updated soon in the Silverlight.net gallery. A video showing this application is available at http://on10.net/blogs/tina/Microsoft-Silverlight-Airlines.

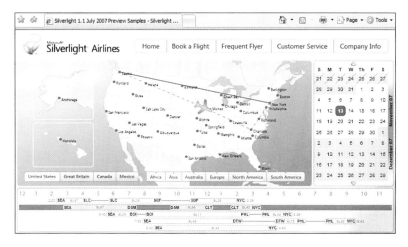

FIGURE 1.5   Airline application

1. Click and hold the departure city. Then, still holding down the button, move the cursor to the target city. You can release the mouse now.

2. Select a date for your trip in the Calendar on the right.

3. The system calculates a number of possible itineraries for your trip. They are shown under the map. Pass your mouse cursor over one itinerary to see it drawn on the screen, and to see a small plane fly from city to city.

This example is interesting, because strictly speaking, Silverlight doesn't offer new functionality here. Online reservation systems are already available today. However, the user interface is better with Silverlight and makes the user experience better and more attractive.

> **NOTE**
>
> Thanks to the goodness of vector-based graphics, you can also resize the window and note how the whole user interface gets resized to fit the screen.

DeepZooming into the Hard Rock Café

At MIX08, probably the most exciting demo was given by the Hard Rock Café and its memorabilia collection of rock souvenirs: How would you like to be able to see high resolution pictures of all the souvenirs normally exposed in various Hard Rock Cafés around the globe (see Figure 1.6)? Even better, how would you like to be able to select them by artist, year, type, and so on? And the most awesome feature of all: Zoom smoothly into the pictures until you are able to see every detail, like small scratches or a handwritten dedication on a guitar! Navigate to http://memorabilia.hardrock.com to try it yourself.

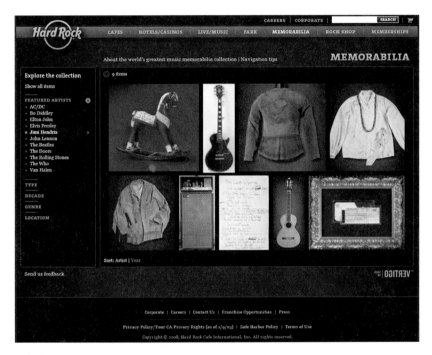

FIGURE 1.6   Hard Rock Memorabilia

This application is enabled by a feature introduced in Silverlight 2, named DeepZoom. A very high resolution picture is prepared by a tool and divided in multiple, lower-resolution pictures. A Silverlight control is loading these images dynamically (according to the level of zoom chosen) and displays them. Additionally, you can pan the image simply by clicking and dragging the mouse, with a lifelike movement. All these seemingly very complex features are made rather easy thanks to Silverlight 2 (though one should not underestimate the value of the developers and designers having created this application!).

Finding More Demos

Many more samples and demos are available online. Make sure to browse through the Silverlight.net gallery and play with demos to see what Silverlight can do at http://silverlight.net/community/communitygallery.aspx.

What Do You Need to Develop Silverlight?

The term "Silverlight" also qualifies the programming platform, which is developed in parallel to .NET 3.5. Since Silverlight is in development now, not all the .NET classes are available yet. In fact, some of them will never make it to Silverlight, as mentioned earlier. However, because the .NET basis is stable now, we can expect to see big improvements in Silverlight in the coming months as Microsoft releases new versions.

We are not going to create standalone applications here. We will only create applications embedded in a web page and unable to run on their own. The nice thing with this way of programming is that distributing (deploying) your application is as easy as copying some files to your web server. If you are adding Silverlight content to an existing web page, you probably already have a web server. If you don't, you will need to get web server space eventually to publish your application. During development, however, you will be able to use the web server IIS built in the Windows operating system. Even better, if you use Expression Blend or Visual Studio 2008, starting a web application is as easy as pressing F5! You learn more about deploying web applications in Chapter 7, "Deploying to a Web Page."

> **WARNING**
>
> Even though the Silverlight runtime is available for multiple platforms, the development environment described in this book (programming, designing, compiling, debugging) is available only for the Windows operating system. There is also a development environment for Linux (Moonlight).

Developing Silverlight can be done with just a text editor. Notepad (or its Mac equivalent) is an option, seriously. You can write your XAML markup (a new programming language we will introduce later) in there, and then run it in the web browser to see the result. However, developing this way can be painful. Fortunately, we now have the support of great tools to make that experience a real pleasure. The best place to start and install the development environment for Silverlight is from http://silverlight.net/GetStarted.

Expression Studio

When Microsoft announced WPF, it also gave us a new suite of tools named the Expression Studio. Included are three important tools for the Silverlight developer: Expression Design, Expression Blend, and Expression Encoder.

> **NOTE**
>
> Expression Studio also contains Expression Web (used to develop web pages) and Expression Media, a tool used to manage media collections (pictures, videos, and so on).

This book uses these tools to create Silverlight content. Expression Blend is studied more in detail in Chapters 4, "Expressing Yourself with Expression Blend," and 6, "Blending a Little More" (and throughout the book). This great tool is located at the border between designers and developers and is used by both professions. It is an almost unavoidable tool when you create WPF and/or Silverlight content. Unfortunately, at the time of writing there is no free edition of Expression Blend. A fully functional demo version can be downloaded from the Microsoft Expression website at www.microsoft.com/expression.

In addition to Expression Blend, we will
be using Expression Encoder in this
book. This application can also be
downloaded from the Microsoft
Expression website.

> **TIP**
>
> If you are a MSDN subscriber, Expression
> Blend is included in the premium edition of
> MSDN, so you don't need to purchase it.

Expression Design can be used to create
XAML-based "assets" (pieces of design). Later, you can import these elements in your
Silverlight application. We will talk about this in Chapter 24.

Visual Studio 2008

Additionally, we will enjoy a better programming tool than Notepad: The powerful
Integrated Development Environment (IDE) Visual Studio 2008 is the tool of choice to
program Silverlight applications. In this book, we will use mostly Visual Studio 2008 and
Expression Blend to program Silverlight applications. A fully functional 90-day demo
version can be downloaded at http://msdn.microsoft.com/en-us/vs2008/products/
cc268305.aspx.

In addition to Visual Studio, you must also install the Silverlight tools available from the
"Get Started" page at http://silverlight.net/GetStarted/.

You learn more about Visual Studio 2008 in Chapters 9, "Understanding .NET" and 10,
"Progressing with .NET" about .NET, and
in following chapters, where we will use
these tools to create C# code-behind.

Microsoft released so-called Express
editions of Visual Studio. Each Express
edition presents a limited set of features
targeted at a specific type of software
development (for example, web applications, C#, VB.NET, and so on). These
limited editions are free to download
and install. According to Microsoft, you
will be able to use these Express editions
to program Silverlight. At the time of
writing, however, an exact release date
was not public.

> **NOTE**
>
> Even though Silverlight supports VB.NET and
> other managed languages, the examples in
> this book are written in C#. I want to person-
> ally apologize for this to all the VB.NET devel-
> opers interested in Silverlight. A translated
> version of the source code is available on
> the book's website at www.galasoft.ch/
> SL2U/Code.
>
> In addition to C# and VB.NET, Silverlight
> supports the so-called *dynamic languages*
> IronRuby and IronPython.

Reading the Documentation

This book does not contain a full reference documentation about Silverlight but will give
you a great head start in this technology. In addition, you will use the Silverlight documentation, available in various forms.

Browsing the Online Reference

The official Silverlight reference is found on MSDN (Microsoft Developer Network) online. You can start at http://msdn.microsoft.com/en-us/library/bb404710(VS.95).aspx (for Silverlight 1.0) and http://msdn.microsoft.com/en-us/library/bb404700(VS.95).aspx (for Silverlight 2).

Finding More Documentation

With the number of classes available in the .NET framework (and even in the Silverlight subset), and with the number of members that each class contains, a comprehensive documentation is a key factor when you program against this framework. Microsoft released a Silverlight 2 Software Development Kit (SDK). It contains technical documentation, libraries and tools to help you in your Silverlight experience.

1. Navigate to the Get Started page at http://silverlight.net/GetStarted

2. Scroll down until you see the link to Microsoft Silverlight 2 SDK. Follow this link and download the SDK setup file.

3. Execute the file "silverlight_sdk.exe" you just downloaded. This will extract the content to C:\Program Files\Microsoft SDKs\Silverlight\v2.0

4. For more information about the SDK, technical documentation, links to external resources, etc., check the "Welcome" page. You find it in your Start menu, under "All Programs / Microsoft Silverlight 2 SDK".

The Silverlight documentation is also available as a compiled HTML file that can be installed locally (see Figure 1.7). The download link is on the SDK welcome page.

FIGURE 1.7   Silverlight documentation

The Search tab allows you easy access to a specific topic. The documentation contains many interesting topics, and it is absolutely worth browsing through it.

Learning with Tutorials

Many tutorial websites are available for WPF, Silverlight, and Blend. The community website Silverlight.net has already been mentioned. Another exciting and innovative site is the Nibbles Tutorials website at www.nibblestutorials.net.

This website does an amazing job of presenting and teaching the technology. Using small, bite-sized tutorials, the Nibbles website allows you to test some of the knowledge acquired in this book.

Additionally, the website's author, Celso Gomes, is a talented graphics designer working for Microsoft, and his tutorials give you the designer's point of view on Silverlight (while this book gives you the developer's point of view).

> **WARNING**
>
> The "Nibbles" website doesn't display any content if Silverlight is not installed. Install Silverlight before you navigate to this site! Like we mentioned before in this chapter, Silverlight-only websites are not recommended because they are only visible on Silverlight-compatible web browsers which speaks against the principles of the World Wide Web.

Looking into Silverlight's Future

Web technologies are evolving fast, and any attempt to look into the future and predict where they are heading in the long term will result in mortifying failure for the psychic...Silverlight is no exception. It's almost impossible to predict where the technology will be five or ten years from now.

One thing is sure, though: Microsoft is putting a lot of effort in Silverlight and porting the .NET framework to multiple platforms. Mobile Silverlight will "hit us" in the very close future. And because so many developers are already active on the .NET platform, we will see more and more Silverlight content soon.

It is also safe to write that Silverlight and WPF will become always more compatible with each other. Silverlight 2 is already delivering a great number of WPF-compatible classes. Learning either WPF or Silverlight will offer an easy passage to the other.

> **NOTE**
>
> At MIX08, in March 2008, Nokia announced a partnership with Microsoft to deliver the Silverlight mobile platform on the Nokia mobile phones.

Is ASP.NET/HTML/JavaScript Dead?

With the advent of Rich Interactive Applications (RIAs) made with Silverlight or Flash, one can wonder if classic ASP.NET will still be available in the future. One thing is sure: ASP.NET is a very strong and important pillar of Microsoft's client application strategy. In fact, Microsoft also released updates to the ASP.NET framework with its .NET framework 3.5 this year.

With "classic" ASP.NET (HTML/CSS/JavaScript) for "thin clients," Silverlight for RIAs and WPF for desktop applications, you cover the whole range of client applications. And since all these platforms run .NET, you can use the same programming language of your choice (amongst C#, VB.NET and many others) to create your libraries.

So in short: No, ASP.NET is definitely not dead, and HTML-based web pages will continue to entertain and inform us on the Internet for many years to come.

Summary

In this chapter, we took a preliminary look at Silverlight and understood where it comes from and what technologies are its "ancestors." We also started playing with demo applications and installed the development environment.

Now it is time to start getting our hands dirty, and to write code. The next chapters introduce you to the new programming language XAML and give you the occasion to write markup and to see your creations running. Gradually, we will build knowledge and help you create more elaborate code. Eventually, we will build applications together, bringing your knowledge of Silverlight to a productive level.

CHAPTER 2

Understanding XAML

What would software development be without acronyms? Let's meet XAML, also known as *eXtensible Application Markup Language* (and pronounced "Zammel"). Located at the border between graphics designers and software developers, this language enables new workflows and allows the designers to *implement markup* instead of working on static screenshots. Optimized for tools like Expression Blend, but still readable (and writable) by humans (with the help of Visual Studio), XAML is a really fascinating new language that admittedly comes with a learning curve. Don't be afraid, though, soon you will have fun mastering this *markup language*!

Using XML for Data

XAML is based on XML, the eXtensible Markup Language. Sometimes we say that XAML is an XML dialect. What does it mean?

Data used to be stored in databases, a special type of file handled by a database system or application. Databases are efficient when it comes to storing and retrieving data. They are fast. But they are complex. Managing a database is so complex that there are engineers who dedicate their job to doing just this. Even the simplest database applications (such as Microsoft Access) are complex, and accessing the stored data from an application can be difficult.

XML, on the other hand, is simple to handle: It's just a text file. If you open an XML file in a text editor, you will see something like the markup shown in Listing 2.1. In fact, a standard text editor will not *color-code* the XML file. More advanced XML editors like the one integrated into Visual Studio use color with XML *tags, attributes, strings* to make it easier to read. The samples in this book follow this practice and all the XML and XAML samples are color coded for clarity.

LISTING 2.1   XML File for Data Storage

```
<!--MyLibrary.xml - All my books-->
<MyLibrary>
  <Authors>
    <Author Name="Zola"
            FirstName="Emile">
      <Books>
        <Book ReleaseYear="1883">
          <Title>Au bonheur des dames</Title>
        </Book>
        <Book ReleaseYear="1885">
          <Title>Germinal</Title>
        </Book>
      </Books>
    </Author>
    <Author Name="Balzac">
      <Books>
        <Book ReleaseYear="1831">
          <Title>La Peau de chagrin</Title>
        </Book>
      </Books>
    </Author>
    <Author Name="Flaubert" />
  </Authors>
</MyLibrary>
```

Let's review the main characteristics of an XML document:

▶ XML is a hierarchic language, where *nodes* contain children nodes. Every node has a parent, except the top one, called the *root node*.

▶ In addition to containing 0 or more children, each node can also have *attributes*. For example, the ReleaseYear is an attribute of the Book node.

▶ A node may be empty; for example the author "Flaubert" is defined, but the library doesn't contain any of his books. Instead of writing an opening tag <Author> and a closing tag </Author>, which would have been possible and allowed, the node is "self-closed" to make the markup more readable and shorter.

▶ Similarly, not all attributes are compulsory. In Listing 2.1, the attribute FirstName is defined only in one of the Nodes. It is an *optional attribute*.

When you have data in an XML file, you must *parse* the file to retrieve the data. Parsing a file is a long and error-prone process. Thankfully, many programming platforms (including JavaScript and .NET) offer built-in ways to handle XML files in a much easier way. If you pass a valid XML file to an XML parser, you can get an object, containing all the nodes, organized in collections just like they are defined in the XML file. XML files can be used as lightweight databases, containing information without the heavy infrastructure of a database system.

Using XML for User Interfaces

Another use for XML is to describe a user interface (UI). The idea of using a markup language for this purpose is not new. The most famous UI markup language is without a doubt HTML (Hypertext Markup Language), but there are other XML-based UI languages, for example, SVG (Scalable Vector Graphics), XUL (XML User Interface Language, a Mozilla project), and so on.

However, HTML is not fully compliant with XML. Trying to load an HTML file with an XML parser will most probably result in errors. But HTML proved that a hierarchic markup language is good at describing complex user interfaces.

XAML obeys stricter rules than HTML. This is a good thing, really. Like XML, XAML must be parsed, and as mentioned already, parsing is a long and error-prone process. If you apply loose rules, the parser must accept many different text strings, and sometimes try to imagine what the programmer actually meant. This is why it is so difficult to write web pages that work the same in different web browsers: The rules of HTML allow too many variations, so the parser implementations use different interpretations, and the same markup can mean different things, depending on which browser loads it.

Understanding XML Namespaces

In XAML as in XML, the rules are defined in *namespaces*. You may have heard this term in relation to .NET, but this is not the same, so don't be confused. .NET namespaces are discussed later in this book. Take a look at the simplest Silverlight file in Listing 2.2:

LISTING 2.2   Simplest Silverlight File Ever

```
<Canvas xmlns="http://schemas.microsoft.com/client/2007" />
```

The `Canvas` element in this (too simple) XAML file uses one XML namespace. Note that the address used here does not correspond to a website. If you enter it in a web browser, you will get a "File Not Found" error (go on, try it!). It is only a URI (Unique Resource Identifier) used to designate a uniquely named

> **WARNING**
>
> If you already took a look at a WPF XAML file, you'll notice that the default namespace is not the same! This is because Silverlight-XAML is a subset of WPF-XAML; different rules must be used for WPF than for Silverlight.

resource, in this case the *schema* in which the XAML structure is defined. The schema is used by the XML parser to validate the file (to make sure that the file complies with the rules). Later, we will see that the schema is also used by XML editors to offer assistance to the user when she is typing XML (and XAML) to make this task easier and to reduce the number of errors.

When a XAML file is loaded into the Silverlight engine, the schema is loaded and checked to see whether a `Canvas` element is defined. If that is the case, the element is read and used to instantiate (create) a `Canvas` object.

Defining Additional Namespaces

The "X" in XML and in XAML stands for "eXtensible." One XML document can refer to multiple XML namespaces, making it possible to mix multiple schemas and to extend the document with elements coming from other sources.

There can be, however, only one default namespace. Additional namespaces must define a *prefix*. For example, XAML typically uses an additional namespace as shown in Listing 2.3:

LISTING 2.3   Additional Namespace

```
<Canvas xmlns="http://schemas.microsoft.com/client/2007"
        xmlns:x="http://schemas.microsoft.com/winfx/2006/xaml" />
```

The second namespace is assigned to the x prefix (that's just a convention; the prefix can be any word as long as it is a valid XML identifier according to XML rules for naming elements that can be found online at www.w3.org/TR/REC-xml). If you want to use elements defined in this second namespace, you must prefix the element's name with x.

For example, the x namespace in Silverlight defines general purpose attributes:

▸ `Name`—Gives a name to the element, used to identify it in the code associated to this markup.

▸ `Key`—When an element is defined in a resource dictionary (a collection of objects), it is identified by a key. This allows retrieving the object later to use it in the code.

▸ `Class`—Used to link a XAML file with a .NET code file. See Chapter 9.

▸ `Other` attributes—These are discussed in the next chapters when needed.

Knowing this, it is easy to assign a name to the root `Canvas`, allowing this object to be referenced in the code later, as shown in Listing 2.4:

LISTING 2.4   Naming the `Canvas`

```
<Canvas xmlns="http://schemas.microsoft.com/client/2007"
        xmlns:x="http://schemas.microsoft.com/winfx/2006/xaml"
        x:Name="MyCanvas" />
```

This syntax allows adding many more namespaces, and these are used later when we create user controls (reusable XAML structures), or when we want to use our own .NET classes in the XAML markup. This is where the XML namespaces meet the .NET namespaces: WPF and Silverlight make it possible to use your code-behind classes in XAML files, like in Listing 2.5! However, we will not use this particular feature before we start using .NET to program Silverlight.

LISTING 2.5   Referencing external assemblies

```
<Canvas
    xmlns="http://schemas.microsoft.com/client/2007"
    xmlns:x="http://schemas.microsoft.com/winfx/2006/xaml"
    x:Name="MyCanvas"
    xmlns:src="clr-namespace:MyOwnClrNamespace"
    xmlns:external="clr-namespace:MyOtherClrNamespace;assembly=MyAssembly" />
```

Creating a Canvas with Children

An empty Canvas is not very useful, however, so Listing 2.6 presents a more complete example.

LISTING 2.6   Canvas with Children

```
<!--SimpleExampleWithChildren.xaml - a simple Canvas with children-->
<Canvas xmlns="http://schemas.microsoft.com/client/2007"
        xmlns:x="http://schemas.microsoft.com/winfx/2006/xaml"
        Background="Red"
        Width="500"
        Height="300">

  <Ellipse Width="400"
           Height="200"
           Fill="Yellow"
           Stroke="Orange"
           StrokeThickness="4"
           Canvas.Left="50"
           Canvas.Top="50"/>

  <TextBlock Text="Hello world"
             FontSize="36"
             Foreground="Blue"
             Canvas.Left="150.763"
             Canvas.Top="122.34"/>

</Canvas>
```

This `Canvas` has three attributes:

▶ `Background` is a brush; in that case, we use a plain red color to "paint" the background of the `Canvas`. We will see later that there are various types of brushes.

▶ `Width` and `Height` define the dimension of the `Canvas`.

The `Canvas` also has two children:

▶ An `Ellipse`, also with the following attributes:

  ▶ `Width` and `Height`—Define the `Ellipse`'s dimensions.

  ▶ `Fill`—Like the `Canvas`'s background, it is also a brush; in that case we use a plain yellow color to paint the `Ellipse`'s insides.

  ▶ `Stroke`—This is again a brush, used to draw the outside border of the `Ellipse`. In this case, we use a plain orange.

  ▶ `StrokeThickness`—Defines the thickness of the outside border of the `Ellipse`.

  ▶ `Canvas.Left` and `Canvas.Top`—These are special, and are discussed later in the chapter.

Another element has been placed in the `Canvas`: a `TextBlock`. Because it appears after the `Ellipse`, the `TextBlock` will be drawn on top of it. The `TextBlock` also defines a few attributes:

▶ `Text`—The string that will be written when the `TextBlock` is rendered.

▶ `FontSize`—This element is self-explanatory.

▶ `Foreground`—This is (again) a brush, in this case a plain blue, used to draw the text.

Attaching Properties: `Canvas.Left` and `Canvas.Top`

The `Ellipse` element doesn't define a `Left` or `Top` attribute. These attributes are specified in the `Canvas` element and "attached" to the `Ellipse` (and later to the `TextBlock`). That's why these properties are called *attached properties* in WPF and in Silverlight. These two specify the location of the `Ellipse` on the `Canvas`, relative to the top-left corner, with the X axis pointing to the right and the Y axis pointing down (as is usual in UI development).

There are multiple benefits to using attached properties: Instead of defining a `Left` and a `Top` in the `Ellipse` object, and another `Left` and another `Top` inside the `TextBlock` object, they are implemented only on the `Canvas` object. Because a `Canvas` can contain a lot of various elements, defining these properties on the `Canvas` and attaching them to the target element are easier. Also, `Left` and `Top` make sense for a `Canvas`, a simple type of panel. But Silverlight supports other types of panels (for example, `Grid`, `StackPanel`, and so on). For these panels, `Left` and `Top` don't make sense, so why define these two proper-ties on the children elements? It makes more sense to define them only on the `Canvas` panel and to attach them when we add children to it.

Documenting Your Markup with XML Comments

XML allows entering comments in the markup. The comments will be parsed, but they do not have any effect on the resulting objects. Commenting your markup (and also your source code as we will see later) is important and is a good programming practice, because:

▶ You will sometimes read markup written by other people, and their way of thinking isn't always the same as yours (yes, yours *is* better, but still…).

▶ You will sometimes read your own code years later and need to remember what the heck you were trying to do.

Writing comments in the XAML markup will help you a lot when you are confronted with these scenarios. XML comments use the following syntax:

> **TIP**
>
> In XML editors, XML comments are usually rendered in green. This makes them easy to recognize.

```
<!--This is a comment-->
```

Testing XAML Markup

That was a lot of theory; now we can put this in practice and experiment with XAML. There are many ways to execute XAML markup. Of course, you can create a Silverlight application (for example, with Expression Blend like we will do later), but that's a bit heavy if you just want to test a few simple (or even not so simple!) XAML constructs.

Thankfully, we have other tools at our disposal.

Using SilverlightPad

Point your browser to the following URL to start the SilverlightPad application, shown in Figure 2.1: http://silverlight.net/samples/1.0/Silverlight-Pad/default.html.

SilverlightPad is a Silverlight sample application, available on the community website Silverlight.net. It can either run online (if you are connected to the Internet) or can be installed locally, with the following steps:

1. Navigate to the Silverlight 1.0 gallery website at http://silverlight.net/community/communitygallery.aspx.

2. Click on View All 1.0 Samples.

3. Locate the SilverlightPad application (see Figure 2.2).

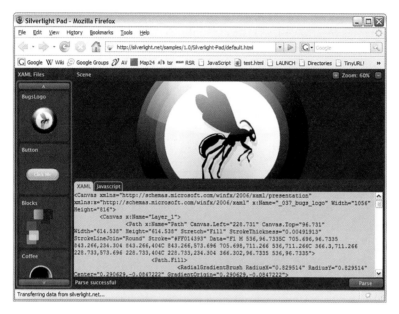

FIGURE 2.1   SilverlightPad

FIGURE 2.2   View or Download SilverlightPad

4. Click on Download It. This triggers the download of a Zip file. Open the file or save it to your hard disk.

5. Extract the Zip file content to a folder on your disk.

6. Navigate to this folder and start index.html in your favorite browser.

If you run SilverlightPad online, you can see sample XAML files on the left, useful to learn complex constructs. In the bottom, you can see (and type) XAML markup. There is also a JavaScript tab, used to attach JavaScript code to the XAML elements. The XAML markup you type is parsed when you click on the Parse button on the bottom right, and the corresponding UI is rendered in the Scene pane. Note also the Zoom controls on the top-right corner. This allows testing the "zoomability" of vector graphics (we'll talk more about that in Chapter 5, "Using Media").

SilverlightPad also allows running animations; for example, if you click on the Blocks XAML file (available if you run SilverlightPad from the Silverlight.net website), you'll see that the blocks are moving. We will program XAML animations in Chapter 3, "XAML Transforms and Animations."

Using KaXaml

SilverlightPad is a great application to train your XAML skills, but it is limited to Silverlight 1. To dig deeper in Silverlight 2 and its XAML markup, you can use the excellent KaXaml created by Robby Ingebretsen.

> **WARNING**
>
> SilverlightPad can be run in any web browser supporting Silverlight 1. However, KaXaml is a Windows application, and can only run on Windows systems.

1. Navigate to the website http://kaxaml.com.

2. Click on the "Download" button and run the installer file.

3. After the installation is complete, run KaXaml from your Start menu. KaXaml appears like in Figure 2.3.

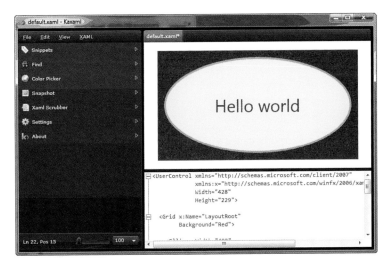

FIGURE 2.3   KaXaml

4. On the right hand side, KaXaml has a XAML markup pane (in the bottom), in which you can type or paste Silverlight markup.

5. On the right hand side, top, the visual rendering of the XAML markup will be displayed.

6. In addition, utilities are available on the left hand side:

   ▶ A collection of "snippets," small pieces of XAML markup that can be dragged to the XAML markup pane.

- ▶ A "Find" dialog handy to look for information in big XAML files.

- ▶ A Color picker including a Color palette.

- ▶ A Snapshot utility, copying the current visual to a PNG image file.

- ▶ A XAML "Scrubber," a utility cleaning up the XAML markup according to user-defined settings.

KaXaml is a very useful tool to learn XAML, and a very fast way to visualize the results of your XAML experiments.

Setting Properties in XAML

Most properties can be set using the XML attribute syntax, but sometimes it is not enough. That's why there is also an *expanded* syntax in XAML. For example, copy Listing 2.7 in SilverlightPad. Then don't forget to click the Parse button to trigger SilverlightPad to render your markup.

LISTING 2.7   Red Canvas

```
<Canvas xmlns="http://schemas.microsoft.com/client/2007"
        xmlns:x="http://schemas.microsoft.com/winfx/2006/xaml"
        Background="Red"
        Width="500"
        Height="300">
</Canvas>
```

This creates an empty, red rectangle. It's red because you set the Background property using the string "Red". Now, modify the markup to look like Listing 2.8:

LISTING 2.8   Another Red Canvas

```
<Canvas xmlns="http://schemas.microsoft.com/client/2007"
        xmlns:x="http://schemas.microsoft.com/winfx/2006/xaml"
        Width="500"
        Height="300">
  <Canvas.Background>
    <SolidColorBrush Color="Red"/>
  </Canvas.Background>
</Canvas>
```

The result is exactly the same. How is that possible? In the first case, using the attribute syntax (also called *simple property syntax*), when the XAML markup is parsed and objects are created, the string "Red" will be converted into an object (of type SolidColorBrush), and assigned to the Background property. Converters in XAML are powerful. They do their best to understand the programmer's intentions and to create the object best suited to reflect the markup.

In the second case, the one with the expanded property syntax, the markup is straightforward. We tell the parser exactly what we want to happen: Create a `SolidColorBrush` object and assign it to the `Background` property of the `Canvas`. Note that one converter is still involved: The one converting the string `"Red"` in a `Color` object, so that this object can be assigned to the `Color` property of the `SolidColorBrush`.

Sometimes, you have to use the expanded property syntax, because it is not possible to define complex objects in just one string so that the converters can create the corresponding objects, as shown in Listing 2.9 and in Figure 2.4.

LISTING 2.9   `LinearGradientBrush`

```
<!--RainbowBrush.xaml - a simple LinearGradientBrush-->
<Canvas xmlns="http://schemas.microsoft.com/client/2007"
        xmlns:x="http://schemas.microsoft.com/winfx/2006/xaml"
        Width="500"
        Height="300">
  <Canvas.Background>
    <LinearGradientBrush StartPoint="0,0"
                         EndPoint="1,0">
      <GradientStop Color="Red" Offset="0"/>
      <GradientStop Color="Orange" Offset="0.25"/>
      <GradientStop Color="Yellow" Offset="0.5"/>
      <GradientStop Color="Green" Offset="0.75"/>
      <GradientStop Color="Blue" Offset="1"/>
    </LinearGradientBrush>
  </Canvas.Background>

  <TextBlock Text="Start" TextWrapping="Wrap"
             Canvas.Top="8" Canvas.Left="8"/>
  <TextBlock Text="End" TextWrapping="Wrap"
             Canvas.Top="8" Canvas.Left="465.717"/>

</Canvas>
```

This markup creates another type of brush, a `LinearGradientBrush`. It produces a gradient, starting in the top-left corner (x=0, y=0) and ending in the top-right corner (x=1, y=0).

The expanded syntax may seem complicated at first, but once you get used to it, you'll notice that it is in fact very logical and well structured.

FIGURE 2.4   `LinearGradientBrush`

Changing Brushes

How can you assign an object of type `SolidColorBrush` to the Background property, and later change that to an object of type `LinearColorBrush`? When we check the documentation online, we see that the `Background` property of a `Canvas` object is of type `Brush`:

http://msdn2.microsoft.com/en-us/library/bb738074.aspx (`Canvas.Background`)

http://msdn.microsoft.com/en-us/library/bb188310.aspx (`Brush`)

In fact, the `Brush` class is *abstract*, meaning that you cannot directly create an object of this type. But there are *derived* types, for example `SolidColorBrush`. Since `SolidColorBrush` and `LinearColorBrush` both *inherit* the `Brush` class, you can say that the `SolidColorBrush` is a `Brush`, and the `LinearColorBrush` is also a `Brush`. This concept is important when you do so-called *Object Oriented Programming (OOP)*, and is called *polymorphism*.

Composing Scenes in XAML

XAML being XML, it is based on the *composition* of objects. This means that every object has a parent (except the topmost one), and a parent may have 0 or more children, as shown in Listing 2.10 and Figure 2.5.

LISTING 2.10   Composing a Scene

```
<!--ComposedScene.xaml - Hierarchical scene-->
<Canvas xmlns="http://schemas.microsoft.com/client/2007"
        xmlns:x="http://schemas.microsoft.com/winfx/2006/xaml"
        Background="Red"
        Width="500" Height="400">

  <Rectangle Width="240" Height="150"
             Fill="Yellow" Margin="40"/>

  <Grid Width="330" Height="250"
```

LISTING 2.10   Continued

```
        Canvas.Left="120" Canvas.Top="110"
        Background="#CCFFFFFF">
  <Ellipse Width="200" Height="140"
           Fill="Orange"
           HorizontalAlignment="Right"
           VerticalAlignment="Bottom"
           Margin="20" />
  </Grid>
</Canvas>
```

FIGURE 2.5   Composing a scene

In Figure 2.5, the yellow `Rectangle` is one of the children of the red `Canvas`. There is also a white `Grid`, defined as another child of the red `Canvas`. You might wonder why you can see through this white `Grid`: The `Background` is set to `#CCFFFFFF`, which creates an 80% transparent white color. You learn more about transparency in Chapter 5, which deals with media in general and colors in particular.

TIP

`Grid` and `Canvas` are two `Panels`, with different functionalities. The various panels available will be reviewed in detail in Chapter 15, "Digging into Silverlight Elements."

▶ A `Grid` is a `Panel` in which you can define rows and columns, a little like a table (or a grid, for that matter).

▶ A `Canvas` is another `Panel`, like a piece of paper, on which you can draw objects with `Top` and `Left` coordinates.

The red `Canvas` has two children, one of them a `Rectangle` and the other one a `Grid`. The half white `Grid` has a child, the orange `Ellipse`. So the XAML markup can be represented as a tree:

- ▶ Red `Canvas`
    - ▶ Yellow `Rectangle`
    - ▶ Half white `Grid`
        - ▶ Orange `Ellipse`

This tree is called the *logical tree* and plays an important role in Silverlight.

Another important thing is that the children of a `Grid` or a `Canvas` appear on top of each other, depending on the order in which they appear in the tree. In Figure 2.5, the yellow `Rectangle` appears under its sibling, the half-white `Grid`. The first child in the tree has a lower `ZIndex` than the second one, which in turn has a lower `ZIndex` than the third one, and so on. You can also change the `ZIndex` in the markup, changing the superposition effect. Change the `Rectangle` markup as in Listing 2.11:

LISTING 2.11   Changed `ZIndex`

```
<Rectangle Width="246"
           Height="152"
           Fill="Yellow"
           Canvas.ZIndex="2"/>
```

This causes the `Rectangle` to appear on top of the half-white `Grid`, as shown in Figure 2.6, (because the `ZIndex` of the `Rectangle` is set to 2, which is higher than the default value of 0 assigned to the half-white `Grid`). Note also that `ZIndex`, like `Left` and `Top`, is an attached property of the `Canvas` class, thus the syntax `Canvas.ZIndex`.

FIGURE 2.6   `Rectangle` in front

Saving Typing, Saving Space

As you already found out, typing XAML can take some time. In fact, XAML was not created for humans. It was created for computer tools (like Expression Blend or Visual Studio), to be used as a storage medium, and then later optimized so that humans can type it anyway without too much pain. In further chapters, we will see how a good editor can help you save time, using a technology called Intellisense, automatic tag completion, and so on.

One such improvement is that for each class, one of the properties can be defined as the default property. In Silverlight, we talk about the *Content Property*. It doesn't need to be explicitly mentioned when you type XAML markup, to save typing and space. For each object in Silverlight, the most used property may be marked as the Content Property by the developer. For example, the `Children` property of each `Panel` is the Content Property, so you can add elements in a `Canvas` without having to use the `Canvas.Children` syntax like in Listing 2.12.

LISTING 2.12   Setting the `Canvas.Children` Explicitly

```
<!--Children.xaml-->
<Canvas
    xmlns="http://schemas.microsoft.com/client/2007"
    xmlns:x="http://schemas.microsoft.com/winfx/2006/xaml"
    Width="640"
    Height="480">
  <Canvas.Children>

    <Ellipse Width="400"
             Height="200"
             Fill="Yellow"
             Stroke="Orange"
             StrokeThickness="4"
             Canvas.Left="50"
             Canvas.Top="50"/>

    <TextBlock Text="Hello world"
             FontSize="36"
             Foreground="Blue"
             Canvas.Left="150.763"
             Canvas.Top="122.34"/>

  </Canvas.Children>
</Canvas>
```

Summary

This chapter gave you a first contact with XAML and some important features of this new language. XAML comes with a learning curve, especially for developers or designers not used to XML. This learning curve can be a little frightening sometimes, but as time goes by, you will learn how to master this language and be productive with it.

In the next chapter, we continue to work with XAML and learn more complex constructs, adding movement to our applications without writing one line of C# or JavaScript. Later, we introduce Expression Blend, a tool that allows you to visually edit the XAML markup. This is where XAML gives us the best of both worlds: a great visual designer and the possibility to act on markup level if we prefer.

CHAPTER 3

Playing with XAML Transforms and Animations

Probably the most exciting feature of Silverlight is the ability to transform and animate visual elements with XAML alone, without writing one line of C# code-behind. In this chapter, we build on the knowledge gained in the previous chapter and learn new constructs to enhance our Silverlight XAML applications.

Transforming Visuals

Silverlight and WPF provide a powerful way to modify the appearance of an element using *transforms*. More specifically, the transforms used in Silverlight and WPF are *affine transforms*, meaning that parallel lines will always remain parallel. This will become clearer as we try all the transforms in SilverlightPad.

To transform an element, you use the `RenderTransform` property of any UI element. The `RenderTransform` doesn't affect the layout of the elements: it is applied to the element *after* all the layout operations have been computed. This means that neighbors of the transformed element will not be affected by the transform, and they will appear just as if the transformed element had not moved at all.

> **NOTE**
>
> WPF knows another transform type, named `LayoutTransform`, computed *before* the layout operations. The `LayoutTransform` affects not only the transformed element, but also its neighbors. This is not available in Silverlight at the moment.

For example, let's enter the XAML markup shown in Listing 3.1 in SilverlightPad.

LISTING 3.1   Transforming an XAML Scene

```
<!--Transforms.xaml - Transforming a scene in XAML-->
<Canvas xmlns="http://schemas.microsoft.com/client/2007"
        xmlns:x="http://schemas.microsoft.com/winfx/2006/xaml"
        Width="640" Height="480">

  <Ellipse Width="190" Height="160"
           Fill="Red" Stroke="Black"
           Canvas.Left="8" Canvas.Top="8" />

  <Grid Width="330" Height="190"
        Background="Orange"
        Canvas.Left="115" Canvas.Top="107"
        RenderTransformOrigin="0.5,0.5">
    <Grid.RenderTransform>
      <RotateTransform Angle="30" />
    </Grid.RenderTransform>

    <TextBlock Text="Hello"
               FontSize="36" Foreground="Gray"
               HorizontalAlignment="Center" />
  </Grid>
</Canvas>
```

Figure 3.1 shows two elements, a red `Ellipse` and an orange `Grid`; the `Grid` contains a `TextBlock`.

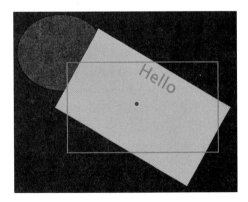

FIGURE 3.1   Transforming an XAML scene

To make things clearer, I added a small blue dot marking the point of origin, and a fine gray line showing the original Grid's position in Figure 3.1 and the next. The following features are important in Figure 3.1:

▶ The orange Grid doesn't appear horizontal like it should. Instead, it is rotated by 30 degrees. Notice how the Grid's child (the TextBlock) is also rotated. Transforms applied to an element also affect the children!

▶ The rotation's point of origin is located in the exact center of the orange Grid, because of the RenderTransformOrigin="0.5,0.5" attribute. The value 0.5 is relative to the element's width, respectively height. The point of origin is the only point that is not modified by the transform.

▶ The default value for RenderTransformOrigin is "0,0", so removing that attribute creates Figure 3.2. The Grid now rotates around its top-left corner.

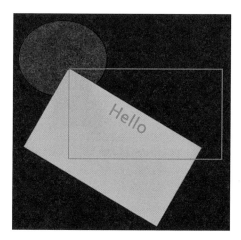

FIGURE 3.2   Default point of origin

Types of Transforms

There are four basic transforms that can be applied to a Silverlight element and modify it in a simple way. We will talk about these basic transforms in this section. Additionally, a more complex mathematic transform can be applied (on its own, or in addition to the basic ones) and modify the element in almost any way possible. Remember however that parallel lines will remain parallel.

RotateTransform

We saw the effect of this transform already. RotateTransform rotates all the points of a figure around the point of origin. The amount by which the figure

> **TIP**
>
> In fact, the value is "limited," from negative 1.79769313486232e308 to positive 1.79769313486232e308 (which is a huge range). The limits are set by the *type* used for the Angle property (the type Double).

is rotated is set by the Angle property. The value (in degrees) can be any number, positive or negative.

You can test variations of this transform:

1. In SilverlightPad (or KaXaml), modify the Angle property of Listing 3.1 to see the effect on the Grid.

2. Since the Angle property is a Double, you can also enter noninteger values. For example, -43.6, 723.2, 465, -512.9 are all valid values.

3. A value of 360 degrees creates a full turn, so that the figure appears unchanged. 720 degrees rotates the figure twice, and so on.

In static transforms, rotating a figure by 360 degrees doesn't make much sense, but it will be useful when we animate the transforms later in this chapter.

TranslateTransform

This transform is slightly less exciting, but can be useful, especially in animations. The effect of a TranslateTransform is to move a figure by a certain amount of pixels along the X, respectively Y axis.

Follow these steps to see how this transform affects the scene:

1. In SilverlightPad, copy again Listing 3.1; then remove the RotateTransform markup and replace with the following TranslateTransform (see Listing 3.2):

LISTING 3.2   TranslateTransform

```
<Grid.RenderTransform>
  <TranslateTransform X="50"
                      Y="40" />
</Grid.RenderTransform>
```

2. The X and Y values are Doubles (like the Angle property before); try entering noninteger values and parse again.

3. Try entering negative values. Notice how a positive value moves the figure along the positive axis, and vice versa.

4. Enter a different value for the RenderTransformOrigin attribute. The scene will not change, because the transform's effect is the same, no matter where its origin is located. The result for a default RenderTransformOrigin is shown in Figure 3.3.

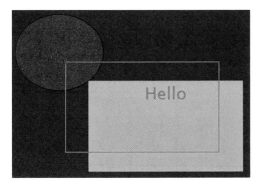

FIGURE 3.3   `TranslateTransform`

ScaleTransform

This transform takes a figure and multiplies its size by a factor (bigger or smaller than 1), along the X and/or Y axis. Let's try a `ScaleTransform` in our scene now with the following steps, and see the result in Figure 3.4:

1. In SilverlightPad, set the `RenderTransformOrigin` to `"0.5,0.5"` again.

2. Replace the `TranslateTransform` with the markup in Listing 3.3. Notice how the `ScaleX`, respectively `ScaleY` properties transform the `Grid`'s apparent size. Notice again how the transform applies to the children too: The `TextBlock` now looks distorted, because the `ScaleX` value is not equal to the `ScaleY` value.

LISTING 3.3   `ScaleTransform`

```
<Grid.RenderTransform>
  <ScaleTransform ScaleX="1.1"
                  ScaleY="1.3" />
</Grid.RenderTransform>
```

3. Try changing the `RenderTransformOrigin` to `"0,0"`, then to `"1,1"` and observe what the effect is: The figure is scaled *relatively* to the point of origin! Here also, the point of origin is the only point that is not modified by the transform.

4. Enter a negative value for the `ScaleX` property. This is probably the most interesting feature of the `ScaleTransform`: A negative value flips the scene and shows it reversed! This will prove useful when we animate a scene!

> **WARNING**
>
> The `RenderTransformOrigin` takes values from 0 to 1, relative to the element's size. The `CenterX` and `CenterY` values, however, are absolute (in pixels)! This can cause difficulties when the element's size is not known at design time.

5. The `ScaleTransform` has two additional attributes `CenterX` and `CenterY`. These have the same effect as the `RenderTransformOrigin`. The figure "grows" relatively to the point defined by these two attributes.

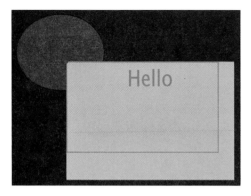

FIGURE 3.4   `ScaleTransform` with origin in "0,0"

SkewTransform

Skewing an element "bends" the borders of the element, keeping them parallel (remember, the transforms in Silverlight are *affine*). The following steps present an example (and the result is shown in Figure 3.5):

1. In Listing 3.1, replace the `RenderTransform` with the markup shown in Listing 3.4:

LISTING 3.4   Transforming an XAML Scene

```
<Grid.RenderTransform>
  <SkewTransform AngleX="30" />
</Grid.RenderTransform>
```

2. As usual, the `AngleX` (and `AngleY`) properties are `Double`, so they can be set to noninteger values and to negative values. Try this in SilverlightPad and observe the effect.

3. Moving the `RenderTransformOrigin` in different locations modifies the action of the skew. Again, the point of origin is the only point that is not modified by the transform.

4. This transform also has `CenterX` and `CenterY` properties. Note that they are slightly confusing: The `CenterY` affects the `AngleX`, and the `CenterX` affects the `AngleY`. Try different values of `CenterY` to see what the effect is on the `SkewTransform` above. Again, remember that `CenterX` and `CenterY` are not relative to the dimensions, but absolute!

5. In SilverlightPad, try combining `AngleX` and `AngleY` and see how you can "distort" an element using the `SkewTransform`.

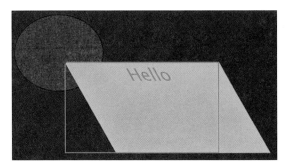

FIGURE 3.5   `SkewTransform` with origin in "0,0"

MatrixTransform

The four basic transforms are actually just a convenience, or simplification of the transformation process. An element is always transformed by a 3x3 matrix, looking like this:

M11	M21	0
M12	M22	0
OffsetX	OffsetY	1

The matrix transformation can be explained in detail with mathematics, but this is not the scope of this book. Fortunately, it's not really complicated. First a few basics:

▶ The transforms in Silverlight are, as already mentioned a few times, affine. This is a simplification, which is sufficient for most cases. This is the reason why the last column in the preceding matrix is set to "0, 0, 1" and cannot be changed.

▶ If more complex transforms are needed, it is possible to move the points of a shape, causing its appearance to be modified in a non-affine way. But that's not possible for every type of element! We'll talk about that in Chapter 11, "Progressing with Animations," in the section about `PointAnimation`.

▶ By setting the values `M11`, `M12`, `M21`, `M22`, `OffsetX`, and `OffsetY`, we can reproduce all the transforms we saw in this chapter. These basic transforms are here to make your life easier, but if you need a more complex transform, you can always resort to the `MatrixTransform`.

▶ If all the values in the matrix's diagonal are set to 1, the effect is the same as doing nothing at all. So by setting `M11` and `M22` to `"1"`, and all other values to `"0"`, you create a void transform.

Let's create a scene now and transform it. Copy the markup shown in Listing 3.5 in SilverlightPad or KaXaml.

LISTING 3.5   MatrixTransform

```
<!--MatrixTransform.xaml - Transform using a Matrix in XAML-->
<Canvas xmlns="http://schemas.microsoft.com/client/2007"
        xmlns:x="http://schemas.microsoft.com/winfx/2006/xaml"
        Width="640" Height="480">

  <Grid Width="330" Height="190"
        Background="Orange"
        Canvas.Left="115" Canvas.Top="107">
    <Grid.RenderTransform>
      <MatrixTransform>
        <MatrixTransform.Matrix>
          <Matrix M11="1" M12="0" OffsetX="0"
                  M21="0" M22="1" OffsetY="0" />
        </MatrixTransform.Matrix>
      </MatrixTransform>
    </Grid.RenderTransform>

    <TextBlock Text="Hello"
               FontSize="36" Foreground="Gray"
               HorizontalAlignment="Center" />
  </Grid>

  <Rectangle Width="330" Height="190"
             Stroke="Gray"
             Canvas.Left="115"
             Canvas.Top="107" />
</Canvas>
```

Listing 3.5 creates an orange Grid with a TextBlock in it. The matrix's values are set to their defaults, so the scene is not transformed (yet). A gray border marks the original location and size of the Grid.

You can experiment more by setting the values M11, M12, OffsetX, M21, M22, and OffsetY to transform the scene. Compose multiple transforms, and try to remember the action of each component.

Composing Transforms

Another way to create complex transforms, next to using a MatrixTransform as in the preceding section, is to compose simple transforms. To do this, we use a TransformGroup.

This object is actually also a transform, like all the basic transforms discussed previously, but its purpose is only to group and combine other transforms! Does it make sense? Consider the example shown in Listing 3.6.

LISTING 3.6   Composing Transforms

```
<!--TransformGroup.xaml - Composing transforms-->
<Canvas xmlns="http://schemas.microsoft.com/client/2007"
        xmlns:x="http://schemas.microsoft.com/winfx/2006/xaml"
        Width="640" Height="480">

  <Grid Width="330" Height="190"
        Background="Orange"
        Canvas.Left="115" Canvas.Top="107">
    <Grid.RenderTransform>
      <TransformGroup>
        <RotateTransform Angle="45" />
        <ScaleTransform ScaleX="1.5"
                        ScaleY="0.5" />
      </TransformGroup>
    </Grid.RenderTransform>

    <TextBlock Text="Hello"
               FontSize="36" Foreground="Gray"
               HorizontalAlignment="Center"/>
  </Grid>
  <Rectangle Width="330" Height="190"
             Stroke="Gray"
             Canvas.Left="115" Canvas.Top="107" />
</Canvas>
```

Figure 3.6 shows the effect of composing a `RotateTransform` and a `ScaleTransform`. The effects of each transform are added. By using additional transforms, a wide range of effects can be achieved.

FIGURE 3.6   Composing transforms

Creating a Basic Animation

The animation system is the "flesh" of
Silverlight. You just saw how to transform an element and a scene by using
static transforms and composing them.
The next step is to animate our static
scene, and that's easy using animations.

> **WARNING**
>
> SilverlightPad is already too limited for
> Listing 3.7. To test it, you should rather use
> KaXaml!

Just as there are multiple types of transforms, there are multiple types of animations. In
fact, there are as many types of animations as there are types of properties to animate.
Because so many properties in Silverlight are of type `Double`, the `DoubleAnimation` is the
one you will use the most. But other types exist, too, and we use some of them later in
this chapter. Let's start with a simple rotating example, shown in Listing 3.7.

LISTING 3.7   Rotating Animation

```
<!--Animation.xaml - Animations in XAML-->
<Grid x:Name="WelcomePanel"
      xmlns="http://schemas.microsoft.com/client/2007"
      xmlns:x="http://schemas.microsoft.com/winfx/2006/xaml"
      Background="#FFFFCA68" Height="150"
      RenderTransformOrigin="0.5,0.5">

  <Grid.RenderTransform>
    <TransformGroup>
      <RotateTransform x:Name="WelcomeRotateTransform"
                    Angle="0" />
    </TransformGroup>
  </Grid.RenderTransform>

  <Grid.Triggers>
    <EventTrigger RoutedEvent="Grid.Loaded">
      <BeginStoryboard>
        <Storyboard RepeatBehavior="Forever"
                AutoReverse="True">

          <DoubleAnimation Storyboard.TargetName="WelcomeRotateTransform"
                        Storyboard.TargetProperty="Angle"
                        From="0" To="360" Duration="0:0:2" />

        </Storyboard>
      </BeginStoryboard>
    </EventTrigger>
  </Grid.Triggers>

  <TextBlock Text="*** Welcome ***"
```

LISTING 3.7   Continued

```
            FontSize="72"
            HorizontalAlignment="Center"
            VerticalAlignment="Center">
  <TextBlock.Foreground>
    <LinearGradientBrush StartPoint="0,0.5" EndPoint="1,0.5"
                         x:Name="ForegroundBrush">
      <GradientStop Color="Red" Offset="0" />
      <GradientStop Color="Lime" Offset="0.5" />
      <GradientStop Color="Blue" Offset="1" />
    </LinearGradientBrush>
  </TextBlock.Foreground>
</TextBlock>
</Grid>
```

As shown in Figure 3.7 the scene contains a Grid with a light-orange background, and a colored TextBlock. The TextBlock's Foreground is set to a LinearGradientBrush.

FIGURE 3.7   Scene for animation

Modify the animation's parameters:

1. If you don't like it, feel free to change the colors, to add GradientStops, to change the text, and so on.

2. Copy Listing 3.7 in KaXaml. The rotating animation starts automatically as soon as the Grid is loaded.

Understanding the Animation's Elements

Let's review the important elements of Listing 3.7:

▶ The Grid.Triggers section defines the way the system reacts to certain events. The EventTrigger is set to "Grid.Loaded". This means that the action will be executed when the Grid is fully loaded, and the corresponding event fires.

WARNING

Unlike in WPF, the Loaded event is the only one that can trigger an animation in XAML. In fact, it's customary to start animations in code in Silverlight.

▶ When the `"Grid.Loaded"` event fires, a `Storyboard` will begin (that's what the `BeginStoryboard` section means). A `Storyboard` is a collection of animations executed together. In our case, the `Storyboard` has only one animation (for now).

▶ The `Storyboard` will never stop, because the `RepeatBehavior` attribute is set to `"Forever"`. Other possible values are `"1x"`, `"2x"`, `"3x"` (for once, twice, three times, and so on). The default value is `"1x"`. Try modifying this attribute to see the difference in KaXaml.

▶ The `Storyboard` will automatically reverse and the scene will go back to its original state. This is because of the `AutoReverse` attribute. The default value for this attribute is `false`, so normally an animation does not reverse!

▶ The `DoubleAnimation` targets an element named `"WelcomeRotate"`. This is the `RotateTransform` of the light-orange `Grid`. This is possible, because the animation will only start after the scene is fully loaded, when all the elements have been created already. Note that the `TargetName` property is an *attached property*, according to the syntax learned in Chapter 2.

▶ The `TargetProperty` (another attached property) specifies which property (here, the `"Angle"` property) will be animated. In this case, we named the targeted transform to allow an easy identification. This is not always possible, in which case the `TargetProperty` will become more complex. You see additional examples and learn more about the `TargetProperty` syntax later in this book.

▶ The `From` and `To` attributes are easy to understand. Note that the `From` value is not compulsory: If you leave this blank, the scene will simply start in the current state and cycle to the `To` value.

▶ You can also replace the `From` and `To` attributes with the `By` attribute. The `By` value specifies by how many units the scene will be modified. `From="0" To="360"` can be replaced with `By="360"`. Try this in KaXaml!

▶ The `Duration` specifies the time it takes for the animation to run. Note that if `AutoReverse` is set to `"True"`, the whole animation (one way and back) takes double as much time. The syntax to set the `Duration` in XAML is DD.HH:MM:SS.mmm with the following meanings:

  ▶ DD—Days

  ▶ HH, MM, SS—Hours, minutes, and seconds

  ▶ mmm—Milliseconds

This is what it takes to make a basic animation. It may sound complex at first, but with time you will grow more comfortable with these parameters, and they will become familiar. Do not hesitate to experiment in KaXaml!

Silverlight knows another kind of animation, using key frames. For example, the equivalent of DoubleAnimation would be DoubleAnimationUsingKeyFrames (long name!). We create key frames animations when we talk about Expression Blend more in detail.

Adding a Scale Animation

Let's add some movement to our animation with a scaling effect. We want the scene to come from far away and to grow while rotating, before going back into the background. The modifications needed to do this are easy. First, we need something to animate, so add a ScaleTransform to Listing 3.7 with the following steps:

> **TIP**
>
> The original Listing 3.7 uses a TransformGroup even though it has only one transform. This is not strictly necessary, but this proves handy when we want to add the ScaleTransform to the scene.

1. In KaXaml, add a ScaleTransform to the TransformGroup section. Note that we start with ScaleX = ScaleY = "0". If we don't animate the scene, we will not see anything, because scaling an element to 0 makes it disappear. The RenderTransform becomes Listing 3.8:

LISTING 3.8   Grouping Transforms

```
<Grid.RenderTransform>
  <TransformGroup>
    <RotateTransform x:Name="WelcomeRotateTransform"
                     Angle="0"/>
    <ScaleTransform x:Name="WelcomeScaleTransform"
                    ScaleX="0" ScaleY="0" />
  </TransformGroup>
</Grid.RenderTransform>
```

2. Then add the following animations to the Storyboard. Simply add the markup under the existing DoubleAnimation (the one targeting the RotateTransform named "WelcomeRotateTransform"). Note that there are two properties to animate (ScaleX and ScaleY), so there are two animations shown in Listing 3.9!

LISTING 3.9   Two Scale Animations

```
<DoubleAnimation
  Storyboard.TargetName="WelcomeScaleTransform"
  Storyboard.TargetProperty="ScaleX"
  From="0" To="1" Duration="0:0:3"/>
<DoubleAnimation
  Storyboard.TargetName="WelcomeScaleTransform"
  Storyboard.TargetProperty="ScaleY"
  From="0" To="1" Duration="0:0:3"/>
```

3. After you make the changes, the animation should start automatically in KaXaml.

4. Notice how the rotation takes 2 seconds, while the scaling animation lasts 3 seconds all together. Also notice how well the animations are coordinated: After the animation reverses, the rotation starts with a 1-second delay. This works because all the animations are placed in the same `Storyboard`, which synchronizes the animations, and because the `AutoReverse` and `RepeatBehavior` attributes are placed on the `Storyboard` and not on each animation separately.

5. To understand the previous point better, try to remove the `AutoReverse` and `RepeatBehavior` from the `Storyboard`, and add them on each animation instead. The animations run and revert independently from each other.

Using Other Types of Animations

Transforms are not the only things you can animate in Silverlight. In fact, you can animate a lot of properties, as long as they are dependency properties (DP). This special type of property is registered with the Silverlight framework. DPs are useful in Silverlight, not only because they can be animated, but also because they enable other useful features such as data binding.

In this section, we add two animations to the scene we are creating. First, we want to introduce a smoother effect by fading the scene in and out. An element (and its children) can be made transparent using the `Opacity` property, which takes a `Double` value from 0 (0%, fully transparent) to 1 (100%, fully visible). Smooth transitions are trendy at the moment, especially in Windows Vista where pretty much all transitions use fade in and fade out to create a better user experience. Follow the steps:

1. Add the animation in Listing 3.10 to the `Storyboard`:

LISTING 3.10   Opacity Animation

```
<DoubleAnimation
    Storyboard.TargetName="WelcomePanel"
    Storyboard.TargetProperty="Opacity"
    From="0" To="1" Duration="0:0:3"/>
```

2. Wait for KaXaml to parse the XAML markup and start the new smooth animation.

Eventually, we will add a shiny effect at the end of the animation, when the scene is fully expanded. We will target the various gradients of the `LinearGradientBrush` with a `ColorAnimation`. That's right, you can also animate colors!

To start the color animation when the `TextBlock` is at its biggest size, we will delay the start of that specific animation using the `BeginTime` property. It uses the same syntax as `Duration` (DD.HH:MM:SS.mmm). Follow these steps:

1. Add the animations in Listing 3.11 to the `Storyboard`. They target specifically the outer gradient stops of the brush. After you add the animations, wait and observe the result.

LISTING 3.11   Color Animations

```
<ColorAnimation
    Storyboard.TargetName="ForegroundBrush"
    Storyboard.TargetProperty="(GradientBrush.GradientStops)[0]
                               .(GradientStop.Color)"
    BeginTime="0:0:3" Duration="0:0:0.100" To="Lime"/>
<ColorAnimation
    Storyboard.TargetName="ForegroundBrush"
    Storyboard.TargetProperty="(GradientBrush.GradientStops)[2]
                               .(GradientStop.Color)"
    BeginTime="0:0:3" Duration="0:0:0.100" To="Lime"/>
```

2. The two animations are similar. But because they target different properties, we need both. The most difficult part to understand is the `TargetProperty`. As we mentioned earlier, this attribute can sometimes be complex. The system needs to find the property it will animate, starting from a given element. This is what the *property path syntax* does.

> **NOTE**
>
> In addition to `DoubleAnimation` and `ColorAnimation`, Silverlight has a `PointAnimation` (we will talk about it in Chapter 11). Another, more complex animation named `ObjectAnimationUsingKeyFrames` (and only available as "using key frames") also exists but it is out of the scope of this book. You can find more information about this animation type in the Silverlight documentation online at http://msdn.microsoft.com/en-us/library/system.windows.media.animation.objectanimationusingkeyframes(VS.95).aspx.

Navigating the Property Path

Until now, we used only simple property paths, for example `"Angle"` or `"ScaleX"`. Here, we need something more complex. We start from the `LinearGradientBrush`, identified by the name `"ForegroundBrush"`. From there, we navigate to the `(GradientBrush.GradientStops)`. This is a collection of `GradientStops`. In the first animation, we target the first stop. This is what the index `[0]` means.

> **WARNING**
>
> In many modern programming languages, the first element of a collection has the index 0. We say that the index is 0-based, as opposed to 1-based as is usual in "normal life." While this may seem strange, it makes many scenarios much easier to program.

Once we have the first `GradientStop`, we target the `Color` property. This is what (`GradientStop.Color`) means.

The full property path is

`(GradientBrush.GradientStops)[0].(GradientStop.Color)`

To avoid having too long lines of markup, the path is broken in two lines. This is perfectly legal and allowed in XML (and XAML). The line-break and the white spaces are simply ignored.

The second `ColorAnimation` does the same, but it targets the last `GradientStop` of the collection. This is the third stop, so it is located at the index `[2]`. The `GradientStop` in the middle (the one with the index `[1]`) remains untouched: It is Lime already!

Deploying the Scene to a Web Page

To show your work to your friends and family, you need to deploy the application to a web server and place the scene on a web page. This is how Silverlight works, remember: We don't create standalone applications, but applications embedded in a web page.

You learn how to deploy XAML and other Silverlight applications in Chapter 7, "Deploying to a Web Page." It involves setting up a web server and creating (or modifying) an HTML page. In the meantime, have patience, and show off your work in KaXaml!

Summary

Without writing one single line of C# or JavaScript code, we were able to create an animated scene, using a combination of transforms, animations, fade in and out, and color effects to bring life into our static scenes.

Transforms and animations are probably two of the most exciting features of Silverlight (and of WPF). With just a few lines of XAML markup, it is possible to create effects that would have taken pages of code in classic technologies (or that would not even have been possible at all). Do not hesitate to experiment more in KaXaml and to explore what the combinations of attributes do to change the scene. You will use this new knowledge a lot in future chapters, when we build applications.

CHAPTER 4

Expression Blend

Together with the new framework come new tools: The Microsoft Expression Studio. This new line of tools is primarily aimed at graphics designers. In fact, Microsoft didn't think that developers would be interested in them, and for some time didn't even market them for developers. Thankfully, after some rather loud reactions in the developer community, Microsoft changed its mind and included Expression Blend in the MSDN subscription, acknowledging the value of this tool for developer work.

> **TIP**
>
> MSDN (Microsoft Developer Network) is a collection of resources for developers, including a subscription system in which subscribers get Microsoft software for development purposes.

The Expression Studio in Short

The Expression Studio is composed of five tools. All these tools can be used for Silverlight development at some level:

▶ Expression Design—Creates graphic design assets and exports them to a number of formats, including XAML.

▶ Expression Blend—Creates WPF and Silverlight applications and provides a visual designer for the UI.

▶ Expression Encoder—Encodes and publishes video, and optionally creates a Silverlight video player for them.

▶ Expression Web—Builds web pages, includes an advanced CSS designer, and an HTML visual designer.

▶ Expression Media—Manages media assets. This is the only tool in the Studio that is not directly useful for Silverlight applications.

Installing Expression Blend

To install Expression Blend 2 SP1, follow these steps:

1. If you didn't do this yet, install the Silverlight tools from the page www.silverlight.net/GetStarted.

2. Go to the URL www.microsoft.com/expression/try-it

3. Scroll down until you find "Expression Blend 2" and click on "Try It".

4. On the same page, locate and install Expression Blend 2 SPI. This service pack gives you the ability to create and edit Silverlight content in Blend.

> **NOTE**
>
> You can choose to install Visual Studio at this time. If you decide to do so, you should install Visual Studio before the Silverlight tools and Blend. Installing Visual Studio also installs .NET 3.5 so you can skip step 4.

Starting Expression Blend

When you start Expression Blend the first time, a Welcome screen displays with options to create a new project, to start the Help system, or to see samples (Figure 4.1). Unfortunately, the samples are all for WPF and not for Silverlight (yet...). Still, you can select the samples to see what you can create using Blend, XAML, and WPF.

A check box asks whether you want to see the Welcome screen every time that you start the application. If you uncheck this box, you can retrieve the Welcome screen by selecting Help, Welcome Screen from the Blend menu.

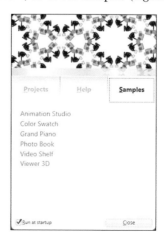

FIGURE 4.1   Expression Blend Welcome screen

Setting Options

Before you create your first project in Blend, you'll want to take a look at the options first with the following steps:

1. Select Tools, Options from the menu.

2. Under Workspace, you can modify the way the application looks with two settings:

   ▶ You can select a theme for your working environment. Currently two themes are available, Expression dark and Expression light. Change the theme and observe how the whole environment's look and feel changes.

   ▶ You can set the zoom factor for the environment. This is especially useful if you have an extra-small screen resolution (for example, when you give a beamer presentation about Expression Blend) or an extra big screen.

   ▶ You can also drag the level of the zoom bar with your mouse to see how WPF handles the resizing. This is done using transforms as you learned in Chapter 3, "Playing with XAML Transforms and Animations."

3. Under Project, you find options related to how Blend creates and saves projects.

   ▶ If you want Blend to require a path for the new project as soon as it is created, check the Save New Projects check box (this is the first check box). It is recommended to check this option.

   ▶ Similarly, it is recommended to use a Grid panel as the default layout for new items. The Grid panel (which we will study more later) is the most flexible and powerful panel available in Silverlight 2.

   ▶ The other options can be left untouched.

4. Under Code Editor, you find settings for the XAML editor.

   ▶ You can choose which font you want to use. Although you can use any font installed on your system in theory, we recommend using a fixed-size font (such as Consolas or Courier New) to enhance readability.

   ▶ You can also use the Tab Size setting and the Insert Space or Keep Tabs setting to specify how your XAML markup will be indented. There is a small religion war going on among developers to decide which settings are the best. A good combination is 2 and Insert Spaces, but you're free to decide for yourself.

   ▶ If you want long lines of markup to wrap according to the size of the application's window, check the Word Wrap check box.

5. Under Event Handlers, specify which editor should be used to implement event handlers in the code-behind. Expression Blend cannot handle C# code on its own. A

good idea is to use Visual Studio for event handlers, if you have it. This setting applies only if you work with Silverlight 2 (with .NET), instead of Silverlight 1 and JavaScript.

> **WARNING**
>
> The Split view comes with a performance hit. It is recommended to use the Design view as default, and to switch to Split view when needed using the vertical tabs on the right side of the Design panel.

6. Under Artboard, you'll find options about Snap grid, Gridlines, default Margin, and default Padding, the color of Blend's background.

7. Under Documents, you can choose the default view for your pages. You can use Split view if your screen is big enough, because it gives a good view on both the XAML markup and the visual representation of the elements.

Creating a New Project

To start a new project, you can either select the Projects tab on the Welcome screen, or select File, New Project from the menu. Then follow these steps:

1. In the Create New Project dialog shown in Figure 4.2, select the version of Silverlight that you want to use. Depending on your installation, you may have the choice between Silverlight 1 Site (with JavaScript only) and Silverlight 2 Application (with .NET).

2. Select the option "Silverlight 2 Application".

3. Enter a name and a location for your project and press "OK". Note that even though Blend allows it, it is not recommended to use spaces in a project's name. It's better to use dots, for example "MyFirm.MyProject".

> **NOTE**
>
> In this book, we will only work with Silverlight 2 applications, even if in the beginning we don't program .NET for Silverlight yet. Silverlight 1 sites have many similarities with Silverlight 2 applications, but also some differences. Except if you have old Silverlight 1 sites to maintain, it's better to start with Silverlight 2 directly.

FIGURE 4.2   The Create New Project dialog box

Understanding the Panels

Blend creates a new Silverlight project and displays the new user control in the central panel. Let's review the panels, as shown in Figure 4.3. Because Blend is a full-fledged WPF application and features two themes, the look and feel of your Blend installation may be slightly different from the one displayed here, depending on the theme setup. You can change the theme in the Options dialog.

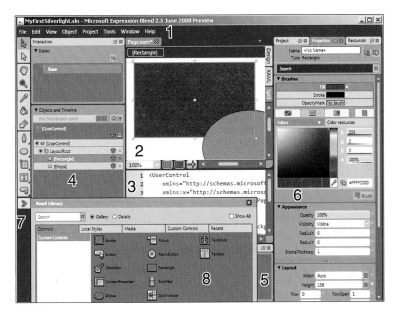

FIGURE 4.3   Blend bars and panels

Figure 4.3 displays the following panels and bars:

1. Menu bar.

2. Designer panel, where the XAML markup is rendered visually.

    Only available in Design or Split mode.

3. XAML editor panel, where the XAML markup can be edited manually.

    Only available in XAML or Split mode.

4. Interaction panel: all the objects in the page are displayed in a tree and animations can be created and managed in the Objects and Timeline category.

    A control's states and transitions can be managed in the States category of the same panel. We'll talk about that in Chapter 17, "Using Resources, Styling, and Templating."

5. Results panel. We will use this panel when we program Silverlight with C#.

6. Project/Properties/Resources panels. The *Project panel* gives easy access to all the files and data in the application. The *Properties panel* allows setting and editing the elements' properties. The *Resources panel* will be used later, when we talk about resources, styles and templates.

7. Toolbar, providing an easy access to all the tools we will use to create visual content.

8. Asset Library, where all the built-in and custom controls can be managed.

Looking at the Files

Let's select the Project panel and take a look at the files that Blend created for us, as in Figure 4.4.

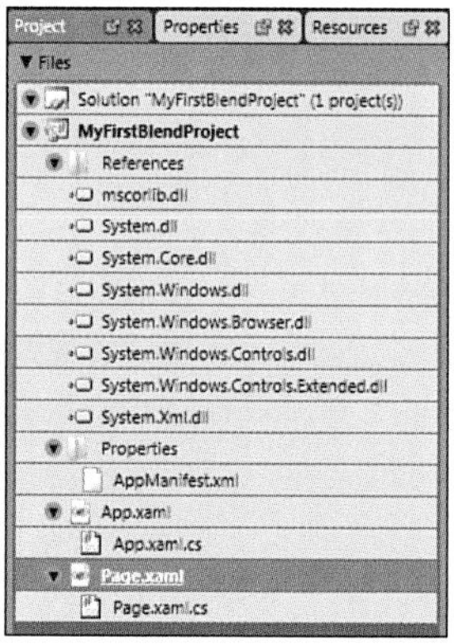

▶ The top file is a *solution* file. We will talk more about solutions in Chapter 9, "Understanding .NET." For the moment, it is enough to remember that a solution is a container for projects. In the file system, the solution file has a .sln extension (for example, MyFirstBlendProject.sln).

▶ Next in the hierarchy is the *project* file. One solution can contain

FIGURE 4.4   Silverlight 2 files

multiple projects, but Blend creates only one by default. The project file is a way to organize all your files neatly and to specify how they are *built* to create the application. Additionally, the project file can contain references to other components. In Windows Explorer, this file has the extension ".csproj" (for a C# project) or ".vbproj" (for a VB.NET project). Again, we detail the project file and its properties in Chapter 9.

▶ The *References* folder contains links to all the components needed to run the application. The components present by default are the *core components* provided by the Silverlight framework. Later we will add references to additional components.

▶ The *Properties* folder contains "meta-information" about the application. This is where we will define later the name of your firm, the copyright information, the assembly's version, etc...

▶ *App.xaml* and the linked file *App.xaml.cs* contain global resources and information valid for the whole application.

> **NOTE**
>
> In previous chapters, we used a `Canvas` as the top level component for our XAML files. In Silverlight 2, the top component is a `UserControl`. You can think of the `UserControl` as a "container" for the main panel of your Silverlight application.

▶ The file *Page.xaml* contains the XAML user interface for your Silverlight application. This is the only file that we will use in this chapter.

▶ The file *Page.xaml.cs* contains the *code-behind* defining the actions and operations of your application.

We spend more time using these files in later chapters. For the moment, we concentrate on the XAML file only.

Executing in the Web Browser

Expression Blend creates the infrastructure needed to run a Silverlight application in the web browser, including a web server embedded in Blend. That's right, you can test your web application in a real web server without installing anything.

1. In Expression Blend, press the F5 key. This will open the page in the default browser defined in your operating system. Notice how a web server was started for your application. The application runs in HTTP!

2. Alternatively, select the menu Project / Test Solution.

The HTML page in which the Silverlight application runs is here for tests only. It is created "on the fly" by Expression Blend. To deploy your application on the Internet, you will need a website or a web application. We will take care of this in Chapter 7, "Deploying to a Web Page," and later.

Of course, a white panel on a white HTML page is not very spectacular. Make sure to run your application again after we create content for your Silverlight page!

Working with Shapes

Blend allows working with three types of primitive shapes: rectangle, ellipse, and line (other shapes such as polyline or path can be created manually, as we'll see later). Use the following steps to draw on the Design panel.

1. To select a `Rectangle`, simply press on the corresponding tool in the toolbar. To select an `Ellipse` or a line, press and hold the same tool. This displays a choice where you can select `Rectangle`, `Ellipse`, or line as you want.

2. After a `Rectangle`, `Ellipse`, or line has been selected, the cursor turns into a cross. You can draw on the white page as shown in Figure 4.5. Draw the line first, then the `Rectangle`, then the `Ellipse` on top of the line.

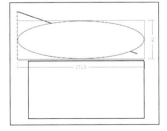

FIGURE 4.5   Drawing shapes in Expression Blend

3. When you draw multiple shapes, you will see that Blend provides a visual aid (red lines) to help you align the shapes, or to space them. Figure 4.5 shows a line, a `Rectangle`, and an `Ellipse`. The `Ellipse`'s width and height appear

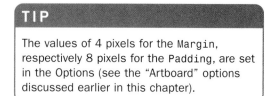

on the screen as you draw. Additionally, a red dashed line appears when the `Ellipse` is lined up with the end of the line. Finally, a thicker light red line appears when the `Ellipse` is exactly 4 pixels away from the `Rectangle`, or 8 pixels away from the container's border (here the container is a `Grid`).

4. Notice how all the objects drawn on the page appear in the Objects and Timeline category as shown in Figure 4.6. It's also interesting to note that a line in Blend is actually a `Path` in Silverlight (there are no line objects in XAML). On the other hand, Silverlight knows a `Rectangle` object and an `Ellipse` object.

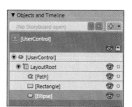

FIGURE 4.6   Simple objects hierarchy

Expression Blend can "remember" a huge number of operations that you perform. By selecting Edit, Undo from the menu (or by pressing Ctrl+Z), you can undo the operations and retrieve a previous state of the scene. Should you change your mind again, selecting Edit, Redo (or pressing Ctrl+Y) will move you forward again in time and re-create everything you just undid.

Other keyboard shortcuts can really speed up your work! The shortcuts are visible when you place the mouse over a tool in the toolbar (in the tooltip), or when you select a menu.

Using the Properties Panel

The Properties panel is a powerful feature of Blend. It allows setting (most of) the attributes of the XAML elements without typing markup, and for some properties, with visual editors, such as in the following steps:

1. Select the `Ellipse` in the Objects and Timeline category. Then select the Properties tab in the Project/Properties/Resources panel on the right of the screen.

2. All the properties that you can set are listed and grouped by category.

3. The Properties panel features a useful Search box. Type a few letters and see how the properties are filtered. Note that you may type any part of the word: For example, typing "tran" leaves the `RenderTransform` and the `RenderTransformOrigin`, because both contain the string "tran".

Using the Color Picker

The color picker is a very useful component of Expression Blend. It allows selecting any color in a variety of ways, and provides visual feedback as shown in Figure 4.7. Later we will see that it allows creating gradient brushes, and changing the transparency of a color.

FIGURE 4.7   Brushes Category and Color Picker

1. The small tabs under the `OpacityMask` property are used to set which kinds of brush you want to use on the selected element. With the `Fill` property selected, select the first tab on the left (the one with "No brush" as a tooltip). If you select this tab, notice how the background color of the ellipse disappears: You can now see the line located underneath.

2. If you select the second tab with the tooltip "SolidColorBrush", you can use the color picker to drag the small dot (currently located in the top-left corner corresponding to the white color). Using the vertical slider on the immediate right of the color picker, you can display other color groups.

3. If you want, you can set the R, G, B and A components of the color directly, or write the hexadecimal code of the color in the box with the "Hex value" tooltip (the one reading "#FFFFFFFF"). You can also type a color name (such as Red or Blue) in the box instead of the hexadecimal code. The value will automatically be converted to the corresponding code (if it exists).

4. If you want to use another color selection system, click on the letters R, G or B to display a choice. You can choose between HLS, HSB, RGB or CMYK.

> **NOTE**
>
> We talk in great detail about colors and transparency in Chapter 5, "Using Media." Do not worry about the color codes for the moment; you learn how to read them soon!

Creating a `LinearGradientBrush`

In Chapter 2, "Understanding XAML," we typed a `LinearGradientBrush` by hand. Needless to say, if your brush has many colors, this can become a tedious job. Fortunately, the color picker can also be used to create gradient brushes, like shown with the steps below:

1. Selecting the third tab allows you to visually edit gradient brushes. This is an exciting feature of Silverlight. The gradient brush editor features a `GradientStop` slider, located directly under the color picker.

2. For the moment, there are only two `GradientStops`, a black one and a white one. By selecting the black one, you can change its color to anything else, using the color picker.

3. By clicking on the `GradientStop` slider bar, you can place additional `GradientStops`.
   By moving them, you can change
   the way the gradient is calculated
   as shown in Figure 4.8. To remove
   a `GradientStop`, move it out of the
   slider.

FIGURE 4.8   `LinearGradientBrush`,
`GradientStop` slider

4. It is not easy to place `GradientStops` exactly on the slider. This is where the XAML
   Split view is useful: Locate the XAML markup corresponding to the `Ellipse`, and
   you can manually edit the position of the `GradientStops`. Try it for yourself! Each
   `GradientStop` can be moved from 0 to 1, using the `Offset` attribute!

The XAML markup created by Blend is not very nicely formatted. In fact, Blend doesn't
care much about the human eye trying to read the markup. Fortunately, after the markup
has been formatted, Blend will not mess it up anymore. Don't lose too much time refor-
matting the markup manually, though. We will see ways to format the XAML markup
automatically when we talk about Visual Studio.

Changing the Gradient Vector

A gradient is defined by a series of `GradientStops`, but also by a direction. In XAML, we
use a `StartPoint` and an `EndPoint` attribute to specify from where to where the gradient
must "flow." Expression Blend has a great tool to help you specify this vector: The Brush
Transform tool (located in the toolbar). To use it, follow the steps:

1. Click on the tool. This adds a vector arrow to the ellipse.

2. Place your mouse next to the
   arrow's tip (or end) until you see
   the small "rotation" cursor. Then
   click and rotate the vector (see
   Figure 4.9). If you press and hold
   the Shift key, it rotates in incre-
   ments of 15 degrees.

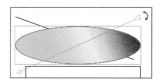

FIGURE 4.9   Rotating the gradient vector

3. Place your mouse on the arrow's middle point (with the small white circle). The
   mouse cursor changes into a cross. You can move this point to change the gradient's
   position.

4. Place your mouse directly on the arrow's tip (or end). The mouse cursor changes
   into a hand. Then drag the tip (or end) of the arrow to the selected location. Note
   that you can place the tip (or end) of the arrow anywhere you want, inside or
   outside the ellipse. This allows creating virtually any gradient you want.

5. In the XAML markup, see how the `StartPoint` and `EndPoint` are set by Blend. The
   points are set relatively to the ellipse "0,0" point, which is the `Ellipse`'s top-left
   coordinate.

Creating a RadialGradientBrush

You can also create another type of gradient: a RadialGradientBrush. Directly under the GradientStop slider, there are two small buttons. The left one (currently selected) is the LinearGradientBrush button. The right one is the RadialGradientBrush. Click on it and see how the Ellipse's fill color changes. Then with the Brush Transform tool still selected, drag the tip, end, or center point of the vector to modify the gradient.

Creating a 3D Border Effect Using RadialGradientBrush

It is interesting to see how brushes can be applied to various objects. In Chapter 3, Listing 3.7, we used a LinearGradientBrush as the Foreground property of a TextBlock. In the steps below, we see how to use a RadialGradientBrush to create a simulated 3D effect for the border of an Ellipse.

1. Select all the elements on the page (keyboard shortcut Ctrl+A) and then press Delete.

> **TIP**
>
> To draw a perfect circle using the Ellipse tool, press and hold the Shift key while resizing the ellipse.

2. Use the Ellipse tool to draw a circle on the page.

3. Select the Fill property and create a brush.

4. In the Appearance category, change the StrokeThickness to 24.

5. Select the Stroke property. For the moment, a solid black color is used.

6. Click on the Gradient Brush tab. Then click on the RadialGradientBrush button.

7. Select a darker color for the outer GradientStop (on the right) and a lighter color for the inner one (on the left).

8. Using the Color eyedropper, you can easily select any color on your screen, even outside Blend! Also, note how the last selected color is available just next to the eyedropper.

9. Move both GradientStops to the far right of the bar. Move them slowly until you get the desired 3D effect (see Figure 4.10).

FIGURE 4.10   Circle with simulated 3D border

Resetting Properties to Their Default Value

It's easy in Blend to reset properties to the default value. When you do so, the corresponding XAML markup will be removed from the source file. This can be a good occasion to clean up your markup with the following steps:

1. There is a small square next to all the properties, for example, the Fill property for the Rectangle object. If the property is set to anything else but the default value, the small square is white. If it is not set, the square is black. Later in this book we will also see that the color can be different: Green if the property is set through a resource, Orange if it is set through a binding.

2. Click on the small square to open the context menu. Select the first item Reset, shown in Figure 4.11, to erase the corresponding XAML markup, thus resetting the value to its default.

FIGURE 4.11   Pop-up menu for the Fill property

Composing the Elements Hierarchy

In Chapter 2, you saw that XAML is a hierarchical language. Some elements can contain children. In turn, some of the children can also contain children. This is reflected in Blend's Objects and Timeline tree. Let's create a new composition:

1. Create a new Silverlight 2 application.

2. Double click on the Grid named "LayoutRoot" until it has a yellow border in the Objects and Timeline category. This special type of selection means that every new element will be added to that selected panel.

3. In the toolbar, click and hold the Grid tool. This is the button right under the Rectangle, Ellipse and Line tool you used before. In the expanding menu, select a Canvas. This doesn't add a Canvas to the page yet. It simply makes the Canvas tool available in the toolbar.

4. Double click on the Canvas button. This adds a Canvas in default size to the LayoutRoot grid.

5. Resize the Canvas to a bigger size, and make it red.

6. Double click on the Canvas to select it with a yellow border.

7. Using the toolbar, add a Rectangle to the Canvas and make it yellow (see Figure 4.13).

8. See how the Objects and Timeline category reflects the hierarchy, called the *Logical tree* (Figure 4.12).

9. Then, select the `Rectangle` in the tree in the Objects and Timeline category. Drag it on the LayoutRoot. See in the Design panel what happened: The rectangle is now placed on the page, outside of the red canvas and overlapping it. Its position has been reset to 0, 0 (that's the default value, see Figure 4.14).

10. In the Objects and Timeline tree, select the `Canvas` and drag it below the `Rectangle`. See how the `Canvas` now appears on top of the `Rectangle`. This is because the tree reflects the markup: The last element in the code is the one with the highest Z-Index and will appear on top of the others.

11. Clicking on the small vertical arrow at the very bottom of the Interaction panel toggles the order of elements between "XAML order" and "Z-Index order".

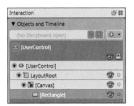

FIGURE 4.12   Logical tree

FIGURE 4.13   Rectangle inside the Canvas

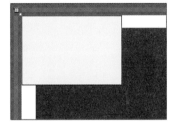

FIGURE 4.14   Rectangle outside the Canvas

Summary

Expression Blend is probably one of the most innovative UI tools developed lately, and it's nice to see a full-featured WPF application used to develop other Silverlight and WPF applications. In this chapter, you had the occasion to play with some of Blend's features. During following chapters, we will keep on using Blend to study additional features and effects.

However, do not give up on typing XAML! Some developers actually prefer to use markup instead of the visual tools. Some others prefer Blend, but all should have a good knowledge of both worlds. Later, we will use Visual Studio and enjoy the comfort of a very good XAML editor, which makes typing much easier than anything we did until now. This way, you can truly enjoy XAML as markup and XAML as visuals!

CHAPTER 5

Using Media

Mixing colors, transparencies, pictures, sounds, and videos to publish rich content—this has been a designer's dream for as long as the Web has existed. Past solutions were never completely satisfying, either because they were slow and heavy, or because they didn't blend well in the HTML page. Silverlight brings new solutions to this old problem.

Mixing Colors

Many converters are involved in the process of parsing a XAML file and transforming it into objects. Colors are a good example of this: Converters have the task of parsing strings formatted like "#AARRGGBB" or "#RRGGBB" and to convert these in colors or in brushes. In WPF and in Silverlight, a color is defined using four elements: Red, Green, Blue (the famous RGB), and another element named *Alpha channel* which we will discuss in a moment.

1. Enter the markup in Listing 5.1 in KaXaml:

LISTING 5.1   White Canvas

```
<Canvas x:Name="parentCanvas"
        xmlns="http://schemas.microsoft.com/client/2007"
        xmlns:x="http://schemas.microsoft.com/winfx/2006/xaml"
        Width="100" Height="100"
        Background="White"/>
```

2. Replace the Background value with the following color names: "Red", "Blue", "Lime", "Green".

3. Now, replace the Background value with the following values:

   "#FF0000", "#0000FF", "#00FF00", "#007F00".

The result is the same.

▶ To code a color in XAML (as in HTML), you can use the color's name when it exists. For example, the colors White, Yellow, Green, Blue, Purple, and Red are all applicable. So you can write Fill="Blue" for a Rectangle. However, not all combinations of R, G, and B have names. The list of all the predefined colors and their code can be found online at http://msdn2.microsoft.com/en-us/library/bb188314.aspx.

▶ If a color isn't named, you must code the colors using the R, G, and B values.

▶ The R, G, and B elements are coded from 0 to 255. Mixing these three fundamental colors can produce all colors from Black (0, 0, 0) to White (255, 255, 255).

Why FF?

Humans count in base 10, or the *decimal* system. We count from 0 to 9, and then we go one step higher from 10 to 19, and so on.

Computers, however, use the *binary* system (base 2). They count with 0s and 1s. For them, the value 0 is coded "0000'0000" and the value 255 is coded "1111'1111". The value 128, for example, is coded "1000'0000". For computers, this is okay, but for humans, it's annoying to type all these 0s and 1s. When humans want to talk to a computer, they would rather use the *hexadecimal* system (base 16). Since 16 is a multiple of 2 (16 = 2*2*2*2), converting from binary to hexadecimal is easy. In base 16, we count from 0 to F as shown in Table 5.1.

TABLE 5.1   Decimal, Binary, Hexadecimal

Decimal	Binary	Hexadecimal
0	0	0
2	10	2
8	1000	8
10	1010	A
12	1100	C
15	1111	F

Similarly, we have:

▶ $128_{[10]} = 1000'0000_{[2]} = 80_{[16]}$

▶ $255_{[10]} = 1111'1111_{[2]} = FF_{[16]}$

With this way of coding, we can represent all numbers from 0 to 255 with just two characters: From 00 to FF! So when we code a color, we can write them like in Table 5.2:

TABLE 5.2   Mixing Colors

White	R=0, G=0, B=0	000000	
Yellow	R=255, G=255, B=0	FFFF00	
Green	R=0, G=128, B=0	008000	
Blue	R=0, G=0, B=255	0000FF	
Lime	R=0, G=255, B=0	00FF00	
Red	R=255, G=0, B=0	FF0000	
-no name-	R=129, G=212, B=208	81D4D0	
-no name-	R=160, G=104, B=24	A06818	

In XAML, when you use a color code (instead of a name), you must use the # prefix, as in HTML. Writing `Fill="Blue"` is exactly the same as writing `Fill="#0000FF"`.

> **NOTE**
>
> **Green or Lime?**
>
> Even though the Green color is named this way, the Green (G) element is not equal to 255, but only 128. The color with R=0, G=255, B=0 is named Lime.

Seeing Through the Transparency Channel

The main difference with HTML regarding colors is the possibility to define the Alpha channel, as mentioned briefly. This additional element specifies the transparency of a color, from 0 (fully transparent) to 255 (totally opaque). The Alpha channel is coded as the first element of a color, and its default value is FF (or 255).

These three expressions are exactly equal:

▶ `Fill="#FF0000FF"` is the same as

▶ `Fill="#0000FF"` is the same as

▶ `Fill="Blue"`.

We can see how to use the transparency in XAML markup in Listing 5.2 and Figure 5.1:

LISTING 5.2   Setting the Transparency

```
<!--Transparency.xaml - Setting the Transparency-->
<Grid xmlns="http://schemas.microsoft.com/client/2007"
      xmlns:x="http://schemas.microsoft.com/winfx/2006/xaml"
      Background="#FFFFFFFF" Width="480" Height="110">

  <!--Text appearing under the squares-->
  <TextBlock Text="THIS IS TEXT" FontSize="72" Margin="10,0,10,0" />

  <!--5 small squares with partially transparent background-->
  <StackPanel Orientation="Horizontal">
    <StackPanel Margin="8,5,8,5">
      <Rectangle Width="80" Height="80" Fill="#19FF0000" />
      <TextBlock Text="10% (#19)" HorizontalAlignment="Center" />
    </StackPanel>

    <StackPanel Margin="8,5,8,5">
      <Rectangle Width="80" Height="80" Fill="#4CFF0000" />
      <TextBlock Text="30% (#4C)" HorizontalAlignment="Center" />
    </StackPanel>
    <StackPanel Margin="8,5,8,5">
      <Rectangle Width="80" Height="80" Fill="#7FFF0000" />
      <TextBlock Text="50% (#7F)" HorizontalAlignment="Center" />
    </StackPanel>
    <StackPanel Margin="8,5,8,5">
      <Rectangle Width="80" Height="80" Fill="#CCFF0000" />
      <TextBlock Text="80% (#CC)" HorizontalAlignment="Center" />
    </StackPanel>
    <StackPanel Margin="8,5,8,5">
      <Rectangle Width="80" Height="80" Fill="#FFFF0000" />
      <TextBlock Text="100% (#FF)" HorizontalAlignment="Center" />
    </StackPanel>
  </StackPanel>
</Grid>
```

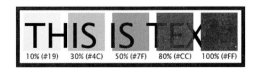

FIGURE 5.1   Setting the transparency

Seeing Through the Opacity

There is another way to make an element transparent in Silverlight: The Opacity property. This is not the same as the Alpha channel! When you set the Alpha channel of a color to 50% (or 7F), this affects only the element using this color. In the opposite, when you set the Opacity of an element to 50% (or 0.5), this affects that element *and its children*! Sometimes you will want to use the Opacity property like in Listing 5.3 and Figure 5.2, but sometimes you will stick with Alpha channels like you did in Listing 5.2.

LISTING 5.3   Setting the Opacity

```
<!--Opacity.xaml - Setting the Opacity-->
<Grid xmlns="http://schemas.microsoft.com/client/2007"
      xmlns:x="http://schemas.microsoft.com/winfx/2006/xaml"
      Width="400" Height="200" Background="#FF97A5FF">

  <Grid.ColumnDefinitions>
    <ColumnDefinition Width="0.5*"/>
    <ColumnDefinition Width="0.5*"/>
  </Grid.ColumnDefinitions>

  <Canvas Background="#7FFF0000" Margin="10,10,10,10">
    <TextBlock Width="161" Height="133"
               TextWrapping="Wrap" Canvas.Left="10" Canvas.Top="10"
               Text="Alpha channel: Even though the Canvas'
                     background is half transparent,
                     the children are fully opaque" />
    <Ellipse Width="98" Height="36"
             Fill="#FF00FF05" Stroke="#FF000000"
             Canvas.Left="72" Canvas.Top="134" />
  </Canvas>

  <Canvas Background="#FFFF0000" Margin="0,10,10,10"
          Opacity="0.5" Grid.Column="1">
    <TextBlock Width="161" Height="133"
               TextWrapping="Wrap" Canvas.Left="10" Canvas.Top="10"
               Text="Opacity: The Canvas and this label are
                     both half transparent" />
    <Ellipse Width="98" Height="36"
             Fill="#FF00FF05" Stroke="#FF000000"
             Canvas.Left="82" Canvas.Top="134" />
  </Canvas>
</Grid>
```

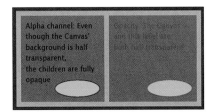

FIGURE 5.2   Setting the opacity affects the children.

Using Vector Graphics

In Silverlight and WPF, all the graphics you create are *vector graphics*. Instead of being a collection of pixels like other *raster graphic* formats (such as BMP, GIF, PNG, JPG, and so on), vector graphics are a set of lines, curves, points, and polygons known as *primitives*. If a zoom factor is applied to such a graphic, the framework calculates a new view of this image in a smooth way, and even the smallest details remain sharp and precise. In the opposite, raster graphics don't resize well, and when you zoom in too much, you'll see pixels appearing. This gives a nasty look to your images. Note that not all graphics are vector graphics in Silverlight. If you import a PNG file to a Silverlight project and use it, the format remains PNG and is not converted to a vector graphic. Let's take a look at a vector graphic:

1. Point your Silverlight-enabled web browser to http://silverlight.net/samples/1.0/ Silverlight-Pad/default.html

2. On the left-hand side, select the Camera file.

3. Use the Zoom buttons in the top-right corner to zoom in and out.

4. You can click on the picture and move the mouse around to "pan" the picture on your screen and observe the details.

Let's compare vector and raster graphics in Figures 5.3, 5.4, 5.5 and 5.6.

FIGURE 5.3   Camera, 100%

FIGURE 5.4   Camera, 7%

FIGURE 5.5   Zoom 700%, vector

FIGURE 5.6   Zoom 700%, raster

Figures 5.3 to 5.6 show clearly that a vector-based graphic zooms much better than a raster-based graphic. As soon as the human eye starts seeing the pixels, the picture becomes unsmooth.

On the other hand, if you zoom out (refer to Figure 5.4), you'll notice that when the picture gets very small, it becomes difficult to recognize the features of the camera. The problem is that there are too many details, and the human eye is not able to differentiate between them to render a clear picture. If a very small zoom factor is applied, it may be necessary to use another, less detailed image. This is just like icon files do (*.ico): saving one image for 32x32 pixels and another, less detailed image for 16x16 pixels.

Adding Media to Your Scenes

As in HTML, images are added to Silverlight using a control especially designed to hold them: the `Image` control. This control accepts a file path as its source. The path may point to a local file (in the same folder as the XAML file, or in a subfolder), or even on a web server somewhere.

Let's create a small gallery of thumbnails in a XAML page and add animations when they get clicked. To control the animations, we will add C# code to the application, without worrying too much about understanding it for the moment. Follow the steps to create this application:

1. Create a Silverlight 2 Application project in Expression Blend. Name this project "Thumbnails".

2. Navigate to the URL http://galasoft.ch/SL2U/Chapter05 and save the four media files pic1.png, pic2.jpg, pic3.jpg and mov1.wmv by right clicking on their name and choosing Save Link As (or Save Target As, or a similar menu) from the context menu. Store these files in a temporary folder on your PC.

3. Open Page.xaml.

4. Make sure that the LayoutRoot `Grid` is selected, and then open the Properties panel.

5. Select the background brush, and set it to No brush. The `Grid`'s background is set to transparent because we want the Silverlight application to display the HTML page's background.

Laying Out the Application

For the moment, we only want to display the media lined up vertically. Some pictures are 240 pixels wide, others are 320 pixels wide. However, we want our Thumbnails gallery to display smaller images. We will use a vertical `StackPanel` for this. Also, later our Thumbnails gallery will have two `TextBlocks` greeting the visitor, and a frame to display the expanded pictures. We want to leave space to host these elements.

1. Using the Selection tool in the toolbar (that's the arrow on top), make sure that the `Grid` named LayoutRoot is selected in the Objects and Timeline category.

2. Pass the mouse over the top-left corner of the `Grid` to make sure that it is in Grid layout mode, and not in Canvas layout mode (see Figure 5.7). If needed, click on the small indicator to switch from one mode to the other.

FIGURE 5.7   Grid or Canvas layout mode

3. Pass the mouse over the light blue border on the left of the `Grid`. You should see an orange horizontal line appear on the `Grid`. Clicking creates a new row in the `Grid`. Set the row's height to approximately two-thirds of the `Grid`'s height (we will set the exact height later in the Properties).

4. Pass the mouse on top of the grid this time to create a new column at approximately two-thirds of the grid's width. You now have a Grid with two rows and two columns.

5. Make sure that LayoutRoot is selected with a yellow border (if needed, double-click on it in the Objects and Timeline category).

6. Using the panel tool in the toolbar (10th tool from the top), add a StackPanel to the Grid. If the Grid tool is selected, you must press and hold on it to display the other panel types. You can either double-click on the StackPanel tool to add it to the Grid in default size and position, or you can directly draw it in the Grid's second column. Don't worry about the panel's size; we will reset it in the Properties panel.

7. Make sure that the StackPanel's Column property is set to 1. This places the StackPanel in the second column of the Grid (remember that XAML uses 0-based indexes).

8. Reset the Height of the StackPanel to Auto, the Margin to "0,0,0,0" and set the RowSpan to 2.

9. Set the StackPanel's Width to 170.

10. If needed, reset the StackPanel's HorizontalAlignment and VerticalAlignment. This sets the actual value to Stretch, which is the default (see Figure 5.8).

FIGURE 5.8   Resetting the alignment

11. Choose the Selection tool again; then place the mouse next to the small lock at the Grid's first row, and click (don't click *on* the lock, but *next* to it, as shown in Figure 5.9!). This selects the whole row. In the Properties panel, set its Height to 340 Pixels (choose the unit "Pixels" from the combo box and enter the value 340). Then select the second row in the same manner and set its height to 1 Star (here too, use the combo box to choose the Star unit, and then set the value 1 in the text box).

FIGURE 5.9   Selecting the row

TIP

Star-sizing

Star means the rest. So 1 Star for a column's width means take the whole rest of the width once all the other columns have been laid out. 0.5 Star means take half of the rest of the width…, and so on.

12. Select the first column and set its Width to 1 Star.

13. Finally, select the last column and set its Width to Auto. The last column will take the exact same width as the StackPanel it contains.

Adding Pictures

We will add a couple of pictures to the `StackPanel`. There are multiple ways to do that in Blend, as shown in the steps below:

1. Double-click to select the `StackPanel` with a yellow border. This is important, because objects dragged to the Designer panel will be added to the "yellow selected" panel.

2. Open the Windows Explorer at the location where you saved the media files earlier.

3. Drag the picture pic1.png from Windows Explorer to the `StackPanel` in the Designer panel. Two things happen:

    ▸ An `Image` control gets added to the `StackPanel` in the Objects and Timeline category.

    ▸ The file pic1.png gets added to the Thumbnails project.

4. Make sure that the `Image` is selected in the Objects and Timeline category and then change to the Properties panel. In the Name text box, enter the name Media0.

Another way to add an image to the `StackPanel` is to do the following:

1. In the Project panel, right-click on the Thumbnails project, and then select Add Existing Item.

2. Select the picture file pic2.jpg in the folder where you saved it earlier. This adds the file to the Thumbnails project in the Project panel.

3. Drag the file pic2.jpg from the Project panel to the `StackPanel` in the Designer panel. Again, this adds a new `Image` control to the `StackPanel` in the Objects and Timeline category. Here too, select the `Image` control and set its name to Media1.

Adding Video

It may sound strange that such an exciting feature as the ability to add video to a web page takes only one small section to describe. There are two reasons:

▸ We will talk more about media (supported codecs and formats, video players) in Chapter 12 "Encoding Videos with Expression Encoder."

▸ It's really easy to add rich media to your Silverlight scene using the following steps!

    1. Drag and drop the video file mov1.wmv from Windows Explorer on the Thumbnails project in the Project panel.

    2. Open the Asset Library by clicking on the last button on the bottom of the toolbar.

    3. Make sure that the check box labeled "Show All" is checked and select the `MediaElement` control.

4. Using the new `MediaElement` tool added above the Asset Library button in the toolbar, add a `MediaElement` control to the `StackPanel`.

5. Select the `MediaElement` in the Objects and Timeline category. In the Properties panel, under the Media category, select the movie file mov1.wmv from the combo box. Then reset the `MediaElement`'s width and height to `Auto`.

6. Notice how the `MediaElement` now takes the whole width of the `StackPanel`, while its actual height changes to keep the movie proportional. If you really want to, you can try and set the `Height` of the `MediaElement` to a non-proportional value to distort the video. Silverlight's video rendering capabilities are powerful.

7. Using the Properties panel, set the `MediaElement`'s name to Media2.

8. Expand the Media category. By using these properties (or by setting them directly in XAML), you can mute the movie, change the sound balance, and change the volume. Later, using C#, you will even be able to control these properties as well as the playback from your application. You can also find a description of all these attributes at the following URL: http://msdn2.microsoft.com/en-us/library/bb188356.aspx.

9. The height of the top user control is set to 480 pixels by Blend when the project is created, and its width to 640 pixels. We want the application to fill the whole web browser's screen, so select the top `UserControl` in the Objects and Timeline category and set its `Width` and `Height` to `Auto`. Note how the first column of the `Grid` collapses to 0 pixels, because it doesn't have any content yet.

> **TIP**
>
> **Design size**
>
> To avoid that empty columns and rows collapse to 0, you can use the Design size feature in Blend. Select the user control and use the special *adorners* (Figure 5.10) to modify the element's size in Blend. The Design size is only used in the visual designer and has no effect at all during runtime.

FIGURE 5.10   Design Size Adorners

Testing the Result Quickly in a Web Browser

We mentioned that Expression Blend allows easy testing in a web browser; let's prove it: Simply press F5. This should start the test web server and then open a new window in your favorite web browser. The video even plays! However, once the video reaches the end, it simply stops. We will change this a little bit later in this chapter.

Note, turn your speakers on, because the movie also has sound!

Refining the Layout

The picture and video thumbnails added to the application look okay, but they could be better. It would be nice to have some space between the thumbnails, and maybe to add a thin frame around each of them. Let's do that now:

1. Double-click on the `StackPanel` until it is selected with a yellow border.

2. In Blend, click and hold the panel tool in the toolbar, and select the `Border` tool.

3. Double-click on the `Border` tool three times. This adds three `Borders` to the `StackPanel`. `Borders` are lightweight containers. They can contain only one child. This child can be any control, or a panel, which in turn can contain multiple children.

4. Select the first image Media0 in the Objects and Timeline category and drag it on the first `Border`. This adds the image to the `Border`. Notice how the image (which used to be the first) now is the third one. This is because the first `Border` was added *after* the two images and the video. In the XAML markup, the first `Border` element comes *below* the video. Reset the `Border`'s and the `Image`'s `Width` and `Height` to `Auto`.

> **WARNING**
>
> **Auto Layout**
>
> When you move an element into a different container in the Objects and Timeline category, Blend assumes that you want its size to be fixed. This is in contradiction with our desire to use auto layout as often as possible. This is why, after you move any element, you should reset its `Width` and `Height` to `Auto`, and check that its `Margin` is set according to your wishes.

5. Drag the second image on the second border and reset its `Width` and `Height`.

6. Then repeat for the video and the third border.

   The result is exactly the same as we had before, because the `Borders`' properties have not been set.

7. Select the first `Border`, and set its `Margin` to left=right=10, top=bottom=5. Notice how the picture gets resized to comply with the `Border`'s new size. Note that in XAML, the `Margin` is defined by "left,top,right,bottom"—for example, "10,5,10,5". The order of the margins in Blend is slightly confusing (left, right, top, bottom).

   The `Border` control also has a `Padding` property. Using the same XAML syntax as the `Margin` property, the `Padding` defines a space *inside* the `Border`, between the `Border` and its child. The `Margin`, on the other hand, is the space *outside* the `Border`, between the `Border` and its container (or its siblings).

   Unfortunately, panels (`Grids`, `StackPanels`, and so on) don't have a `Padding` property. If you need padding, you can enclose the panel inside a `Border` and set the padding on the `Border`.

8. With the `Border` selected, set the `BorderBrush` to a `SolidColorBrush` of #FFA9A899 and the `BorderThickness` to "2,2,2,2". Notice how you can choose a different thickness for each side of the `Border`!

9. Repeat the operation for all three `Borders`. Note that you can select multiple elements in the Objects and Timeline category and apply the same properties to all of them. To select multiple elements, hold down the Ctrl key when you click on them.

It is annoying to have to set similar properties on all the controls. This is exactly what styles are for: You can define a set of Properties in a style and then simply apply the style to the controls. We will talk about styles in Chapter 17 "Using Resources, Styling, and Templating."

Adding Yet Another Image

Expression Blend allows copying parts of the logical tree and pasting it somewhere else in the document. In XAML you can also copy an element (including its children) and paste it, but it's sometimes a little difficult to keep an overview of where you are located. Blend makes this operation easy thanks to the Objects and Timeline category. Follow these steps to add a new image:

1. Add the last image, pic3.jpg, to the Thumbnails project.

2. In the Objects and Timeline category, select the first `Border` and choose Edit, Copy (or press Ctrl+C).

3. Make sure that the `StackPanel` is selected with a yellow border.

4. Select Edit, Paste (or press Ctrl+V).

5. Here too, Blend assumes that you want to fix the new `Border`'s `Width` and `Height`. Make sure that you reset these to `Auto`, and set the `Margin` just like for the other three borders!

6. In the Objects and Timeline category, select the `Image` control into the last `Border`.

7. In the Properties panel, select pic3.jpg in the `Source` property combo box.

8. If needed, set the `Image` control's name to Media3.

> **TIP**
>
> **Drilling into the Elements Tree**
>
> Instead of using the Objects and Timeline category, you can "drill into" the controls by double-clicking on them. For example, with the `StackPanel` selected, double-clicking on the last picture selects the `Border` first. Double-clicking again selects the `Image` control into the `Border`.

You may use JPG or PNG pictures; these two formats are supported by Silverlight at the moment. More formats should be supported in future versions.

Controlling Sound and Video

Three things are annoying regarding the video in our Thumbnails gallery:

▶ The movie automatically starts when the page is loaded, which is distracting for the user.

▶ The movie runs until the end; then stops and cannot be restarted.

▶ Once the movie starts, there is no way to pause it.

To correct these issues, we need to set properties, and also a little code-behind. This is our first contact with C#, so don't expect to fully understand everything we do here. Everything will become clearer in future chapters!

Switching Auto-Play Off

The very first thing you do is to prevent the movie to start automatically when the page is loaded, with the following steps:

1. Select the `MediaElement` named Media2 in the tree.

2. In the Properties panel, set the `AutoPlay` property to false (in the Miscellaneous section, uncheck the check box). At the time of writing, there is a bug in Expression Blend. You might need to click the `Autoplay` check box two or three times to set its actual value to false.

Creating an Endless Loop

Let's force the movie to start again once it reaches the end. This needs a little code to work. Simply follow the steps:

1. Select the `MediaElement` named Media2.

2. On top of the Project panel, click on the button with the small lightning bolt (Events), as shown in Figure 5.11.

FIGURE 5.11   Events button

This displays a list of all events for this element. The one that interests us is `MediaEnded`. This event is *raised* when the video comes to an end. At this moment, we want to restart the video to create an endless loop.

3. Click once in the text box next to the MediaEnded label. Then enter the event handler name `MediaElement_MediaEnded` and then click outside of the box to remove the focus.

This action modifies the XAML markup by adding the MediaEnded event handler:

```
<MediaElement x:Name="Media2"
  Source="mov1.wmv" AutoPlay="False"
  MediaEnded="MediaElement_MediaEnded" />
```

If you installed Visual Studio previously, this action also starts the development environment, opens the Thumbnails application in it and places a snippet of C# code into the Thumbnails application's Page class. If you don't have Visual Studio installed, the snippet of C# code gets placed in the Clipboard and must be pasted in the C# code-behind file.

The integration between Studio and Blend is great when it works, but some problems have been reported on some systems. If this happens to you, use the Options dialog in Blend to disable the integration (under Event handlers), and use the Clipboard instead with the following steps:

1. Open the file Page.xaml.cs in a text editor (for example Notepad).

2. Paste the code snippet in the Page block.

Then modify the *event handler* named MediaElement_MediaEnded to restart the video. Conveniently, the MediaElement at the origin of the event is passed to the event handler (this is the sender parameter). Also, when the video comes to an end, it stays positioned at the end. So we will stop the video first and then start it again, as shown in Listing 5.4.

The rest of the code is irrelevant for now; we will learn much more about C# later (in Chapter 9 "Understanding .NET" and later chapters), and you will be able to understand everything we do here!

LISTING 5.4   Thumbnails Application, MediaEnded Event

```
public partial class Page : UserControl
{
  public Page()
  {
    // Required to initialize variables
    InitializeComponent();
  }

  private void MediaElement_MediaEnded(object sender,
    System.Windows.RoutedEventArgs e)
  {
    (sender as MediaElement).Stop();
    (sender as MediaElement).Play();
  }
}
```

Pausing and Playing the Video

Finally, we will start the video when the MediaElement is clicked, and pause it the next time it is clicked. Again, we need to add an event handler to the MediaElement: In Blend, select the MediaElement and enter the name MediaElement_MouseLeftButtonDown in the box labeled MouseLeftButtonDown. This copies the code in Visual Studio (or in the Clipboard). If needed, open the file Page.xaml.cs in a text editor. Paste the code in Listing 5.5 in the Page class, under the existing event handler MediaElement_MediaEnded:

LISTING 5.5   Thumbnails Application, MouseLeftButtonDown Event

```
private bool _isPaused = true;
private void MediaElement_MouseLeftButtonDown(object sender,
  System.Windows.Input.MouseButtonEventArgs e)
{
  if (_isPaused)
  {
    (sender as MediaElement).Play();
    _isPaused = false;
  }
  else
  {
    (sender as MediaElement).Pause();
    _isPaused = true;
  }
}
```

In short, we save a variable named _isPaused which can be either true or false. If it's true, when the MediaElement is clicked, we play the video and then set the _isPaused variable to false. If the variable is false when the MediaElement is clicked, the video is paused, and the variable is set to true. Easy, no?

Setting a "Hand" Cursor

Just to make it more obvious that the user can click on the MediaElement, we will change the appearance of the cursor when the mouse passes over it with the following steps:

1. In Blend, select the MediaElement.

2. In the Properties panel, click on the Properties button (next to the Events button we clicked earlier, on top of the panel).

3. Find the Cursor property and select Hand.

To check all this, press F5 in Blend. The C# code we entered previously will be *compiled* by Expression Blend.

If you want to play audio instead of video, simply set the `Source` attribute of the `MediaElement` to any supported sound file. The supported formats in the current version are

- ▶ (Sound)—MP3, WMA (WMA7, WMA8, and WMA9)

- ▶ (Video)—WMV (WMV1, WMV2, WMV3, WMVA, and WMVC1)

Additionally, at the time of writing, support for H.264 and AAC have been announced for a later version of Silverlight (but not in Silverlight 2 yet).

Checking the Other Properties

A few other properties govern the appearance and behavior of media in Silverlight.

Filling the Space

You can control the way an image (or a video) fills the space by using the `Stretch` property (see Figure 5.12). There are four possible values:

- ▶ `None`—The image doesn't get resized or distorted at all whatever the container size is. It may be cropped.

- ▶ `Uniform`—The whole picture will be displayed. The aspect ratio is preserved, but the picture may be resized if needed.

- ▶ `Fill`—The whole picture will fill the whole container whatever happens. It is never cropped, will get resized as needed, and may be heavily distorted.

- ▶ `UniformToFill`—The picture will fill the whole container, but without being distorted. It may be cropped, however.

FIGURE 5.12   Using the `Stretch` attribute

Hiding the Media from Mouse Input

Sometimes you want to place an image or a video on a scene, but hide it temporarily. We saw already how to use the `Opacity` attribute to hide the element visually. However, when an element's opacity is set to 0, it will still receive the mouse input, and possibly block elements underneath from receiving the click.

To avoid this, there are two possibilities:

- ▶ You can set the `Visibility` property to `Collapsed`. This not only hides the element, but it won't even influence the layout anymore, or receive mouse input. This is not always satisfactory, however. Sometimes the Collapsed value has nasty side-effects, as we will see in the next section about video brushes.

▶ Alternatively, you can set the IsHitTestVisible attribute to false. In that case, any mouse click on the element will be ignored. This attribute is not just available for images and videos, but for a lot of Silverlight elements.

Using Media to Write

An interesting way to use media is to write text to your web pages! Yes, you can write with images and videos. Let's try it! For a change, we will now work a little in the XAML editor.

Writing with Video

Let's start with video and the following steps:

1. In the Designer panel, click on the XAML tab. This displays the XAML editor instead of the visual designer.

2. *Under* the first panel, but still *inside* the LayoutRoot Grid, add the markup in Listing 5.6:

LISTING 5.6   Thumbnails Application, Adding a TextBlock

```
<StackPanel Grid.Row="1">
  <TextBlock Text="Welcome to my Gallery!"
             Margin="10,0,10,0" FontSize="48" TextWrapping="Wrap"
             FontWeight="Bold" FontFamily="Arial">
    <TextBlock.Foreground>
      <VideoBrush SourceName="Media2" />
    </TextBlock.Foreground>
  </TextBlock>
</StackPanel>
```

The VideoBrush used to "paint" the text makes reference to the element Media2 added previously. It is synchronized with this MediaElement: When the video plays, you'll see movement in the TextBlock as well. So it is possible to control the VideoBrush by controlling the MediaElement that it references.

The new StackPanel gets added to the first column of the Grid, because we didn't specify the Grid.Column attached property. The default value for Grid.Column is 0, which corresponds to column number 1.

Using an Invisible Video to Paint Text

Sometimes you want to use a video that is not displayed in your scene, in which case you can do the following:

1. Add a `MediaElement` anywhere and set its `Source` to a video file.

2. Set the `IsMuted` property to true if you don't want this video to be heard.

3. Set the `MediaElement`'s `Opacity` to 0 to hide it. You cannot simply set the `Visibility` property of the source `MediaElement` to Collapsed. If you do, the `VideoBrush` won't show anything.

4. To avoid unwanted effects when the user clicks on the area in which the `MediaElement` is placed, use the `IsHitTestVisible` and set it to false.

```
<MediaElement Source="mov1.wmv"
              IsMuted="True"
              Opacity="0"
              IsHitTestVisible="False"
              x:Name="InvisibleMedia"/>
```

Then you can use this `MediaElement`'s `Name` as the `SourceName` property for the `VideoBrush`.

Writing with Images

Instead of a `VideoBrush`, we can also use an `ImageBrush` to write text.

Add the `TextBlock` in Listing 5.7 just under the one we added in the previous section, but still *inside* the `StackPanel` container.

LISTING 5.7   Thumbnails Application, Adding Another `TextBlock`

```
<TextBlock Text="Have some fun!"
           Margin="10,0,10,0" FontSize="48" TextWrapping="Wrap"
           FontWeight="Bold" FontFamily="Arial">
  <TextBlock.Foreground>
    <ImageBrush ImageSource="pic1.png" />
  </TextBlock.Foreground>
</TextBlock>
```

Note that you can use a `VideoBrush` or an `ImageBrush` everywhere you can use any other type of brush (such as `SolidColorBrush`, and so on). Run the application. The result is displayed in Figure 5.13.

FIGURE 5.13   Media gallery, writing with media

Transforming Media

WPF and Silverlight bring graphics and media to a whole new level, with the possibility to transform images and even videos. All the transforms we studied earlier can be applied to the `Image` and `MediaElement` controls. It also means that these elements can be animated, for example rotated, skewed, or flipped (in which case the video will be displayed from behind). By combining transforms, you can reach the kind of simulated 3D effects that are used in this rather impressive demo:

www.telerik.com/demos/silverlight/#Examples/Cube/FirstLook.

Using Web-Based Media

You can also use a web-based image as the source of your images (or of your media elements). However, the following points are important:

▶ You can access media located on another server. For example, if your Silverlight application runs in www.galasoft.ch/mysilverlightapplication (this is just an example), you can add an image (or a movie) located on www.microsoft.com.

▶ When you access an image, the path must be using the same scheme! For example, a Silverlight application running in HTTPS cannot access an image in HTTP.

If your application runs in HTTP, you cannot access a file located on the local file system (for example c:\temp\pic1.jpg). Similarly, if your application runs locally, you cannot access pictures from the Web.

Your application runs in the FILE scheme when you open the file by double-clicking it. You will see an address starting with "file:" or "C:" in the browser's address bar. When you use a web server to test your applications (for example by pressing F5 in Blend), they run in the HTTP scheme.

Table 5.3 lists what is allowed and what is not:

TABLE 5.3   Accessing Media

Silverlight Scheme	Media Scheme	OK
FILE file:///C:/temp/Project1/Default.html C:\temp\Project1/Default.html	HTTP/HTTPS http://www.domain.com/pic1.jpg https://www.domain.com/pic1.jpg	NO
FILE file:///C:/temp/Project1/Default.html C:\temp\Project1/Default.html	FILE file:///C:/temp/pic1.jpg C:\temp\pic1.jpg	OK
HTTP http://www.domain.com/Default.html	HTTP http://www.domain.com/pic1.jpg	OK
HTTP http://www.domain.com/Default.html	HTTPS https://www.domain.com/pic1.jpg	NO
HTTPS https://www.domain.com/Default.html	HTTP http://www.domain.com/pic1.jpg	NO
HTTP http://www.domain.com/Default.html	FILE file:///C:/temp/pic1.jpg C:\temp\pic1.jpg	NO
HTTP / DOMAIN 1 http://www.domain1.com/Default.html	HTTP DOMAIN 2 http://www.domain2.com/pic1.jpg	OK
HTTPS / DOMAIN 1 https://www.domain1.com/Default.html	HTTPS DOMAIN 2 https://www.domain2.com/pic1.jpg	NO

For more information about accessing media and permissions, check the following page on MSDN: http://msdn2.microsoft.com/en-us/library/bb820909.aspx.

Summary

In this chapter, you learned how to use colors and transparency to create advanced designs. Then you used images, videos, and sound to enhance your HTML pages with rich media. Silverlight is a platform of choice to create rich web pages, because of the advanced graphics capabilities it offers, and because of the unique possibility to blend this rich content within HTML elements.

CHAPTER 6

Blending a Little More

We already learned to know Expression Blend as a creative tool allowing us to design, compile, and run Silverlight (and WPF) applications. Later we will use this tool in collaboration with Visual Studio (for the source code), but for now we will continue to create XAML markup visually in Blend.

Creating Transforms

We studied the transforms available in Silverlight in Chapter 3, "Playing with XAML Transforms and Animations," and saw how to apply them to UI elements. Using Blend, it is easy to create all these transforms using the following steps:

1. Create a new Silverlight 2 Application project in Expression Blend.

2. Add a rectangle in the visual designer, and change its color and borders to make it look colorful.

3. Make sure that the rectangle is selected. Place the mouse cursor next to one of its corners, and observe how it changes to a "rotate" cursor. Click and drag to rotate the rectangle.

4. Place the mouse on the small white dot located in the center of the rectangle. The cursor changes into a cross. You can move the point to another location. This is the RenderTransformOrigin point we saw in Chapter 3. Move it to a different location and try rotating the rectangle again.

5. Now place the cursor next to the point in the middle of the rectangle's short side. See how the cursor changes to a "skew" symbol. By clicking and dragging along the side of the rectangle, you apply a `SkewTransform`.

6. Since we're talking about the small decorations (called *adorners*; see Figure 6.1) placed around the rectangle, see what happens when you select the small dot at the end of a scattered line near the rectangle's angle: This will round the corners. You can also set the values in the Properties panel, using the `RadiusX` and `RadiusY` properties under the Appearance category. (It's not strictly speaking a transform, so forgive me for placing it in this part of the text.)

FIGURE 6.1   Adorners and `SkewTransform` cursor

You can also create more transforms using the Properties panel by following these steps:

1. In the Properties panel, click on the Transform category to expand it if needed.

2. See all the transforms we studied in Chapter 3 (except the matrix transform, which Blend cannot handle!). Try to play with the various transforms to see the effect on the rectangle.

3. Notice how the last tab, Flip, uses transforms to change the rectangle's aspect.

When you create a simple transform in Expression Blend, the tool creates a `TransformGroup` in XAML, and sets all the basic transforms to their default values. This produces more XAML markup than needed, but this markup may safely be removed manually if you want.

Creating an `OpacityMask`

Brushes can be used for a variety of effects: backgrounds, foregrounds, fills (for shapes), strokes, and so on. There is an additional effect that we haven't studied yet: `OpacityMask`.

We saw already how an element's `Opacity` property can be used to make it (fully or partially) transparent. This setting applies to the whole element (and its children). But sometimes, you want to define an element's opacity following a certain pattern. This is where `OpacityMask` can be useful, with the following steps:

1. In Expression Blend, create a new project (Silverlight 2 Application).

2. Make the LayoutRoot's background a plain yellow.

3. Create a blue ellipse.

4. Create a `Grid` next to the ellipse, overlapping it; set its `Background` property to a plain Red.

5. In the `Grid`, add a `TextBlock`. You can select the `TextBlock` tool and draw on the `Grid`. Alternatively, you can double-click on the `Grid` in the Objects and Timeline category until it gets a yellow border. Then you can double-click the `TextBlock` tool.

6. Set the `TextBlock`'s `Text` property to Hello and its `HorizontalAlignment` property to Center.

7. Set the `TextBlock`'s font to 48, and its `Foreground` property to Orange.

8. Select the `Grid`, and then its `OpacityMask` property. For the moment, it is set to No brush.

9. Select the Gradient brush tab.

10. In the gradient bar, select the left gradient and set its Alpha channel to 0%. This creates the result shown in Figure 6.2. Note that even though `OpacityMask` is a brush, the colors you define will be ignored, and only the Alpha channel matters.

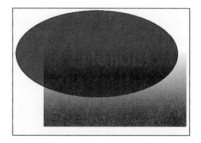

FIGURE 6.2   Grid with linear `OpacityMask`

Just like the `Opacity` property, an `OpacityMask` applies to the element and its children! The `TextBlock` we added to the `Grid` is also changed by the `OpacityMask`.

By adding gradient stops to the gradient slider, or by moving them, you can achieve different effects. Also, don't forget the Brush Transform tool in the toolbar, to change the orientation of the gradient (we worked with this tool in Chapter 4, "Expressing Yourself with Expression Blend," in the section "Changing the Gradient Vector").

For some elements, it can be interesting to use a `RadialGradientBrush` instead of a `LinearGradientBrush` for the `OpacityMask`. Try it:

1. Select the red `Grid`. Make sure that the `OpacityMask` property is selected.

2. Using the small buttons under the gradient bar, select the Radial gradient.

3. Now the center of the `Grid` is transparent, and you can see all the way down to the blue ellipse. The edges of the `Grid` are opaque.

4. Here also, you can change the aspect of the mask by using the brush transform tool, or by adding or moving gradient stops in the gradient slider (see Figure 6.3).

FIGURE 6.3   Grid with radial `OpacityMask`

We will reuse this scene in the next chapter, so make sure that you save your project carefully!

Using Paths

After you're finished playing with ellipses and rectangles, you will likely feel the need for more. Thankfully, we are not limited to these two primitives, but using drawing tools like Expression Design and Expression Blend, we can create any shape we want in XAML, and use them in Silverlight.

Creating a Path from Scratch

In Blend, paths are created using the Pen tool (P) or the Pencil tool (Y), as shown in Figure 6.4. Both tools are available in the tool group in the eighth button from the top in the toolbar.

FIGURE 6.4   Pen and Pencil tools

You can draw a path with the following steps:

1. Select the Pencil tool, and draw freehand on the page. Alternatively, you can use the Pen tool to create polygons.

2. Using the color picker, set the Fill color to Red. See how the Fill is disposed, to cover all the inner areas of Figure 6.5.

3. Select the Pen tool in the toolbar. Notice how additional "markers" appear along the path. These are the *anchor points* defining the shape.

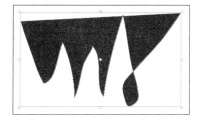

FIGURE 6.5   Freehand path with Solid Color Fill

4. With the Pen tool selected, move the cursor near an anchor point. Notice how the Pen cursor changes depending on whether you are passing over an anchor point, next to it, or on the path or not.

Blend offers many ways to modify a path by adding, removing, or moving anchor points, and by changing curves. These operations are triggered by a combination of the tool chosen, the position of the mouse, and keyboard shortcuts. A complete list of all the possible operations is given in Expression Blend help, available by selecting Help, Keyboard Shortcuts from the menu, and then choosing the hyperlink titled Pen and selection shortcuts in Expression Blend.

Using Splines to Modify a Path

Drawing freehand shapes is difficult, especially if you don't have a graphic tablet. It is easier to start with one or more paths, and to modify them, for example with the following steps:

1. Delete everything and then draw a rectangle on the screen.

2. From the menu select Object, Path, Convert to Path. This turns the `Rectangle` object into a `Path` object. This command is also available for ellipses.

3. Select the Pen tool from the toolbar.

4. Place the cursor on one of the rectangular path's long sides, and press the Alt key. This turns the cursor into the Convert Segment cursor.

5. Click and drag the long side and see how it turns into a curve.

6. Click on the Direct Selection tool (A) in the toolbar. Use this tool to click and drag the *tangent* anchored on the corner point (see Figure 6.6).

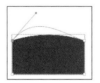

FIGURE 6.6   Tangent and spline

Combining Shapes

Sometimes, you want to use existing paths and combine them to create a more complex one. The steps below show you how.

> **TIP**
>
> **Hidden tangent**
>
> To display the tangent again if it is hidden, use the Direct Selection tool (A) and click on an anchor point.

1. Delete everything on the screen and draw a blue rectangle. Then draw a red ellipse overlapping the rectangle.

2. Select both paths. You can do this either by selecting the two paths with the Shift key pressed, or with the Ctrl key pressed, or by clicking anywhere on the LayoutRoot grid (outside a path) and dragging the selection rubber band to touch both the rectangle and the ellipse (see Figure 6.7).

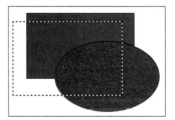

FIGURE 6.7   Selection rubber band

3. From the menu select Object, Combine to make one single path out of the rectangle and the ellipse. As you see, you have the following options: Unite, Divide, Intersect, Subtract, and Exclude Overlap.

4. Select Unite from the menu and see the result. Then press Ctrl+Z to undo the last operation, and try all the other possibilities. Notice how the unified shape takes the color of the last element you select (either the blue rectangle, or the red ellipse).

5. From the menu select Object, Path, Release Compound Path. This splits the combined path into two objects, as shown in Figure 6.8.

FIGURE 6.8   Two shapes—Exclude Overlap and Release Compound Path

Clipping Path

When we started talking about Silverlight, we mentioned an exciting feature: It is possible to create nonsquare areas, so that not only the *visual* but also the *hit test area* is nonsquare. This allows you to easily create nonsquare controls.

The support for nonsquare shapes is extensive, and it is actually possible to give any shape to any element, even images and videos! This amazing feat is accomplished using *clipping paths*. Follow these steps.

1. Set LayoutRoot's color to yellow.

2. In Blend, in the Project panel, right-click on the project file (the one directly under the solution) and select Add Existing Item.

3. Use the File Explorer to select a WMV file on your disk. If you don't have a WMV file available, you can download one from www.galasoft.ch/SL2U/Chapter05.

4. Drag the movie from the Project panel to the LayoutRoot grid. This creates a new MediaElement. Alternatively, use the method we mentioned in Chapter 5, "Using Media," in the section titled "Adding Video." Position this new element on the grid and size it.

5. Make sure that the MediaElement is selected and set the Cursor property to Hand.

6. Use the shape created previously (refer to Figure 6.8) and place it on the MediaElement. You may need to change the order of the elements in the Objects and Timeline category so that it appears on top of the MediaElement, and you may need to resize it.

7. Make sure that both the MediaElement and the shape are selected. Then from the menu select Object, Path, Make Clipping Path.

8. Run the project in the web browser by pressing F5 (see Figure 6.9).

FIGURE 6.9   MediaElement with clipping path

Notice how the clipping path modifies even a video element. The underlying LayoutRoot is visible in the excluded overlap, and the cursor only turns to a Hand when it is on the visible video. The hit test area follows the shape exactly, and if you click on an excluded area, you will effectively click on the element underneath.

The ability to modify not only an element's shape, but also its hit test area opens the door to creativity without any limits. Any XAML shape can be turned into a movie screen. Later we will see how we can use *templates* to create controls (buttons, check boxes, and so on) from scratch. Here too, we can use paths to shape the control and blend it in the environment.

Paths in XAML

In XAML, paths are created with a specific notation named *Path Markup Syntax*. An example of the Path Markup Syntax can easily be seen in Blend with the following steps:

1. Right-click on the clipped `MediaElement` created in the previous section and select View XAML.

2. In the XAML editor, scroll until you see a property named `Clip`, which contains an apparently incoherent suite of numbers and letters. In fact, this is a code, which translates the visual path into a text form. This is called the *Path Mini Language*.

Explaining this notation is outside the scope of this book, but more details can be found at http://msdn2.microsoft.com/en-us/library/bb412389.aspx.

Grouping Controls

Often, when you design an application, you suddenly realize that some components belong together. You may want to move them together, resize the group, and so on. Other times, you want to duplicate a group of controls and copy the group multiple times in your application, with just minor changes. Blend can assist you in these tasks and make them easier.

Grouping Elements

Every good drawing application allows grouping elements together. In Blend, you can do this too but remember that we don't draw a static picture, we create XAML markup. Grouping elements modifies the markup too, as shown in the following steps:

1. Create a new Silverlight 2 Application in Blend.

2. Create a few elements on the screen (rectangle, ellipse, path, button, and so on).

3. Select some of the elements by pressing the Ctrl key and clicking on the ones you want to group. Make sure to leave some elements unselected.

4. In the scene shown in Figure 6.10, the black-orange ellipse, the red path, and the button are selected. The two other elements are not part of the selection.

5. Once done, from the menu select Object, Group Into, Grid.

6. The three elements selected are now part of a new Grid, as shown in Figure 6.11, which was inserted in the tree (see the Objects and Timeline category).

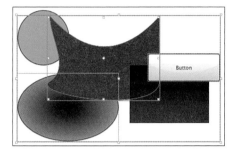

FIGURE 6.10   Scene with paths and button

Notice how the Button now appears *under* the black-red rectangle. This is because the Grid is inserted between the green circle and the black-red rectangle. Thus the Z-Index of the Button is now the highest within the Grid but lower than the black-red rectangle's Z-Index.

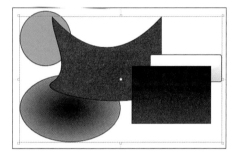

FIGURE 6.11   Elements grouped into a Grid

1. Select the bottom-right corner of the selected Grid containing the three grouped elements, and resize it.

2. Then move the group to another location (see Figure 6.12).

The three elements now act as a group, and can get resized or moved together. If you resize the group too small, some elements may disappear out of sight!

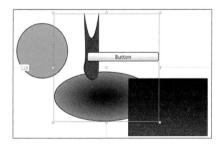

FIGURE 6.12   Resized group

Trying Other Panels

When choosing Object, Group Into from the menu, you can select different types of panels. For example, selecting a StackPanel will stack the three elements above each other, creating a very different effect. We will study all the panels and their features in Chapter 15, "Digging into Silverlight Elements."

One useful choice is the `ScrollViewer`. If a scene is too big for a given area, the `ScrollViewer` can host it and will display horizontal and/or vertical scrollbars if needed for example with the following steps:

1. Press Ctrl+Z a few times until you restore the scene as it was in Figure 6.10.

2. Now choose Object, Group Into, ScrollViewer from the menu.

   By default, only the vertical scrollbar appears. The horizontal one is disabled. You can enable it by selecting the `ScrollViewer` and then setting the property `HorizontalScrollBarVisibility` to Visible (it is located under the Miscellaneous section).

3. If you now resize the `ScrollViewer`, the scene contained into it doesn't get resized, but the scrollbars will appear.

4. Try enabling and disabling the scrollbars, and resizing the scene to understand how the `ScrollViewer` reacts to resizing.

5. Finally, run the application and use the scrollbars to scroll the scene (see Figure 6.13).

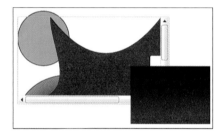

FIGURE 6.13   Scene with `ScrollViewer`

Scrolling the Thumbnails

Remember our Thumbnails application? We have four thumbnailed media elements into a `StackPanel`. If you run that application and resize the web browser to a small width, the thumbnails on the bottom will disappear. One solution to that problem is to set them into a `ScrollViewer` with the following steps:

> **NOTE**
>
> `ScrollViewer`, `Border` **and** `Panel`
>
> A `ScrollViewer` is not a panel. Like a `Border`, it can contain only one single element. When you group multiple elements into a `ScrollViewer`, Blend adds a `Grid` in the `ScrollViewer`, and then adds the elements into the `Grid`. You can see this by expanding the Objects and Timeline category.

1. Open the Thumbnails application into Expression Blend.

2. In the Objects and Timeline category, select the `StackPanel` containing the four `Borders`.

3. Right-click on the `StackPanel` in the Objects and Timeline category.

4. Select Group into, ScrollViewer from the menu. Technically, we didn't "group" anything, since we have only one element. This is just a convenient way to insert a `ScrollViewer` in the scene.

5. When the logical tree gets modified, Blend often modifies the layout properties. Select the `ScrollViewer`, and in the Properties panel, make sure that the `Margin` is set to 0,0,0,0. The `Width` and `Height` should be `Auto`. The `Column` should be 1 and the `RowSpan` should be 2. The `HorizontalAlignment` and `VerticalAlignment` properties should be set to Stretch.

6. Under the Layout category, expand the advanced properties and check that the `HorizontalScrollBarVisibility` is Disabled and the `VerticalScrollBarVisibility` is Visible (this is the default).

7. Finally, reset the `StackPanel`'s `Height` to `Auto`. Leave its `Width` set to 170.

8. Run the application and resize the browser window to be less high than the four thumbnails; notice how the vertical scrollbar can be used to scroll if needed.

Making a User Control

Grouping elements into a panel is a nice feature, but it doesn't cover all scenarios. Sometimes, you want to reuse a group of elements in your application. Granted, you could simply copy/paste the group of elements. But this is not satisfactory if the group contains a great number of elements. Also, the instances of this group may vary slightly in their behavior. It would be nice if each instance of the group could get a code-behind file to give some "intelligence" to the group. This is what a `UserControl` does.

In Silverlight 2, each Silverlight application's top container is in fact a `UserControl`. This provides a nice model throughout the Silverlight application: A main `UserControl` contains XAML elements and other controls. We talk more about user controls and other types of controls in Chapter 19, "Creating User Controls and Custom Controls." In this section here, we study the automatism that Blend provides to create a new user control.

Creating a User Control

With the following steps, we will build a control named a `SpinButton`, and then use it to build a basic (and nonfunctional) date picker, composed of three such `SpinButtons`.

1. Create a new Silverlight 2 Application in Blend and name it DatePickerControl.

2. Copy the `Grid` in Listing 6.1 inside the top `UserControl` container. This creates the scene shown in Figure 6.14.

LISTING 6.1   Spin Button and Date Picker

```
<!--Page.xaml - SpinButton and DatePicker-->
<Grid x:Name="LayoutRoot">

  <Grid.RowDefinitions>
    <RowDefinition Height="25" />
```

LISTING 6.1   Continued

```
    <RowDefinition Height="*" />
  </Grid.RowDefinitions>

  <Grid.ColumnDefinitions>
    <ColumnDefinition Width="75" />
    <ColumnDefinition Width="75" />
    <ColumnDefinition Width="75" />
    <ColumnDefinition Width="*" />
  </Grid.ColumnDefinitions>

  <!--Spin Button Basis-->
  <Border HorizontalAlignment="Stretch" VerticalAlignment="Stretch">
    <Grid>
      <Grid.RowDefinitions>
        <RowDefinition Height="0.5*" />
        <RowDefinition Height="0.5*" />
      </Grid.RowDefinitions>
      <Grid.ColumnDefinitions>
        <ColumnDefinition Width="*" />
        <ColumnDefinition Width="20" />
      </Grid.ColumnDefinitions>

      <Button Grid.Column="1" Cursor="Hand" />
      <Button Grid.Column="1" Grid.Row="1" Cursor="Hand" />
      <TextBox Grid.RowSpan="2" Text="10" FontSize="14" />
    </Grid>
  </Border>
</Grid>
```

3. Select the `Border` immediately under LayoutRoot in the Objects and Timeline category.

4. From the menu select Tools, Make Control or press the F8 key.

5. In the Make Control dialog, enter the name SpinButton. The Leave Original Content check box should be unchecked.

This creates two new files: SpinButton.xaml and SpinButton.xaml.cs. Additionally, a new

FIGURE 6.14   SpinButton

> **WARNING**
>
> **Rebuild needed**
>
> The newly created SpinButton instance is only visible in Page.xaml after you save everything and rebuild the project. Choose Project, Build Solution from the menu.

instance of the SpinButton control is placed instead of the Border we had previously. The SpinButton will need some code to work. In the current implementation, nothing happens when you click on the Up or Down buttons. However, we don't know how to write this code yet and will not implement the functionality.

Using the User Control

Now we will use our SpinButton to create an additional control with the following steps:

1. Open Page.xaml and open the Asset Library by pressing the corresponding button (it is the lowest button in the toolbar).

   The Asset Library (see Figure 6.15) contains all the controls that you can use in Silverlight 2, including those that we know already: all the panels, the TextBlock, the TextBox, the Button, and so on.

2. Click on the Custom Controls tab. This tab contains all the controls that you create yourself (in addition to the top Page).

FIGURE 6.15   Asset Library

3. Select the SpinButton. This places the corresponding tool in the toolbar, just above the Asset Library button.

4. Make sure that LayoutRoot is selected with a yellow border; then double-click twice on the SpinButton tool. This adds two new controls to the Grid.

5. In the Objects and Timeline category, select the second SpinButton in the tree. In the Properties panel, set the Column to 1, and if needed reset the HorizontalAlignment and VerticalAlignment to Stretch.

6. Do the same with the third SpinButton, but this time set the Column to 2.

   You now have all three SpinButton instances neatly lined up.

7. Finally, select all three SpinButtons, and choose Tools, Make Control from the menu. Name the new control DatePicker.

After saving, selecting Page.xaml and having rebuilt the application, you see now only one control in LayoutRoot, and this control is named DatePicker. Notice also how its ColumnSpan property is set to 3 (meaning that the control is spread over there columns) to replace the layout we had before we created that control.

> **NOTE**
>
> **Not Perfect**
>
> The Make Control feature is not perfect by a long shot. For example, the three `SpinButtons` inside the `DatePicker` don't resize neatly when the `DatePicker` is set to a different width. Obviously, the tool cannot guess exactly what the developer wants. Nonetheless, F8 is a convenient shortcut to speed up development.

Working on the Thumbnails Gallery

We are going to reuse what we learned to enhance our Thumbnails gallery with additional features. In Blend, open the Thumbnails project again.

Adding a Display Frame

We will use this display frame only in Chapter 10, "Progressing with .NET," but let's add it already with the following steps.

1. Open the file Page.xaml in the XAML editor.

2. Copy the XAML markup in Listing 6.2 into the main `Grid`, at the very end, after the `StackPanel` containing the `TextBlocks`. Make sure that this markup is *inside* the LayoutRoot.

LISTING 6.2   Thumbnails Application, Display Frame

```
<Grid Width="340" Height="260" Margin="30,30,0,0"
      VerticalAlignment="Top" HorizontalAlignment="Left">
  <Rectangle Fill="#FF000000" Opacity="0.5" Margin="20,20,-20,-20" />
  <Rectangle Fill="#FF000A70" />
  <Rectangle x:Name="DisplayBackground" Margin="10,10,10,10">
    <Rectangle.Fill>
      <LinearGradientBrush StartPoint="0,0.5" EndPoint="1,0.5">
        <GradientStop Color="#FFABABAF" Offset="0" />
        <GradientStop Color="#FFABABAF" Offset="1" />
        <GradientStop Color="#FF767499" Offset="0.5" />
      </LinearGradientBrush>
    </Rectangle.Fill>
  </Rectangle>
  <Rectangle x:Name="Display" Margin="10,10,10,10" Fill="Transparent" />
</Grid>
```

▶ We add a shadow under the display frame. This is done by placing a rectangle in the `Grid`, behind all other elements (that's the first rectangle). We set its background to black, its opacity to 50%, and then we use margins to move it down and to the right. Note that if an element has negative margins, parts of it will appear out of its parent container.

▶ We will display the expanded thumbnails in the Display rectangle. Note that it is fully transparent for the moment.

▶ Right underneath it, we place a background rectangle, which will be visible if no media is displayed, or if the expanded media is smaller than the whole frame (for example for narrow pictures). Note the LinearGradientBrush used for this rectangle's Fill.

Adding a Reflection under the Thumbnails

Now that we know how to use VideoBrush and ImageBrush (studied in Chapter 5), transforms (studied in Chapter 3), and the OpacityMask (studied earlier in this chapter), we have all we need to make a cool reflection effect next to our Thumbnails with the following steps:

1. In the Objects and Timeline category, select the first of the four Borders containing the thumbnailed media.

2. Right-click and choose Group Into, Grid.

3. Select the newly created Grid around the Border, and reset the Width and Height to Auto. Make sure that HorizontalAlignment and VerticalAlignment are both set to Stretch. Then set the Margin to 10 (left), 10 (right), 5 (top) and 5 (bottom).

4. Double-click on the Grid until it is surrounded by a yellow border. Make sure that this Grid is in Grid layout mode (refer to Figure 5.7).

5. In the toolbar, make sure that the Selection tool is selected. Then pass the mouse on the light blue border on top of the Grid. Using the orange vertical line that appears, create a column at approximately two-thirds of the Grid's width as shown in Figure 6.16. Do not worry if this messes up the layout somehow. We will take care of this in a moment.

FIGURE 6.16   Creating a column

6. Click just next to the small lock on the left and set its width to 0.75 Star (this is 75% of the whole width). Then set the second column to 0.25 Star.

7. In the Objects and Timeline category, expand the Grid you just created and select the Border it contains.

8. Make sure that the Column is set to 0 (the first column); reset the ColumnSpan to 1 and the Margin to "0,0,0,0". The layout should look better again now.

9. With the small `Grid` still selected with a yellow border, add a `Border` to it and use the Properties panel to place it in `Column` 1 (the second column). Reset its `Width` and `Height` to `Auto` and its `Margin` to "0,0,0,0".

10. Double-click on that new `Border` to select it with a yellow border and add a `Rectangle` to it. Again, set its `Width` and `Height` to `Auto`, `Margin` to "0,0,0,0", `HorizontalAlignment` and `VerticalAlignment` to Stretch.

11. Open the Designer in Split mode by clicking on the small tab on top-right of the Designer panel.

12. In the Objects and Timeline category, select the `Rectangle` you just added. The XAML markup of this rectangle is now shown in the XAML panel.

13. Replace this `Rectangle` with the markup in Listing 6.3:

LISTING 6.3   Thumbnails Application, `ImageBrush`

```
<Rectangle>
  <Rectangle.Fill>
    <ImageBrush ImageSource="pic1.png"/>
  </Rectangle.Fill>
</Rectangle>
```

You should now see a smaller Matterhorn directly next to the bigger thumbnail. We will now transform it to make it look like a reflection.

14. Now we want to flip the reflection rectangle. Make sure that it is selected in the Objects and Timeline category (not the `Border`, but the `Rectangle`!).

15. In the Transform category (in the Properties panel), select the rightmost tab, Flip, and then use the corresponding button to flip along the X axis.

16. We will now use the `OpacityMask` to make this reflection look more real: Select the `Rectangle`'s `OpacityMask` property, and click on Gradient brush.

17. The new gradient brush is oriented from top to bottom. Use the Brush Transform tool (G) to rotate the gradient so that it points from left to right.

18. In the gradient bar, set the right gradient stop's Alpha channel to 0%.

19. Set the left gradient stop's Alpha channel to 90%. If needed, move the gradient stops, or use the Brush Transform tool to make the reflection look more real.

    Finally, we will "skew" the reflection. This way it will look as if it is reflecting on a nonflat surface. Follow these steps:

20. Select the `Border` containing the reflection.

21. Find the Skew transform and set the Y angle to 30.

22. In the Properties panel, locate the `RenderTransformOrigin` property (under the Miscellaneous category) and reset it to "0,0". This is the top-left corner, the corner that should remain unchanged by our transform.

The next picture is going to stand in front of the reflection, somehow breaking the effect. This is why you will take care of repeating the steps for all the images.

Reflecting Video

Using the same steps, but replacing the `ImageBrush` with a `VideoBrush`, you can add a reflection effect under the video thumbnail. The reflection will play when the original media element plays too. That's a rather impressive effect!

▶ Execute steps 2 to 13 in the preceding list of steps for the third `Border`, containing the video.

▶ Then, enter the markup in Listing 6.4 for the rectangle:

LISTING 6.4   Thumbnails Application, VideoBrush

```
<Rectangle>
  <Rectangle.Fill>
    <VideoBrush SourceName="Media2" />
  </Rectangle.Fill>
</Rectangle>
```

▶ Then, execute steps 14 to 22.

To see your changes, press F5 in Blend. Make sure that you click on the video thumbnail to start the video and see the video reflection!!

Just One Last Thing

When you run the application and resize the browser window to test the scrolling, you'll see that the last reflection is cut on the bottom side. This is because the "skewed" reflection does not count when the total height of the `StackPanel` is computed. The reflection is outside its normal boundaries.

To avoid cutting the last reflection, we can simply add a margin on the bottom side of the `StackPanel` containing the thumbnails with the following steps.

1. In the Objects and Timeline category, select that `StackPanel` (inside the `ScrollViewer`).

2. Set the bottom `Margin` to 60.

3. Run the application again. The reflection should now appear uncut (see Figure 6.17).

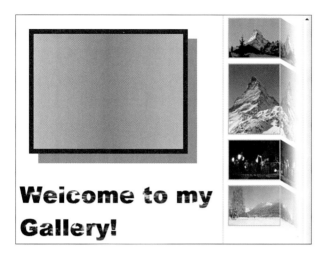

FIGURE 6.17   Video and image reflections

Summary

In this chapter, we built on our basic knowledge of Expression Blend and expanded it to create advanced graphics effects and animations. We saw how the tool can make the programmer's life easier by supporting us when we create complicated XAML markup visually.

CHAPTER 7

Deploying to a Web Page

Deploying a Silverlight application to a web page is an exciting step: You share your work with the world! Depending on your past experience, you may already have a website. In that case, you probably know about FTP and publishing HTML already, and some sections of this chapter will feel like a refresher.

Creating a Test Page

When you create a new Silverlight application in Blend and run it by pressing F5, an HTML page is automatically created for you. The first thing we will do is copy the test page's code and create a new one, which we can modify as we want. Later (in Chapter 14, "Letting .NET and JavaScript Talk") we see how Visual Studio can generate a website and the corresponding HTML page for you so that you don't need to copy the generated HTML page every time you create a new Silverlight application. For now, simply follow these steps.

1. Create a new Silverlight 2 application in Blend. Name it TestObjectTag.

2. Change the background color of the main grid named LayoutRoot to Red.

3. Build the application by selecting the Project, Build Solution from the menu. This step is needed to generate the files we want.

4. Right-click on the project in the Project panel (just under the solution), and select Open Folder in Windows Explorer.

5. You should now see all the files included in the project, for example App.xaml, App.xaml.cs, Page.xaml, Page.xaml.cs, and so on.

6. Navigate to the folder [Project Root]\bin\Debug. You should now see a bunch of generated files, including a file named TestObjectTag.xap (we'll talk about this file later) and a file named Default.html.

7. Copy the file Default.html into the project root (the folder where you have the XAML and CS files). We don't want to edit the original one, because it is regenerated by Blend every time you compile the application, and your changes would be overwritten.

8. Right-click on the file Default.html that you just copied, and select Open With, Notepad. This opens the HTML file in a text editor. Alternatively, you can choose any text editor you prefer.

9. Since we moved this file, we need to edit the path to the XAP file. Locate the line starting with `<param name="source"` and change the value from `"TestObjectTag.xap"` to `"bin/Debug/TestObjectTag.xap"`. Depending on your editor, the text color might be different, but the content is the same. This is a URL! You must use the forward slash "/" to separate the folders, and not Windows backslash.

10. In Windows Explorer, double-click on the file Default.html you just modified. You should now see your red Silverlight application in your favorite browser.

NOTE

When you run the application by pressing F5, Blend starts a so-called *development web server* for you. This way, the HTML page with your Silverlight application is served using conditions as real as possible, using the HTTP protocol. You may have noticed a small icon in your Tray bar, saying "ASP.NET Development Server – Port XXXX." This is where you can control the web server that Blend just started. If you start multiple applications together, each will have a separate instance of the web server, with a different port.

When you double-click on the file Default.html, it runs instead in "file" mode. The address in the browser's location bar doesn't start with "http:". It's not exactly the same as running the file in the development web server, like we discussed in Chapter 5, "Using Media," and like we will also see later in this book. The main difference is that the *site of origin* of the Silverlight application is local, and that it will not get the same permissions as a web-based application.

Understanding the `object` **Tag**

The file Default.html has the following sections:

▶ In the header, three CSS rules to style the page and the Silverlight application. *CSS (Cascaded Style Sheets)* is outside the scope of this book. It is enough to say that you can "style" a Silverlight `object` tag and its enclosing `div` element. For example, use the rule named `#silverlightControlHost` to set the size, position, or other features of the `div` element with the same id.

▶ Still in the header, a JavaScript function named `onSilverlightError`. It will be called if an error occurs with your Silverlight application. You don't need to worry about this for the moment.

▶ In the `body` section, a `div` element with the id `errorLocation`. The JavaScript function `onSilverlightError` will display additional information about the possible errors in this element. In normal conditions, this element is invisible.

▶ The main `div` element (id: `silverlightControlHost`), containing an `object` tag. This is where the magic occurs.

Attributes

`object` tags are used to create an instance of a plug-in. This is also the mechanism used, for example, by Adobe Flash or by Java applets to run on a page. It contains a series of attributes that define the behavior of the plug-in. Let's talk about the most important ones.

The `type` **Attribute**
This attribute is important because it helps the plug-in to decide whether a newer version is needed to run the current content. For example, if the `type` attribute specifies `application/x-silverlight-2`, it means that version 2 of Silverlight is the minimum needed to run this application. If only version 1 is installed, the Install Microsoft Silverlight button will be displayed (see the later section "Detecting Silverlight" for details).

The `width` **and** `height` **Attributes**
These attributes can be used to set the size of the Silverlight application. It is better to leave these two attributes set to `100%` and to use the CSS rule `#silverlightControlHost` to change the size of the application. Do not remove these attributes however, they are mandatory.

The `id` **Attribute**
The `id` must be unique within your whole HTML page. Though this `id` is not generated by the HTML test page, it is a good idea to uniquely identify your Silverlight object, in order to access it later, either through JavaScript or CSS.

Parameters

The `object` tag also has children (remember, HTML is very close to XML, so the hierarchy also exists here), a series of `param` tags used to pass information to the plug-in.

The source **Parameter**

This parameter tells the plug-in where to look for the content to be displayed. It is mandatory and cannot be omitted.

The onerror **Parameter**

This parameter contains the name of a JavaScript function, which will be executed if there is an error when creating or running the Silverlight application. In the generated test HTML page, the JavaScript function is already available. It has two parameters, `sender` and `args`. This last parameter contains additional information about the error, such as the error type, error message, and so on. The generated error handling function displays the error message to the user. You can of course modify this function to customize the error message or to display it in another way.

The onload **Parameter**

This parameter is not created by default, but you can add it. It follows the exact same syntax as the `onerror` parameter. The JavaScript function that it references will be called when the Silverlight application has been fully loaded and is completely ready to start working.

The background **Parameter**

This sets the color of the Silverlight application's background. This color will be visible only if you set the `windowless` parameter to `true` as explained in the next section.

The `background` parameter is a XAML color, not an HTML color. It means that you can also set the Alpha channel, as we saw in Chapter 5.

In addition to these generated parameters, you can create additional ones as discussed in the following sections.

The windowless **Parameter**

This parameter is tricky. To keep it simple, let's say that if `windowless` is false, even if you set the background color of your XAML page to Transparent, you will not see what is underneath the Silverlight plug-in. We say that the plug-in is "windowed." On the other hand, if `windowless` is true, the plug-in is integrated with the HTML markup, and you can even place HTML elements on top of the Silverlight scene.

Additional Parameters

There are additional parameters and attributes not mentioned here. You can find their description in Silverlight's documentation (see Chapter 1, "Introducing Silverlight," in the section called "Installing the Documentation"). Look for the documentation page titled "Instantiating a Silverlight Plug-In (Silverlight 2)".

Modifying the Attributes and Parameters

We saw the most important attributes in the preceding sections. There are a few other ones, and you should definitely read the documentation about them to learn more. For the moment, let's just play a little with the attributes we know and observe their effect. First let's prepare our application with the following steps:

1. In Blend, in the application TestObjectTag, set the width and height of the top user control to 300, respectively 200.

2. Place a small rectangle in the bottom-right corner of the grid LayoutRoot. We will use this rectangle as a "marker." The bottom-right corner of the rectangle should be placed in the bottom-right corner of the Grid.

3. Build the application.

Playing with the Size

Let's experiment with the application's (and its container's) size first with the next steps:

1. Go back to the file Default.html that we copied before.

2. Change the CSS rule for the HTML page's body as in Listing 7.1:

LISTING 7.1   Body CSS Rule

```
body {
    padding: 0;
    margin: 0;
    background-color: Green;
}
```

3. Change the CSS rule #silverlightControlHost as in Listing 7.2:

LISTING 7.2   silverlightControlHost CSS Rule

```
#silverlightControlHost {
  height: 180px;
  width: 280px;
}
```

4. Change the value of the background parameter of the Silverlight
object tag to Blue.

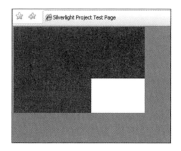

5. Double-click on Default.html to
run it in your favorite browser. You
should see the red Silverlight application, but notice how you see
only part of the "marker" rectangle
as shown in Figure 7.1. The size of
the Silverlight application remains
300x200. The rest of the applica-
tion is hidden, as well as the blue background we just set.

FIGURE 7.1   Silverlight plug-in is too small.

6. Now change the #silverlightControlHost CSS rule as in Listing 7.3:

LISTING 7.3   silverlightControlHost CSS Rule, Modified

```
#silverlightControlHost {
    height: 220px;
    width: 320px;
    background-color: yellow;
}
```

7. Refresh the page in the web
browser. You should now see a
border of blue between the red
Grid and the green body background (see Figure 7.2). The yellow
color never appears, because the
div element is completely filled by
the Silverlight application, and the
application itself is completely
filled by the red Grid.

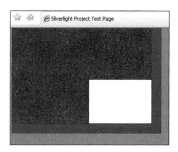

FIGURE 7.2   Silverlight plug-in is too big.

In general, you want to match the size of the silverlightControlHost div element with
the size of the Silverlight application. In our case, the rule would be as in Listing 7.4:

LISTING 7.4   silverlightControlHost CSS Rule, Modified

```
#silverlightControlHost {
    height: 200px;
    width: 300px;
    background-color: yellow;
}
```

The last experiment is to modify the size of the Silverlight plug-in within the div element. In other words, we will now see the div element's yellow background:

1. Change the width and the height attributes in the object tag to 50%. The width and height attributes in the object tag use the same syntax as CSS width and height, so you can use %, px, and so on.

2. Refresh the page in the web browser. You should now see that the Silverlight plug-in occupies only one quarter of the yellow div. As we said before, you usually want the Silverlight plug-in to occupy the whole div element, but controlling these two attributes might come in handy in some occasions.

Colors, Transparency, and windowless

Let's try diverse transparency settings with the following steps:

1. In Blend, set LayoutRoot's background color to red, but with the Alpha channel set to 50% like we did in Chapter 5.

2. Build the application.

3. Open the file Default.html in your web browser. You should see a purple background for your application (see Figure 7.3). The reason is that the red Grid is half

FIGURE 7.3 Half-transparent red Grid on blue background.

transparent, so the red color is mixed with the Silverlight plug-in's blue background (blue + red = purple).

4. Change the value of the `background` parameter in the `object` tag to `Transparent`. Since this is a XAML color, `Transparent` is a valid value.

5. Then, add a parameter as follows:

```
<param name="windowless" value="true" />
```

6. Refresh the page in the web browser. You should now see an orange background: The blue background is gone, and since the Silverlight application is `windowless`, the HTML element `div` is visible underneath. This `div` has a yellow background (yellow + red = orange).

7. Just out of curiosity, change the `windowless` parameter from `true` to `false` and refresh the web page. Depending on your operating system, the results will vary:

   ▶ In Windows, you will see a dark red background. This is because the non-windowless Silverlight plug-in appears as a black element (half transparent red + black = dark red).

   ▶ On Macintosh computers, you shouldn't see any difference, because the `windowless` parameter is ignored.

These small exercises are important to understand the hierarchy of all the elements needed to represent a Silverlight application. From the web page's body, to the `div` host, to the Silverlight plug-in, to the main user control, to the LayoutRoot and its children, all these elements have a size and a color that will influence the end result.

Deploying with JavaScript

There is an alternative way to deploy your application on an HTML page, using JavaScript. We see this alternative in the next chapter (Chapter 8, "Programming Silverlight with JavaScript"), where we talk more about this fascinating (and often misunderstood) programming language.

Detecting Silverlight

We saw already in Chapter 1 that Silverlight can detect whether the Silverlight plug-in is installed. In fact, it can even detect whether the installed version is recent enough to play the downloaded content. If that is not the case, an Install Microsoft Silverlight button is displayed. Often, however, you want a more creative message.

For example, imagine that you have a low-resolution video posted on an online video service. Since you know that Silverlight offers a better user experience, you want to offer this video in high-definition to your end user. If Silverlight is installed on the client, the high-resolution video must play; if it isn't, you want to display the low resolution video instead. Let's see what steps are needed.

1. In TestObjectTag, in Default.html, change the `type` attribute from `application/x-silverlight-2` to `application/x-silverlight-3`. Then refresh the page in the web browser. You should now see the button asking you to install Silverlight. This is because you requested a version of Silverlight that is not installed on your PC (in fact, it is not even available on the market yet).

2. With Default.html open in a text editor, go down to the line starting with:

```
<a href="http://go.microsoft.com/fwlink/?LinkID=115261"
```

3. This is where the browser finds the content to be displayed, in this case an Install Microsoft Silverlight picture enclosed in a link. In fact, the whole HTML markup included between the last `param` element and the closing `</object>` tag will be displayed. This is where you can be creative and display any HTML content you want.

4. As you probably noticed, the content displayed by default is hosted by Microsoft.com. It means that the Get Silverlight button will not be displayed if you are offline. In most cases, however, you want to host the content yourself.

5. Don't forget to change the `type` attribute back to `application/x-silverlight-2`!

Integrating Silverlight in an Existing Web Page

Adding Silverlight content to an existing web page is actually pretty easy because of the fact that the `object` tag is just a standard HTML tag. Also, the `source` parameter accepts a XAP file even if it's not located on the same web server as the HTML page hosting it.

This fact is especially important in case you want to integrate Silverlight content in a blog, for instance. Many providers allow you to add custom HTML content to some sections of your blog, but do not allow you to save any external files (apart from pictures) on their server. With this ability, you can save the Silverlight content on your own web server and reference it on your blog.

> **WARNING**
>
> Some blog sites (such as Google's blogger.com) or community websites (such as facebook.com or myspace.com) do not allow HTML tags to be added to the user's content on a blog they host. Checking whether a community site or a blog site accepts Silverlight content is an important part of choosing a host for your public content!

Understanding the Original Code

In the following example, you edit an existing web page and replace the central image with an animated Silverlight application. Follow the steps.

1. Download the original code located at www.galasoft.ch/SL2U/Chapter07/ SilverlightBookCover.Original.zip.

2. Extract the content of the Zip file to a local folder.

3. Open the file index.html in a web browser. You should see Figure 7.4.

FIGURE 7.4   Original Silverlight book cover page

4. If you open index.html in a text editor of your choice, you see that the page has four main areas:

   ▶ The HTML header with the included CSS file.

   ▶ A Silverlight logo (picture). This image is positioned using CSS so that it appears "on top" of the central image if the page is resized to a very narrow size.

   ▶ The Silverlight book cover picture that we want to replace.

   ▶ A `div` with a promotional message.

Getting the XAP file

The whole Silverlight application is packaged as an XAP file. This includes the XAML markup, the C# code-behind (compiled in a DLL), a small Silverlight logo movie displayed in the top-left corner, and the book cover, which will be animated.

To use the XAP in the web page you are modifying, you need to get the XAP file with the following steps:

1. Download the XAP file from www.galasoft.ch/SL2U/Chapter07/ SilverlightBookCover.xap.

2. Save this file in the resources folder, located in the same directory as the file index.html that you are editing now. Make sure that it is really named SilverlightBookCover.xap. Sometimes the web browser adds a ".zip" extension to the file name. If that's the case, you must remove this extension!

That's it, you have everything you need!

The steps needed to create the book cover animation are not listed here. It is a standard Silverlight 2 application, created using Expression Blend. If you want to study the code, you can download it from www.galasoft.ch/SL2U/Chapter07/SilverlightBookCover. Source.zip. Simply extract the content to a local folder, and then open the file SilverlightBookCover.sln in Blend.

If you don't want to use the proposed animation but instead create your own XAP file, feel free to do so. After you build the application, the XAP file is found in the bin/debug folder.

> **TIP**
>
> You must remember to update the `source` parameter in the `object` tag when you move the XAP file to another location!

Modifying the Markup

To include the new Silverlight logo, open the file index.html in a text editor of your choice, and follow these steps:

1. The original markup we want to replace is in Listing 7.5:

LISTING 7.5   Original Image

```
<!--Book cover-->
<img src='resources/SL2U-web.png'
    alt='Silverlight 2 Unleashed'
    title='Silverlight 2 Unleashed'
    style='width: 470px;height: 445px;' />
```

2. Replace this markup with the markup as in Listing 7.6:

LISTING 7.6   Animated Logo

```
<!--Silverlight-enabled book cover animation-->
<div id="silverlightControlHost">
  <object data="data:application/x-silverlight,"
          type="application/x-silverlight-2"
          width="100%" height="100%">
    <param name="source" value="resources/SilverlightBookCover.xap"/>
    <param name="background" value="Transparent" />
    <param name="windowless" value="true" />

    <!--"Static" book cover-->
    <img src='resources/SL2U-web.png'
         alt='Silverlight 2 Unleashed'
         title='Silverlight 2 Unleashed'
         style='width: 470px;height: 445px;' />

  </object>
</div>
```

3. See how we keep the original `img` tag within the Silverlight `object` tag? This is the content that will be displayed if Silverlight is not available.

4. To display the Silverlight logo in the center of the screen, we need to add some CSS code. In the header section, on top of the page, under the other .css file, add the code in Listing 7.7:

LISTING 7.7   silverlightControlHost CSS Rule

```
<!--Silverlight Animated Logo-->
<style type="text/css">
  #silverlightControlHost
  {
    height: 445px;
    width: 470px;
    margin: auto;
  }
</style>
```

Testing the Result

Open the file index.html in a web browser.

▶ You should now see the animated book cover, as well as the famous Silverlight logo running as a movie in the top-left corner. Notice also that the `TextBlock` "Powered by Microsoft Silverlight" has a color animation.

▶ If you resize the browser window to a very narrow size, the Silverlight logo (an image) appears on top of the book cover, which is exactly what we wanted.

▶ Try and open this page on a computer without Silverlight, and see that the original static picture is indeed displayed. On Internet Explorer, you can simulate this behavior by deactivating the Silverlight plug-in with the following steps:

   1. Select Tools, Manage Add-ons, Enable or Disable Add-ons.

   2. Locate Microsoft Silverlight under Add-ons Currently Loaded in Internet Explorer.

   3. Select the Disable radio button and click OK.

   4. Refresh the page. You may have to close and restart the web browser to see the change.

   5. Keep this code; we will reuse it in the next chapter!

Referencing a XAP on Another Web Server

We mentioned before that Silverlight can display a XAP file located on an external web server. This can be handy if you want to add Silverlight content to a website on which you cannot load any XAP files—for example, a blog. Depending on your blog provider, you may be able to add the `object` tag, but you must host the XAP content yourself.

In the preceding example, we downloaded the XAP file from the website www.galasoft.ch. Let's see whether we can now reference this XAP file directly, without downloading it first. Follow these steps:

   1. In the file index.html that we just edited, replace the `source` parameter in the `object` tag with the following:

```
<param name="source"
value="http://www.galasoft.ch/SL2U/Chapter07/SilverlightBookCover.xap"/>
```

   2. Reload the page index.html in the web browser.

   3. The Silverlight application doesn't show up.

So what happened? This is a permission problem. We mentioned earlier that there are some differences between running your application in File mode or in HTTP mode. This is one of them: A web page running in File mode may not execute Silverlight code loaded over HTTP.

As a workaround, you can copy the file index.html as well as the folders "resources" and "layout" to your own web server, as explained later in this chapter. If the file index.html runs in HTTP mode, you can load the XAP from the GalaSoft website and you will see the animated logo.

Because the remote XAP file needs more time to load, you may see a subtle animation showing the download percentage (see Figure 7.5). This animation is built-in in the Silverlight plug-in, and you don't need to do anything to make it appear.

FIGURE 7.5   Silverlight download animation

Getting Web Space

A web server must be online 24/7, be resilient to errors, be able to sustain a lot of traffic without crashing, and in the worst case, be able to "crash gracefully" and either restart on its own, or give the provider enough information to be able to put all the websites online, fast.

This is not an easy task for a computer to fulfill. In fact, servers usually run on specialized systems (hardware and software) and are set up and monitored by specialists.

Fortunately, improvements in hardware and software, as well as intense competition, has made commercial web server space very affordable. Space on a typical, high-quality web server costs less than $10 a month, including server space around 1GB or more, email server, around-the-clock support, and so on.

> **WARNING**
>
> Cheaper or even free offers are also available, but are often financed by advertising (over which you have no control). Additionally, such providers often offer poor (or no) support. Support is critical when you run your own website, so sometimes paying a little more is really worth it.
>
> Often, the Internet service provider (ISP) you get your Internet connection from also includes free web server space in the package. While such a space is typically small (50MB or less), it is sufficient to get started and even to store multiple Silverlight applications.

A website such as www.free-webhosts.com can help you in your quest for inexpensive or free web space.

Web Server Requirements

Serving a Silverlight application requires *no special equipment* (software or hardware) what-soever. Since the code is executed on the web client, the Silverlight runtime needs to be present only on the client.

It is perfectly okay to serve Silverlight from any web server, such as Apache running on Linux, Unix, and so on. For the web server, a Silverlight application is just a collection of files, which will be sent on request. The whole work is done on the client only.

> ### TIP
>
> There is one little thing to do on the web server so that the XAP file is identified correctly by the web browser: You must register the MIME type for the XAP file. Explaining this is outside the scope of the book, so if you don't know what MIME is, ask the person who is managing your web server. Chances are that this MIME type is already registered.
>
> You can find more information about this on Brad Abrams' blog: http://blogs.msdn.com/brada/archive/2008/03/14/using-silverlight-2-on-a-production-web-server.aspx.

Finding a Provider

That's the tricky part. There are just so many of them. A search online for "cheap web server provider" returns hundreds of thousands of addresses. In general, it's a good idea to try a few providers before settling on one. Most of them offer trial periods. A few rules can make the choosing process easier:

▶ Try to find out where the support is located. Do they even speak your language? Are they in your time zone? Can they be reached by phone, or only by email, or using a web-based ticketing system? Is support available round the clock?

▶ Try placing a request and see how fast the support answers. You may want to ask for your password, for example. Do you get a standardized answer (or no answer at all), or is someone really answering?

▶ During the trial period, try to access your website often. Is the web server down sometimes? If it is, did you get a notice? Is the outage documented in a log?

▶ Try to find user reviews about the provider you choose. Sometimes you can find interesting information in forums. Users who have had bad experiences are readier to share them, so no review may be a good review.

▶ Ask your friends and your peers. Many of them have stories to share.

▶ Compare, compare, compare. The provider's site should give a clear indication of what they're selling. Don't forget, there are many of them, so as the customer, you can afford to be picky!

To sum up, reputation, good technical support, and few (or no) outages are the criteria you're looking for.

Getting Started with FTP

After you get server space, your provider will give you the following information:

▶ FTP host—This can be an address such as ftp.myprovider.com or an Internet Protocol (IP) address like 167.247.4.32.

▶ A username and password for your account.

This information is needed to connect to your web server using an application called an *FTP client*.

> **NOTE**
>
> This is not *really your* web server. In fact, except if you purchased this option specifically (and paid more money), you are most probably sharing a server with other users. Most of the time, it's not an issue, except if you plan on running large scale applications, or have very specific needs.

Setting Up an FTP Client

A few good FTP clients are available. Depending on the operating system you are using, you will need a specific FTP client. A good search on the Internet allows you to get a good free (or cheap) client. While the illustrations will be different for your FTP client, it should be easy to adapt them to your case.

For the purpose of the demo, we use a free application named Core FTP for Windows, which provides all the functionality you need for no money. This application can be downloaded from www.coreftp.com and installed with the following steps:

1. After downloading the setup program, execute it and follow the instructions to install the application. You can select all the default options.

2. Start the program. The dialog shown in Figure 7.6 is displayed.

3. If it's the first time you start the program, or if you just got a new server, you must set up a connection:

    ▶ Site name—This is just a friendly name for this connection.

    ▶ Host/IP/URL—This information is given to you by your provider.

    ▶ Username/Password—This information is also given to you by your provider. Do *not* check the Anonymous check box.

FIGURE 7.6   Setting up a new connection

▶ If you prefer, you can check
   the Don't Save Password
   check box. This is recommended if you are using the
   FTP client on a public unpro-
   tected computer.

▶ All the other information
   can be left untouched.

> **WARNING**
>
> Be very careful with your FTP username and
> password! A malicious user getting this infor-
> mation can access your web server and
> damage your website or publish illegal mater-
> ial under your name!

4. Click the Connect button.

Connecting to Your Server

The FTP client displays two lists of folders (see Figure 7.7):

▶ On the left-hand side, you see your local file system. You can use this panel to navigate to the folder containing your Silverlight application.

▶ To navigate upwards from a given folder, double-click on the folder named "..", or
   click the Up Directory button.

▶ On the right-hand side, you see the web server's file system. You can only navigate
   in your own space and cannot see or access other users' folders. Using this panel,
   you can manage (create, rename, delete) folders and files on the server.

▶ The bottom panel displays information about the current transfer (if there is one).

▶ The top panel shows a log of the current connection. In most cases, you can ignore
   this information.

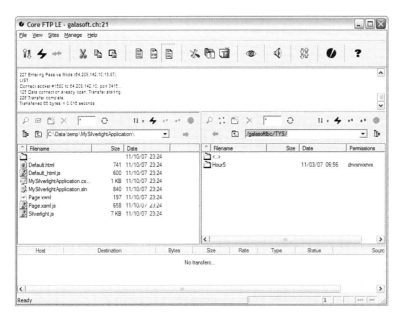

FIGURE 7.7   FTP client main window

Copying Your Silverlight Application

Silverlight 2 makes deploying a Silverlight application easy. All files needed are packed in the XAP file. That said, your application will typically need additional files, such as HTML, JavaScript, images and videos, and so on.

Table 7.1 gives an overview of all the file types found in a typical Silverlight application, with a short explanation. Some file types will become clearer as we progress in our exploration, but this table should already provide a handy guide as to what you should and should not copy to the web server.

Even though a file or folder is marked "not needed," it doesn't harm your web server if you copy it anyway. In some cases, it can even be a good idea to copy all the files to the web server—for example, for tests, as a backup, and so on.

> **NOTE**
>
> Unless you specify otherwise, the images and videos used by a Silverlight application are packed into the DLL or into the XAP file.
>
> Often, however, you want your media files to be outside the application and load them dynamically. This way, you don't have to modify and recompile the application every time you add new media, for example. In that case, the images and videos are available as loose resources and must be copied to the web server separately! We will do this in Chapter 19, "Creating User Controls and Custom Controls."

TABLE 7.1   Copying Files to the Web Server

File/Folder	Description
ClientBin (folder) bin (folder)	Contains compiled files, some resources as well as the XAP output.
	This folder is **not** needed on the web server (but the XAP file is needed!!).
obj (folder)	Contains temporary files created when the application is compiled.
	This folder is **not** needed on the web server.
Properties (folder)	Contains code files. They will be compiled into your application.
	This folder is **not** needed on the web server.
Any file ending with ".csproj" or ".csproj.user"	These are the *project files*, with all the information needed to create and compile your Silverlight application.
	This file is **not** needed on the web server.
Any file ending with ".xaml"	The XAML files contain the markup for user interface.
	These files are **not** needed on the web server (the XAML file is packed in the XAP).
Any file ending with ".cs"	The code-behind files contain the code needed to run the application. These files are *compiled* into a binary file (DLL), which is then packed into the XAP.
	These files are **not** needed on the web server.
.xap file	Contains the compiled code for your Silverlight application, as well as some resources such as videos, images, and so on.
	Must be copied to the web server!
Any file ending with ".html" or ".aspx"	HTML and ASPX files are needed, at least the one hosting your Silverlight application. They **must be copied** to the web server.
Any file ending with ".js"	JavaScript files contain code needed to create the Silverlight application and to interact with it.
	Must be copied to the web server!
	Note: JavaScript files are not strictly needed for Silverlight 2, but may provide additional functionalities.
Video files Image files	If the files are included in the XAP, they do not need to be copied again to the web server. We discuss this in more detail in Chapter 19.
Any additional folder/file	Additional folders or files added by you for the purpose of your Silverlight application (for example movies, pictures, and so on) **must be copied** to the web server.

7

To upload the files, follow these steps:

1. In the right-hand panel, navigate to the folder in which you want to *upload* your Silverlight application.

2. On the right-hand panel, click the Make Directory button to create a new directory for your application if needed.

3. Select a file, a group of files, or a whole folder in the left-hand panel.

4. Click the Upload button.

It is actually easy to check whether a given video or image file must be copied as a loose file to the web server, with the following steps:

1. Open the XAP file with WinZip or any other Zip utility. Since the XAP is simply a Zip file, you can see the content and check whether the video or image file is included.

2. Alternatively, do not copy them to the web server first and then test the application. If the media is displayed correctly, everything is fine. if not, you need to copy it to the web server. Call this an empiric method.

Testing Your Work

After you copy all the files mentioned in Table 7.1 to your web server, you can test your work in the web browser.

The address you enter in your web browser depends on the location in which you copied the Silverlight files. The *entry point* for your application is the HTML file in which the `silverlightControlHost` element is placed.

If you copied your Silverlight files on your web server http://www.mydomain.com and placed them in the folder Silverlight/MyFirstApplication, then the complete address is: http://www.mydomain.com/Silverlight/MyFirstApplication/Default.html.

Summary

In this chapter, you got a better understanding of the `object` tag needed to place a Silverlight application in an HTML page. You saw how a XAP file is used to pack the items needed to make the Silverlight application work. You also learned what you can do if Silverlight is not installed, or if the version installed is too old for your application's needs.

Then you used that knowledge in a small practical exercise and added a "rich island" of Silverlight functionality within standard HTML content. Importantly, you learned how Silverlight can load XAP files located on an external web server, and how this feature can be used to add Silverlight content to a blog or another website.

In the second half of the chapter, we talked about web space, web providers, and FTP clients needed to deploy the Silverlight application to a web server.

After this chapter, you should be ready to enhance your web page with Silverlight! In the next chapters, we see how Visual Studio can assist us to make the deployment even easier, but you are now already able to deploy some applications manually.

7

Programming Silverlight with JavaScript

Some say that JavaScript is probably the most misunder-stood programming language. First, let's clear things up: JavaScript has nothing to do with Java. Some time ago, a marketing guy thought it would be cool to ride the Java wave and so that name was given to the language formerly named LiveScript. Even though Java and JavaScript share some syntax (like all the other languages having evolved from the original programming language C), the relation-ship stops there. If you know JavaScript, you still don't know Java. And if you know Java, you will still need to learn a lot to master JavaScript.

Second, even though it's a script language, it is actually complex. It is in fact very different from C#, VB.NET, or Java, very different from most other "high-level" object-oriented languages available today.

One chapter is not enough to learn JavaScript. If you want to use a lot of JavaScript in your web pages, you should look for specialized books, for instance *Sams Teach Yourself JavaScript in 24 Hours* by Michael Moncur. For the purpose of this book, we concentrate on the objects and features that are especially useful in relationship with Silverlight applications.

In this chapter, we also define concepts and syntax elements that will be useful later, when we learn C# and .NET. It's a good preparation, and it's really not "just" about script!

NOTE

If you never programmed JavaScript before, this chapter might be a little tough. It introduces many concepts that will be reused in other sections of this book, so don't be afraid. You will have plenty of occasions to understand all this better.

Learning the Basics

As mentioned earlier, JavaScript uses a syntax based on the C programming language. This makes our job easier, because C# (the language we use later in this book to program Silverlight with .NET) is also based on this same programming language. Many constructs are similar in both languages, but there are also some differences that we will highlight.

Comments

In JavaScript like in C#, you can write *comments* in the code, to make it easier to understand (remember, you can do that in XAML too, but with a different syntax). In C-based languages, comments can be written in two ways:

```
// This is a line-comment
/* This is a block comment */
```

A line comment means that everything placed between the `//` sign and the end of the line is a comment. There may be code before the `//` sign, but not after it.

A block comment means that only text between the `/*` sign and the `*/` sign is a comment. There may be code before the `/*` sign and after the `*/` sign.

Semicolons

A JavaScript application consists of a series of *statements*. Each statement must be clearly separated from the next one, or there is a risk of misunderstanding what the programmer really meant.

In JavaScript, a statement can be terminated by an "end-of-line" (carriage return), or by a semicolon ";". The semicolon is not compulsory in JavaScript! The following code is legal:

```
var counter = 0
alert(counter)
```

However, the following code causes an error:

```
var counter = 0 alert(counter)
```

To put multiple statements on one line only, you must separate them with a semicolon:

```
var counter = 0;alert(counter)
```

WARNING

In C# (as well as in Java and other C-like languages, and unlike in JavaScript), it is *compulsory to end every statement with a semicolon.*

The best guideline to follow regarding semicolons is to end every statement with a semi-colon systematically for two reasons:

- ▶ You will not have any issues doing it in C#.

- ▶ The code will be cleaner and easier to read.

In general, avoid putting more than one statement on a single line. This makes the code more difficult to read. Structuring your code neatly makes it easier to maintain. Beautiful code works better.

Case Sensitivity

JavaScript, C#, and other C-based languages are case sensitive! That means that you can write:

```
var myObject = 1;
var myobject = 2;
alert(myObject);
alert(myobject);
```

However this is not recommended, because it's rather easy to miss the difference (did you see it?).

When you write code, it is better to use guidelines, and to name your functions, classes, variables, and so on, according to certain rules. JavaScript guidelines can be found on the Internet by using your favorite search engine. In this book, we try to stick as much as possible to recommended JavaScript coding guidelines.

Variables

Like all programming languages, JavaScript uses *variables* to store data. A variable is declared by the keyword `var`. However, one thing is special: A JavaScript variable does not have a clearly defined type. The following is perfectly legal in JavaScript:

```
var untypedVariable = 123.4;
// ...
untypedVariable = "this is a string";
//...
untypedVariable = function()
{
  // Do something
}
```

At the beginning, `untypedVariable` contains a number. Later, it holds a character string, and eventually it holds a function. This kind of code couldn't even be compiled in C#, but it is legal in JavaScript.

Functions

Functions are declared with the keyword `function`.

A function is used to group a suite of operations that have a common purpose. Typically, you use functions to store operations that you want to reuse throughout the application. You can also use functions to separate the operations logically, to create smaller chunks of code that are easier to manage and to maintain.

> ### TIP
>
> A good rule of thumb in modern software engineering is that, if a function or a method is longer than a computer screen, it should probably be split in multiple functions.

Prototype, `this`, `new`

JavaScript is a special language, as you understood already. Contrary to other object-oriented languages, JavaScript uses *prototype based objects.* Without going into too many details, let's just say that JavaScript is a *dynamic language.* It allows modifications of the types during runtime, through a property called `prototype`.

Once a method or an attribute has been added to the prototype of an object, instances of this object can access the new member by using the keyword `this` followed by a dot "." and the name of the member.

When an object is defined, it is still just a blueprint. If you want to create an instance and initialize it with data, you need to use the keyword `new`. This keyword allocates space in the memory to store the instance. We say that it *constructs* the object's instance. We see a practical example a little bit later in this chapter.

> ### WARNING
>
> In fact the keyword `this` represents the *context* in which the current function is executed. In most cases, the context is the object that contains the function, but sometimes the context is different from what you would expect, as we see later in this chapter. For the moment, you can just assume that `this` is the object that contains the method you execute.

Types

While a JavaScript variable is not strongly typed, JavaScript does, however, know the following types:

- ▶ `Number`—JavaScript does not differentiate between *integer* numbers (for example 123) and *floating point* numbers (for example 123.45).

- ▶ `String`—A character string in JavaScript can be defined in two different ways, using either the double quote delimiter (`"`) or the single quote delimiter (`'`):

  ```
  "This is a JavaScript string"
  'This is another string'
  ```

- ▶ `Boolean`—Such a variable can hold either `true` or `false`.

- ▶ `Date`—This object allows date/time calculation.

▶ Function—In JavaScript, even functions are objects. You can pass a function from one object to another and execute it.

▶ Array—This special type of object contains other variables and objects, organized in a cell-like structure, and referenced by an index.

▶ Object—They are user-defined types, as we see in a moment.

In addition, JavaScript has a Math object. This object cannot be *instantiated* but contains many useful functions for mathematical operations.

Built-In Objects and Libraries

JavaScript is "just" a programming language. That's not enough to program an application: You also need a *framework* to execute the code and to provide the basic operations and objects! The JavaScript language is not only used in web browsers: You can also use JavaScript on web servers in ASP (though nowadays you probably want to use ASP.NET instead). You can use JavaScript on .NET (JScript.NET), and so on.

In the version of JavaScript that we use here, the framework is running in a web browser. It contains a set of built-in objects (libraries) that are vital to any web application. It also contains libraries that you can use to make your programming life easier (utilities, basic functions, and so on). Learning to use these libraries is an important part of a programmer's life.

You usually can find technical documentation on the Internet. For example, the two most popular web browsers' documentation can be found here:

▶ http://developer.mozilla.org/en/docs/JavaScript

▶ http://msdn2.microsoft.com/en-us/library/hbxc2t98.aspx

alert

One example of framework functionality available in the web browser is the alert function. It creates a message box displaying the string passed as parameter. This is a helpful functionality when you debug your application.

More important, you can also pass a variable containing a string, and the message box will show the string. So the following calls are equivalent, and create the box shown in Figure 8.1:

FIGURE 8.1   JavaScript alert

```
alert("Hello world");
var hello = "Hello world";
alert(hello);
```

undefined

A variable in JavaScript can have multiple values during its lifetime. One particular value is undefined: This is the value of the variable before it has been initialized by the script application. For example:

```
alert(newVariable);
var newVariable;
alert(newVariable);
newVariable = 15;
alert(newVariable);
```

The first and second calls to alert display the value undefined in a message box. The last call displays the value 15 as expected. When the variable is used the first time, the scripting engine doesn't know it because its declaration has not been parsed yet. That's why the special value undefined is used by the engine.

The value undefined can be tested against the Boolean value false (and also against the value null described in the next section). This provides a handy way to test for the existence of a variable or of an object, or even of a functionality in the web browser. Let's see an example in Listing 8.1.

LISTING 8.1   Feature Detection

```
if (document
  && document.body
  && document.body.style)
{
  document.body.style.backgroundColor = "Red";
}
else
{
  // ...
}
```

So here we say: *If* there is a global variable named document, *and* document has a property named body, *and* document.body contains a variable named style, *then* set the backgroundColor to "Red". Or *else*, do something else.

> **TIP**
>
> The sign && is a logical And. We will talk more about the logical operators when we talk about .NET.

With that strategy (named *feature detection*), it is possible to protect your code from errors in case a variable or a function doesn't exist, for example, in an older browser.

null

Another interesting value for a variable is `null`. This is the value that an object has when it is defined, but not initialized yet.

In other languages (such as C#), this status is clearly defined. In JavaScript, the value `null` is similar to the value `undefined`. There is, however, a difference: The type of `null` is `Object`, while the type of `undefined` is `undefined` as shown in Listing 8.2.

LISTING 8.2   Comparing `undefined` and `null`

```
 1  var test1;
 2  if (test1 == null)
 3    alert("test1 compares positively with null");
 4  if (typeof(test1) == "undefined")
 5    alert("but test1 is not null, it's actually undefined");
 6
 7  var test2 = null;
 8  if (test2 == null)
 9    alert("test2 compares positively with null");
10  if (typeof(test2) == "undefined")
11    alert("but test2 is not null, it's actually undefined");
```

The alert at lines 3, 5, and 9 are displayed, but not the alert at line 11. `null` does compare positively with `undefined`, but its type is not `undefined`! Don't worry too much about that though. The difference is really rather subtle, and you probably won't need that before you finish this book.

Handling Events

What would a modern application be without events? They are used to trigger an action in response to user interaction. Some of them are fired by the web browser during the page's life span (for example `onload` on the `body` tag). Others are fired only when the user explicitly performs a certain operation (`onclick` on the `button` tag, for example).

For every event, you can specify an event handler, which is a snippet of JavaScript code that will be executed (see Listing 8.3).

LISTING 8.3   Event Handlers

```
<!--Event handlers-->
<html>
  <head>
    <title>Event handlers</title>
    <script type="text/javascript">
      function handleOnLoad()
      {
        alert("Page is loaded and ready");
```

LISTING 8.3   Continued

```
      }
      function clickButton_onClick()
      {
        alert("Button was clicked");
      }
    </script>
  </head>
  <body onload="handleOnLoad();">
    <form action="http://www.galasoft.ch">
      <input type="button" id="ClickButton"
             value="Click me"
             onclick="clickButton_onClick();" />
    </form>
  </body>
</html>
```

The onload event on the body tag deserves a special mention: It is very useful! When it is fired, you can be 100% sure that all the JavaScript, CSS, and HTML objects needed for the page to work are loaded and ready. This is the ideal place to start your JavaScript computations!

> **WARNING**
>
> When the JavaScript body onload event fires, the Silverlight application may not be ready yet. This is why you should only start interacting with the Silverlight application when Silverlight's own onload event fired, as mentioned in Chapter 7 "Deploying to a webpage."

Note that JavaScript can also register for events raised by the Silverlight application itself. We see examples of that later, especially in Chapter 14, "Letting .NET and JavaScript Talk."

Understanding the Concept of Objects

We often use words such as "object," "attribute," "method," and so on. We talk much more about these in Chapters 9, "Understanding .NET" and 10, "Progressing with .NET." For now, let's just establish the following definitions:

▶ Object—A self-enclosed piece of software code, designed to fulfill certain functionalities. When people talk about objects, they sometimes talk about the type (or the class), and sometimes about the instance (see definition later in this list).

▶ Type (or class)—The object's definition, the blueprint. This is where the object's members are defined.

▶ Instance—When a class is created in memory, and filled with data, we say that it is *instantiated*. There can be multiple instances of the same class. One instance has a life span, between its *creation* and its *destruction*.

- Attribute (or property)—A variable belonging to an instance, storing some data.

- Method—A function that belongs to an object. It is executed in the context of the object and can access the object's attributes.

- Static—The functionality or the data is shared by all the instances of the same class.

- Namespace—A logical grouping of classes according (in general) to their purpose. It is good practice (though not compulsory) to define namespaces instead of leaving all the classes in the *global* namespace. This avoids *name conflicts*, for example, between two classes.

These (very rough) definitions will help you understand the following sections. Contrary to what many people believe, you can use objects in JavaScript, though differently as in other more "standard" languages such as C# or Java.

Interfacing with Other Instances

Instances can communicate by calling each other's methods. They can also access each other's attributes, though it's not recommended to do so. When an object accesses another object's attribute directly, the attribute's owner has no control about what's happening. If the access is executed through a function, the owner can control the access.

Other programming languages offer ways to protect an object against unwanted access of its attributes, but these ways are not available in JavaScript.

Storing Stuff Globally

In JavaScript, you can avoid using objects altogether (but it's not recommended, especially for complex applications). In that case, you are storing everything in the so-called *global object*.

For web browsers, the global object is actually the browser's window. There are multiple ways to refer to the global object: For instance, you can use the keywords window or self or even nothing at all. If they are executed in the global context, the lines of code in Table 8.1 are exactly equivalent.

> **NOTE**
>
> As a matter of a fact, even when you create a global variable or a global function, you are actually just adding members to the global object! Told you JavaScript uses objects a lot!

TABLE 8.1   Equivalent Lines of Code

`var globalVariable = 56;`	`window.globalVariable = 56;`
`self.globalVariable = 56;`	`globalVariable = 56;`

This means that a window is a pretty encapsulated world for JavaScript: A global variable in a window is invisible to a script running in another window. In fact, it's pretty safe to consider that a window is a closed world when it comes to JavaScript. That said, there are possibilities for windows to communicate with each other using JavaScript, but that's really outside the scope of this book.

> **WARNING**
>
> You can declare a new variable without using the keyword `var`, but it's not recommended because of nasty side effects. As a rule, always declare new variables using the `var` keyword.

Also, when a web browser window is refreshed, the global object is deleted, and the script is reloaded from scratch. If the application needs state information to be stored between page refreshes, special measures must be taken.

JavaScript stores objects, variables, and functions in a hierarchy starting at the global object, as shown in Table 8.2:

TABLE 8.2   JavaScript Hierarchy

Global object	`window`
Global variable (member of global object)	`var globalVariable1 = 123.4;` or `window.globalVariable2 = 345;`
Global function (member of global object)	`function doSomething() {/*...*/}` or `window.doSomething() {/*...*/}`
Local variable	`var localVariable = "hello";`
New object	`Converter = function() {/*...*/}` `Converter.prototype = {/*...*/}`
Attribute	`this.creationTime = new Date();`
Method	`convert: function(anyString) {/*...*/}`
New namespace	`window.Utilities = {};`
New object with attributes and methods	`Utilities.Converter2 = {};` `Utilities.Converter2.prototype = {/*...*/}`

Using the Literal Notation JSON

JavaScript allows creating objects using the so-called *literal notation*. With the explosion of communication between computers, this notation became popular to encode the exchanged information. The JavaScript community talks of *JavaScript Object Notation, JSON* (pronounced "Jason").

JSON makes use of three great features:

▶ JavaScript can create an object by assigning its properties explicitly in code. This allows defining and constructing objects during runtime.

- ▶ JSON is a compact notation.

- ▶ JavaScript has the utility method `eval` which can be used to transform any character string into a JavaScript call. When the string is formatted according to JSON, `eval` can be used to transform this character string into an instance of a class.

Web services are often (mis)labeled "AJAX" (for Asynchronous JavaScript and XML), but XML is probably not the best protocol for lightweight, light-fast communication, for two reasons:

- ▶ XML is verbose and needs more characters to describe the same object than JSON.

- ▶ For a web browser without additional ".NET power," converting an XML message to a JavaScript object (*deserialization*) is slower than deserializing the same object encoded with JSON.

Thankfully, even though JSON sometimes replaces XML in AJAX scenarios, nobody was geeky enough (yet?) to name that "AJAJ."

Many existing web services are exchanging JSON-encoded messages with web clients. Even though a standard Silverlight application uses XML to communicate, it is also able (with a little bit of code) to decode JSON-encoded messages, and you can simply reuse existing JSON services directly. We will implement an example in Chapter 23, "Placing Cross-domain Requests and Handling Exceptions."

Creating Objects with JSON

JSON is not "just" useful for web services, but also provides a handy way to create new objects in a compact way (see Listing 8.4).

LISTING 8.4   JavaScript Object Notation and Objects

```
 1   <script type="text/javascript">
 2     var myNewObject =
 3     {
 4       property1 : "Value",
 5       property2 : 12345
 6     }
 7
 8     function doSomething(settings)
 9     {
10       if (settings.value1)
11       {
12         alert(settings.value1)
13       }
14       else
15       {
```

LISTING 8.4   Continued

```
16        alert("Default value 1")
17      }
18
19      if (settings.value2)
20      {
21        alert(settings.value2)
22      }
23      else
24      {
25        alert("Default value 2")
26      }
27    }
28
29    doSomething({
30      value1 : "Hello"
31    });
32
33  </script>
```

▶ Lines 2 to 6 assign a new object to a local variable myNewObject. This object is created on-the-fly and has two properties.

▶ Another great use of JSON is to pass parameters to functions (or methods), especially when you don't know exactly how many parameters you will get:

  ▶ Lines 8 to 27 create a function doSomething taking one parameter settings.

  ▶ This parameter, however, is structured and may contain multiple properties.

  ▶ This is handy because you can add properties at a later point without breaking anything for existing users of this function.

This notation may be a little confusing at first, but it is powerful and handy. For settings, it allows you to specify only the parameters you want to explicitly set, while ignoring the others. Big JavaScript developers such as Google (for example, Google Maps) are also using JSON as a way to construct objects and parameters.

Static Members

Static members in object-oriented programming languages are members shared by all the instances of the class. This could be a utility method used by all instances in the same way, or a static attribute conditioning how every instance of that class works, and so on.

In JavaScript, static members are simulated by adding a member to the class instead of the prototype. For example in Listing 8.5:

LISTING 8.5   Static Method

```
Utilities.Converter._defaultInstance = null;

Utilities.Converter.getDefaultInstance = function()
{
  if (Utilities.Converter._defaultInstance == null)
  {
    Utilities.Converter._defaultInstance = new Utilities.Converter();
  }
  return Utilities.Converter._defaultInstance;
}
```

The method `getDefaultInstance` is stored in the `Utilities.Converter` class. Note, however, that in JavaScript this is strictly speaking more of a logical grouping than a static method.

To sum up:

► Members added to a class (static) are shared by all the instances of the class.

► Members added to the prototype (nonstatic) are specific to each instance of the class.

Loading Scripts in a Web Page

Scripts are not compiled, they are *interpreted*. This is (almost) the only difference between a script and an application: You can very well write a compiled application using JavaScript as a programming language (in fact, you can do this in .NET, using a slightly different version of JavaScript named JScript.NET).

An *interpreter* is an engine loading the script file (or *segment*), *parsing* it, creating the in-memory variables and functions according to the script's definition, and then *executing* the commands. An HTML page gets loaded according to the (slightly simplified) following steps:

1. The web browser loads the HTML page and starts parsing it.

2. When the web browser's HTML engine encounters a `script` tag, the JavaScript interpreter is triggered (refer to Listing 8.3).

3. The interpreter loads the content of the `script` tag and parses it. Objects are created in memory according to the script's specifications.

> **WARNING**
>
> `script` tags may very well point to an external script file, located in the same folder, in an external folder, or even on another web server! *The location of the script doesn't matter; it will be executed in the context of the HTML page in which it is loaded!*

4. If global code (that is, code that doesn't belong explicitly to a function) is found during the parsing, it is executed.

5. The `body onload` event is fired, and if an event handler was defined, it is executed.

In parallel to the HTML and JavaScript loading process, the Silverlight application(s) (if they are found on the page) are started. Again, remember that when the web page is loaded (and the `onload` event fires), it doesn't necessarily mean that Silverlight is ready to run! That's why the Silverlight plug-in exposes its own `onload` event.

Understanding the Context

One recommended way to create new objects in JavaScript is to create a function and modify its prototype. We mentioned before that the keyword `this` represents the *context* in which the method is executed. This is a little difficult to understand, but can be illustrated by a simple example (see Listing 8.6):

LISTING 8.6   Method Execution Context

```
1   <script type="text/javascript">
2     document.body.name = "DocumentBody";
3
4     MyClass = function()
5     {
6       this.name = "MyClass";
7     }
8
9     MyClass.prototype =
10    {
11      sayMyName : function()
12      {
13        alert(this.name);
14      }
15    }
16
17    var myObject = new MyClass();
18    myObject.sayMyName();
19
20    document.body.onclick = myObject.sayMyName;
21  </script>
```

The `onclick` event (like any other event) can be handled simply by passing a method to it (line 20). Remember, methods (functions) are objects in JavaScript. Here *we do not call* the method (that would be `myObject.sayMyName()` with parentheses); instead, we pass a reference to the method.

With this syntax, whenever the event is raised (when you click in the window), the method is executed, and the value contained in `this.name` is displayed.

To test this code, create an empty HTML document and copy Listing 8.6 within the `body` tag. Then load the page in a web browser. When you run this code, an alert window displays the name MyClass. This is the result of calling `myObject.sayMyName()` directly at line 18. The keyword `this` references the instance itself.

But if you click anywhere in the window, the message box shows the name DocumentBody, but the same code is executed! So what happened? Well, the context is different. When the event handler is executed, the context is `document.body`! Since we set its name to `"DocumentBody"` on the first line of the script, this is what is displayed.

To "recenter" the context on the instance of `MyClass`, a little utility method is needed: `createDelegate`. This method is not part of the JavaScript framework, so if you want to use this, you must make sure that you add the code shown in Listing 8.7 to your application:

LISTING 8.7   createDelegate Method

```
if (!window.MyClass)
    window.MyClass = {};

MyClass.createDelegate = function(instance, method) {
  return function() {
    return method.apply(instance, arguments);
  }
}
```

`createDelegate` takes two parameters:

- ▶ `instance` is any instance of a class; it is the context in which the method will be executed.

- ▶ `method` is any method to be executed when the event is raised. In this method, any use of `this` will actually refer to the other parameter `instance`.

How this method works is called "closure" and is outside the scope of this book. For the purpose of Silverlight, we only need to know that it takes care of the context problem.

Integrating Silverlight in an Existing Web Page Using JavaScript

As an alternative to placing the `object` tag directly on a web page, you can use JavaScript to create the tag and its parameters dynamically. Microsoft released a JavaScript file named Silverlight.js containing all the code needed for this operation. Let's see how to find this file and use it.

> **NOTE**
>
> For ASP.NET developers, there is yet another alternative: The `Silverlight` and `MediaPlayer` server controls can be placed in an ASPX page and will create all the code needed to get Silverlight running on the client. We talk about these two server-side controls in Chapter 24, "Silverlight: Continuing the Journey."

Finding Silverlight.js

The file Silverlight.js released by Microsoft is a part of the Silverlight Software Development Kit (SDK) that we installed in Chapter 1, "Introducing Silverlight," in the section titled "Finding More Documentation."

After you install the SDK, you can locate the file Silverlight.js in the folder C:\Program Files\Microsoft SDKs\Silverlight\v2.0\Tools.

Using Silverlight.js

In this example, we will use Silverlight.js with the following steps to check whether the correct version of Silverlight is installed, and if this is the case, to replace the Silverlight book cover on the HTML page that we edited in Chapter 7.

1. Navigate to the folder where you saved and edited the SilverlightBookCover application in Chapter 7.

2. In the same folder, next to "layout" and "resources," create a folder named "script" and copy the file Silverlight.js in this new folder.

> **TIP**
>
> It is customary to group all script files in a "script" folder, but this is not compulsory. You can save the script files in any place you want, as long as it is reachable from your HTML page. In fact, script files can even be included from external web servers.

Editing the HTML

We will now include the Silverlight.js file into our HTML page and use the functions included into it with the following steps:

1. Open the file index.html in a text editor.

2. Change the `head` section as shown in Listing 8.8. Note that we refer to a file named SilverlightBookCover.js that is not created yet. We will implement this file in a minute.

LISTING 8.8   SilverlightBookCover HTML Header

```html
<head>
  <title>Silverlight 2 Unleashed</title>

  <link rel="stylesheet"
        type="text/css"
        href="layout/style.css" media="all" />

  <!--Silverlight-enabled book cover animation-->
  <style type="text/css">
    #silverlightControlHost
    {
      height: 445px;
      width: 470px;
      margin: auto;
    }
  </style>

  <script type="text/javascript" src="script/Silverlight.js"></script>
  <script type="text/javascript" src="script/SilverlightBookCover.js"></script>
</head>
```

3. Change the content of the silverlightControlHost div element to look like Listing 8.9:

> **WARNING**
>
> Even though the script tag is empty, you cannot use the "self-closing" form that XML allows. Browsers are funny that way, and some will cause an error if you try to do this.

LISTING 8.9   Call to createSilverlight

```html
<!--Silverlight-enabled book cover animation-->
<div id="silverlightControlHost">
  <script type="text/javascript">
    SilverlightBookCover.createSilverlight("resources/SilverlightBookCover.xap",
      "silverlightControlHost",
      "silverlightControl");
  </script>
</div>
```

After including two external JavaScript files in the HTML page, we replaced the object tag by a call to a JavaScript method named SilverlightBookCover.createSilverlight. This method doesn't exist yet, so if you open the HTML file in a web browser, it causes an error.

Editing the JavaScript

Let's do some JavaScript now:

1. Create a new text file in the "script" folder and name it SilverlightBookCover.js.

2. Open this file in a text editor, and create the object in Listing 8.10.

LISTING 8.10   SilverlightBookCover JavaScript Object

```
1   if (!window.SilverlightBookCover)
2     window.SilverlightBookCover = {};
3
4   SilverlightBookCover.Page = function()
5   {
6     this.loadMessage = "Welcome to this application";
7   }
8
9   SilverlightBookCover.Page.prototype =
10  {
11    handleLoad : function(sender, args)
12    {
13      // This method will get called when the
14      // Silverlight application is fully loaded.
15      alert(this.loadMessage);
16    },
17
18    handleError : function(sender, args)
19    {
20      // This method will get called if the
21      // Silverlight application has an error.
22    }
23  }
24
25  SilverlightBookCover.createSilverlight = function(xapUrl, hostId, controlId)
26  {
27    if (!window.Silverlight)
28    {
29      alert("Silverlight.js can't be found");
30      return;
31    }
32
33    if (Silverlight.isInstalled("2.0"))
34    {
35      var page = new SilverlightBookCover.Page();
36
```

LISTING 8.10   Continued

```
37      Silverlight.createObjectEx({
38        source: xapUrl,
39        parentElement: document.getElementById(hostId),
40        id: controlId,
41        properties: {
42          width: "100%",
43          height: "100%",
44          version: "2.0",
45          isWindowless : "True",
46          background : "#00000000"
47        },
48        events: {
49          onLoad: SilverlightBookCover.createDelegate(page, page.handleLoad),
50          onError: SilverlightBookCover.createDelegate(page, page.handleError)
51        }
52      });
53    }
54    else
55    {
56      document.writeln("<img src='resources/SL2U-web.png'"
57        + "alt='Silverlight 2 Unleashed'"
58        + "title='Silverlight 2 Unleashed'"
59        + "style='width: 470px;height: 445px;' />");
60    }
61  }
62
63  SilverlightBookCover.createDelegate = function(instance, method) {
64    return function() {
65      return method.apply(instance, arguments);
66    }
67  }
```

Let's review what happens here:

▶ Lines 1 and 2 create a new namespace named `SilverlightBookCover` inside the global object (`window`). This is a little tricky: To simulate a namespace, we actually create an empty object (using the literal notation discussed earlier). Thanks to the `if` clause on line 1, we only create the new namespace if it doesn't exist already in the window object (or else we would overwrite the old namespace, including every object we stored there!).

▶ We use the `window` syntax here, even though we said that `window.SilverlightBookCover` is equivalent to `SilverlightBookCover`. However, simply testing for `SilverlightBookCover` throws an error. You must explicitly use the `window` syntax when you check for the existence of a global object.

▶ Lines 4 to 7 define a new class named `Page` inside the `SilverlightBookCover` namespace. Here again, this is tricky: We actually define a new *function*, not an object!! In fact, in JavaScript, the best way to define an object is to create a new function, and then to modify its *prototype* (line 9 and below) by adding new variables and methods. In "conventional" object-oriented languages, the method used to create a new instance of a class is called a *constructor*, so this is also how we refer to this function.

▶ To create an instance of the object we defined here, we use the keyword `new` when we call the function. This keyword notifies the framework that this function is used as a constructor.

▶ Lines 9 to 23 define a new *prototype* for the class. By adding two methods `handleLoad` and `handleError`, we make these methods available to each instance of the class. Notice the syntax used: This is the JSON notation we discussed earlier.

▶ Lines 25 to 61 create a new static method that we call in the HTML file to create the plug-in. This method `SilverlightBookCover.createSilverlight` takes three parameters as follows:

  ▶ `xapUrl` is the URL of the XAP file (relative to the HTML file, or absolute).

  ▶ `hostId` is the HTML ID of the `div` element containing the call to `SilverlightBookCover.createSilverlight`.

  ▶ `controlId` is the ID that will be given to the Silverlight control when it is created.

▶ Line 33 makes sure that the correct version of Silverlight is installed. If it is not available, lines 56 to 59 are executed (see the next section for details).

▶ Line 35 creates a *new* instance of the class we just defined.

▶ Lines 37 to 52 are the call to the method `Silverlight.createObjectEx`. This method is included in the file Silverlight.js that we got from Microsoft.

▶ Lines 48 to 51 create a new object with the JSON notation. This object is assigned to the events property of the first (and only) parameter of the JavaScript method `createObjectEx`. Note how we use the method `createDelegate` that we discussed earlier to make sure that the context is correctly set to the page instance. This way, whenever `handleLoad` or `handleError` are called, you can use the keyword `this` to access attributes of this instance. In this sample, the

> **NOTE**
>
> Why can we call a method from the file Silverlight.js into our own file SilverlightBookCover.js? Because both files have been included in the HTML code. Silverlight.js comes before SilverlightBookCover.js, so its content is parsed first and is available when our own code needs it. Remember that all the script files are loaded and executed in the same context!

method `handleLoad` will display a welcome message defined on line 6 and stored in the `SilverlightBookCover.Page` class.

Just to be clear:

▶ We pass only one parameter to the `Silverlight.createObjectEx` constructor (lines 37 to 52). This parameter starts at the opening curly bracket "{" on line 37 and ends at the closing curly bracket "}" on line 52. This parameter is an instance of a dynamically created object. It contains five properties, `source`, `parentElement`, `id`, `properties`, and `events`. These two last properties are themselves objects built with the JSON notation and also contain properties.

▶ This dynamically created object is not defined anywhere. There is no blueprint for it. JavaScript is a dynamic language and allows this kind of operation: creating objects on-the-fly.

▶ We already talked about the properties and events in Chapter 7, when they were included in the HTML `object` tag. For more details about these, consult the documentation we installed in Chapter 1.

You can open index.html in a web browser now. You should be greeted by a JavaScript alert, and then see the same animation as before.

Detecting Silverlight Versions

In Chapter 7, we saw how to display alternate content when Silverlight is not available (or its version is too old). We need to do the same when the Silverlight application is created with JavaScript.

Fortunately, this is easy: Microsoft did the work for you. Simply use the method `Silverlight.isInstalled(versionNumber)` where `versionNumber` is a string formatted like (for example) `"1.0"` or `"2.0.30226.2"`.

In Listing 8.10 earlier in this chapter, we detect whether a user has Silverlight version 2.0 installed, and we create the Silverlight control if a sufficient version is found. If Silverlight is not installed, or if the version is too old, we display the static `img` tag using the built-in JavaScript method `document.writeln`. This method can be called when a page is not fully loaded yet. It writes HTML code to the page; the HTML code will be rendered as if it was written directly. Using JavaScript, you have the possibility to output different HTML code depending on certain conditions.

TIP

The Silverlight version number has four positions. The first position (Major) is used for major changes to the application. The second position (Minor) is used for small, backwards compatible changes. The third position (Revision) is used for bug correction. Finally, the last position (Build) changes every time a new version of the application is compiled. For example, V1.0.20926.0 is bigger than V1.0, but smaller than V2.0.

Detecting JavaScript

Of course, all this is useless if JavaScript is not enabled on the web browser! The Silverlight plug-in will not be created, and the code you added in the `document.writeln` section earlier in the chapter will not be written.

To create a user-friendly web page even for those users without JavaScript enabled, you can modify the call to the method `createSilverlight` as in Listing 8.11:

LISTING 8.11   Call to `createSilverlight` with `noscript` Content

```
<div id="silverlightControlHost">
  <script type="text/javascript">
    SilverlightBookCover.createSilverlight("resources/SilverlightBookCover.xap",
      "silverlightControlHost",
      "silverlightControl");
  </script>
  <noscript>
    <img src='resources/SL2U-web.png'
      alt='Silverlight 2 Unleashed' title='Silverlight 2 Unleashed'
      style='width: 471px;height: 498px;' />
  </noscript>
</div>
```

The content of the `noscript` tag will be displayed only if JavaScript is disabled.

Modifying the Web Page During Runtime

With the collaboration of JavaScript, CSS, and the so-called Document Object Model (DOM), it is possible to modify the structure of a web page even when it is running, and even after it has been fully loaded in the web browser. Many AJAX-based applications use this feature to update their content without reloading the whole page.

Because Silverlight can also access the DOM, it can just as well modify the web page's content. We will demonstrate this in Chapter 21, "Taking Silverlight 2 Even Further."

Debugging

Debugging JavaScript is not very easy, due to the dynamic nature of the language. Thankfully, two very good debuggers are available:

- ▶ For Firefox—http://www.mozilla.org/projects/venkman.
- ▶ For IE—Visual Studio can debug JavaScript code running in Internet Explorer.

For more information about installing and using these debuggers, please refer to the debugger's technical documentation. In addition, we will use the JavaScript debugger in Visual Studio in Chapter 21.

Summary

JavaScript is a powerful and often misunderstood programming language. Some love it and some hate it (very much like the XAML language, in fact). But all web developers need to use it, at one point or another. With the new Web 2.0 era, many web applications are now using AJAX, DHTML to become richer and richer.

Silverlight plays well with JavaScript. In this chapter, we learned a lot about the JavaScript syntax, how to create new Silverlight applications, and how to react to events. We also learned object-oriented programming concepts, which will help us when we use C# to program Silverlight. We will use advanced JavaScript in Chapter 14, where Silverlight will communicate with JavaScript.

CHAPTER 9

Understanding .NET

.NET was officially released in 2002 and was a small revolution in the Windows programming world. Inspired in many ways by the Java programming language, but learning from and improving on Java's weaknesses (especially the speed of startup and of execution), the so-called "managed languages" (C#, VB.NET, and so on…) also brought with them a tremendous gain in productivity towards classic Windows programming technologies.

Together with .NET, many libraries and thousands of objects were released. It can be a little overwhelming at first, but thankfully we have the help of a great tool, a so-called *Integrated Development Environment (IDE)*: Visual Studio.

When we tried to learn JavaScript in one chapter, you were warned that it was an ambitious goal, and yet we managed to understand enough JavaScript to program Silverlight. Now the task is even bigger! We dedicate more time to .NET and its use in Silverlight, but again this is not a definitive guide. Other books will help you to understand .NET in depth if needed. This introduction and the examples in further chapters will enable you to feel confident with basic and not so basic .NET operations.

History of .NET

The .NET framework contains multiple parts. The most famous are

▶ A web server framework, to program web applications, called ASP.NET

▶ A Windows programming framework named Windows Forms

▶ (From .NET 3.0) A Windows programming framework named Windows Presentation Foundation (WPF)

▶ (From .NET 3.0) A unified communication framework named Windows Communication Framework (WCF)

▶ (From .NET 3.5) Silverlight

Versions, Versions, Versions

At the time of writing, there are 5 major versions of .NET available: 1.0, 1.1, 2.0, 3.0 and 3.5. Let's review them shortly.

1.0, 1.1

.NET 1.0 was released in 2002. This version is not really current anymore, and most people upgraded to .NET 1.1 (or higher). Many existing applications still use version 1.1 of the framework, which requires Visual Studio 2003.

> **NOTE**
>
> Up to Visual Studio 2008, a version of the .NET framework was linked to a version of Visual Studio. If you wanted to upgrade your application, you had to install a newer version of the IDE. Thankfully, this is not the case anymore, and Visual Studio 2008 can handle .NET 2.0, 3.0, and 3.5 (but not .NET 1.0 and 1.1).

2.0

A big improvement was brought about with .NET 2.0 (Visual Studio 2005): additional libraries, improvement to the .NET programming languages, and so on. Upgrading an application from .NET 1.1 to .NET 2.0 was relatively painless, even though some constructs were marked *deprecated*.

.NET 2.0 is still very current. Many client applications are written in ASP.NET and Windows Forms 2.0.

> **TIP**
>
> *Deprecated* means that a functionality still works in the framework's new version, but you should consider upgrading to a newer functionality, better suited for the task.

3.0

.NET 3.0 was released in 2006, as a set of additional libraries on top of .NET 2.0. Some argued that this was not really a new version of the framework, rather an addition, but this is not really important.

More important is that the .NET 2.0 code base is stable and allows Microsoft to build new frameworks (such as WPF or WCF) without changing the core libraries.

3.5

.NET 3.5 was released officially in February 2008, but developers received the official RTM (Release To Market) version in December 2007. .NET 3.5 was released together with Visual Studio 2008, the latest (and best) installment of the IDE.

.NET 3.5 brings multiple improvements over .NET 3.0, especially the new so-called Language Integrated Query (LINQ), but also increased stability and a whole row of improvements in many areas.

In summer 2008, Microsoft released a major overhaul of .NET 3.5 under the name .NET 3.5 Service Pack 1 or .NET 3.5 SP1. This Service Pack addresses many concerns in .NET 3.5 and especially Windows Presentation Foundation, such as increased performance and stability, new controls, and so on.

Silverlight

Silverlight 2 is developed in parallel to the "full" .NET framework. You probably heard already that Silverlight is a subset of WPF. In fact, the Silverlight .NET framework is a subset of the .NET framework 3.5. With this, we mean that not all the libraries of the .NET framework 3.5 are available in Silverlight. It also means that Silverlight is widely compatible with .NET 3.5.

> **WARNING**
>
> With two frameworks being developed in parallel, there may be small incompatibilities between .NET for Silverlight and .NET 3.5. These small differences should gradually disappear as both frameworks progress together.

Managed Versus Unmanaged

Traditional Windows applications were (and still are) often programmed using a framework called *Microsoft Foundation Classes (MFC)*. This code compiles to *machine code*, which is low-level, machine-near computer code. It is called *unmanaged* because it is directly executed by the processor, without an additional layer.

.NET code is different. The application is made of *assemblies* (EXE and DLLs) containing code written in *intermediate language (IL)*. This code is not machine code. When the application runs, the code is executed by the .NET runtime, which in turn executes the corresponding machine code. The code is *managed* by the .NET runtime.

Managed code is typically slower than machine code, because of the additional layer between the code and the machine. However, the .NET framework offers many advantages over unmanaged code:

- ▶ A huge number of built-in high level libraries.

- ▶ Stable code with fewer errors thanks to new safer programming languages. Most errors will be found when you compile the application already, instead of appearing only at runtime.

- ▶ Because the .NET runtime *abstracts* the machine (that is, stands between the machine and the code), the code doesn't have to care about differences between processors, or even differences between operating systems.

6

In theory, .NET is *machine-independent*, and the same code can run on PC, Macintosh, Linux, and so on (as long as there is a .NET runtime available for these platforms). In practice, however, it's not that easy. Silverlight is a big step forward in direction of the *write once, run everywhere* philosophy already applied to Java.

Downloading and Installing Visual Studio 2008

Maybe some of you already installed Visual Studio 2008 in Chapter 1, "Introducing Silverlight," of this book, or even earlier. If you did, you are almost ready to program Silverlight! The links to Visual Studio 2008 (trial edition) and to all the tools needed to program Silverlight can be found at www.silverlight.net/GetStarted. At this point, you should install Visual Studio 2008 and the Silverlight Tools for Visual Studio 2008.

Creating a Silverlight 2 Application in Visual Studio 2008

We created Silverlight 2 applications in Expression Blend already, and now we will do the same in Visual Studio 2008 with the following steps.

1. Start the Visual Studio 2008 application.

2. From the menu select File, New, Project.

3. In the dialog, select Silverlight and then select Silverlight Application.

4. Enter a name (for instance MyFirstSilverlight) and a path for the new Silverlight Application, and then click OK (see Figure 9.1).

5. The next dialog prompts you to create either a Web Site, a Web Application, or an HTML test page to host the new application. Select the Add a New Web... button and then select Web Site from the Project Type combo box (see Figure 9.2).

> **TIP**
>
> You can choose between a Web Site and a Web Application. The differences between these two project types are outside scope of this book (but a good ASP.NET book will tell you all about it). A Web Site gives you a little less flexibility, but is a little easier to publish.

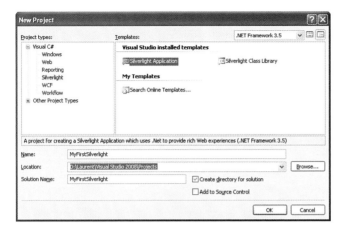

FIGURE 9.1   The New Project dialog in Visual Studio

FIGURE 9.2   The Add Silverlight Application dialog

Building and Running the Application

▶ Before running a Silverlight 2 application (or any other .NET application), you need to *build* it. This process (also called *compiling*) takes the source code (the *.xaml and *.cs files) and transforms them into one or more *assemblies*.

▶ An *assembly* is either an EXE or a DLL file, containing *intermediate language* code. This code is not machine code (as discussed earlier) but is loaded by the .NET framework and executed.

▶ The assemblies needed to run the application are copied to the bin folder. In addition, Silverlight 2 applications are "packed" in a XAP file, which is essentially just a

Zip file with all the files needed for the Silverlight application to run. The XAP file will be sent to the client web browser, and executed.

▶ In Visual Studio, you can run the application in *debug mode* (by pressing F5) or in *runtime mode* (by pressing Ctrl+F5). In debug mode, the application runs in the debugger, and you can step into it and inspect variables. We talk about the debugger later.

Finding Compilation Errors

Unlike JavaScript, .NET is compiled, and errors can be detected before the application even runs. Follow these steps to test it yourself:

1. Open the file Page.xaml.cs and try to modify the Page *constructor* as in Listing 9.1:

LISTING 9.1   DoSomething

```
public Page()
{
  // Required to initialize variables
  InitializeComponent();
  DoSomething();
}
```

2. Choose Build, Build Solution from the menu (press Ctrl+Shift+B). An error is displayed as shown in Figure 9.3.

3. A compilation error is displayed in the Error List pane. In that case, the error is that the code attempts to call a method that is not defined anywhere.

FIGURE 9.3   Compilation error

4. To correct the error, you can remove the call to the nonexistent method DoSomething.

Most compilation errors are displayed with enough information to find the cause relatively easily. Also, double-clicking on the error message will "jump" in the code at the error location. Remove the call to DoSomething and you should be able to build.

Exploring the Files

Let's review the most important files created by Visual Studio in both the Web Site project and in the Silverlight project.

Web Site Project

This project, when published to an ASP.NET-enabled web server, will "serve" dynamic and static web pages. The contents of the dynamic web pages (ASPX) are modified by a .NET application before they are sent to the web browser.

> ## WARNING
>
> Even though ASP.NET also executes .NET code, it is important to understand the major difference between the ASP.NET code-behind, running on the web server ("up there") and the Silverlight code-behind, running in the web browser ("down here"). For example, if you save an object in ASP.NET, you cannot access it from Silverlight without sending a request through a web service, for example.
>
> Also, the code on the ASP.NET web server is "full" .NET while Silverlight is only a subset.

In the context of Silverlight, we will use the ASP.NET Web Site project as a test environment for our application. A test page containing a Silverlight `object` tag will be sent to the web browser. Only when the page reaches the browser will the Silverlight control be created and the Silverlight application will start.

The most important files created by Visual Studio are shown in Table 9.1.

TABLE 9.1   Files Created by Visual Studio

Default.aspx	This is a dynamic ASP.NET page. It contains a mix of HTML code and of ASP.NET code. Together with the code-behind file Default.aspx.cs, this page creates the HTML (and JavaScript and CSS) code that will be sent to the web browser.
	Note that in the current test project, the page Default.aspx doesn't do anything.
MyFirstSilverlightTestPage.aspx	This page is also a dynamic ASP.NET page. It is created as a test page for your Silverlight application. We talk a little more about it in just a minute.
MyFirstSilverlightTestPage.html	This static HTML page is also a test page for your Silverlight application.
ClientBin\MyFirstSilverlight.xap	This file (and the ClientBin folder) is only available after the first time you build the solution.
	Because there is an invisible link between the Web Site project and the Silverlight project, the output of the Silverlight project will automatically be updated in the Web Site project every time you build. This is handy, because you can simply deploy the Web Site project files (including the XAP file) to the target web server.

The other files and folders are not relevant for the moment.

Static HTML Versus Dynamic ASPX

ASP.NET is outside the scope of this book. We will however talk about two ASP.NET controls used in the context of Silverlight in Chapter 24, "Silverlight: Continuing the Journey." The main differences between an HTML page and an ASPX page are

▶ The HTML page is sent "as is" to the web browser, without any modification. The ASPX page, on the other hand, has parts that are built dynamically.

▶ The ASPX page typically has a source code file (code-behind) attached. This is not compulsory, but it's usually the case.

For example, if a user wants to choose from a bicycle catalog, but only wants the bicycles suited for kids between 5 and 8 years old, you don't want to have a separate HTML page for this kind of scenario. Instead, you will build just one ASPX page and use the code-behind to query a database and generate the corresponding HTML code in the dynamic page.

▶ If you open the page MyFirstSilverlightTestPage.aspx in Visual Studio, you will see a tag named `asp:Silverlight`. This instructs the ASP.NET framework to generate (or *render*) the `object` tag that we studied earlier. Using the Silverlight *ASP.NET control* is handy, because you can use code-behind to set parameters before the actual HTML code is sent to the web browser. We talk more about this control in Chapter 24.

▶ On the other hand, the HTML page looks better known to us: It is pretty much the same HTML code as in the test page that we opened in Chapter 7, "Deploying to a Web Page."

The Silverlight Project

The files created for Silverlight 2 are similar to a Silverlight 2 application created by Expression Blend. Since we are already familiar with most of these files (we studied them in Chapter 4, "Expressing Yourself with Expression Blend"), let's just mention the solution file and the AssemblyInfo file:

▶ The Solution file (top-level file in the Solution Explorer) now contains two projects: The Web Site project used to test the application, and the Silverlight project.

▶ The Properties folder contains the file AssemblyInfo.cs. This C# file will be compiled into the binary output file. It contains information

> **TIP**
>
> If you don't see the Solution Explorer in Visual Studio, it might be closed or collapsed.
>
> To open it if it is closed, select View, Solution Explorer from the menu.
>
> To expand it if it is collapsed, check the side bar (it should be on the far right of the main window) and pass the mouse over the Solution Explorer tab (see Figure 9.4).

FIGURE 9.4   Collapsed Solution Explorer tab

about the application, such as Title, Description, Company, Copyright, Version, and so on. After compilation, this information is encoded in the file ClientBin/ [ApplicationName].xap/[ApplicationName].dll visible for example in Windows Explorer.

The other files have been mentioned already. For details about these files, refer to Chapter 4.

Running the (Empty) Application

Let's change our application so that we have something to see, and run it with the following steps:

1. In Visual Studio, open the file Page.xaml.

2. The very first time that you open an XAML file in Visual Studio, it opens in split view between the XAML editor and the visual designer. However, this mode is very slow and you probably shouldn't use it at the moment. After all, we have Blend for visualizing our application. You can close the preview panel by clicking on the Swap Panes button to put the XAML view on top (Figure 9.5) and then on the Collapse Pane button (Figure 9.6). This setting is saved by Visual Studio, and XAML files will open faster.

FIGURE 9.5   Swap Panes button

FIGURE 9.6   Collapse Panes button

3. Find the `Grid` named `LayoutRoot` and select the word `White` (content of the `Background` property).

4. Start typing the word `Red`. Enter the letter "R". A box should appear, with a list of all the colors starting with the letter "R". This feature is called Intellisense (see Figure 9.7).

5. Set the page's background to `Red`, so that we see something.

6. Add a `TextBlock` to the `Grid`. We will use this as a status line, displaying the result of our calculations.

FIGURE 9.7   Intellisense in XAML editor

```
<TextBlock x:Name="StatusLine"
           Text="Initializing..."/>
```

7. Right click on the web site MyFirstSilverlightWeb and choose Set as Startup Project from the context menu. Then right click on MyFirstSilverlightTestPage.html and choose Set As Start Page from the context menu. The startup project is displayed in bold in the Solution Explorer. You should always make sure that the correct project is selected as startup!

8. The first time you run the web site in debug mode, Visual Studio asks you if you want to modify it for debugging. Select the radio button labeled Modify the Web.config file... and click on OK.

9. Press F5. This *builds* the application and starts your favorite browser, displaying a red grid and the text "Initializing".

We use and extend this application in the course of this chapter.

Intellisense

When you type code in Visual Studio's editors, Intellisense offers you a choice of words automatically. This feature is called *Intellisense*. It helps you to write code faster and to avoid errors by proposing to you a choice according to what you are currently writing.

When Intellisense proposes a choice to you, you can use the key combination Ctrl+Spacebar to complete the word you started to type. Intellisense is used in multiple circumstances:

▶ When you declare a new variable by typing a class name, Intellisense offers you a choice of all the types currently available, grouped by namespace. A short documentation is also displayed (if available).

▶ When you want to use a variable declared somewhere else, Intellisense proposes all variables currently accessible, as well as documentation, if available (see Figure 9.8).

▶ When you type a class name followed by a period, or an instance name followed by a period, Intellisense presents all the methods available in the class (static methods) or in the instance. It also indicates the *method's signature* (the number and type of the parameters) and the number of overloads (or method with the same name, but a different signature); here also, a short documentation about this method is shown, if available (see Figure 9.9).

FIGURE 9.8   Intellisense for types and variables

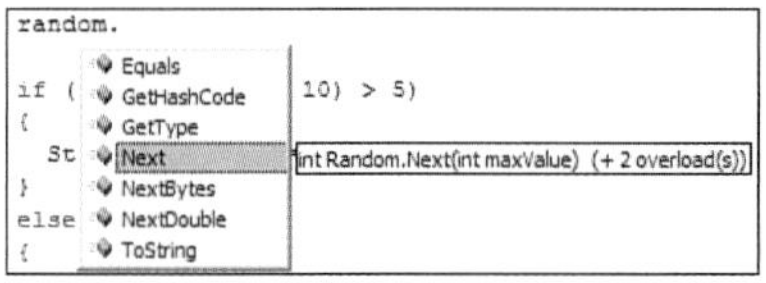

FIGURE 9.9   Intellisense for methods

► By passing the mouse cursor (without clicking) on any method, type, instance, parameter, and so on, Intellisense displays the short documentation for this member (if available).

Intellisense is really an invaluable tool. With time, you will learn to use it to its fullest to improve your developer skills.

> **TIP**
>
> When an Intellisense pop-up is displayed, pressing the Ctrl key makes the pop-up transparent, so that you can read the code underneath.
>
> You can also make an Intellisense pop-up appear at the cursor's location by pressing Ctrl+Spacebar.

Programming C# with Basic Constructs

Mastering the basic constructs is the first step for every programming language. All of them support these constructs and operators in one form or another, because they are the basis needed to implement any algorithm.

We already saw some of the constructs discussed in the following section in Chapter 8, "Programming Silverlight with JavaScript," and you will see that the C# syntax is similar. Both languages are descendants of the C programming language.

Types

.NET offers a very large choice in types, stored in libraries. Some of them are called *basic types* and are an intrinsic part of the .NET programming languages. Others are objects and can be compared to building blocks, which you will use to implement your applications.

> **NOTE**
>
> .NET specifies a list of basic types that have to be implemented by all the .NET programming languages. In addition, C# specifies *built-in types* such as `int`, `long`, `bool`, and so on. In a first approach, you can consider that C# built-in types are equivalent to the corresponding .NET type.
>
> For more information go to http://msdn2.microsoft.com/en-us/library/ya5y69ds.aspx.

Integer Types

An integer is a nonfractional number. There are various types of integer that you can use:

► byte—(System.`Byte`, 0 to 255)

► sbyte—(System.`SByte`, -128 to 127)

► short—(System.`Int16`, -32,768 to 32,767)

► ushort—(System.`UInt16`, 0 to 65,535)

► int—(System.`Int32`, -2,147,483,648 to 2,147,483,647)

► uint—(System.`UInt32`, 0 to 4,294,967,295)

▶ long—(System.Int64, –9,223,372,036,854,775,808 to 9,223,372,036,854,775,807)

▶ ulong—(System.UInt64, 0 to 18,446,744,073,709,551,615)

As you can see, these types are different by their *range* (minimum value and maximum value); also, some types allow negative values and others don't.

WARNING

Since `long` covers such a large range and allows for negative values, why do we need other types? In fact, every type is optimized for a certain use.

The fastest and most efficient type on 32-bit operating systems such as Windows Vista 32 and Windows XP is the `int` type, and this is probably the one you will use the most.

`long` is less efficient because of the way the memory is organized on 32-bit systems, but if you need to deal with very big numbers, then this is the right choice.

Finally, unsigned integers can be very useful, for example to handle binary files.

Floating Point Types

The integer types we just saw are very useful, but we need more:

```
int result1 = 5 / 2; // stores 2 in result
```

The preceding operation stores 2 instead of 2.5 as expected, because integer types cannot handle fractional results. This is what *floating point types* are for!

```
double result2 = 5 / 2;    // stores 2.0 in result
double result3 = 5.0 / 2.0; // stores 2.5 in result
```

Why does `result2` contain 2.0 instead of 2.5 as expected? Because 5 and 2 are integer values, and dividing two integers produces an integer value too. On the other hand, 5.0 and 2.0 are explicitly floating point values.

Because .NET handles type strictly and wants to avoid any confusion, non-integer values must be marked explicitly to specify their type. For instance, 42.34567m is stored as a `decimal` (because of the "m" suffix) while 42.34567 is stored as a `double` (because this is the default type for floating point values).

▶ decimal (System.Decimal, $\pm 1.0 \times 10^{-28}$ to $\pm 7.9 \times 10^{28}$)

```
decimal myDecimal = 42.34567m;
```

This type is useful for operations where precision is important.

▶ double (System.Double, $\pm 5.0 \times 10^{-324}$ to $\pm 1.7 \times 10^{308}$)

```
double myDouble1 = 5.0;
double myDouble2 = 5D;
```

▶ float (System.Single, $\pm 1.5 \times 10^{-45}$ to $\pm 3.4 \times 10^{38}$)

```
float myFloat = 5F;
```

Here also, choose the type corresponding to the operation you want to perform. The type double is the standard floating point type. Note also that float has the lowest precision, and decimal the highest precision.

Other Types

In addition, .NET has two types for dealing with text, and the boolean type.

▶ char (System.Char)—This type can store single characters of text.

```
char myChar = 'a';
```

▶ string (System.String)—Contains chains of characters.

```
string myString = "Hello";
```

▶ bool (System.Boolean)—This well-known type can store the values true or false.

Type Conversion

You cannot simply assign an object from a type to a variable of another type. If there is a way to transform a type into another type, you must use it explicitly. Transforming a variable of one type into another type is called *casting*. For example, the type long cannot implicitly be converted into the type int.

```
long longNumber = 12;
int shortNumber = (int) longNumber;
```

The cast operator () transforms one type into another. You can use this operator on primitive types or on any object.

Another way to cast an object from one type into another type is the as operator. When you don't know for sure what the type of an object you receive is, you can use the as operator in conjunction with the is operator, which returns true if an instance is of a certain type. The following code accepts an instance of type UIElement. But depending on whether it's a TextBlock or another UIElement (such as Button, Checkbox, and so on), the code will execute different operations. Contrary to the cast operator (), the as operator applies only to objects, not to basic types, like in Listing 9.2:

LISTING 9.2   is and as Operators

```
public void MyMethod(UIElement control)
{
  if (control is TextBlock)
  {
    (control as TextBlock).Text = "Hello";
  }
  // ...
}
```

if then else

This conditional construct enables the programmer to execute a series of operations if a condition is true, and another series if the condition is false. For example, implement the following steps:

> **NOTE**
>
> The fact that a TextBlock is also a UIElement is an application of an important principle of object-oriented programming called *polymorphism*. We talk more about this in next chapters.

1. Open the file Page.xaml.cs of the application MyFirstSilverlight in Visual Studio.

2. Modify the Page constructor to look like Listing 9.3:

LISTING 9.3   if...then...else

```
 1  public Page()
 2  {
 3    // Required to initialize variables
 4    InitializeComponent();
 5
 6    Random random = new Random();
 7    if (random.Next(0, 2) == 0)
 8    {
 9      StatusLine.Text = "Smaller";
10    }
11    else
12    {
13      StatusLine.Text = "Bigger";
14    }
15  }
```

3. Execute the code by pressing Ctrl+F5.

4. In the web browser, refresh the page by pressing the F5 button.

Let's take a moment to review the code:

- At line 6, we create an instance of type Random. This built-in object is used to generate pseudo-random numbers. We name this new instance random, which is allowed because C# is case-sensitive.

- When we write the call to the method Next on line 7, Intellisense shows that this method has three overloads. We choose the one where we can specify the maximum value and the minimum value. Careful: The minimum value is *inclusive*, and the maximum value is *exclusive*. So in fact, the values will be either 0 or 1.

- If you refresh the web page, you will see the text "Smaller" appear approximately 50% of the time.

> **WARNING**
>
> Do not get confused! F5 in Visual Studio compiles the code and runs the application in debug mode. F5 in the web browser refreshes the page and restarts the Silverlight application.
>
> Every time you modify the C# code or the XAML markup, you need to rebuild the application!

for

Every programming language offers a number of *loops*. The most well-known is the for loop: A series of operations is executed a certain number of times, for example in Listing 9.4:

LISTING 9.4   for

```
public Page()
{
  // Required to initialize variables
  InitializeComponent();

  int counter = 1;
  for (int index = 0; index < 5; index++)
  {
    counter = counter * 2;
  }
  StatusLine.Text = counter.ToString();
}
```

The preceding code displays the value 32 which is the value of 1*2*2*2*2*2.

Here again, a few notes:

- We loop from 0 (inclusive) to 5 (not inclusive). So we loop five times altogether. This way of doing is customary in C-based languages.

▶ index++ means the same as index = index + 1. So we start at 0, and increase index by 1 at every loop. The value of index gets evaluated, and as long as the condition index < 5 is true, the loop continues.

▶ As in JavaScript, we can place multiple operations on one single line, as in the for loop definition (the variable index is defined, assigned, tested against, and incremented, all on one line). The semicolon ";" is used to separate the operations.

▶ Note that in C#, the semicolon at the end of an operation is compulsory!

foreach

Here is a variation of the for loop. This loop takes every member of a collection and performs a series of operations on each.

There are multiple collections in .NET, and we will encounter some of them in later chapters. The simplest collection is the array: A group of "cells," each cell of the same type as all others, such as in Listing 9.5:

LISTING 9.5   foreach

```
 1  public Page()
 2  {
 3    // Required to initialize variables
 4    InitializeComponent();
 5    string[] words = new string[5] { "Hello", "to", "all",
 6      "Silverlight", "fans" };
 7    string display = "";
 8    foreach (string word in words)
 9    {
10      display = display + word + " ";
11    }
12    StatusLine.Text = display;
13  }
```

▶ Lines 5 and 6 create an array of five strings and initialize the content with five words.

▶ Line 7 creates a new variable of type string and initializes it with an empty string. Initializing the variable with an empty string is needed, or else the compiler will refuse to build the application. .NET doesn't like unassigned variables, because their state is not clear.

▶ Lines 8 to 11 loop through the string array. At each loop, a temporary variable named word is created and is initialized with the content of the current cell.

▶ Line 10 adds the content of the variable word to the string named display, and then adds a "space." The result is stored in display again. The strings (like any other variables) are moved and copied in memory by the Silverlight runtime.

▶ The variable `word` is discarded at the end of every loop. It is *local* only to the block between lines 9 and 11.

▶ The variable `display` is local to the block between lines 2 and 13, and thus can be used outside the `foreach` loop.

▶ Running this code displays the string "Hello to all Silverlight fans".

while

Here is another loop! `while` executes a series of operations as long as a condition is true as shown in Listing 9.6. Note that depending on the condition, it is possible that the loop is never executed! It is also possible that the loop never ends once started (we will see an example of this in Chapter 24).

LISTING 9.6   while

```
 1  public Page()
 2  {
 3    // Required to initialize variables
 4    InitializeComponent();
 5
 6    string display = "";
 7    int index = 0;
 8    while (index < 10)
 9    {
10      display = display + index + " ";
11      index++;
12    }
13    StatusLine.Text = display;
14  }
```

▶ The variable `index` is created at line 7 and initialized to 0.

▶ At line 8, the value of `index` is compared to 10. If it is strictly smaller the loop will execute.

▶ Line 10 adds the current value of index and a space to the string display.

▶ Line 11 increases the value of index by 1. If you forget this line, you'll have an infinite loop! The *end condition* will never be met,

NOTE

Even though .NET is very strict about types, it is possible to "add" (concatenate) a string (display) and an integer (index). To do this, the integer must be converted to a string thanks to the built-in method `ToString()`. This method is available on every .NET object.

As a developer, when you create your own types, you may want to *overload* the built-in ToString method with your own.

6

and the application will run
forever.

▶ Running this code will display "0 1
2 3 4 5 6 7 8 9".

do…while

This is a variation of the `while` loop discussed previously, as in Listing 9.7:

LISTING 9.7   do…while

```
public Page()
{
  // Required to initialize variables
  InitializeComponent();

  string display = "";
  int index = 0;
  do
  {
    display = display + index + " ";
    index = index + 1;
  }
  while (index < 10);
  StatusLine.Text = display;
}
```

The preceding code creates exactly the same output as the corresponding `while` loop. The
only difference is that the operations in the loop will be executed once before the condition is even checked!

switch…case

This condition operator is a handy shortcut to replace multiple `if… then…else` operations.
Often, you want to execute various operations depending on a condition, for example in
Listing 9.8:

LISTING 9.8   switch…case

```
1  public Page()
2  {
3    // Required to initialize variables
4    InitializeComponent();
5
6    string display = "";
7    int index = 0;
```

LISTING 9.8   Continued

```
 8    while (index < 10)
 9    {
10      switch (index)
11      {
12        case 1:
13          display = display + "one ";
14          break;
15        case 2:
16          display = display + "two ";
17          break;
18        case 3:
19        case 4:
20        case 5:
21          display = display + "345 ";
22          break;
23        default:
24          display = display + index + " ";
25          break;
26      }
27
28      index = index + 1;
29    }
30    StatusLine.Text = display;
31  }
```

- According to the value of the variable `index`, a different `case` is executed.

- A series of operations in a `case` must be terminated by a `break`.

- Note that you can group multiple values, like we do at lines 18, 19, and 20: The same code is executed for the values 3, 4, and 5.

- If no corresponding `case` is found, the programmer can specify (optionally) a `default` series of operations.

- The code outputs the string "0 one two 345 345 345 6 7 8 9".

We could have reached the same result by nesting a series of `if…then…else` operations, but a `switch` is really easier to maintain and extend, and easier to read.

Operators

C-based languages mostly share the same operators, and we already used some of them in JavaScript. Again, a great advantage of using C# and JavaScript for Silverlight!

Mathematical Operations

The usual operators +, -, *, and / are pretty obvious. Let's just mention the fact that in C#, a developer can specify the way these operators act for a custom type. For example, a custom type `Tree` can specify that adding a `Tree` plus another `Tree` returns a `Forest`. Remember before, we added a string and an integer, and we got a string in return. This is the same type of operation.

In addition, C# offers useful operators such as the well-known ++ operator that gave its name to the famous language C++. This operator is a shortcut, and the following two lines are equivalent:

```
index++;
index = index + 1;
```

The operator -- is also available and means `index = index - 1;`.

One operator deserves a special mention, because it is not well known: The modulo operator—%. It returns the remainder of a division. For example in Listing 9.9:

> **WARNING**
>
> The operators ++ and -- can be used before and after the variable they apply to. If they are placed before (++index), it means "increase by one and then perform an operation." In the other case, it means "perform an operation and then increase by one" (index++).

LISTING 9.9   Modulo Operator

```
int result = 5 % 3; // 5 modulo 3, stores 2 in result
result = 6 % 3; // Stores 0 in result
result = 7 % 3; // Stores 1 in result
```

Assignment

There are multiple ways to *assign* a value to a variable:

▶ If you don't want to modify the assigned value, you simply use the = operator:

```
anyNumber = 5;
```

▶ It often happens that you want to modify the value stored in a variable, and to assign the modified value to the same variable again. For instance:

```
anyNumber = anyNumber + 10;
```

▶ This way of writing is annoying, however, because you must repeat the name of the variable. This is what the other assignment operators can help you with:

```
anyNumber += 10;
```

▶ The preceding line has the same result as the previous statement. It adds 10 to the number already contained in the variable `anyNumber`.

▶ Other such operators exist for each of the basic mathematical operations:

```
anyNumber *= 2;
anyNumber /= 4;
anyNumber -= 10;
```

Conditional and Logical Operators

When handling *boolean* values, you want to be able to test for a value, but also to modify it. This is what conditional and logical operators are for.

The three main operators acting on boolean values are shown in Listing 9.10:

▶ `&&`—AND, returns `true` only if both operands are `true`.

▶ `||`—OR, returns `true` if at least one of the operands is `true`.

▶ `!`—NOT, returns `true` if the single operand is `false`, and returns `false` if it is `true`.

LISTING 9.10   Conditional and Logical Operators

```
bool value1 = true;
bool value2 = !value1;         // stores false into value2
bool value3 = value1 && value2; // stores false into value3
bool value4 = value1 || value2; // stores true into value4
```

Relational and Equality Operators

These operators are used to test how a value compares to another, for example in Listing 9.11:

LISTING 9.11   Relational and Equality Operators

```
int number1 = 100;
int number2 = 1000;
bool test1 = (number1 < 100);    // stores false in test1
bool test2 = (number1 <= 100);   // stores true in test2
bool test3 = (number1 > 90);     // stores true in test3
bool test4 = (number1 == number2); // stores false in test4
bool test5 = (number1 != number2); // stores true in test5
```

Conditional Operator

This last operator is a little confusing for beginners. It is a handy way to write an `if...then...else` operation in a short and elegant way. Using the conditional operator, you can add a conditional check in a line already containing other operations.

If a condition is `true`, the expression *before* the colon is evaluated. If it is `false`, the expression *after* the colon is evaluated. The evaluated expressions may be simple values or complex calculations, for example in Listing 9.12:

LISTING 9.12   Conditional Operators

```
bool value = true;
int result1 = value ? 1 : 2; // stores 1 into result1
int result2 = (result1 == 2)
    ? (result1 * 2)
    : (result1 + 5); // stores 6 into result2
```

Using Parentheses

Parentheses have multiple purposes in C#. We saw before that they can be used to *cast* a variable from one type into another type. Another important use is to specify the order of the executed operations. For example:

> **NOTE**
>
> C# has additional operators that are not presented here. A complete list of the C# operators can be found online, at http://msdn2.microsoft.com/en-us/library/6a71f45d.aspx.

```
int result1 = 5 + 2 * 3;   // stores 11 in result1
int result2 = (5 + 2) * 3; // stores 21 in result2
```

The first result calculates 2 * 3 first, and then adds 5. This is because the multiplication operator has precedence over the addition operator.

When in doubt, use parentheses to explicitly set the order of the operations you want to execute.

Summary

In this chapter, we studied important basic concepts of programming in C# and .NET. Even though it was a lot of theory, this step will allow you to get a good understanding of the programming concepts. We continue this quest during the next chapter, and we use this knowledge to build applications. .NET has huge potential, and it is only the beginning of a long and wonderful journey.

CHAPTER 10

Progressing with .NET

In Chapter 9, "Understanding .NET," we learned what we need to create basic .NET applications, but now we need more structure. This chapter introduces objects in .NET and explains how to program them in C#.

Programming with Objects in C#

In Chapter 8, "Programming Silverlight with JavaScript," we saw a few definitions about object-oriented programming applied to JavaScript. The definitions we learned are valid in C#, too, though the implementation might be different. In the first part of this chapter, we define additional concepts.

Breaking Your Problem into Smaller Ones

Before object-oriented programming (OOP) took off, applications were written in a *procedural* way. The application had an entry point, which was calling global methods and saving data in global variables.

This way of programming proved to be difficult to maintain and to extend. When a bug was found, looking for the cause took a lot of time, due to the structure (or the lack of…) of the code.

OOP breaks the problems in much smaller structures, so you can concentrate on one problem after the other. Objects can be tested independently from the rest of the application, making it easier to isolate bugs, find their cause, and test the code in unusual circumstances.

Our environment is made of objects, each with a specific *behavior*. Building a plane is difficult. But a plane has two wings, so if you build one wing, you pretty much know how to build the second one. The differences between both wings can be expressed by a set of *properties*. They communicate with the rest of the plane using *interfaces*.

In turn, each wing is composed of a set of smaller, simpler objects. Similarly an application can be broken down into components and objects.

> **NOTE**
>
> When you start doing serious OOP work, you probably want to take a look at UML (Unified Modelling Language) editors. Many of them are available, varying in quality, features, and price. The most sophisticated can even generate code in various programming languages; they can also import existing source code and "reverse engineer" a visual representation. Other simpler editors allow drawing objects and their relationships to make analysis easier.

Namespaces and the `using` Directive

Namespaces are logical groups of objects, used to organize objects according to their functionality. Namespaces in C# don't have an impact on the object they host other than simply offering them a place to dwell.

Namespaces can be spread over multiple assemblies, and one assembly can contain multiple namespaces.

You can only use namespaces defined in *referenced assemblies*. These are assemblies that the current project explicitly links to. Later we see how to reference an external assembly to access the functionality it contains. In Visual Studio, referenced assemblies can be seen in the References folder. Do not modify the content of this folder, or your Silverlight application will stop working!

A top namespace is automatically defined when you create a new project in Studio or Blend. By default, the top namespace is equal to the project name. For example, for a project named MySilverlightApplication, the top namespace will be MySilverlightApplication, and the assembly will be named MySilverlightApplication.dll.

This is a good convention, and it is recommended to keep it this way. Additionally, you may define *subnamespaces* in the same assembly, for example: MySilverlightApplication.Services and MySilverlightApplication.Utilities.

```
namespace MySilverlightApplication.Services
{
  // ...
}
```

Adding a `using` Directive

If you want to use a namespace located in the current assembly or in a referenced assembly, you need to specify it explicitly in the source code. This is what the `using` directive is for.

In any Silverlight source code file created with Visual Studio 2008, you will see such a section, automatically added:

```
using System;
using System.Windows;
using System.Windows.Controls;
using System.Windows.Shapes;
// …
```

By adding a namespace with a `using` directive, you expose all the public code it contains without explicitly mentioning it. For example, the `Rectangle` class is located in the namespace `System.Windows.Shapes`. If you use a `Rectangle` in your code, you can type:

```
Rectangle myRectangle = new Rectangle();
```

If you remove the directive `using System.Windows.Shapes;` you cannot compile the code anymore, unless you mention the namespace explicitly:

```
System.Windows.Shapes.Rectangle myRectangle
  = new System.Windows.Shapes.Rectangle();
```

Visual Studio assists you in adding `using` directives with the following steps:

1. Having removed the statement `using System.Windows.Shapes;`, simply type the word `Rectangle` in your code.

2. Notice a small red underline appearing on the bottom right of the word `Rectangle`, as shown in Figure 10.1.

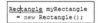

FIGURE 10.1   Automating a using directive (1)

3. Pass your mouse on this underline, and choose using System.Windows.Shapes (to add a `using` directive), as shown in Figure 10.2, or System.Windows.Shapes. Rectangle (to use the full name).

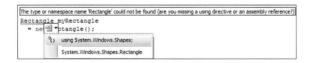

FIGURE 10.2   Automating a using directive (2)

4. You can expedite things by pressing the key combination Shift+Alt+F10 when the small red underline is displayed, instead of using the mouse.

Visibility

We saw that JavaScript cannot protect an object's members against unwanted access. In C#, however, you can control who is allowed to use attributes, properties, and methods.

▶ private—This is the most restrictive qualifier. Private members can be used only inside the class that defines them. This is also the default visibility: If you don't define it explicitly, private visibility will be used.

WARNING

Unlike the Java programming language, C# does not have a visibility restricted to the current namespace only.

▶ protected—These members can be used inside the class that defines them, and inside any derived class (see the "Inheritance" section later in this chapter).

▶ internal—These members can be used only by classes located inside the same assembly as the class that defines them.

▶ public—These members can be used by anyone, anytime, any place.

Properties

A property is a member somewhat between attributes and methods.

▶ Attributes should never be accessed directly, because the class that exposes them has no control over the way the accessing class uses or modifies them. That's why attributes usually are private.

▶ Methods offer better control, there is a *body* that is executed, and the class exposing the method can control what happens. But if you just want to get and set the value of an attribute, you need two methods (a setter and a getter) for each attribute, which is annoying to program.

▶ Properties are right in the middle: They expose a setter and a getter, but also have a body, so the class exposing the property can control what happens and what value is set.

▶ In C# 3.5, you can either declare a body for the property, or let the framework take care of it (if this is a simple setter/getter property). This is called an *automatic* property as shown in Listing 10.1:

LISTING 10.1   Automatic Property

```
1  protected double Area1
2  {
3    get;
4    private set;
5  }
6
7  private double _area2;
8  protected double Area2
9  {
```

LISTING 10.1   Continued

```
10    get
11    {
12      return _area2;
13    }
14    set
15    {
16      if (value < 0)
17      {
18        value = 0;
19      }
20      _area2 = value;
21    }
22  }
23
24  public void UseProperties()
25  {
26    Area1 = 20.0;
27    Area2 = 40.0;
28    DoSomething(Area2);
29  }
```

▶ Lines 1 to 5 define an automatic property with default setter and getter. Notice that even though the property itself is public, the setter is private, so it may only be used from inside the class itself. Note also that there is no attribute to store the value of Area1. The storage is taken care of by the framework.

▶ Line 7 creates a private attribute. Because it is private, it can only be used inside the class that owns it.

▶ Lines 10 to 13 define a getter for the attribute. It simply returns the value of the attribute _area2. Since the whole property is protected, it can only be used in this class and classes deriving from it.

▶ Lines 14 to 21 define a setter for the attribute. Because it is not explicitly set, its visibility is also protected. Note that value is a keyword, and represents what the setter's caller passes to it (for example 40.0). In this setter, we check the value passed to the property, and if it is negative, we set it to 0.

▶ Eventually, lines 26 to 28 use the properties we defined. Notice how a property can be used just like an attribute.

▶ Area1 and Area2 have been created differently, but the result is exactly the same. Area1 uses the new way allowed by .NET 3.5.

▶ By convention, attributes are often written with a preceding underline "_" and a small letter. Properties start with a capital letter.

10

Inheritance

Inheritance is a key concept in OOP. An object can have an *ancestor* (*base type*) and *derived types*.

Let's consider a plane wing again: A 747 jet, a Cessna, and an F16 fighter all have wings. They do have shared characteristics, but they are also very different from each other. The basic physics is the same, however. So why not create a class `Wing` to take care of the basic functionality?

Then, we can create derived classes `JumboWing`, `CessnaWing`, and `FighterWing`. Each refines the base functionality, making it possible to adapt a `Wing` to any type of plane.

In Silverlight, the most obvious use of inheritance we have seen so far is within the framework itself, and the fact that (for instance) a `TextBox` is also a `UIElement`. Other Silverlight controls are also `UIElement`s. This base class defines the base functionality, and the inherited control classes refine the implementation.

The fact that a `TextBlock` is also a `UIElement` thanks to inheritance is called *polymorphism* ("multiple shapes" in Greek), another key concept in OOP.

Checking the Inheritance Path

To check the inheritance path of a given element, the best place is the Silverlight documentation that we installed in Chapter 1, "Introducing Silverlight." Follow the steps:

1. Open the CHM file by double-clicking on it.

2. Select the Search tab.

3. Enter the word "TextBlock" in the Search box and click on List Topics.

4. In the search results, scroll down until you find the topic TextBlock Class and double-click on it.

5. On top of the `TextBlock` class page, you find the namespace to which it belongs (System.Windows.Controls) as well as the assembly in which this class is defined (System.Windows.dll). This DLL is part of the default assembly set included in every Silverlight application by Visual Studio. You don't need to do anything to use this element.

> **NOTE**
>
> In .NET, every element automatically inherits `System.Object`, even if this is not explicitly specified. This allows the developers to make certain assumptions about any instance in any application.

6. If you scroll down on the `TextBlock` class page, you see the inheritance hierarchy. We see that a `TextBlock` is also a `UIElement`, a `FrameworkElement`, a `DependencyObject`, and finally an `Object` (see Figure 10.3).

- **Inheritance Hierarchy**
  System.Object
   System.Windows.DependencyObject
    System.Windows.FrameworkElement
     System.Windows.UIElement
      System.Windows.Controls.TextBlock

FIGURE 10.3   TextBlock inheritance hierarchy

7. The See Also section located at the bottom of the documentation page leads you to other related subjects. It is always interesting to check this section and to start browsing.

Adding Interactivity to the Thumbnails Application

Our Thumbnails application (we worked on it in Chapter 5, "Using Media," and Chapter 6, "Blending a Little More") is already a Silverlight 2 application, but now we want to add some interactivity. The user already has the possibility to play and pause a video thumbnail. We also want to use the Display frame we added in Chapter 6, and display an expanded version of the media, be it video or image.

Adding Event Handlers in Code

Every thumbnail in the application should do something when clicked. Our first move is to add a generic event handler that will handle all the `Image` and `MediaElement` controls. We will do this in Visual Studio with the following steps:

1. In the file Page.xaml, find the `MediaElement` named `Media2` and remove the event handler for the `MouseLeftButtonDown` and the `Cursor` attribute. We need to remove the "old" event handler, because we will now use a generic event handler for all the images and videos, and take care of this in C# code. The new `MediaElement` code is shown in Listing 10.2:

LISTING 10.2   Updated `MediaElement`

```
<MediaElement x:Name="Media2"
  Source="mov1.wmv" AutoPlay="False"
  MediaEnded="MediaElement_MediaEnded />
```

2. In Page.xaml.cs, modify the `Page` constructor as in Listing 10.3:

LISTING 10.3   Updated `Page` Constructor

```
private FrameworkElement _expandedMedia = null;

public Page()
{
  // Required to initialize variables
  InitializeComponent();

  FrameworkElement media = null;
  int index = 0;
  do
  {
```

10

LISTING 10.3   Continued

```
    media = this.FindName("Media" + index++) as FrameworkElement;
    if (media != null)
    {
      media.Cursor = Cursors.Hand;
      media.MouseLeftButtonDown
        += new MouseButtonEventHandler(media_MouseLeftButtonDown);
    }
  }
  while (media != null);
}
```

3. Note the presence of the attribute _expandedMedia. Because we want that attribute to store an Image or a MediaElement, we use the class FrameworkElement, which is the base class for both types. So we can say that an Image is a FrameworkElement, and a MediaElement is also a FrameworkElement.

Displaying the Expanded Media

1. Delete the whole method MediaElement_MouseLeftButtonDown (including the private attribute _isPaused) and replace it with the code in Listing 10.4:

LISTING 10.4   Updated MouseLeftButtonDown Event Handler

```
1   void media_MouseLeftButtonDown(object sender,
2     MouseButtonEventArgs e)
3   {
4     FrameworkElement castedSender = sender as FrameworkElement;
5
6     // If needed, pause movie
7     if (_expandedMedia != null)
8     {
9       if (_expandedMedia is MediaElement)
10      {
11        (_expandedMedia as MediaElement).Pause();
12      }
13      // Hide currently displayed media
14      Display.Fill = new SolidColorBrush(Colors.Transparent);
15      FrameworkElement currentMedia = _expandedMedia;
16      _expandedMedia = null;
17
18      if (castedSender == currentMedia)
19      {
20        return;
```

LISTING 10.4   Continued

```
21      }
22    }
23
24    // Set size and position of DisplayRectangle
25    double sizeFactor
26      = castedSender.ActualWidth / castedSender.ActualHeight;
27    Display.Width = Display.ActualHeight * sizeFactor;
28    double sideMargin
29      = (DisplayBackground.ActualWidth - Display.Width) / 2;
30    Display.Margin
31      = new Thickness(sideMargin, 10, sideMargin, 10);
32
33    // Set the Display and start movie (if needed)
34    if (castedSender is MediaElement)
35    {
36      VideoBrush brush = new VideoBrush();
37      brush.SetSource(castedSender as MediaElement);
38      (castedSender as MediaElement).Play();
39      Display.Fill = brush;
40    }
41    if (castedSender is Image)
42    {
43      ImageBrush brush = new ImageBrush();
44      BitmapImage source
45        = (castedSender as Image).Source as BitmapImage;
46      brush.ImageSource
47        = new BitmapImage(source.UriSource);
48      Display.Fill = brush;
49    }
50
51    _expandedMedia = castedSender;
52  }
```

2. To make this code work, you need to add a reference (a using) to the namespace System.Windows. Media.Imaging. To do this, place the cursor on the BitmapImage on line 44 and follow the steps we described earlier in the section titled "Adding a using Directive."

> **NOTE**
>
> You will need to add using statements often in the course of this book (remember the Shift+Alt+F10 trick). We will not mention it explicitly every time, so make a mental note now for later!

10

▶ The method `media_MouseLeftButtonDown` is called every time the user clicks on one of the thumbnails, because the event handler was added dynamically to each media thumbnail in the `Page` constructor.

▶ Since we don't know whether the *event sender* is an `Image` or a `MediaElement`, we will mostly work with a parent class of these two objects: `FrameworkElement`. This parent class contains information about the sender's size, its position, and so on. Since the `sender` is of the most generic type `object`, we *cast* (transform) `sender` to the `FrameworkElement castedSender` (line 4).

> **NOTE**
>
> Even though we have multiple references to the sender parameter, they all point to the same instance in memory. On line 4, we do not create a new instance, we merely store a reference to the same instance under a different name (and a different type, but that's okay because of polymorphism).

▶ Lines 6 to 22 check whether an element is already displayed. Since the *attribute* `_expandedMedia` is initialized to `null`, this section will not be executed the first time the code runs. If, however, the `_expandedMedia` is not `null`, we check first whether the stored element is a `MediaElement` (using the `is` operator discussed in Chapter 9, in the section titled "Type Conversion"). If it is, we pause the movie.

▶ On line 14, we reset the `Fill` property of the `Display` element (that's a rectangle we created in the XAML markup) to a solid `Transparent`. Effectively, this simply hides the displayed element.

▶ Lines 15 and 16 store the reference to the current element in a local variable `currentMedia`, and then we set the attribute `_expandedMedia` to `null`. In doing this, we break the reference between this private attribute and the actual element (see line 51).

▶ Finally, we check whether the saved `currentMedia` is the same as the sender. That would be the case if the user clicks on the same element that is currently being displayed. In that case, we exit the method by calling `return`. Usually, `return` is used to *return* a value to the method's caller, but in that case we don't have anything to return (that's why our method is marked `void`).

> **TIP**
>
> We have multiple references to the same object in memory. When we set one of these references to `null` like we just did, the system will check whether other references are still available for this object. If that is the case, the object remains in memory. If, however, all the references to that object have been removed, the object is marked for *garbage collection* and will soon be removed from memory.

▶ Lines 24 to 31 calculate the size and position of the `Display` rectangle in which the expanded media is going to be shown. This is needed, because we have some vertical (narrow) and horizontal (wide) images. The calculation computes the size factor using the small thumbnail that we received as the `sender`. Since the `object` type doesn't have any indication about the element's size, we use instead the same element *casted* to the `FrameworkElement` type. Based on this calculation, we can position the element in the middle of the `DisplayBackground` rectangle using margins.

▶ Notice how we use the `ActualHeight` instead of `Height`. This is because `Height` might be set to Auto, in which case we don't get a numeric value. On the other hand, `ActualHeight` is really useful, because it is always set to the real numeric size (in pixels) of the element!

▶ Lines 36 to 39 are executed only if the event's sender is a `MediaElement`. In that case, we set the `Display` rectangle's `Fill` property to `VideoBrush`. We also start the movie.

▶ If on the other hand the sender is an `Image`, we build an `ImageBrush` instead. Note that the syntax to build an `ImageBrush` is different from a `VideoBrush`: Instead of using the `MediaElement`, we need to build a new `BitmapImage` object. The new `BitmapImage` object has the same `Source` as the sender.

▶ Finally, on line 51, we store the sender in the private attribute `_expandedMedia`. Remember that we needed this attribute to stop a playing movie (if needed) from line 7 onward.

You can now execute the code by pressing Ctrl+F5.

▶ Click on the thumbnails to see the expanded view in the display, and see how the movie gets played/paused.

▶ If you click twice on the same element, the image (or video) is displayed first, and then hidden.

> **NOTE**
>
> As you can see, a lot of conversions (casts) take place in this code. C# is strongly typed and will not compile if the types are not explicitly defined. This is a major difference from JavaScript. Generally, C# code needs to be more precise and explicit than JavaScript code.

Typing this code will show you how Intellisense helps you. Take some time to train your Intellisense skills, and you can type your C# code much faster and more accurately.

Overloading Methods

As mentioned a few times before, C# is very strongly typed. Because of this, a method made for a certain type (for example `string`) cannot be used for another type (for example `int`) as in Listing 10.5.

LISTING 10.5   Non-overloaded Method

```
public void DoSomething(string myString)
{
  // ...
}
```

10

LISTING 10.5   Continued

```
public void UseMyMethod()
{
  DoSomething("hello"); // OK
  DoSomething(2);       // doesn't compile
}
```

We already talked briefly about polymorphism ("multiple shapes") earlier when we mentioned that a `TextBlock` is also a `UIElement` and a `FrameworkElement` (by inheritance). Another type of polymorphism is used to *overload* methods with multiple signatures. For example, you can write Listing 10.6:

LISTING 10.6   Overloaded Method

```
 1   public void DoSomething(string myString)
 2   {
 3     // ...
 4   }
 5   public void DoSomething(int myInt)
 6   {
 7     // ...
 8   }
 9   public void UseMyMethod()
10   {
11     DoSomething("hello"); // OK
12     DoSomething(2);       // OK
13   }
```

Thanks to the clearly defined type, the C# compiler knows that it must call the first method (with the `string` parameter) on line 11, and the second method (with the `int` parameter) on line 12.

This way to code has one disadvantage: If you want to handle multiple types, you need multiple methods, and that's not really nice. Another solution is to use *generics*. We talk about generics in Chapter 20, "Taking Silverlight 2 One Step Further."

Raising Events and Using Delegates

When an object wants to notify another object that something occurred, a good way is to raise an event.

▶ For the event's sender, it is handy because it doesn't need to know who is interested in the event. The event is raised, and all subscribers will be notified without the need for a direct reference.

▶ For the event's subscriber, you just need to register once, and you will get all the notifications asynchronously.

We already saw how to register for an event exposed by another class:

```
media.MouseLeftButtonDown
  += new MouseEventHandler(media_MouseLeftButtonDown);
```

with:

```
void media_MouseLeftButtonDown(object sender, MouseEventArgs e)
{
  // Do something
}
```

But how do we expose and consume a custom event in our own classes?

Creating an EventArgs

Often, you want to pass additional information to the event's subscribers. By convention, an event always has two parameters:

▶ The event's sender (declared as an object)

▶ An instance of EventArgs or of another class deriving from EventArgs.

If you don't want to pass any information, simply create an empty instance of EventArgs and use it when you raise the event. This avoids breaking any application if you decide to change it later and to pass information using your own flavor of EventArgs.

For example, if you want to pass the date and time at which the event occurred, create the class in Listing 10.7:

LISTING 10.7   SomethingOccurredEventArgs Class

```
public class SomethingOccurredEventArgs : EventArgs
{
  public DateTime When
  {
    get;
    internal set;
  }
}
```

Notice how SomethingOccurredEventArgs inherits the EventArgs class (that's what the ":" means on the first line), and defines an additional property to store information about the event.

By convention, the name of any class deriving from `EventArgs` will be suffixed with "EventArgs".

Declaring the Event

First, we need to create a *delegate*. This special declaration looks much like a method but doesn't have a body. In fact, it is a *contract* between the class raising the event and the class subscribing to it. It says *"If you want to receive my event, you need to have, somewhere, a method looking like this delegate."*

Delegates have other uses than for event handlers (though it's probably their main use). A delegate is something like a "method object" (sometimes people refer to delegates as a "method pointer"). You can pass a delegate to another object, and this object can *invoke* the method that the delegate represents.

By convention, the delegate's name (for an event handler) ends with the suffix "Handler" to signify that this is an event handler, as in Listing 10.8:

LISTING 10.8   SomethingOccurredHandler Delegate

```
public delegate void SomethingOccurredHandler(object sender,
   SomethingOccurredEventArgs e);
```

Now we can declare the event itself in the class that will raise it. The event's type is the delegate that we created just before (see Listing 10.9):

LISTING 10.9   EventRaiser Empty Class

```
public class EventRaiser
{
   public event SomethingOccurredHandler SomethingOccurred;
}
```

The last task that the `EventRaiser` class needs to do is provide a method to raise the event. By convention (again), such a method is named with the prefix "On" followed by the name of the event (like in Listing 10.10). This convention is not very strictly followed, and the "raising" method is often named differently.

If a method wants to raise the SomethingOccurred event, it can do so by creating a new SomethingOccurredEventArgs instance and then call the method OnSomethingOccurred:

WARNING

Before raising the event, you need to make sure that there is at least one susbscriber. If nobody subscribed yet, the event SomethingOccurred will be null, and should not be raised.

LISTING 10.10   Updated EventRaiser Class

```
public class EventRaiser
{
  public event SomethingOccurredHandler SomethingOccurred;

  public void OnSomethingOccurred(SomethingOccurredEventArgs e)
  {
    if (SomethingOccurred != null)
    {
      SomethingOccurred(this, e);
    }
  }

  public void DoSomething()
  {
    // ...
    SomethingOccurredEventArgs e = new SomethingOccurredEventArgs();
    e.When = DateTime.Now;
    OnSomethingOccurred(e);
    // ...
  }
}
```

Subscribing to the Event

Subscribing to the event is simple, especially with the help of Intellisense (see Listing 10.11):

> **TIP**
>
> When you type the string _raiser. SomethingOccurred and then add the += operator, Intellisense offers to automatically create an event handler with the correct signature. Simply press the Tab key twice to get a free event handler!

LISTING 10.11   EventReceiver Class

```
public class EventReceiver
{
  private EventRaiser _raiser;
  public EventReceiver()
  {
    _raiser = new EventRaiser();
    _raiser.SomethingOccurred
      += new SomethingOccurredHandler(_raiser_SomethingOccurred);
  }

  void _raiser_SomethingOccurred(object sender,
```

10

LISTING 10.11   Continued

```
  SomethingOccurredEventArgs e)
{
  Status.Text = "Something occurred at " + e.When.ToShortDateString()
    + " " + e.When.ToLongTimeString();
}
}
```

Storing Data on the Client

In classic web applications made with HTML, JavaScript, and CSS, data persistence on the web client is achieved by saving a small piece of text called a *cookie*. This small text can be retrieved at a later time and is even saved if the browser is closed. This mechanism is rather primitive, however, and not suited to saving complex structures.

In Silverlight, a real file system is made available to the application. You can create or delete directories, save data (text or binary), and read or delete files.

Understanding the Isolated Storage Security Restrictions

The isolated storage is, like the name shows, isolated. The application has no way to find out where the files are located on the client computer. Code located in an application can only access the isolated storage for this particular application. Other files located on the client computer may not be accessed. Only the isolated storage is made available, for obvious security reasons.

The isolated storage is limited in size. However you can find out how much space remains in the store, and even require more space from the user. For more information about these advanced functionalities, check the documentation we installed in Chapter 1, especially the page titled "IsolatedStorageFile Class."

Remember that you cannot be sure whether files saved on the client will be available the next time the application runs. If the data saved is critical, you should save it on the server, for example, in a server-side file or in a database.

Creating Objects

Following the advice to "break our problem into smaller ones," we will create two objects to perform specific tasks:

▶ The User object will store the date and time of the last visit. This may seem a trivial task for an object, but it will be useful when we extend the application with multiple users in a later chapter.

▶ The `DataFile` object will take care of reading and writing the information from and to the isolated storage.

The `User` Class

To create and implement this specialized class, follow the steps:

1. Open the Thumbnails application in Visual Studio and right-click on the Thumbnails project in the Solution Explorer.

2. Select Add, New Folder and name this folder Data.

3. Right-click on the Data folder and select Add, Class.

4. Enter the name "User.cs" and click Add; the file opens automatically.

5. In the `User` class, add the property in Listing 10.12:

> **NOTE**
>
> The `User` class is automatically placed in a new namespace `Thumbnails.Data`. While this is not an obligation, it is strongly recommended to create one class per C# file only, and to place each file in a folder corresponding to its namespace. This creates a cleaner file structure.

> **TIP**
>
> The ? is not a typo! The type `DateTime`? is called a *nullable DateTime*. Prior to .NET 3.5, a member of type `DateTime` always contained a value. With .NET 3.5, however, a nullable `DateTime` instance can be set to `null`. Similarly, other nullable types have been introduced, for example `bool?`, `int?`, and so on.

LISTING 10.12   `LastVisit` Property

```
public DateTime? LastVisit
{
  get;
  private set;
}
```

6. Add two constructors to the `User` object as in Listing 10.13. The first one is used to create a new, empty `User`. The second overload takes a line from the saved data file and uses this information to initialize the `LastVisit` property.

LISTING 10.13   Two Constructors for the User Class

```
public User()
{
  LastVisit = null;
}
public User(string line)
{
  try
  {
    LastVisit = DateTime.Parse(line);
```

10

LISTING 10.13   Continued

```
  }
  catch (ArgumentNullException)
  {
    LastVisit = null;
  }
  catch (FormatException)
  {
    LastVisit = null;
  }
}
```

▶ The second constructor tries to parse the line parameter and catches two different exceptions

▶ ArgumentNullException is thrown by the DateTime.Parse method if the line is null.

▶ FormatException is thrown (also by the DateTime.Parse method) if the format is not recognized as a valid DateTime. In both cases, we catch the exception (avoiding that the application crashes), and we set the LastVisit to null.

7. An additional method is created to set the LastVisit property to the current date and time. This will be used before saving the information to the data file.

```
public void SetLastVisit()
{
  LastVisit = DateTime.Now;
}
```

8. Finally, we want the User class to provide a method converting an instance of this class to a string. This process is called *serialization*. In this simplified example, we simply convert the LastVisit property to a string. Later, this method will be extended to convert additional properties too. Every .NET object inherits the basic class object (even though this is never explicitly specified in the class declaration). This is why each and every .NET object has a basic set of methods; one of them is the ToString method, used to serialize the instance to a string. However, the original ToString method cannot serialize the User instance and returns only a generic string with the class's name. This is why we need to *override* this method and provide our own, in Listing 10.14:

LISTING 10.14   Overriden `ToString` Method

```
public override string ToString()
{
  if (LastVisit == null)
  {
    return "";
  }
  else
  {
    return LastVisit.ToString();
  }
}
```

Our `ToString` method checks the value of `LastVisit`. If the nullable `DateTime` is null, we simply return an empty string. If it is set, we use the `ToString` method that the `DateTime?` type also defines. Build the application to check if there are any errors.

The DataFile Class

The other new class we create is responsible for handling the writing and reading to the isolated storage. Follow the steps to create and implement it:

1. Again, add a C# class to the Data folder. Name this DataFile.cs.

2. In the class, add a constant to store the name of the data file we will read from and write to.

   ```
   private const string DATA_FILE_NAME = "ThumbnailsData.txt";
   ```

We will add two methods to this class (see Listing 10.15):

▶ The first method, `LoadUser`, reads the data file and creates the `User` instance.

▶ The other method, `SaveUser`, saves the `User` information to the data file.

Some of the namespaces we use in this class have to be added explicitly to the `using` section. Remember the Shift+Alt+F10 trick we learned before!

LISTING 10.15   `LoadUser` and `SaveUser` Methods

```
1  internal User LoadUser()
2  {
3    User user = null;
4
5    // Try to get the information about the last visit
6    using (IsolatedStorageFile store
7      = IsolatedStorageFile.GetUserStoreForApplication())
8    {
9      if (store.FileExists(DATA_FILE_NAME))
```

LISTING 10.15   Continued

```
10      {
11        using (IsolatedStorageFileStream streamRead
12          = store.OpenFile(DATA_FILE_NAME, FileMode.Open))
13        {
14          using (StreamReader reader = new StreamReader(streamRead))
15          {
16            string line = reader.ReadLine();
17            if (line != null)
18            {
19              user = new User(line);
20            }
21            else
22            {
23              user = new User();
24            }

25          }
26        }
27      }
28      else
29      {
30        user = new User();
31      }

32    }
33    return user;
34  }
35
36  internal void SaveUser(User user)
37  {
38    using (IsolatedStorageFile store
39      = IsolatedStorageFile.GetUserStoreForApplication())
40    {
41      using (IsolatedStorageFileStream streamWrite
42        = store.OpenFile(DATA_FILE_NAME, FileMode.OpenOrCreate))
43      {
44        using (StreamWriter writer = new StreamWriter(streamWrite))
45        {
46          writer.WriteLine(user.ToString());
47        }
48      }
49    }
50  }
```

Let's review this code.

Reading from the Isolated Storage

▶ Lines 6 and 7 get a reference to the IsolatedStorageFile corresponding to this application. As we mentioned, one application can only write to a given store, and you cannot know where it is located on the client machine.

▶ Line 9 checks whether the file we want to read from already exists. If it doesn't, we create a new empty User on line 26.

> **NOTE**
>
> Lines 6 and 7 create the IsolatedStorageFile instance by means of a using statement. This is *not the same* as the using section we discussed earlier in this chapter.
>
> In this context, using allows creating special objects like readers and writers, and makes sure that all the files and other resources are closed properly when they are not needed anymore.

▶ Lines 11 to 12 create a Stream in the isolated storage. A Stream is an object you can write to or read from. In this particular case, what you read from the stream comes from a file located in the isolated storage. Note that we created the Stream in the Open mode. This mode is good to read from an existing file. Note also that we use the constant DATA_FILE_NAME we defined earlier.

▶ Line 14 uses the Stream we just created and wraps a StreamReader object around it. This object is good for reading text (as opposed to reading binary data).

▶ Lines 16 to 20 read the first line from the text file and use it to create an instance of User. When a StreamReader reaches the end of the file (for example, if the file exists but is empty), it doesn't create an error, but it returns null. In that case, we create a new empty user on line 19.

▶ Line 17 is where the line is actually read from the file. The method ReadLine reads the current line until it finds an "end-of-line" character. Then it moves the cursor to the next line.

▶ Finally, line 30 returns the User instance we just created to the caller. This instance's LastVisit may be initialized to a valid DateTime (if the file was found and parsed successfully), or to null (if the file was not found).

Writing to the Isolated Storage

The method SaveUser accepts a User instance as parameter and saves it to the file in the isolated storage.

▶ Lines 38 to 39 get the IsolatedStorageFile for this application.

▶ Lines 41 to 42 create a new Stream, this time in OpenOrCreate mode. This mode creates a new file if no existing file is found. If the file already exists, however, it reopens it and *overwrites* the content with the new data.

10

▶ Line 44 creates a `StreamWriter`, a good class to write text content to a stream.

▶ Line 46 uses the `ToString` method on the `User` instance to save the content of the instance to the data file.

Build the application and see if everything is OK. You'll have to add two `using` directives.

> **NOTE**
>
> Here, we see the advantage of breaking our problem into smaller chunks. If we decide to add information to the `User` class, we don't need to modify the `DataFile` class. This class is responsible for saving information to a file, and nothing else. The way the information is formatted is the responsibility of the `User` class only.

Updating the User Interface

We still need to add a way to display the information to the user, and of course trigger the reading and saving of this information to the data file. Follow the steps:

1. Open the file Page.xaml.

2. Right after the `TextBlock` saying "Have some fun" (and in the same `StackPanel`), copy the following code:

```
<TextBlock x:Name="LastVisitTextBlock"
           Margin="10" />
```

3. Open the file Page.xaml.cs.

4. At the end of the `Page` constructor, below the `do…while` loop initializing the media elements, add the code in Listing 10.16:

LISTING 10.16   Reading and Writing the Data File

```
1  DataFile dataFile = new DataFile();
2  User user = dataFile.LoadUser();
3  if (user.LastVisit == null)
4  {
5    LastVisitTextBlock.Text = "(This is your first visit)";
6  }
7  else
8  {
9    LastVisitTextBlock.Text = "(Your last visit: "
10     + user.LastVisit.Value.ToShortDateString()
11     + " " + user.LastVisit.Value.ToLongTimeString() + ")";
12  }
13  user.SetLastVisit();
14  dataFile.SaveUser(user);
```

▶ On line 1, we create a new `DataFile` instance. (You'll have to add the `Thumbnails.Data` namespace to the `using` section.)

▶ On line 2, we load the `User`. Note how we don't need to know any specifics. The `DataFile` class could be modified to save the data to a server without needing to change the user interface code.

▶ Lines 3 to 12 check the value of the `LastVisit` property:

  ▶ If it's `null`, we set the `LastVisitTextBlock` to a default message.

  ▶ If it's set, we use its `Value` to construct a message displaying the date and time in a readable form.

Run the application now (after adding yet a few more `using` directives). Every time that you run it, or that you refresh the page, your last visit will be listed. Since the data is saved to a file, you can close the web browser, and even switch your computer off. The data will be there the next time. This simple example could be solved with a cookie too, but more complex files (such as binary files, complex XML files, etc...) can also be saved to the isolated storage while a cookie wouldn't be able to take care of these.

Multibrowser Compatibility

Interestingly, the isolated storage is allocated per application, but it doesn't matter which web browser the application is running on. The following steps demonstrate this:

1. From Visual Studio, execute the Thumbnails application by pressing Ctrl+F5.

2. Without closing the Internet Explorer (or Firefox) web browser, copy the address displayed in the location bar.

3. Open Firefox (or Internet Explorer) and paste this address in the location bar; then press Enter to start the application.

4. The Last visit `TextBlock` is set correctly, even though your last visit was in another web browser. The isolated storage is *shared* between all the browsers on a given computer.

Summary

In this chapter, we used .NET for some exciting tasks. Reacting to events, storing and reading data—these are is the basis for any advanced application, and our Silverlight applications will evolve to become more and more complex. In addition, we had a "crash course" in object-oriented programming. Hopefully this will give you a taste for this fascinating way to create code and encourage you to study it more. Learning OOP is a long but rewarding process!

10

Progressing with Animations

In Chapter 3, "Playing with XAML Transforms and Animations," we learned how to create animations in XAML. Back then, we mentioned that Expression Blend creates a different type of animation, using keyframes. In fact, you can also type a `DoubleAnimationUsingKeyFrames` by hand in XAML if you want (everything you do in Blend can be done in XAML directly), but it's not very easy. In such a case, using a tool is a better idea.

Animating Elements in Blend

The main difference in an animation using keyframes is that instead of defining the *duration* of the timeline, you specify how an element looks at given points in time. The Silverlight framework calculates the transition to be applied to the scene between the *keyframes*. Let's try it together with the following steps:

1. Open Expression Blend and create a new Silverlight 2 application. Name it AnimationInBlend.

2. In the Objects and Timeline category, select the top `UserControl` and name it TopUserControl (the Name text box is on top of the Properties panel).

3. In the `Grid` LayoutRoot, add an ellipse and set its `Fill` brush to a `LinearGradientBrush` from black to red (see Figure 11.1).

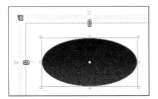

FIGURE 11.1   Ellipse with Linear Gradient Fill

4. In the Objects and Timeline category, next to the (No Storyboard open) box, as shown in Figure 11.2, click on the + sign to create a new storyboard.

FIGURE 11.2   Manage storyboards

5. In the dialog, enter the name EllipseStoryboard and click OK.

6. Notice how the workspace is now in Timeline recording mode: A red border appears around the Design panel, and a small red dot (similar to the Record button of a sound recorder) is displayed in the title bar (see Figure 11.3).

7. At this point, you may want to change the workspace layout to get more space: You can do this by selecting Window, Active Workspace, Animation Workspace from the menu. You can also switch between workspaces by pressing the F6 key.

> **TIP**
>
> When we talk about animations in Silverlight, you will hear the words "timeline," "animation," and "storyboard." In fact, they are similar. Animation and storyboard are types of timelines. A storyboard is a group of one or more animations.

FIGURE 11.3   Timeline Recording mode

8. Move the vertical yellow timeline to "2" (this is 2 seconds). Alternatively, you can enter the time "0:02.000" in the playhead position text box.

9. Click on the Record Keyframe button. This is the small button with a green "+" icon, next to the playhead position text box. Figure 11.4 shows the button with a black circle around it. This adds a keyframe at 2 seconds for the ellipse.

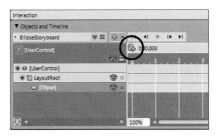

FIGURE 11.4   Timeline workspace

If your element didn't have a name before, Blend automatically names it when you create an animation for it. In our case, the ellipse is automatically named "ellipse."

10. Without touching anything else, modify the ellipse so that it looks like it should appear after 2 seconds:

   ▶ Resize the ellipse on the Designer panel to make it smaller than it is now.

   ▶ Move it to the bottom-right corner of the page.

   ▶ In the Properties panel, select the `Fill` property. Then, select the red gradient stop and change its color to yellow.

   ▶ In the Transform category, rotate the ellipse by 360 degrees.

11. To test your animation, click on the Play button located above the playhead position text box. You should see the ellipse move, shrink, rotate, and change color as you specified. As you can see, it is possible to animate even the gradient stops of a gradient brush (be it a `Background`, an `OpacityMask`, and so on).

Testing the Application

Blend creates the storyboard as a *resource* in the top `UserControl`. You can verify this by checking the XAML panel in Blend. The `EllipseStoryboard` should be placed towards the top of the page, in the `UserControl.Resources` section.

This is all very nice, but we need to *trigger* the storyboard now. For example, we want the animation to run when the user clicks on the ellipse, with the following steps:

1. Save all your files in Blend by choosing File, Save All (Ctrl+Shift+S) from the menu. Then, right-click on the Solution in the Project panel and select Edit in Visual Studio. This starts Visual Studio.

2. Open the file Page.xaml.

3. Locate the ellipse in the XAML markup, and add an event handler for `MouseLeftButtonDown`. To do this, simply start typing "Mouse" and see how Intellisense helps you to enter the correct event.

4. Notice how, after you enter the `MouseLeftButtonDown` event, Visual Studio presents a button that you can click to create a new event handler, as shown in Figure 11.5. If you had a list of event handlers in your code already, Visual Studio would also ask you to choose from this list.

FIGURE 11.5   New event handler in XAML

5. The new event handler is automatically named `ellipse_MouseLeftButtonDown`. This is a good convention, and it is recommended to keep the event handlers' names this way.

TIP

Remember that you can also add the new event handler in Blend. We did something similar in Chapter 8, "Programming Silverlight with JavaScript." You can either choose to copy the event handler code to the clipboard, or to use the integration with Visual Studio.

6. Right-click on the event handler `ellipse_MouseLeftButtonDown` in the XAML editor, and select Navigate to Event Handler from the context menu. This opens the file Page.xaml.cs and positions the cursor in the new event handler.

7. Now get the storyboard from the resources and start it. This is what Listing 11.1 does:

LISTING 11.1   MouseLeftButtonDown Event

```
private void ellipse_MouseLeftButtonDown(object sender,
  MouseButtonEventArgs e)
{
  Storyboard ellipseStoryboard
    = TopUserControl.Resources["EllipseStoryboard"] as Storyboard;
  ellipseStoryboard.Begin();
}
```

The Resources collection contains elements of type `object`. This allows you to store just about anything in resources, but it also means that you need to cast the element back to `Storyboard`.

8. Run the code by pressing Ctrl+F5. You should now be able to start the animation by clicking on the ellipse.

Editing the Animation's Properties

This animation is a little too linear to be really interesting. Additionally, it would be nicer if it was reversing to come back to its original state. Let's do this with the following steps:

1. Save everything in Studio. Then, in Blend, check whether the name EllipseStoryboard appears on top of the Objects and Timeline category. If it's the case, jump to step 5.

2. If no storyboard is open, you should see the words "(No Storyboard open)" in the box. On the right-hand side of this box, click on the button with an arrow pointing down (Open a Storyboard).

3. In the storyboard management pop-up, select the EllipseStoryboard. This reopens the storyboard and puts Blend in recording mode.

4. We don't want to change the timeline, but only edit some properties of the storyboard. Switch the Timeline recording mode off by clicking on the red Record button on top of the workspace (refer to Figure 11.3).

5. Click on the storyboard's name, EllipseStoryboard.

6. In the Properties panel, check the AutoReverse check box.

7. Run the application to see the result (press F5). When one "run" of the storyboard is completed, you can click again on the ellipse to repeat it.

8. In Blend, set the `RepeatBehavior` property to 3x, as shown in Figure 11.6. Then run the application. The ellipse will now go back and forth three times before stopping.

FIGURE 11.6   Animation properties

9. If you change the value of RepeatBehavior to Forever, the animation will never stop.

Easing In and Out

You can also edit the way an animation is "eased" in and out with the following steps, to make it look more lifelike and less linear.

1. In the Objects and Timeline category, expand the elements until you find the translation animation. It should be under LayoutRoot/ellipse/RenderTransform/Translation.

2. Click on the Translation. In the Properties panel, you'll see the Easing graph. Using the small yellow dots, move them with the mouse until the KeySpline looks like Figure 11.7.

3. You can also enter the x1, y1, x2, and y2 values manually. Each value pair (x,y) defines the position of a yellow point, between (0,0) and (1,1).

> **WARNING**
>
> Blend generates a Rotation animation (under which you see the `Angle` property), a Scale animation (with its `ScaleX` and `ScaleY` properties), and the Translation animation we want to edit (with `X` and `Y` properties).

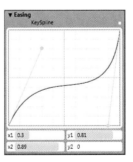

FIGURE 11.7   Easing the Translation animation

4. Click on the Play button. See how the ellipse's movement decelerates first, and then accelerates again, following the Easing line: When the line is steep, the animation goes faster; when it is flat, the animation decelerates.

Synchronizing Animations

Animations grouped into a storyboard are synchronized. They all run relatively to each other. To demonstrate this, we create a shorter animation with the following steps, and see how it "waits" on the longer one before reverting.

1. Add a green rectangle to the LayoutRoot grid, below the ellipse.

2. Make sure that the EllipseStoryboard is open.

3. In the Objects and Timeline category, select the green rectangle.

4. Move the vertical yellow line to 1 second.

5. Add a keyframe at 1 second, by clicking on the Record Keyframe button.

6. If the workspace is not in Timeline recording mode anymore, you can set it again by clicking on the small recording dot (refer to Figure 11.3). It should be red.

7. Select the `Opacity` property and set it to 0%.

8. Play the animation. Notice how the opacity animation "waits" on the ellipse before it reverts to the original state: The animations are synchronized because they belong to the same storyboard.

9. Stop the recording mode by clicking on the small recording dot in the title bar.

Understanding the Animation Elements

The Objects and Timeline category offers a nice way to see and interact with each animation element separately. Follow the steps:

1. Expand all the elements under the top user control.

2. The tree displays many animation elements, each with a double arrow icon (this icon is shown in Figure 11.9 for a different Silverlight application).

3. Using the tree, you can understand how the animations are structured. Try to compare this with the XAML markup. For example, the ellipse gets animated by six separate animations. One of them is shown in Listing 11.2 (some values might vary in your version though):

> **WARNING**
>
> The animation elements are displayed only if the storyboard is selected in the Objects and Timeline category. If you don't see these elements, reopen the storyboard like we did before.

LISTING 11.2   DoubleAnimationUsingKeyFrames

```
<DoubleAnimationUsingKeyFrames
  Storyboard.TargetName="ellipse"
  Storyboard.TargetProperty="(UIElement.RenderTransform)"
```

LISTING 11.2   Continued

```
                          .(TransformGroup.Children)[3]
                          .(TranslateTransform.X)"
  BeginTime="00:00:00">
   <SplineDoubleKeyFrame KeyTime="00:00:02" Value="434.5" >
     <SplineDoubleKeyFrame.KeySpline>
       <KeySpline ControlPoint1="0.3,0.814000010490417"
                  ControlPoint2="0.889999985694885,0"/>
     </SplineDoubleKeyFrame.KeySpline>
   </SplineDoubleKeyFrame>
</DoubleAnimationUsingKeyFrames>
```

▶ The XAML markup was formatted to fit these pages.

▶ The animation targets the element named ellipse.

▶ As usual, the property path is the most complex element:

  ▶ The path starts from the ellipse (which is a UIElement), and then targets its RenderTransform.

  ▶ In this case, the RenderTransform is a collection of transforms. So the property path targets the TransformGroup.Children and selects its children of index 3 (that's the fourth child in a zero-based collection). Because the transforms are generated by Blend, it is possible that the index is set to something different.

  ▶ That fourth child is a TranslateTransform, and the animation targets the X property. This is what will be animated.

▶ The animation above starts 0 seconds after the storyboard.

▶ A keyframe of type SplineDoubleKeyFrame is added to the animation, at a key time of 2 seconds. The value of the X property is set to 434.5 (your value might be different) which is located on the right of the page. If we had defined additional keyframes, they would be visible under this one.

▶ Because we "eased" the translation animation, the SplineDoubleKeyFrame contains a KeySpline with four coordinates. These define the two yellow points we set earlier in the Easing graph (refer to Figure 11.7).

As you can see from this example, creating an animation using keyframes is complex in markup. As for "normal" animations, the most complex task is to get the property path right. The easiest way to create animations is to create the basis in Expression Blend, and if needed to tweak the XAML markup to refine the animation's behavior.

Reversing a Storyboard

Blend has a really great feature that allows you to easily create an animation running exactly in the opposite way to an existing one. Simply follow these steps:

1. In Blend, select the EllipseStoryboard. If you don't remember how to select it, check the "Editing the Animation's Properties" section earlier in this chapter.

2. Uncheck the AutoReverse check box.

3. In the Objects and Timeline category, select the ellipse and add a keyframe at 0 seconds. This is needed to specify a known state for when we will be reversing the storyboard. Don't touch anything else. If needed, you can switch off the Timeline recording mode.

4. Just on the right of the + button located next to the storyboard's name, there is a menu that you can expand. From this menu, select Duplicate. This creates a copy of the current storyboard. Note that the original is untouched.

5. From the same menu, choose Reverse.

6. Play the animation. Notice how the Ellipse goes from the end position back to the start.

This feature is useful when you need to restore an object's initial state.

PointAnimation

We already saw that many properties of many objects can be animated in Silverlight: You can rotate, translate, skew, add colors, adjust opacity, and so on.

However, just as working with graphics primitives (rectangle, ellipse, and so on) is sometimes (often) not sufficient, working with basic animations is also not enough, and you need to create more advanced animations. This is where the `PointAnimation` comes in handy. In this section we learn how to use such an animation to create a collapse effect with the following steps:

1. In Blend, create a new Silverlight application, named PointAnimationTest.

2. Create a rectangle; set its `Width` to 640 and `Height` to 480.

3. Reset the rectangle's `Margin` to 0,0,0,0 and position it so that it covers the whole user control.

4. Reset the rectangle's `Fill` to No Brush.

5. Right-click on the project in the Project panel; select the menu Add Existing Item and use it to add a 640×480 picture to your project. If you don't have such a picture handy, you can download one here: www.galasoft.ch/SL2U/Chapter11/pic.jpg.

6. Locate the rectangle in the XAML editor, and modify the markup like in Listing 11.3. If needed, change the value of `ImageSource` to match your picture's name.

LISTING 11.3   Rectangle with ImageBrush

```
<Rectangle Width="640" Height="480">
  <Rectangle.Fill>
    <ImageBrush ImageSource="pic.jpg"/>
  </Rectangle.Fill>
</Rectangle>
```

7. Make sure that the rectangle is selected, and select Object, Path, Convert to Path from the menu.

8. Select the Pen tool in the toolbar. Make sure that the path is selected in the Objects and Timeline category.

> **TIP**
>
> To locate the rectangle element easily in the XAML editor in Design mode, right-click on the element in the Objects and Timeline category, and select View XAML.

9. Add a number of points to the path. To do this, move the cursor anywhere on the path's border until it turns into the Pen insert cursor (a pen with a small + sign). Then, click to add a new point. Repeat this operation until you have 15 points or more, all around the path.

10. Create a new storyboard using the exact same process we used in the section titled "Animating Elements in Blend." Name it CollapseStoryboard. The environment should be in Timeline recording mode.

11. Move the yellow timeline to 1 second (0:0:1) and add a keyframe at this position using the Record Keyframe button.

12. Click on the Direct Selection tool. Start moving points closer together, to create a new smaller nonrectangular path (see Figure 11.8).

13. Add a new keyframe after 2 seconds, and continue collapsing the path by closing up the points.

14. Eventually, add a last keyframe and collapse the path until all the points are just next to each other.

FIGURE 11.8   Collapsing an ImageBrush

15. For this last keyframe, set the `Opacity` to 0%, so that the animation ends nicely by a fade-out effect.

16. Press the Play button to observe the effect.

This basic example can be expanded to other, more complicated paths, and allow a great range of advanced animations.

> **WARNING**
>
> If you want to run this animation in the web browser, you need to trigger it, like we did with the ellipse's animation in the section titled "Testing the Application." You can do this by adding a `MouseLeftButtonDown` event handler on the path.

Starting and Stopping the Animation

In this chapter, we saw in the section titled "Testing the Application" how to get a stored storyboard from the resources, and to "begin" it in code.

In Windows Presentation Foundation, there is another way to start a storyboard, using triggers. In Silverlight 2, however, triggers are not completely supported. There is a way to trigger a storyboard when a control is loaded (we did that in Chapter 3, Listing 3.7), but the Silverlight documentation recommends against it. It is better to not use triggers in Silverlight 2 altogether, and to use code-behind instead.

Sometimes, you also need to stop the storyboard. When a storyboard is animating a property, it has a tight grip on that property as long as it is running. In fact, the animation system has a high precedence on the property's value.

If your application wants to set a property while it is being animated, it needs to stop the storyboard first. For example, consider the markup in Listing 11.4 (you can copy this in a new Silverlight application to test it yourself):

LISTING 11.4   Ellipse with Opacity Animation

```
<Grid x:Name="LayoutRoot" Background="Orange">
  <Grid.Resources>
    <Storyboard x:Name="EllipseStoryboard"
                AutoReverse="True" RepeatBehavior="Forever">
      <DoubleAnimation Storyboard.TargetName="ellipse"
                       Storyboard.TargetProperty="Opacity"
                       To="1" Duration="0:0:2" />
    </Storyboard>
  </Grid.Resources>
  <Ellipse Height="100" Width="200" Fill="#FFFF0000"
           x:Name="ellipse" Opacity="0.2"
           MouseLeftButtonDown="ellipse_MouseLeftButtonDown" />

  <Button Height="50" Width="150"
          VerticalAlignment="Bottom"
          Content="Make Transparent"
```

LISTING 11.4   Continued

```
        x:Name="MakeTransparentButton"
        Click="MakeTransparentButton_Click" />
</Grid>
```

and the code-behind in Listing 11.5:

LISTING 11.5   MouseLeftButtonDown Event and Click Event

```
private void ellipse_MouseLeftButtonDown(object sender,
  MouseButtonEventArgs e)
{
  Storyboard ellipseStoryboard
    = LayoutRoot.Resources["EllipseStoryboard"] as Storyboard;
  ellipseStoryboard.Begin();
}

private void MakeTransparentButton_Click(object sender,
  RoutedEventArgs e)
{
  ellipse.Opacity = 0;
}
```

If you start the storyboard by clicking on the Ellipse, and then try to set the Opacity with the Button, it will fail. The storyboard continues undisturbed.

To force the Opacity, you need to stop the storyboard first. This can be done with the code in Listing 11.6:

LISTING 11.6   Modified Click Event

```
private void MakeTransparentButton_Click(object sender,
  RoutedEventArgs e)
{
  Storyboard ellipseStoryboard
    = LayoutRoot.Resources["EllipseStoryboard"] as Storyboard;
  ellipseStoryboard.Stop();
  ellipse.Opacity = 0;
}
```

First we get the running storyboard from the resources; then we stop it, and eventually we can modify the Opacity property.

Working on the Thumbnails Gallery

Our Thumbnail application is already interactive; let's face it, though, the user experience is not the best. How about leveraging some of Silverlight's features to make it smoother and nicer to watch? Open this application in Visual Studio first.

Making a Scenario

In the current state, the clicked media element is displayed in a display rectangle, which doesn't move. It is only there as a placeholder for the media. Now we want a smoother animation:

▶ We need a placeholder in addition to the Display frame. This placeholder will be animated when a thumbnail enters the stage. This way we can use an animation to create a smooth user experience.

▶ The "expanding" animation will be started when the user clicks on a thumbnail. The placeholder will move smoothly from the clicked media's original place to the display frame. Additionally, the placeholder's opacity will go from 0% to 100% in the same time.

▶ If the clicked media is a video, the video will start playing when the user clicks on it.

▶ If a media is displayed in the Display frame, it will fade out when it needs to be removed from the scene.

Setting the Stage

For the placeholder to move easily, we place a `Canvas` panel in front of everything. To avoid disturbing the application, the `Canvas` must fulfill two criteria:

▶ It must be transparent.

▶ It must not block any mouse click.

We know already how to realize this. Let's simply add a transparent `Canvas` to the `Grid` LayoutRoot and make sure that its property `IsHitTestVisible` is set to false. Because the `Canvas` must appear in front of the whole application, add the XAML markup in Listing 11.7 *inside* the LayoutRoot `Grid`, but at the very end of it, after the `Grid` with the display frame that we added in Chapter 6, "Blending a Little More."

Additionally, we create one rectangle in XAML to serve as placeholder.

LISTING 11.7   Canvas and a `Rectangle`

```
<Canvas Grid.RowSpan="2" Grid.ColumnSpan="2"
        IsHitTestVisible="False" x:Name="AnimationCanvas">
  <Rectangle Height="120" Width="160"
             Opacity="0" x:Name="ThumbDisplay1"
```

LISTING 11.7   Continued

```
          RenderTransformOrigin="0,0">
  <Rectangle.RenderTransform>
    <TransformGroup>
      <ScaleTransform />
      <SkewTransform />
      <RotateTransform />
      <TranslateTransform />
    </TransformGroup>
  </Rectangle.RenderTransform>
 </Rectangle>

</Canvas>
```

Also, we need to address the main user control by name, so let's add a property x:Name to it. If your user control has additional properties, just add the x:Name property and leave the others; they have been added by Expression Blend.

```
<UserControl xmlns="http://schemas.microsoft.com/client/2007"
            xmlns:x="http://schemas.microsoft.com/winfx/2006/xaml"
            x:Class="Thumbnails.Page" x:Name="TopUserControl">
```

Making the Draft Animation

We use two animations, as mentioned previously. One is simple, and we create it in code-behind directly. The other is more complex, and we create a draft in Blend. Then, we adapt this draft to the clicked thumbnail in the code-behind. Follow the steps:

1. If it's not done already, open the Thumbnails project in Expression Blend.

2. In the Objects and Timeline category, double-click on AnimationCanvas until it is selected with a yellow border. Then expand it and select the rectangle named ThumbDisplay1.

3. Set the rectangle's Fill property to red and its Opacity to 100%, so that you see it better (it is in the top-left corner).

4. Add a new storyboard and name it ExpandStoryboard.

5. Move the yellow timeline to 1 second and add a keyframe.

> **TIP**
>
> Working with the same project open in both Visual Studio and Blend is a common scenario when you develop Silverlight applications. To open a Solution in Blend from Visual Studio, the easiest way is to right-click on the Solution in Visual Studio. Then select Open Folder in Windows Explorer. Then right-click on the file Thumbnails.sln in Windows Explorer and choose Open With, Microsoft Expression Blend.

6. Move the rectangle on top of the display frame. Don't worry if it's not perfect, we will set the exact coordinates in code later. Don't resize it yet! Make sure that you select only the rectangle in the Design panel, not any other element. If you are unsure, you can also move the rectangle using the keyboard's arrows.

7. In the Transform category of the Properties panel, set the Scale to X=2 and Y=2.

8. Move the timeline to 0 seconds and add a keyframe. The rectangle moves back in place and "shrinks" back to its original size.

9. At this keyframe, move the red rectangle on top of the first thumbnail. Here also, no need to be exact; this is only a draft animation. Do not resize the red rectangle, we'll do that in code.

10. Set the red rectangle's `Opacity` to 0%. When the animation starts, we want the placeholder to be transparent.

11. Move the yellow timeline to 0.5 seconds. Do *not* add a keyframe. The rectangle is now half transparent, and half expanded.

12. In the Transform category, add a `RotateTransform` of 15 degrees. Make sure that the `RenderTransformOrigin` (in the Miscellaneous category) is set to "0,0", or we will have a problem with the `ScaleTransform`.

13. Play the animation to make sure that it is okay. Then switch the Timeline recording mode off.

14. Reset the rectangle's `Fill` property back to No Brush. You must change this property only after the Timeline recording mode has been switched off, or the system will make this change part of the story-board, which we don't want.

> **WARNING**
>
> If you add a keyframe manually at 0.5 seconds, this additional keyframe is added to each animation, which will cause problems later. By simply setting the `RotateTransform`'s `Angle`, we add a keyframe only for this animation, and not for the others.

We now have a draft storyboard placed in the user control's resources. You can take a look at the markup in the XAML editor. When we need this storyboard, we will get it in code and customize it.

Easing the Translate Animation

In this section, we will ease the animation to make it look more natural with the following steps:

1. In Blend, make sure that the storyboard named ExpandStoryboard is open, then expand the tree until you find the translate animation (see Figure 11.9). This is the animation we want to ease.

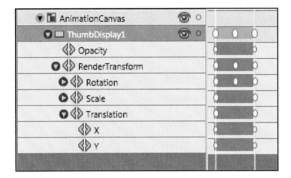

FIGURE 11.9   Finding the Translate animation

2. Click on the translate animation in the tree and open the Properties panel. Blend displays a warning in the Easing category. Click on the hyperlink labeled "Click here to deselect keyframes at time 0."

3. Set the Easing properties as shown in Figure 11.10. Note that this will ease both the X and Y animations with the same parameters.

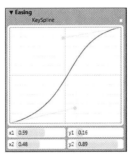

FIGURE 11.10   Easing the Translate animation

Triggering the Animation in Code

The next step is to modify the code-behind to use the animation we just created.

Initializing

Let's prepare the code first with the following steps:

1. Open Page.xaml.cs in Visual Studio.

2. On top of the class, just below the _expandedMedia declaration, add the following two attributes as shown in Listing 11.8. They will hold information while animations are executed:

LISTING 11.8   Two Attributes

```
private double _expansionFactor = 1.0;
private Storyboard _fadeStoryboard = null;
```

3. In the Page constructor, right after the call to InitializeComponent, place the code in Listing 11.9:

LISTING 11.9   Registering the Event Handler

```
Storyboard expandStoryboard
  = TopUserControl.Resources["ExpandStoryboard"] as Storyboard;
expandStoryboard.Completed
  += new EventHandler(expandStoryboard_Completed);
```

This adds an event handler that will be called when the storyboard ends. The code for this event handler is shown in Listing 11.10. Add it below the Page constructor and try to build the application to check that there are no errors.

LISTING 11.10   Completed Event Handler

```
void expandStoryboard_Completed(object sender, EventArgs e)
{
  Canvas.SetLeft(Display, Canvas.GetLeft(ThumbDisplay1));
  Display.Width = ThumbDisplay1.ActualWidth * _expansionFactor;
  Display.Fill = ThumbDisplay1.Fill;
  Display.Opacity = 1;
  if (_fadeStoryboard != null)
  {
    _fadeStoryboard.Stop();
    _fadeStoryboard = null;
  }
  ThumbDisplay1.Opacity = 0;
  (sender as Storyboard).Stop();
}
```

This code is executed when the placeholder finished its "expansion" and is located on top of the Display frame. Since there might be margins on the sides of the Display (we calculate these margins later in code), we reposition the Display rectangle and resize it. Then, we assign the placeholder's Fill (an ImageBrush or VideoBrush) to the Display rectangle. We stop the "fade" storyboard if needed, and hide the placeholder. Finally, we stop the expanding storyboard.

These operations are needed because Silverlight requires that you stop the storyboards when they are not in use, to avoid that they keep their "grip" on the values as we saw earlier in this chapter.

Note that this method relies on knowledge of what we do later in code. For example the attribute _expansionFactor is calculated in Listing 11.11 below. Also, the Display rectangle will be faded in code, in Listing 11.16.

Handling the `MouseLeftButtonDown` **Event**

We already added an event handler to each media, and we have a handler in code, named `media_MouseLeftButtonDown`. We can reuse this and just modify it to trigger the animation.

1. Calculate the position of the placeholder when it is expanded, because not all pictures have the same width. We did that already in Chapter 10, "Progressing with .NET;" now we need to adapt the code. Replace the seven lines coming after the comment `Set size and position of DisplayRectangle` with the code in Listing 11.11. Instead of setting the position of the `Display` rectangle immediately after the thumbnail is clicked, we store the value locally for later use. We also calculate the factor by which we need to expand the placeholder to fill the `DisplayBackground` rectangle's height or width. There might be a margin on each side or on the bottom of smaller pictures.

LISTING 11.11   Size and Position of `DisplayRectangle`

```
// Set size and position of the displayed media
double sizeFactor
  = castedSender.ActualWidth / castedSender.ActualHeight;
double newHeight = DisplayBackground.ActualHeight;
double newWidth = newHeight * sizeFactor;
double sideMargin
  = (DisplayBackground.ActualWidth - newWidth) / 2;
_expansionFactor
  = DisplayBackground.ActualHeight / castedSender.ActualHeight;

if (sideMargin < 0)
{
  newWidth = DisplayBackground.ActualWidth;
  newHeight = newWidth / sizeFactor;
  sideMargin = 0;
  _expansionFactor
    = DisplayBackground.ActualWidth / castedSender.ActualWidth;
}
```

2. Now set the size of the placeholder to be the exact same size as the clicked thumbnail. Remember that we casted this `sender` to a `FrameworkElement`, so we can read its `ActualHeight` and `ActualWidth`. Add the code in Listing 11.12 after what we wrote in step 1.

LISTING 11.12   Setting the Placeholder's Size

```
// Set the placeholder's size and calculate its proportions
ThumbDisplay1.Width = castedSender.ActualWidth;
ThumbDisplay1.Height = castedSender.ActualHeight;
```

3. Here is a tougher part: We need some coordinates. Remember how the placeholder is moving on a transparent Canvas? We need to know exactly where the clicked thumbnail is located in relation to this Canvas. That will be our starting point, and we also need to know where the ending point is. This is the location of the DisplayBackground rectangle (plus possible margins) relative to the Canvas. The code in Listing 11.13 comes right below what we inserted in point 2. Then, build the application.

> **NOTE**
>
> Getting these coordinates is relatively easy when you know how, but explaining how it works exactly is rather complex. It relies on the Visual class, which is a representation of the space occupied by the UI element on the screen, and on a MatrixTransform.

LISTING 11.13   Getting Coordinates

```
// Getting the coordinates of the clicked thumbnail
GeneralTransform gtStart =
  castedSender.TransformToVisual(AnimationCanvas);
Point offsetStart = gtStart.Transform(new Point(0, 0));
ThumbDisplay1.SetValue(Canvas.LeftProperty, offsetStart.X);
ThumbDisplay1.SetValue(Canvas.TopProperty, offsetStart.Y);

// Getting the coordinates of the DisplayBackground rectangle
GeneralTransform gtDisplay =
  DisplayBackground.TransformToVisual(AnimationCanvas);
Point offsetDisplay = gtDisplay.Transform(new Point(0, 0));
```

Setting the Animations' Properties

Now it's time to set all the animations' parameters according to our calculations. Note that some of the animations do not need to be parameterized:

▶ The opacity animation is always the same for all the thumbnails.

▶ Similarly, the RotateTransform animation doesn't need to be parameterized.

Add the code in Listing 11.14 to the method media_MouseLeftButtonDown, right under the spot where we calculated the value of offsetDisplay.

LISTING 11.14   Setting the Animation's Parameters

```
1  // Get the storyboard and set the animations' parameters
2  Storyboard expandStoryboard
3    = TopUserControl.Resources["ExpandStoryboard"] as Storyboard;
4
5  foreach (Timeline child in expandStoryboard.Children)
6  {
```

LISTING 11.14   Continued

```
 7    string property = Storyboard.GetTargetProperty(child).Path;
 8    if (property.IndexOf("TranslateTransform.X") > -1)
 9    {
10      (child as DoubleAnimationUsingKeyFrames).KeyFrames[0].Value = 0;
11      (child as DoubleAnimationUsingKeyFrames).KeyFrames[1].Value
12        = offsetDisplay.X - offsetStart.X + sideMargin;
13    }
14    if (property.IndexOf("TranslateTransform.Y") > -1)
15    {
16      (child as DoubleAnimationUsingKeyFrames).KeyFrames[0].Value = 0;
17      (child as DoubleAnimationUsingKeyFrames).KeyFrames[1].Value
18        = offsetDisplay.Y - offsetStart.Y;
19    }
20    if (property.IndexOf("ScaleTransform.ScaleX") > -1)
21    {
22      (child as DoubleAnimationUsingKeyFrames).KeyFrames[0].Value = 1;
23      (child as DoubleAnimationUsingKeyFrames).KeyFrames[1].Value
24        = _expansionFactor;
25    }
26    if (property.IndexOf("ScaleTransform.ScaleY") > -1)
27    {
28      (child as DoubleAnimationUsingKeyFrames).KeyFrames[0].Value = 1;
29      (child as DoubleAnimationUsingKeyFrames).KeyFrames[1].Value
30        = _expansionFactor;
31    }
32  }
```

▶ Lines 2 and 3 get the storyboard from the resources.

▶ We loop through all the animations in the storyboard. Remember how we added the DoubleAnimationUsingKeyFrames in XAML in the storyboard tag? Effectively, this filled the Children collection with the animations. In code-behind, we can use this collection in a foreach loop.

▶ The Children collection is of type TimelineCollection (you can see this by holding the mouse over the Children in the C# editor, and read the Intellisense documentation).

▶ Line 7 stores the attached property Storyboard.Target in a local variable. Note the use of the method Storyboard.GetTargetProperty to get this attached property. Since this method returns an instance of type PropertyPath, we use its Path property of type string.

► Lines 8 to 13 check whether the current child is the X (horizontal) translate animation. If that's the case, we set the value of the first keyframe to "0". At the beginning of the animation, the placeholder is firmly placed on top of the clicked
thumbnail (we moved it there in code earlier). As for the second keyframe (after 1
second), we place the placeholder on top of the DisplayBackground rectangle. Note
how we use the sideMargin value we calculated before to align the expanded media
in the middle of the display frame.

► Lines 14 to 19 do the same operation for the Y (vertical) translation.

► Lines 20 to 31 set the scaling factor that we calculated earlier for the scale animation. At the first keyframe, the value is always "1" because we set the placeholder to
the exact same size as the clicked thumbnail earlier in code. At the second keyframe
(after 1 second), the placeholder must have grown to the size of the
DisplayBackground rectangle.

Remember that all the animation types in Silverlight inherit the Timeline basic class. By
using the generic Timeline type in the loop, we make our code able to handle other kinds
of animation if needed. We could use the DoubleAnimationUsingKeyFrames type instead,
(since we know that all the animations in the storyboard are of this type), but this way
we just made our code more robust and extendable.

Setting the Placeholder's Fill
The last change we must do for the "expanding" animation is set the Fill property on
the placeholder instead of the Display rectangle. Below the code shown in Listing 11.14,
we check if the clicked thumbnail is a MediaElement or an Image. This code was already
added in Chapter 10. Replace both lines reading Display.Fill = brush; with
ThumbDisplay1.Fill = brush;

This last operation assigns the VideoBrush or the ImageBrush to the placeholder instead of
the Display frame directly. This way, we can animate the placeholder to create a smooth
transition.

Starting the Animation
Now we are ready to start our storyboard and see the "expanding" animation work.
Starting a storyboard in Silverlight is easy: Simply call the method
expandStoryboard.Begin. This call (Listing 11.15) is placed right before the end of the
method:

LISTING 11.15   Beginning the Storyboard

```
_expandedMedia = castedSender;
//Start the Storyboard
expandStoryboard.Begin();
}
```

Now you can run the application by pressing Ctrl+F5. Click on a thumbnail and see how the animation runs to move and expand the thumbnail on the display frame.

Creating the "Fading" Animation in Code

In this section, we fade the currently expanded media (in the Display frame) to ensure a smooth transition when a thumbnail is clicked. Follow the steps:

1. Find the code starting with `If needed, pause movie` in the method `media_MouseLeftButtonDown`. Delete the whole `if` block and replace it with the code in Listing 11.16:

LISTING 11.16   Pausing the Movie, Fading the Display

```
1   // If needed, pause movie and fade display
2   if (_expandedMedia != null)
3   {
4     if (_expandedMedia is MediaElement)
5     {
6       (_expandedMedia as MediaElement).Pause();
7     }
8
9     FrameworkElement currentMedia = _expandedMedia;
10    _expandedMedia = null;
11
12    _fadeStoryboard = new Storyboard();
13    _fadeStoryboard.Completed += new EventHandler(_fadeStoryboard_Completed);
14
15    DoubleAnimation anim = new DoubleAnimation();
16    Storyboard.SetTarget(anim, Display);
17    Storyboard.SetTargetProperty(anim, new PropertyPath("Opacity"));
18    anim.Duration = new Duration(TimeSpan.FromSeconds(0.9));
19    anim.To = 0;
20    _fadeStoryboard.Children.Add(anim);
21
22    _fadeStoryboard.Begin();
23
24    if (castedSender == currentMedia)
25    {
26      return;
27    }
28  }
```

▶ Lines 4 to 7 pause the media if needed. Of course this is only done if the currently expanded media is a video. Remember that we store a reference to the expanded media at the end of the method `media_MouseLeftButtonDown`.

▶ Lines 9 and 10 store the currently displayed media and then set the stored reference to that media to null. This way, we don't keep an unneeded reference. The garbage collector can only free an object from memory if it is not referenced anywhere in the code. Setting the references to null when they are not needed anymore is a good programming practice!!

> **NOTE**
>
> The most attentive readers will notice that this storyboard's creation could be optimized. Because the storyboard must be created only once and never changes, we could perform this step in the Page constructor. Alternatively, we could also define the storyboard in XAML. Creating a new storyboard every time that a thumbnail is clicked is not optimal for static storyboards.

▶ In lines 12 to 22, we create a whole new storyboard in code. We set its Completed event to a new event handler named fadeStoryboard_Completed which we will implement in just a moment.

▶ On lines 15 to 19, we create a new DoubleAnimation in code, targeting the Display frame that must be faded.

▶ On line 18, notice the usage of the static method TimeSpan.FromSeconds. Other static methods of the TimeSpan class allow constructing various durations.

▶ To work, the animation must be added to the storyboard. This is what we do on line 20. Notice how we use (again) the Children collection.

▶ On line 22, the storyboard starts. 0.9 seconds later, the expanded media will be totally transparent, and the fadeStoryboard_Completed event handler will be called.

▶ On lines 24 to 27, we check if the clicked thumbnail is the media that is already displayed. If so, we just exit the method. The media must fade out, but no new media must be displayed.

The last step before we run our application is to implement the event handler _fadeStoryboard_Completed. The code is simple: We reset the Display to transparent (by setting its Fill property to null) and stop the running storyboard (this is the event handler's sender). Add the code in Listing 11.17 under the method media_MouseLeftButtonDown but still inside the Page class.

LISTING 11.17   Completed Event Handler

```
void _fadeStoryboard_Completed(object sender, EventArgs e)
{
  Display.Fill = null;
  (sender as Storyboard).Stop();
}
```

You can now run the application and test the thumbnails to make sure that the implementation works fine.

Summary

The animation system is probably one of the most exciting features of Silverlight (and WPF). Without a visual tool, complex animations can be difficult to program, however. Expression Blend offers a great interface to create animations, which can be "polished" by editing the XAML markup later. This interaction between the visual tools and the XAML (text) editors is one of the major strengths of the new UI framework.

11

CHAPTER 12

Encoding Videos with Expression Encoder

When Microsoft released Silverlight 1, they understood the need for the runtime framework to be available on as many computers as possible, and fast. If you want developers and designers to create content for any new platform, they need an audience. This is why the first release targeted Windows and the Macintosh operating system, making it potentially available on more than 95% of the market. (With Silverlight 2 being available for Linux too, this number is of course even higher.)

Something more was needed, though: The user needs a reason to install the runtime! Even though the installation experience is fast and rather painless, if the content is not attractive enough, the user won't install. According to research, the most attractive online content nowadays is video, and this is exactly what Silverlight 1 targeted in the first place.

Today, the experience is even better. Expression Encoder 2, the tool that we use in this chapter, was released in May 2008 and brings video encoding and Silverlight integration one big step further.

Before We Start...

Expression Encoder is not the only application that can save videos in Silverlight format. The well-known publisher of video encoding applications Roxio released a new version of its video editor Roxio Buzz, which can upload encoded videos directly to Silverlight streaming websites.

This application (built in WPF) can be found at this website: www.roxio.com/enu/products/buzz/standard/features.html.

You will need video files to follow the steps described in this chapter. The best is to have three of them: One main file for the encoding part itself, one small file (for example a title) for the header, and one small file (for example credits) for the footer. If you don't have video files, you can find some at www.galasoft.ch/SL2U/Chapter12.

Introducing Expression Encoder

This application's main purpose is not directly related to Silverlight: Expression Encoder is there to encode video files. It is not a video editor though it has some video editing capabilities. It is not a Silverlight application editor, though it can produce Silverlight content.

Expression Encoder can be installed from the Expression website: www.microsoft.com/expression/try-it.

After the trial period expires, you will need to purchase the product (available currently for $199). Expression Encoder is also part of the full Expression Studio (available for $699 as of this writing). Unfortunately, Expression Encoder is currently not available in any MSDN subscription.

In this chapter, we discover how we can use Expression Encoder in relation with Silverlight. This is not a complete reference about video encoding, but rather a guide to creating videos that can be watched from a web page.

Setting Options

As usual when starting a new application for the first time, it is a good idea to check the options. In Encoder, the Options dialog can be displayed by selecting Tools, Options from the menu.

The Options dialog shows the following sections:

- ▶ Workspace—There is a similar section in Expression Blend. You can change the application's skin and resize the workspace, in case you're working on extra big or extra small screens. This is a hint that the application's user interface was programmed in WPF.

- ▶ Logging—When you encode a lot of movies, it is interesting to create log files. The encoding process can last a long time, and if an error occurs, it is important to understand what happened exactly to correct the error. This section gives you the possibility to set up which attributes you want to log, and in which location the logs should be saved. You can also set a size limit, to avoid filling your hard disk too fast (though if you encode videos a lot, you'll need more disk space soon anyway!).

- ▶ Metadata Attributes—Custom attributes can be added in this section. These can be set later in your encoded video files. We learn more about metadata attributes later in this chapter.

▶ Compatibility—Many video formats are available on the market, and many of them are installed on your PC by third-party applications! When you import a video in Encoder, these filters can be used to convert the video to a format that Encoder understands. In some cases, this can cause compatibility issues. Using this section, you can disable specific filters in Expression Encoder. This section also features a check box enabling or disabling hardware acceleration when you import a video. Usually, hardware acceleration is enabled to speed up the process, but if you have issues, you may want to disable it.

Understanding the Panels

The application has four main panels, as shown in Figure 12.1 and described in Table 12.1.

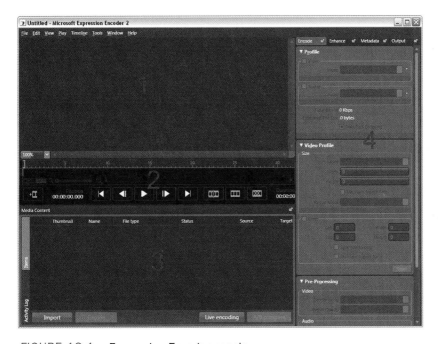

FIGURE 12.1   Expression Encoder panels

TABLE 12.1   Expression Encoder Panels

1   Viewer panel—Displays the video being encoded.

2   Timeline panel—Displays the video's timeline, and various controls which we study in a moment.

3   Media content panel—Displays the content you imported in the application as well as the logs (if available).

4   Encode/Enhance/Metadata/Output panel—Here you can set up the way the video will be encoded. We review these sections soon.

Most of the commands available in the panels are also available as menus from the menu bar.

Importing a Video

The first operation you need to perform when you want to encode a video for Silverlight is to import it in the workspace.

Expression Encoder can read a lot of video types. In fact, you can import all the videos for which Encoder can find a filter. This means that if you can read the video in Windows Media Player, you can probably import it in Encoder too.

If you try to import a video for which you don't have a filter installed, you get an error, as shown in Figure 12.2. The best way to solve this kind of issue is to attempt to find on the Internet the *codec* corresponding to the video type you are trying to import.

FIGURE 12.2   Error when importing a video

To import a video in Expression Encoder, follow the steps:

1. In the Media Content panel, click on the Import button.

2. Select one or more video file(s) to import. If the file you want to import is not visible, set the Files of Type box to All Files (*). Even video files with an unknown extension may be imported if a suitable filter is found.

3. Click on Open. The file is analyzed and, if the import is successful, the video appears in the Viewer panel.

4. Using the controls shown in Figure 12.3, you can do the following (from left to right):

   FIGURE 12.3   Video controls

   ▶ Go back to the previous marker (or to the beginning of the video, if no marker is found).

   ▶ Go back to the previous frame.

   ▶ Play the video.

   ▶ Go to the next frame.

   ▶ Go to the next marker (or to the end of the video, if no marker is found).

5. If you want, you can also zoom the video in and out, using the combo box located in the bottom left of the Viewer panel. Note that you can also click and drag on this combo box to choose a zoom factor (see Figure 12.4).

FIGURE 12.4   Video zoom combo box

12

Saving your Changes

Before you start, it is useful to know how you can save all your changes, so that your work is preserved should anything happen. Simply follow the steps:

1. At any time, you can choose File, Save Job (Ctrl+S) from the menu.

2. If this is the first time you save your work, you will be asked to enter a name and location for the file.

> **NOTE**
>
> Encoder jobs files are saved with a .xej extension. In fact, they are saved in XML format. Remember when, in Chapter 2, "Understanding XAML," we said that XML could be used for data? Here's a real-life example!

3. If you exit the application (or if it crashes), you can reopen the saved XML file at a later time (by selecting File, Open Job from the menu). This reloads all the settings you saved.

4. If you want to make a copy of your current job, save it by selecting File, Save As.

Specifying the Output Type

Expression Encoder uses *profiles* to save the video encoding settings. If no profile is loaded, you must specify all the settings manually with the following steps:

> **TIP**
>
> Like Expression Blend, Expression Encoder saves a huge number of operations in memory, so that you can *undo* them if needed. Simply press Ctrl+Z to undo (select Edit, Undo from the menu), or Ctrl+Y to redo (select Edit, Redo from the menu).

1. In the Encode panel, choose a video format (see Figure 12.5). There are many predefined formats, from High Definition (HD 720p Intranet) to Motion thumbnail. As usual when you encode video, you must accept a trade-off between definition and file size. If you plan on putting your video on the Internet, a lower definition and smaller size are preferred.

FIGURE 12.5   Video and Audio profile settings

2. Did you notice that there is an "expander" right under the Video setting? Here you can see what each predefined profile means. This helps you to choose a profile suited for your needs, or to tweak the profile to suit your specific needs.

3. For each video profile, an audio setting is proposed. If you want to change this, uncheck the Default Profile check box and select a different audio format. Here you can expand two Advanced Properties sections.

4. You may notice a Two Pass Encoding check box. For a higher definition (but also a longer encoding time), you can check this check box. This check box is disabled for some video/audio profiles.

Explaining all the advanced properties is outside the scope of this book. If you need to modify the default settings for a profile, the user documentation can help you (select Help, User Guide from the menu), especially the sections under "Encode Your Video for Microsoft Silverlight and the Web."

Editing the Video Size and Aspect

Even though Expression Encoder is not a video editor, some editing functionalities are available. These are very good for simple edits, or for last minute changes before encoding the video.

Changing the Size and Aspect Ratio

Under the Video Profile section, you can refine your settings for the current job with the following steps:

1. You may choose a different size for your video. You can choose between the following:

   ▶ Profile Adaptive—Resizes the video to the default size specified in the profile, but analyzes the video to find the video aspect ratio.

   ▶ Profile—Resizes to the default profile size.

   ▶ Source—The original video's size will be used.

   ▶ Custom—You may select the size you want.

2. If you select Custom, you can resize the video directly in the Viewer panel, using a yellow border. If you uncheck the Maintain Aspect Ratio check box and set the Resize Mode to Stretch, you can even distort the video output.

3. In the advanced properties under the expander, you can select a different aspect ratio (4:3 or 16:9, or even set your own custom aspect ratio).

> **WARNING**
>
> Resizing a video works well when you make it *smaller* than the original. If you make it bigger, you will start seeing pixels, and the result will not be smooth. Remember, videos are *raster graphics*. We talked about that in Chapter 5, "Using Media," in the section titled "Using Vector Graphics."

Cropping and Trimming the Video

You can crop the video to make it smaller or to focus on a certain region, for example with the following steps:

1. To change the output video's size, you can use the Crop functionality. Check the Crop check box.

2. Using the red border in the Viewer panel, select which area of the video you want to output.

3. By unchecking the Maintain Aspect Ratio check box, you can select any shape you want (well, as long as it's rectangular!).

4. Depending on the aspect ratio you selected for the output, Encoder might add some black borders. If you want to remove them from the output video, check the Sync Size to Crop check box.

> **WARNING**
>
> If you select a small crop area, and depending on the chosen output size, the output video might appear *pixelized*. Make sure you check the video output carefully before you encode the video. We see in a moment how you can test the settings on a small portion of the video.

You may also want to trim the video or remove parts of it. To do this, you can either use the Timeline panel, or set a new Start Time and End Time in the Clip Edits section of the Enhance panel.

To use the Timeline panel, follow these steps:

1. Under the blue timeline, on the left-hand side, locate the Show Cut Regions (or Hide Cut Regions) button. Make sure that this button is set so that the cut sections are displayed.

2. Move both ends of the blue timeline bar until you select the segment that you want to encode (see Figure 12.6).

3. Using the Zoom % controls, you can zoom in and out of the timeline. This can be useful if you want to trim the output to a short segment of the initial video.

FIGURE 12.6   Cropping and Trimming the video

4. You can delete any edit you make to the video by moving the playhead on that section (that's the orange rectangle located on top of the red/blue timeline bar). Then click the button with the Remove the Edit at the Playhead ToolTip.

Note that you can select multiple segments in a video. Follow these steps:

1. To add a segment, position the playhead inside one existing segment (blue section of the timeline).

2. In the Enhance panel, in the Clip Edits section, click on the Add button.

3. Move the ends of the new segment in the Timeline panel to set the start and end positions.

Advanced Processing and Codec Settings

These settings are outside the scope of this book. More information about them can be found in the Expression Encoder user guide (from the menu select Help, User Guide). In most standard cases, you can just leave the default settings untouched.

Adding a Leader and Trailer Video

You may want to add a leader and/or trailer video segment. This can be useful to add a title, credits, and so on. Follow the steps:

1. Click on the Add Leader to Source button, under the zoom controls below the timeline (see Figure 12.7).

FIGURE 12.7   The Add Leader button

2. Alternatively, you can also use the Auto Stitch section in the Enhance panel.

3. Select the video file you want to add. Here also, it can be any of the supported input formats, even a XAML animation. We will create XAML animations in Chapter 13, "Progressing with Videos," for overlays. The same technique can be used for leaders and trailers.

> **NOTE**
>
> You cannot edit the leader/trailer video much. If you need to crop, trim, or otherwise edit that video, you must do it before you choose it as a leader/trailer.

4. If the leader or trailer video segment is of a different size, it must be resized to fit your video. You can set the resize mode to Letter Box (the aspect ratio will be preserved, and a black mask will be applied) or Stretch (the leader/trailer will fill the space, but may be distorted).

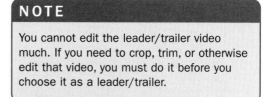

5. The leader or trailer appears in the Timeline panel (see Figure 12.8).

FIGURE 12.8   Video with a 15 seconds leader

Testing Before Encoding

Probably the most exciting feature of Expression Encoder is the ability to see the end result before you encode the whole video, and even to compare it with the original video file with the following steps!

1. In the Media Content panel, click on A/B Compare.

2. The video is "split," with the original on the left, and a (currently) black pane on the right.

3. Using a combo box on top of the Media Content panel, you can change the Compare Mode from Split (one image only) to Side by Side (two images).

4. In the timeline, use the white markers to select a segment of the video you want to test (see Figure 12.9).

FIGURE 12.9   Segment for A/V Compare mode

5. In the Media Content panel, click on Build Preview. This encodes the portion of the video that you selected, and displays the output next to (or below) the original quality video (see Figure 12.10).

The preview builds faster than the real thing (that's the idea!), so you can visualize the result.

FIGURE 12.10   A/B Compare mode

▶ Notice how you can move the yellow splitter to compare what you will get with great precision.

▶ Of course, you can also move the playhead to a specific position within the encoded segment.

▶ And you can even play the video to see the differences!

▶ To change the orientation of the yellow splitter, double-click on it!

You can also try encoding with different settings! Perform the following steps:

1. Without exiting the A/B mode, select another profile in the Encode panel.

2. Click on the Build Preview button.

3. You now see Encoded 2 in the video.

4. Using the combo boxes on the left of the Build Preview button, you can switch between Original, Encoded 1, Encoded 2, and select the best result.

After you verify that your settings are okay, you can exit the A/B Compare mode by clicking the corresponding button in the Media Content panel.

Setting Metadata

Using the Metadata panel, you can specify information that will be encoded in your video file. This is interesting if you want to publish your video on the Internet, for example, and embed your name, copyright information, and other such details.

<blockquote>
WARNING

Adding metadata to a video doesn't mean that it cannot be "stolen." The metadata information in the video file can be modified or deleted by malicious users. Once again, the old saying is true: If you don't want anyone to steal your work, don't publish it.
</blockquote>

The following metainformation can be entered:

- Title, Author (your name), Copyright, Rating, Credits, and Description (see Figure 12.11).

- And a lot of other information, which you can see if you expand the Advanced Properties section, right under the Description box.

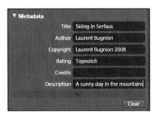

FIGURE 12.11   Metadata

For example, on Windows computers, this information is displayed in Windows Explorer in Details mode (see Figure 12.12). This information is also displayed in a ToolTip that appears when you place the mouse over the file.

FIGURE 12.12   Metadata displayed in Windows Explorer

Adding Your Own Metainformation

In the "Setting Options" section earlier in this chapter, we mentioned a section titled "Metadata Attributes" where you can specify custom metadata attributes. After you create them, they are available in the Metadata panel (you must expand the advanced properties to see the custom attributes).

If you enter a value for the custom attribute, it will be visible encoded in the video file's metainformation, and can be retrieved by other video editing tools (see Figure 12.13).

This can be useful for specific cases, but in general, it is better to try and "stick" with the standard attributes. When you load your videos on another device, for example, a pocket video player, the custom attributes will probably be ignored, while the device can work with standard attributes (for example, displaying the video's author and description).

FIGURE 12.13   Custom metainformation

Creating Chapters

If your video is long enough, it can be interesting to divide it into chapters. When you publish your video in Silverlight format, the chapters will be available in a built-in dialog, allowing the viewer to skip to a given section easily. Follow the steps:

1. In the Timeline panel, place the yellow playhead on the position in which you want to add a chapter.

2. In the Metadata panel, in the Markers section, click the Add button.

3. Expression Encoder adds a marker (see Figure 12.14). Note that you may enter "only" 1,000 markers to a video (including chapters, captions, and so on).

4. If you want this marker to be a keyframe, check the corresponding check box (by checking the check box on top of the column, you force all markers to be keyframes).

> **TIP**
>
> A *keyframe* is a frame for which the whole picture information is saved in the video. For other frames, only the differences between the previous frame and the current frame are encoded. This reduces the size of the video, but also makes it more difficult to work with that particular frame.

5. Enter a name for the chapter in the Value text box.

6. If you want Encoder to create a thumbnail of the video at this particular moment, check the Thumbnails check box. Here also,

FIGURE 12.14   Creating chapters

checking the check box on top of the column forces the value for all markers.

7. If you want the Silverlight player (that we create later) to display a chapter list, you must create a thumbnail for each chapter.

8. To specify the look of the thumbnails, expand the Advanced Properties section just under the buttons Add, Remove, and so on. You can specify the format of the thumbnail (for example, JPG, PNG, GIF, BMP), its quality, and its size.

9. You can export (and import) markers using the corresponding buttons. The markers will be saved in XML format. We will see a use for the markers file in Chapter 24, "Silverlight: Continuing the Journey," in the section titled "Using the MediaPlayer ASP.NET control."

Creating Captions

How cool would it be to provide subtitles for your video, and to display them in the Silverlight player? With Expression Encoder, it is easy. You can use the captions as a way to translate your video, as titles for a given section of the video, and so on. You can add captions with the following steps:

1. In the Timeline panel, move the yellow playhead to the position in which you want to display a caption.

2. In the Metadata panel, in the Script Commands section, click on the Add button.

3. Set the type of the command to Caption. You might need to type this in the combo box in the Type column.

4. Enter the text you want to display in the Command column (see Figure 12.15).

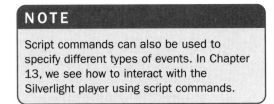

> **NOTE**
>
> Script commands can also be used to specify different types of events. In Chapter 13, we see how to interact with the Silverlight player using script commands.

FIGURE 12.15   Creating captions

If you want the caption to disappear from the screen after a certain time (for example, after 2 seconds), you must enter a new empty caption 2 seconds later. Follow these steps:

1. Move the timeline approximately 2 seconds after the caption you want to remove from the screen.

2. Add a new caption.

3. Select Caption from the Type combo box.

4. Delete the content of the Command text box.

Here also, you can export and import captions using the corresponding buttons.

Encoding the Video for Silverlight

After this rather long preparation, it's time to specify the output and to encode it with the following steps:

1. In the Metadata panel, select the Output tab.

2. In the Thumbnail section, you can set Expression Encoder to create a thumbnail for your video:

   ▶ Specify the thumbnail's type: You can choose the best frame of your video, the first frame, or any other time of your video. If you choose the Custom type, you can choose the time in the Timeline panel (yellow marker).

   ▶ Specify the output format and quality.

   ▶ Specify the thumbnail's size.

3. The Timeline panel displays all the markers, captions, thumbnail and so on (see Figure 12.16).

> **TIP**
>
> If you let Encoder export a thumbnail, it will be displayed in the Silverlight viewer while the video is buffering.

FIGURE 12.16   Timeline with two chapters (white), 2 captions (periods delimited by gray circles), and one thumbnail marker (yellow)

Now is the time to choose a player for your video. Expression Encoder lets you choose from a set of predefined Silverlight templates. We will experiment with these templates later.

1. In the Job Output section, you can choose from a set of Silverlight templates for the video player (see Figure 12.17). If you choose None, the video will be encoded, but no additional files will be created to play it.

2. Select the directory in which your video should be saved.

3. If you want the video to open automatically in your favorite web browser after it is encoded (to test the result), check the Preview in Browser check box.

FIGURE 12.17   Selecting a Silverlight template

> **TIP**
>
> Depending on the size of the video, the speed of your PC, and the power of your graphics card, the encoding can take a long time. It's wise to test your settings on smaller portions of the video before you encode the final result.

4. If you want all the settings to be saved in the same folder as the video output, check the Save Job File check box.

5. If you want the video to be saved in a separate subfolder, check the Subfolder by Job ID check box. The video will be saved in a folder named [PC NAME] [DATE] [TIME].

6. In the Media Content panel, click on the Encode button.

Checking the Result

You did it: You just encoded your first video for Silverlight. Let's check the result with the following steps:

> **NOTE**
>
> Depending on the template you chose, the results may vary. The template displayed here is called the Expression template.

1. If the file is not already visible in your web browser, go to the location where you saved the video output, and double-click the file Default.html.

2. In the web browser, notice how the player occupies the whole window. If you resize the window, the player resizes too. In Chapter 13, we see how to include the player in an existing web page.

3. In the top-left corner, notice a small button. If you click it, the list of chapters opens.

4. In the bottom of the video, the video controls are hidden. Pass your mouse over this area of the screen to make the controls visible. You can play, pause, fast forward, rewind, and control the volume.

5. While the video is playing, notice how the captions appear and disappear, bringing additional information to the viewer (see Figure 12.18).

FIGURE 12.18   Silverlight video player in Firefox

Playing the Video in Full Screen

One nice feature of Silverlight is the ability to change to full-screen display. This is available for any Silverlight application (unless it was explicity disabled by the application), and the video players created by Expression Encoder also offer this functionality.

To test this, simply double-click on the movie being played. To exit the full-screen mode, press the Esc key.

Unfortunately, this function is not very intuitive. Additionally, some player templates have a Full Screen button, but the Expression template we use in this chapter doesn't, and you cannot see anywhere on the screen that double-clicking the movie will switch to full screen. In Chapter 13, we see how to add a Full Screen button to the player.

Advanced Parameters

Before we finish this chapter, let's follow the steps and take a look at advanced parameters you can see when you encode the video.

1. In the Output panel, in the Job Output section, open the expander at the very bottom.

2. The first option (Cue Video on Page Load), if checked, initiates a download as soon as the Silverlight application is loaded in the web browser. If you uncheck this option, the video player shows a Start button, as shown in Figure 12.19. The video download will start only when this button is clicked.

FIGURE 12.19   Start button

3. The option Automatically Start Video When Cued is self-explanatory. If it is unchecked, the video will be loaded by the browser, but it will not start until the user clicks the Play button.

4. Check Allow Closed Captions to Show if you want captions to be visible. If you uncheck this option, the closed captions (subtitles) will not be displayed when the video is playing.

5. Mute Player on Start is another self-explanatory option. Check this option to turn off sound.

6. Check Player Background Color to choose a color for the HTML page in which the Silverlight player is included. Note, however, that the player's color is not modified by this option. We see in Chapter 13 how to edit a player template and how to modify its look and feel.

Summary

In this chapter, we learned how to encode a video to your hard disk (including a Silverlight player) and watch it locally in the Silverlight video player. We also learned how to add captions in your video to provide your viewers with more information, and how to divide your video into chapters.

In the next chapter, we learn how to publish on a perfectly standard website, how to add video to existing web pages, and even how to host short videos on Microsoft's own streaming servers. Adding video to your website is easy with Expression Encoder!

CHAPTER 13

Progressing with Videos

After having encoded videos in Chapter 12, "Encoding Videos with Expression Encoder," the next step is to publish them on the Internet and place the viewer on web pages, to make your videos available to many users.

The solutions commonly available for online video publishing are often not very satisfying. By publishing your videos on any of the normal online video providers, you pretty much give away your content to this firm. Your videos will be resized and converted to a lower quality. Additionally, they will often add their own logo on your video, which is annoying.

Silverlight video, on the other hand, is fully in your possession. You decide in which quality your movies must be delivered, and which look and feel the player should have. You are the sole owner of your content.

Why Streaming?

First, it is important to remember what we studied before: Silverlight runs on the client; that is on *the user's* computer, and not on the web server. Even when we publish a Silverlight video application on a web server, the user must *download* the Silverlight application and any additional files (including videos) to his computer. The application sends a *request* to the web server. In response, the server sends the first bytes of the video. Often, however, the user decides that the video is not what she wants and stops the player after a few seconds.

Here lies the critical difference between streaming a video and downloading it: When a server sends a video for download, it sends the whole file, no matter what. If the user stops the video after just a few seconds, the rest of the file gets sent anyway to the client, and that is a waste of bandwidth.

On the other hand, if the server is streaming, it sends small packets after small packets, and can interrupt the transmission if the video player is not interested anymore.

Note that with modern video players (including Silverlight), *progressive download* is supported. This term simply means that the player can play the video as soon as enough content has been downloaded. Users often mistake progressive download for streaming, because it's hard to tell the difference without checking what's really going on under the hood.

There are a few differences between streaming and downloading:

▶ If a video is streamed, it is not saved on the client. It requires less disk space, but it also means that it cannot be viewed offline.

▶ If a video is downloaded, even if progressive download is supported, the user cannot simply skip ahead to a portion of the movie. The player must wait until the file download reaches this portion to be able to display it. On the other hand, if the video is streamed, the server can skip ahead and start sending the corresponding parts.

▶ For live video broadcast (live webcast, live TV shows, and so on), the video must obviously be streamed.

▶ Streaming servers can optimize the transmission based on a number of parameters (connection speed, capability of the player, and so on). Download servers, on the other hand, simply send packets as fast as possible. If a big number of clients connects simultaneously, this can lead to "traffic jams."

▶ Last but not least: Renting streaming server space costs more money than regular server space.

The Silverlight video players support both progressive download and streaming, so it's up to you to choose the best solution for your application.

Publishing on Your Own Website

You might be surprised to see no XAP or C# files in the output created by Expression Encoder. The reason is simple: It targets Silverlight 1! The video playing capabilities of this Silverlight version are absolutely sufficient to support all the functionalities of the players created by Expression Encoder. It means that we will deal mostly with XAML and JavaScript files in this chapter.

Copying the Files

Publishing a Silverlight video on your own website is easy. You just need to upload some files, and you're set. Let's review the procedure in the following steps:

1. For information about setting up your web server and installing and setting up the FTP client, check Chapter 7, "Deploying to a Web Page."

2. Start your FTP client and connect to your web server.

3. Create a new folder for your video on the server.

4. On the client side, navigate to the folder in which the encoded video and all the output files are placed.

5. Copy all the files to the web server.

Expression Encoder creates the following files:

▶ ExpressionPlayer.js, MicrosoftAjax.js, player.js, Silverlight.js, SilverlightControl.js, SilverlightMedia.js—Contain application files for the Silverlight player. Do not modify these files, or your Silverlight player could stop working correctly.

▶ PlayerString.js—Contains messages for the user. If needed, these can be translated.

▶ StartPlayer.js—This script file is created especially for your video. This is the file in which we will work later to customize your application.

▶ Marker thumbnails—These files are the thumbnails you specified for chapters. Their name varies according to your movie name, the time in the movie at which the corresponding chapter is placed, and the format you choose for the image—for example: skiing_7.369.jpg.

▶ Any other image file—Depending on the video player you choose, additional image files are created. For example, some video players use a file named buffering.jpg to display an animation when the video content is being downloaded.

▶ player.xaml—This XAML file contains the video player's user interface.

▶ Default.html—This HTML file is a test page where the Silverlight video player is displayed in full size. You can upload this file to your web server if you want to test the video without integrating it in your own page first, or if you want to point an HTML `iframe` to it.

▶ MediaDefinition.xml—This XML file contains information about the video and its chapters. It is not strictly needed on the web server, however, because this information is also encoded in the video file, but it doesn't harm uploading it.

Adding an Overlay

Adding an overlay to a video can be a great way to give an identity to such a file, for example, with a company logo.

However, don't forget that everything you're doing here will be "burned" into the video file. It might not be an appropriate way to display a message that must change often, such as an advertisement. In that case, a better solution would be to set your Silverlight application so that the advertisement is displayed on top of the media element in which the video is playing. A nice touch is also to resize the media element while the advertisement plays, so that it is not covered by the ad, which would reduce the user experience.

Overlays are well suited, on the other hand, when you want to mark the video with your print, either for branding, to add disclaimers, or for copyright purposes. Since the overlay is burned into the video file, it is not possible to remove it.

Adding an Icon or a Video

One type of overlay is a "static" image or even a video file. You can add one with the following steps:

1. Open Expression Encoder and prepare a video for encoding like we did in Chapter 12.

2. In the Overlay category of the Enhance panel, check the Add Overlay check box.

3. Using the File controls, click on the "…" button to display a file dialog.

4. In the Open dialog, select Files of Type, Media Files.

5. Select an image or a video file for the overlay. Do not worry about the size; you can resize it in Encoder.

6. You should now see the overlay in the Viewer panel. Move it to the desired location. You can also resize it using the green border, or the corresponding section in the Overlay category of the Enhance panel.

7. You can make the overlay partly transparent using the Opacity control.

8. If your media overlay has a solid color background, you can ask Expression Encoder to remove it. Simply check the Use Transparent Background check box.

9. Note that a video overlay is always muted.

> **WARNING**
>
> Encoder samples the pixel located on the top-left corner of the overlay (at location 0x0). Then it removes this color from the whole media. Only use this feature if the background uses a solid color, and if this color is not used anywhere else in the media.

Setting Advanced Properties

As usual in Encoder, an advanced section is also available for the overlay. To display it, open the expander located under the Overlay category in the Enhance panel. The following properties are available in the advanced section:

▶ Specify whether the overlay should apply to the whole video or to parts of it:

  ▶ Main Video Only—The overlay will be visible during the whole video, but not during a leader or trailer sequence.

- ▶ Whole Sequence—The overlay will always be visible.

- ▶ Custom—Allows you to specify a start and end time for the overlay. You can move the yellow playhead to a position in the video where the overlay should appear. Click the Update button next to the Start text box. Then move the playhead again and do the same for the End position.

▶ If the overlay is a video, it will play in a loop if the Loop Overlay check box is checked.

▶ If you checked the Loop Overlay check box, you can also specify a gap between the loops. During the gap, the video overlay will be hidden. After the gap is expired, the video overlay will appear and play again.

▶ Instead of letting the overlay appear aggressively, use the Fade In and Fade Out boxes to specify a smoother transition. You can also use the playhead and the Update button!

You can test the result directly in Encoder by positioning the playhead and using the Play/Pause button.

Adding an XAML Overlay

The ability to use a static icon or a video for an overlay is already pretty exciting, but let's see now how to add XAML to the picture—literally! Note that in addition to being used as an overlay, a XAML file like we create here can also be added as a leader or a trailer for a video. This is great to create animated titles or credits, for example. Follow the steps:

1. Start Expression Blend.

2. Select File, New Project from the menu.

3. Select the first option: WPF Application (.exe). We are not really going to create a WPF application here, but we will use Blend to create a XAML animation that we can import into Expression Encoder.

4. Set the location where this (temporary) application must be saved, give it a name and click OK.

5. Add an image to the `Grid` named LayoutRoot. Remember you can simply drag and drop an image file from Windows Explorer. Typically, you can add your company's logo, for example.

6. Make sure that the `Image` is selected in the Objects and Timeline category.

7. Set the following properties:

   - ▶ `HorizontalAlignment` and `VerticalAlignment`: Center

   - ▶ `Margin`: 0 0 0 0

   - ▶ `Stretch`: Uniform

8. Select the Window in the Objects and Timeline category, and reset its `Height` and `Width` to Auto. Of course you can also add other XAML elements if you want, such as texts, shapes, etc...

9. Add a storyboard and name it LogoStoryboard.

10. Using what you learned in previous chapters, create an animation with your logo. Use `ScaleTransform`, `RotateTransform`, or any other animation.

11. Save all your files. Then, right-click on the Solution and select Edit in Visual Studio.

12. In Studio, select the menu File, New, File and add a new text file to the project.

13. Copy the whole XAML markup from Window1.xaml to the next text file you just added.

14. Save the text file under the name Animation.xaml. Make sure that the file is saved in the same folder as all the other project files, including the picture you're displaying in your animation.

15. Remove from the markup the properties `x:Class`, `x:Name`, and `Title`.

16. Everywhere in the markup, replace the word `Window` with `Grid`. Expression Encoder cannot use a `Window` as the top-level element. By replacing with a `Grid`, we allow Encoder to load the XAML markup. Then save all your files.

> **TIP**
>
> In Studio, you can search and replace using Edit, Find and Replace, Quick Replace (Ctrl+H) from the menu.

17. Change to Expression Encoder and create a new job. Import a video.

18. In the Overlay category of the Enhance panel, follow the same procedure as before to add an overlay, but instead of choosing a video overlay, select the XAML file we saved (and edited) before (Animation.xaml).

FIGURE 13.1   Video with XAML overlay. The orange bar indicates the duration of the overlay.

19. All other parameters can be set just like the video overlay's parameters. The animation runs like a video. You can set it to loop, to fade in and out, and you can specify for how long it should run. In the end, you have an XAML overlay as shown in Figure 13.1.

> **WARNING**
>
> Unfortunately, at the time of writing, Expression Encoder ignores the value of the `AutoReverse` attribute for a Storyboard. If you want your animation to reverse to the original state, you must do it manually in Expression Blend.

Letting Your Users Choose the Player

Given the number of player templates available in Expression Encoder, and thanks to the possibility to edit their source code, it is fairly easy to let your users choose which player they want to use.

Copying the Files

The first action is to get the template files from Encoder, and to copy them to a location where we can edit them. Follow the steps:

1. On your PC, create the following structure:

```
[root]
    VideoPlayer
        MyVideo
        Templates
            script
```

2. In Expression Encoder, in the Output panel, select any template—for example, Minimalist.

3. Using the small white square located on the right of the Template combo box (see Figure 13.2), open the context menu and select Open Template Location.

4. From the Minimalist template folder, go up one level in Windows Explorer. You should see a collection of folders, one for each installed template.

FIGURE 13.2   Minimalist Silverlight video player template

5. Copy Minimalist and CorporateSilver from the folder Microsoft Expression\Encoder 2\Templates\en to the folder VideoPlayer\Templates that we created earlier.

Modifying the Files

The rest of the work happens on the files we just copied. Make sure you don't delete or modify the original files! If you delete files from the original template location, you won't be able to use this template in Encoder anymore.

1. Some files are common to all the players, and we will *move* them from the Minimalist folder into the script folder: ExpressionPlayer.js, MicrosoftAjax.js, Silverlight.js, SilverlightControl.js, and SilverlightMedia.js.

2. You can *delete* these files from the CorporateSilver folder too.

3. Other files are not needed anymore. In the Minimalist folder and in the CorporateSilver folder, you can *delete* the files Default.html, MediaDefinition.xml, and StartPlayer.js.

4. We need some additional "intelligence" to be able to switch between the templates. For this, create a new text file in the script folder, and name it MyVideoPlayer.js. Then, open this file in a text editor and copy Listing 13.1 to this file.

LISTING 13.1   Selecting a Video Template with JavaScript

```
// MyVideoPlayer.js - Selecting a Silverlight video template

 1  if (window.MyVideoPlayer == null)
 2    window.MyVideoPlayer = {};
 3
 4  MyVideoPlayer.TEMPLATE_PARAMETER = "template";
 5  MyVideoPlayer.templateName = "Minimalist";
 6
 7  if (window.location != null
 8    || location.search != null
 9    || location.search.indexOf(MyVideoPlayer.TEMPLATE_PARAMETER) > 0)
10  {
11    // Remove the "?"
12    var searchString = location.search.substring(1);
13    // Separate the queries
14    var queries = searchString.split('&');
15
16    for (var index = 0; index < queries.length; index++)
17    {
18      var query = queries[index].split('=');
19      if (query[0] == MyVideoPlayer.TEMPLATE_PARAMETER)
20      {
21        MyVideoPlayer.templateName = query[1];
22      }
23    }
24  }
25
26  document.writeln("<script type='text/javascript' src='../Templates/"
27    + MyVideoPlayer.templateName
28    + "/PlayerStrings.js'></" + "script>");
29  document.writeln("<script type='text/javascript' src='../Templates/"
30    + MyVideoPlayer.templateName
31    + "/player.js'></" + "script>");
```

- After creating a namespace, we define one constant `TEMPLATE_PARAMETER` and a static variable `templateName`.

- The constant is just a value that we will use in a few places, so it makes sense to define it once. It should not be modified by the code. The variable will receive the template name. By default, it is initialized to Minimalist, so this is the template we'll use if nothing else is specified.

- In fact, JavaScript doesn't have constants. Any variable can be modified in the code (other programming languages can mark a variable as constant, and so prevent any modification). By convention, we use capitals to name constants (or pseudoconstants like here) and to notify other developers that they should not modify the value of this member.

- At lines 7 to 24, we check the built-in object `location` to see whether the user entered a query string in the URL. The query string comes after a "?" in the page's URL. You can use it to pass parameters to a JavaScript application, for example. We use the built-in function `indexOf` to check whether the string `"template"` is found in the query string. This method returns -1 if the string is not found, or it returns the index at which the string is found. This code would work with a URL like http://www.mydomain.com/player?template=Minimalist.

- At line 12, we remove the leading "?" from the query string, using the built-in function `substring`. We take everything except the first character (the one with index 0).

- Between lines 16 and 23, we use a `for` loop to split the query string and find the value of the parameter `template`. We use this code because we don't know whether the query string contains additional parameters. This brings *flexibility and extensibility*.

- After this work is done, we use the built-in method `document.writeln` to dynamically include the script files according to the chosen template.

> **WARNING**
>
> The browsers' JavaScript engines are not very clever, and some cause an error when a string contains the word `</script>`. This is why we split this word in two when we call the method `document.writeln`.

Creating the Video

Now that our script is ready, we can prepare to encode a video and modify the generated HTML file to handle multiple players with the following steps:

1. In Expression Encoder, create a Silverlight video application as we did in Chapter 12, choosing any template. Then, from the output folder, copy the following files into the MyVideo folder that we created before: Default.html, MediaDefinition.xml, the WMV output file, all the JPG thumbnails, and StartPlayer.js.

2. If you use one template that uses additional images (such as buffering.jpg), you must also copy these to the MyVideo folder.

3. Open the file Default.html in a text editor, and modify it as shown in Listing 13.2.

LISTING 13.2   File Default.html for Multiple Video Templates

```
<!DOCTYPE HTML PUBLIC "-//W3C//DTD HTML 4.01 Transitional//EN"
 "http://www.w3.org/TR/1999/REC-html401-19991224/loose.dtd">
<html xmlns="http://www.w3.org/1999/xhtml">
<head>
<script type='text/javascript'
       src="../Templates/script/MicrosoftAjax.js"></script>
<script type='text/javascript'
       src="../Templates/script/Silverlight.js"></script>
<script type='text/javascript'
       src="../Templates/script/SilverlightControl.js"></script>
<script type='text/javascript'
       src="../Templates/script/SilverlightMedia.js"></script>
<script type='text/javascript'
       src="../Templates/script/ExpressionPlayer.js"></script>
<script type="text/javascript"
       src="../Templates/script/MyVideoPlayer.js"></script>
<script type='text/javascript' src="StartPlayer.js"></script>
<title></title>
<style type="text/css">
    html, body { margin: 0; padding: 0; height:100% }
    #divPlayer_0 { min-height: 100%; height:100%;  }
</style>
</head>

<body style="background-color:black;margin:0,0,0,0;overflow:auto;">
    <div id="divPlayer_0">
        <script  type='text/javascript'>
            var player = new StartPlayer_0();
        </script>
    </div>
</body>
</html>
```

4. Finally, in the same folder, open the file StartPlayer.js in a text editor. Locate the function StartPlayer_0 and modify it like Listing 13.3:

LISTING 13.3   Modified Function `StartPlayer_0`

```
function StartPlayer_0(parentId) {
    try {
        eval('document.body.style.backgroundColor="#000000"');
    } catch(e){}

    this._hostname = ExpressionPlayer.Player._getUniqueName("xamlHost");
Silverlight.createObjectEx( { source: '../Templates/'
 + MyVideoPlayer.templateName
 + '/player.xaml',
 parentElement: $get(parentId ||"divPlayer_0"),
 id:this._hostname,
 properties:{ width:'100%',
  height:'100%',
  version:'1.0',
  background:rgbToHex(document.body.style.backgroundColor),
  isWindowless:'false',
  inplaceInstallPrompt:true },
  events:{ onLoad:Function.createDelegate(this, this._handleLoad) } } );
    this._currentMediainfo = -1;
}
```

We almost didn't modify the function: We simply refer to the attribute `MyVideoPlayer.templateName` to set the correct XAML file as the `source` parameter.

How Does It Work?

Once all this is done, you can test the player in a web browser: If you simply double-click the file Default.html, the Minimalist player will be used. If you want to use another player, call the URL with a *query string*—for example:

file:///C:/VideoPlayer/MyVideo/Default.html?template=CorporateSilver

or

www.mysite.com/VideoPlayer/MyVideo/Default.html?template=CorporateSilver

The script we wrote in the file MyVideoPlayer.js reads the template name from the URL and dynamically includes the correct JavaScript files (those in the CorporateSilver folder, or those in the Minimalist folder). Because of the way the JavaScript and XAML files are structured, it is sufficient to include the correct script files in the HTML page to change the video player's look and feel.

If you want to include more player templates in your video player, simply repeat the steps we entered under "Copying the Files" earlier in this chapter. With a little additional work, you can construct a nice flexible video application for your users, and even save their preference in a cookie.

To add more videos, encode them and repeat the steps listed in the section "Creating the Video," earlier in the chapter. Copy the files into another folder, for example MyOtherVideo instead of MyVideo. You can create multiple videos, all using the same players.

Publishing on Microsoft Silverlight Streaming Servers

We explained before the advantage of publishing video from a streaming server. However, one major issue was also mentioned: Renting space on a streaming server can be expensive, and less attractive for a private user.

Thankfully, to promote the use of Silverlight, Microsoft launched a service called Silverlight Streaming (http://silverlight.live.com). This service is still in beta, meaning that the exact terms of use are not final yet.

At the moment, the following restrictions apply:

▶ The encoded file may not be longer than 10 minutes.

▶ The encoded file must have a maximum bit rate of 1.4Mbps.

▶ The encoded file may not be bigger than 105MB.

This service does not replace a professional streaming host, but can be useful for private use. Additionally, the Silverlight applications are copied to a vast array of mirror servers worldwide, so that the viewer has the best viewing experience possible.

Additionally to videos, you can also copy nonvideo Silverlight applications to the streaming servers and enjoy the benefit of the mirror servers! As the service grows more mature, it will offer unlimited conditions with advertising, or against a nominal fee.

Signing Up

Before you can publish a Silverlight streaming application, you need to create an account with the following steps:

1. Navigate to http://silverlight.live.
com and click the Get It Free
button (see Figure 13.3).

FIGURE 13.3   The Get it Free button

2. Follow the website's directions to sign up for the service.

After you are signed up, you need to write down two IDs:

▶ Your account ID.

▶ Your account key.

These two IDs can be found on the page Manage Account, after you are logged in to the Microsoft Silverlight Streaming website.

Installing, Setting Up the Plug-in, Publishing

Microsoft created a plug-in for Microsoft Encoder, which makes publishing the videos on the streaming web server even easier! This plug-in can be downloaded from the Microsoft Expression web page, at www.microsoft.com/expression. Click on the link labeled "Silverlight Streaming plug-in for Expression Encoder 2" to reach the download page and install the plug-in. Then, follow the steps:

1. Start Expression Encoder.

2. On the Output panel, you should see a new category named Publish, as shown in Figure 13.4.

3. Select Silverlight Streaming from the Publish To combo box.

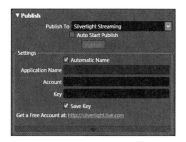

FIGURE 13.4   Publish from Encoder

4. Under Settings, enter your account ID in the Account text box, and your account key in the Key text box.

5. If you want, click the Save Key check box to save your key and avoid having to enter it every time you run the application.

6. Encode an application as we did in Chapter 12, including a Silverlight template of your choice.

7. If you want, enter a name for your application. You need to uncheck the Automatic Name check box first.

8. When everything is ready, click the Publish button.

9. After the video has been success-fully published, you can see the result using the Preview screen. Notice that thanks to the magic of Silverlight, all the buttons are fully operational even in the small preview screen!

> **WARNING**
>
> Publishing a large video can take a lot of time. Typically, the "upstream" of a high-speed Internet connection is slower than the "downstream" so have patience.

Testing the Output

To test the output, you have multiple possibilities. The easiest one is simply copying and pasting a URL in your web browser with the following steps:

1. Under the Publish category, click on the Code tab (next to the Preview tab).

2. The snippet typically looks like this (the SILVERLIGHT_URL is actually a URL depending on your account ID and the application name):

```
<iframe
  src="SILVERLIGHT_URL"
  scrolling="no"
  frameborder="0"
  width="1024"
  height="508"></iframe>
```

This snippet creates an HTML iframe, which can be used to display content from a web server in a page located on a different server. It can be copied and pasted into an existing web page if you want. In the next section, "Adding the Application in an Existing Web Page," we see how to use this markup, but for the moment we only want to test.

3. Copy the URL to your Silverlight application (the one in the src attribute, in place of the SILVERLIGHT_URL) to your web browser. This should automatically start the video from the streaming web server.

Alternatively, you can manage and test all your applications from the Silverlight Streaming home page with the following steps.

1. Navigate to http://silverlight.live.com and sign in to the service.

2. After you're signed in, click on Manage Applications.

3. Locate the new application you just created in the list, and click on its name.

4. To test the application, click on the Launch Application Test Page link.

5. After you successfully test the video stored on the server, you can safely delete the local output to save space on your computer.

The Application Properties page also allows you to update your application or delete it. We use the rest of the page (under "Add this Application to a Web Page") later when we integrate the video into our existing web pages.

Adding the Application in an Existing Web Page

After your movie and its Silverlight player are published, either on Microsoft's streaming servers or on your own web space, you have one more step to fulfill to integrate the video in your own web pages. As mentioned earlier, Silverlight content created by Expression Encoder targets version 1 of the framework. There is no XAP file to be included. You can decide between two strategies:

▶ Using an `iframe` to embed the HTML application page with a minimal impact on your own web page

▶ Adding the content directly to your page with JavaScript and a so-called *Live Control*.

This decision should be based on the level of control that you have over the page in which you want the application to run. If the web page belongs to you, it is preferable to use the second method, which offers a better user experience. In the case of a community website, a blog, and so on, you may have to use the `iframe` method instead.

Using an `iframe`

The `iframe` markup you need to include in your HTML page is the one we got from the Publish category earlier (see the section "Testing the Output" earlier in the chapter). If you forgot to write down that markup, you can retrieve it by performing the following steps:

1. Under Publish, set the Publish To combo box to Silverlight Streaming.

2. Expand the Advanced Properties under the Publish category. You should see an Applications list.

3. If the list is empty, click on the Refresh button. Note that you must be online to execute this function, and you must have published at least one application!

4. Select the application for which you need the `iframe` markup.

5. Copy the `iframe` markup to your HTML page, for example, in a `div`, a table cell, or any other container you choose for the movie.

6. You can also get the `iframe` markup from the Silverlight Live website. Follow the steps in the next section, "Using JavaScript and a Live Control," and you'll find this markup!

The `iframe`'s `src` attribute points to the test page, which is automatically created by Expression Encoder. Note that the video player automatically fills the whole `iframe`, so that you can change its size (for example, with CSS, or even dynamically with JavaScript), and the video will automatically be resized.

This `iframe` markup can be copied to Windows Live Writer and included in a blog article, for example. Copying and pasting the `iframe` markup is a simple process to add rich content to your blog!

James Clarke of the Expression Encoder team published a plug-in for Windows Live Writer named Jet Fuel. This plug-in makes it even easier to encode and publish videos using Silverlight on your blog. Jet Fuel can be found at www.clarkezone.net.

13

Using JavaScript and a Live Control

The Silverlight streaming administration web page gives you the code needed to include a Silverlight video application directly in your website using a so-called Live Control with the following steps:

1. As before, navigate to http://silverlight.live.com and sign in to the service.

2. Click on Manage Applications.

3. Select the application you want to integrate.

4. Under Add this Application to a Web Page, you'll find the steps required. Simply follow the indications on the page.

Firing Script Commands (and Catching Them)

As we saw in Chapter 12, you can use the Script Commands category in Expression Encoder to embed caption texts in the video. The same mechanism can also be used to fire events that JavaScript (or C#) can catch and handle. This can be useful if you need to synchronize an action with a certain scene in the video, or if you want to parameterize a method based on the video that is currently played.

In this example, we change the color of the HTML page containing the video player based on a command saved in the video movie. This way, you can modify the color based on the movie's mood: Dark red for suspense, pastel colors for a love scene, and so on. Follw the steps:

1. In Expression Encoder, prepare a video for encoding as we did previously. From the Job Output tab, select the Clean template.

2. Before you encode, select a scene in the video and add a script command (just as we added a caption earlier). As Type, enter ChangeColor, as shown in Figure 13.5.) As Command, enter #FF0000 (this is a bright red).

3. If you want, add more commands at various times, with the same type, but a different color.

4. Encode the video locally.

> **NOTE**
>
> ChangeColor is a name that we just made up. The script handling the event must be informed of this name and react accordingly. We implement this in just a moment.
>
> In fact, it's just like with Caption: The Silverlight player created by Expression Encoder knows that it must react to this command and display the text passed as parameter.

FIGURE 13.5   ChangeColor commands

> **TIP**
>
> We use these colors to set the HTML page's background. In HTML, colors only have the R, G, and B channels, and not the Alpha channel as in Silverlight. You can use the colors we saw in Table 5.2 in Chapter 5, "Using Media."

5. After the video is encoded, locate it on the disk, and open the file StartPlayer.js in a text editor or in Visual Studio

6. Find the call to the method `Silverlight.createObjectEx`, and replace it with the code in Listing 13.4:

LISTING 13.4   Modified Method `Silverlight.createObjectEx`

```
Silverlight.createObjectEx( {    source: 'player.xaml',
  parentElement: $get(parentId ||"divPlayer_0"),
  id:this._hostname,
  properties:{ width:'100%',
               height:'100%',
               version:'1.0',
               background:"Transparent",
               isWindowless:'true',
               inplaceInstallPrompt:true },
  events:{ onLoad:Function.createDelegate(this, this._handleLoad) } } );
```

7. Find the lines where the event handlers (such as `mediaEnded` and `mediaFailed`) are added, and modify this code to look like Listing 13.5.

LISTING 13.5   Modified Event Handlers

```
{ // event handlers
  markerReached: Function.createDelegate(this, this._onMarkerReached),
  mediaEnded: Function.createDelegate(this, this._onMediaEnded),
  mediaFailed: Function.createDelegate(this, this._onMediaFailed),
  playPreviousVideo: Function.createDelegate(this, this._onPlayPreviousVideo),
  playNextVideo: Function.createDelegate(this, this._onPlayNextVideo)
},
```

8. Then create the event handler _onMarkerReached just before _onMediaEnded (see Listing 13.6).

LISTING 13.6   Event Handler _onMarkerReached

```
_onMarkerReached: function(sender, eventArgs) {
  if (eventArgs._marker.Type == "ChangeColor")
  {
    document.body.style.backgroundColor = eventArgs._marker.Text;
  }
},
```

13

We need a minor adjustment in the file player.xaml. This is just a cosmetic change only:

1. Open the file player.xaml.

2. On line 2 of this file, set the `Background` property of the `Canvas` element to `Transparent`.

Finally, we make the video player a little bit narrower to make the change in the background color of the page more obvious:

1. Open the file Default.html in a text editor, and modify the `div` of the player to look like this:

```
<div id="divPlayer_0" style="margin: 0 50px 0 50px;">
```

2. Open the file Default.html in a web browser: The video starts, and you see the background color change according to the saved markers.

This simple example shows how a video file can communicate with its host by sending script commands.

NOTE

We saw earlier (in Chapter 5) how to handle the event `MediaEnded` on the MediaElement control in C#. You can do the same with `MarkerReached`. This allows you to react to embedded script commands in your Silverlight 2 application with .NET.

In JavaScript, the event is named `markerReached` while in C# (and in XAML) it is named `MarkerReached` (with a capital "M"). The difference in naming is due to historical reasons and naming guidelines. Don't mix them up.

Modifying the Player Template in Blend

One great feature of Silverlight, especially when you use it to play videos, is the ability to go full screen. All the video players support this feature, but sometimes it is not very well documented: In the Expression video player, you must double-click the video screen to make it go full screen. In this section, we add a Full Screen button to this template in Expression Blend.

Adding a Full Screen Button

Since the player is made of XAML, you can edit it in Blend. Here we will add a button to the player with the following steps. Silverlight 1 (which is what Expression Encoder creates) doesn't have controls; the button is simulated using a `Canvas` to stay in line with the rest of the player's controls.

1. Prepare a video for encoding; then in Expression Encoder, in the Output panel, select the Expression template.

2. Using the small white square located on the right of the Template combo box (refer to Figure 13.2), open the context menu and select Edit Copy in Expression Blend.

3. Give a name to the copy of the template you want to edit—for example, ExpressionFullScreen. Click OK. Expression Blend starts and opens the file player.xaml.

4. Expand the top `Canvas`, and make sure that the `Canvas` directly underneath is selected with a yellow border as shown in Figure 13.6 (double-click on that `Canvas` until this occurs).

FIGURE 13.6   Canvas selected

5. In the top-right corner, add a new button. To do this, add a small `Canvas` and set its `Width` to 18 and `Height` to 15.

6. Line the new button up with the existing ChapterToggleButton (`Top` = 27.5743) and set its `Left` property to 598.

7. Name this `Canvas` FullScreenToggleButton.

8. Set its `Cursor` property to Hand.

9. Select FullScreenToggleButton until it gets a yellow border, and then add a rectangle with the following:

    ▶ The same width and height as the button's canvas (18×15)

    ▶ `Fill` = #FF555355

    ▶ `Stroke` = #FFAAAAAA

    ▶ `StrokeThickness` = 1.33

    ▶ `RadiusX` = `RadiusY` = 1

10. In the same `Canvas`, on top of the background rectangle, add two small rectangles, as shown in Figure 13.7.

11. Right-click on the `Canvas` FullScreenToggleButton and select View XAML. This command is visible only in Design mode. If you set Blend in Split mode, the XAML editor automatically displays the XAML markup corresponding to your selection.

FIGURE 13.7   Full Screen button in Blend

12. In the `Canvas`'s XAML markup, add the following event handler:

```
MouseLeftButtonDown="ToggleFullScreenButton_MouseLeftButtonDown"
```

Handling the Event in Script

We need to make a few changes to the JavaScript code to toggle the full screen mode. In fact, Microsoft planned that you would want to modify the existing templates, and provides a player.js file where you can add your own code with the following steps:

1. Back in Expression Encoder, click on the small white square next to the Template. Select Open Template Location.

2. Open the file player.js in a text editor.

3. Modify the constructor `ExtendedPlayer.Player`. We need to save a reference to the instantiated player for further use, as in Listing 13.7:

LISTING 13.7   Modified Constructor `ExtendedPlayer.Player`

```
ExtendedPlayer.Player = function(domElement) {
    ExtendedPlayer.Player.initializeBase(this, [domElement]);
    ExtendedPlayer.Player.instance = this;
}
```

4. Finally, implement the event handler declared in the XAML markup for the FullScreenToggleButton. This event handler uses the instance of Player that we just saved and calls its method `_onToggleFullScreen`.

LISTING 13.8   Event Handler `ToggleFullScreenButton_MouseLeftButtonDown`

```
function ToggleFullScreenButton_MouseLeftButtonDown(sender, args)
{
  if (ExtendedPlayer.Player.instance != null)
  {
    ExtendedPlayer.Player.instance._onToggleFullScreen();
  }
}
```

To keep it simple, we didn't create a different look for the "mouse over" state or the "pressed" state. The point of this section is to show that a Silverlight video player is in no way different from any other Silverlight application, and that the XAML file can be edited in Blend just like any other XAML-based content.

You can learn a lot about the Silverlight 1 video players created by Expression Encoder by opening the XAML and JS files of the other templates. Even though the code looks a bit "messed up" sometimes, using other templates as examples will help you creating your own video players for Expression Encoder!

Testing the Result

To test the result, save everything, and then encode a video using the newly created template ExpressionFullScreen. Any change you just made to the XAML and JavaScript will be applied when you use this template. Once the player is displayed, click on the new button to show the video in full screen.

Summary

In this chapter, we learned how to take advantage of Expression Encoder 2 to create customized videos and to enhance the viewing experience. Expression Encoder has other advanced features that we didn't study here—for example, the capability to stream live events directly to Silverlight players.

One attractive thing about Expression Encoder is that it is really easy to get a result, fast. Once this is done, you can spend hours refining the result (especially if you are as obsessed with details as this author).

13

Letting .NET and JavaScript Talk

Interoperability is a vast and complex subject in the history of software development. Many technologies are available and "letting them talk" is crucial and sometimes difficult.

Over time, JavaScript has grown to be a key component of the web client. It is present in all the major web browsers, it is mostly enabled, and it is mostly standardized. Silverlight 1 relies heavily on JavaScript to create and interact with all the Silverlight controls in the web page. In Silverlight 2, JavaScript is less crucial to the operation, but communication between Silverlight and JavaScript opens a world of possibilities.

Making .NET Available to JavaScript

Interoperability in Silverlight goes in both directions, as we will see in the course of this chapter. Let's start by considering how JavaScript can directly interact with the .NET environment in Silverlight.

Using the ScriptableMember Attribute

Attributes in .NET are used to *decorate* classes, methods, or other elements to add information without modifying their body or their signature. For example, we need to signal the Silverlight framework that some of the methods, properties, and events in our .NET objects are "scriptable"—that is, that they can be used from JavaScript.

To make a public .NET member scriptable, simply add `[ScriptableMember]` before the member's declaration as in Listing 14.1:

LISTING 14.1   ScriptableMember

```
public class AnyObject
{
  [ScriptableMember]
  public int Index
  {
    get;
    set;
  }
}
```

> **WARNING**
>
> The attribute `ScriptableMember` belongs to the namespace `System.Windows.Browser`. To make this namespace available to your .NET object, you must add it explicitly to the `using` section as we saw in previous chapters! You will also have to add other `using` directives later in this chapter.
>
> The attribute can either be referenced as `ScriptableMember` or `ScriptableMemberAttribute`. By convention, you can always omit the `Attribute` suffix when you reference an attribute.

Similarly, any method, event, or property that you want to make available to JavaScript must also be marked with the `ScriptableMember` attribute.

> **WARNING**
>
> The `RegisterScriptableObject` method must be used only if at least one `ScriptableMember` method, property, or event is defined in the class. If that's not the case, an error will occur!

Registering the Object

In addition to using the `ScriptableMember` attribute, you must register the .NET object with the Silverlight application as in Listing 14.2.

LISTING 14.2   Call to RegisterScriptableObject

```
public Page()
{
  InitializeComponent();
  AnyObject myObject = new AnyObject();
  HtmlPage.RegisterScriptableObject("MyObject", myObject);
}
```

The first parameter of the `RegisterScriptableObject` method is a name that can be used in JavaScript to address the object. We see an example in the next section.

Handling .NET Events in JavaScript

We saw in Chapter 10, "Progressing with .NET," how to create and raise events, and how a .NET object can subscribe to events raised by another .NET object. Now we will see how we can raise events in .NET and catch them in JavaScript! This enables an elegant one-way communication (a bit later we see how to communicate back from JavaScript to .NET).

Preparing the scriptable Class

Let's create a new Silverlight class that will be used to communicate with JavaScript with the following steps:

1. Start by creating a new Silverlight 2 application in Visual Studio. Name it JavaScriptDotNet.

2. In the Add Silverlight Application dialog (refer to Figure 9.2), select the Add a New Web to the Solution option, and select Web Site as the Project Type.

3. Open the file Page.xaml.cs. Under the `Page` class, create a new class deriving from `EventArgs`. We use this class to pass additional information about the event. Because we want to access the `CounterValue` from JavaScript, we need to decorate this property with the `ScriptableMember` attribute. This class (see Listing 14.3) must be placed *inside* the namespace `JavaScriptDotNet`.

LISTING 14.3   Class `CounterTickedEventArgs`

```
public class CounterTickedEventArgs : EventArgs
{
  [ScriptableMember]
  public int CounterValue
  {
    get;
    internal set;
  }
}
```

4. Under the `CounterTickedEventArgs` class, create a delegate specifying the signature of the `CounterTicked` event handler:

```
public delegate void CounterTickedHandler(object sender,
  CounterTickedEventArgs e);
```

Let's take care of the `Page` class itself now (see the code in Listing 14.4):

1. Declare the `CounterTicked` event and mark it as a `ScriptableMember`.

2. Implement the `OnCounterTicked` method.

3. In the `Page` constructor, register the Page object with the Silverlight application. We simply use the name `Page` as an identifier for JavaScript.

4. After you enter the code, build your application to check if everything is fine.

LISTING 14.4   JavaScriptDotNet Application, `Page` Class

```
public partial class Page : UserControl
{
  [ScriptableMember]
  public event CounterTickedHandler CounterTicked;

  public void OnCounterTicked(CounterTickedEventArgs e)
  {
    if (CounterTicked != null)
    {
      CounterTicked(this, e);
    }
  }

  public Page()
  {
    InitializeComponent();
    HtmlPage.RegisterScriptableObject("Page", this);
  }
}
```

Raising the Event

We will raise the `CounterTicked` event every time the user clicks five times on a button. Implement this with the following steps:

1. First, let's add the button (Listing 14.5) in Page.xaml, inside the LayoutRoot:

LISTING 14.5   New Button

```
<Button x:Name="CounterButton"
        Width="80" Height="40"
        Content="Count" Click="CounterButton_Click"
        HorizontalAlignment="Left"
        Margin="100,20,0,0" />
```

2. In the `Page` class in Page.xaml.cs, declare a private attribute for the counter value. This attribute will be incremented every time the button is clicked (see Listing 14.6).

3. In addition to incrementing the counter, the event handler `CounterButton_Click` will check the value. If it is a multiple of 5, the `CounterTicked` event will be raised. This uses the modulo operator `%` that we introduced in Chapter 9, "Understanding .NET." You can build the application again.

LISTING 14.6   Event Handler `CounterButton_Click`

```
private int _counter = 0;
private void CounterButton_Click(object sender, RoutedEventArgs e)
{
  _counter++;
  if ((_counter % 5) == 0)
  {
    // true every time the counter is a multiple of 5
    CounterTickedEventArgs args = new CounterTickedEventArgs();
    args.CounterValue = _counter;
    OnCounterTicked(args);
  }
}
```

Subscribing to the Event on the JavaScript Side

Now comes the time of *interoperability*. We will implement a JavaScript class that will call subscribe to the Silverlight event we created with the following steps.

1. Open the test page JavaScriptDotNetTestPage.html.

2. Enter the code shown in Listing 14.7 in the `script` section, right under the function `onSilverlightError`.

LISTING 14.7   JavaScriptDotNet Application, JavaScript Code

```
1   JavaScriptDotNet = function(page)
2   {
3     page.CounterTicked
4       = JavaScriptDotNet.createDelegate(this,
5         this.handleCounterTicked);
6   }
7
8   JavaScriptDotNet.createDelegate = function(instance, method)
9   {
10    return function()
11    {
```

LISTING 14.7   Continued

```
12      return method.apply(instance, arguments);
13    }
14  }
15
16  JavaScriptDotNet.prototype =
17  {
18    handleCounterTicked : function(sender, e)
19    {
20      alert("Counter ticked: " + e.CounterValue);
21    }
22  }
23
24  var jsDotNetInstance;
25  function onSilverlightLoaded(sender, args)
26  {
27    jsDotNetInstance
28      = new JavaScriptDotNet(sender.getHost().Content.Page);
29  }
```

▶ On lines 1 to 6, we define a constructor for our new JavaScript object. Note that it takes a parameter called page. This parameter is the "gateway" to the Page object that we registered on the .NET side when we called the method HtmlPage.RegisterScriptableObject.

▶ On lines 3 to 5, we register a JavaScript method for the .NET event CounterTicked. That's right, we can cross the language boundaries this easily!

▶ Lines 8 to 14 define the method createDelegate that we studied earlier (in Chapter 8, "Programming Silverlight with JavaScript"). It is defined as a "static" method.

> **WARNING**
>
> There is another way to register multiple event handlers for one event, using the JavaScript method addEventListener. We see examples in Chapter 21, "Taking Silverlight 2 Even Further."

▶ Lines 16 to 22 define the object's prototype. It has only one method, called handleCounterTicked. This method creates a JavaScript alert every time it is called.

▶ Notice how the parameter e is a JavaScript representation of the CounterTickedEventArgs instance that we created on the .NET side: You can access the property CounterValue, because we marked it as a ScriptableMember.

▶ Lines 24 to 29 define a global function named onSilverlightLoaded. Due to the Silverlight event model, this method has to be global. It is as simple as possible: It creates a new instance of the class JavaScriptDotNet, saves it in a global variable, and lets it do the rest of the work.

▶ Notice the complicated syntax to get the Page control that we registered earlier:

  ▶ `sender.getHost()` returns the instance of the Silverlight control. This is in fact a reference to the `object` tag in the HTML page.

  ▶ This "host" has a property named `Content` that is the entry point on the XAML page and all the objects registered for JavaScript, as we see in the next section.

Finally, we need to "hook" the global function `onSilverlightLoaded` to the `onload` event of the Silverlight object. Simply add the following parameter in the HTML page, in the `object` tag, under the other event handler named `onerror`:

```
<param name="onload" value="onSilverlightLoaded" />
```

Testing the Code

And now comes the exciting part, testing what we just implemented. Follow the steps:

1. Right-click on the website JavaScriptDotNetWeb and select Set As StartUp Project.

2. Right-click on the file JavaScriptDotNetTestPage.html and select Set As Start Page.

3. Press Ctrl+F5 to run it.

4. Click five times on the button. This raises the .NET event and triggers the alert. If you click OK and then click on the button five more times, the alert will be triggered again (see Figure 14.1).

FIGURE 14.1   .NET event handled in JavaScript

Calling JavaScript Methods from .NET

In addition to raising events from .NET to JavaScript, you can also simply call JavaScript methods from the .NET code with the following steps:

1. Modify the JavaScriptDotNet object prototype as follows. We now only declare a second method with Listing 14.8.

LISTING 14.8   Method saySomething

```
JavaScriptDotNet.prototype =
{
  handleCounterTicked : function(sender, e)
  {
    alert("Counter ticked: " + e.CounterValue);
  },
  saySomething : function(message1, message2, message3)
```

LISTING 14.8   Continued

```
  {
    alert(message1 + "/" + message2 + "/" + message3);
  }
}
```

2. In Page.xaml, add a new button under the one we added before (see Listing 14.9):

LISTING 14.9   Another Button

```
<Button x:Name="SaySomethingButton"
        Width="80" Height="40"
        Content="Say" Click="SaySomethingButton_Click"
        HorizontalAlignment="Right"
        Margin="0,20,100,0" />
```

3. and in Page.xaml.cs (Listing 14.10):

LISTING 14.10   Event Handler SaySomethingButton_Click

```
private void SaySomethingButton_Click(object sender,
  RoutedEventArgs e)
{
  ScriptObject instance
    = HtmlPage.Window.GetProperty("jsDotNetInstance") as ScriptObject;
  instance.Invoke("saySomething",
    new object[] { "Hello", "World", DateTime.Now });
}
```

▶ The class `HtmlPage` is a useful entry point from .NET to the HTML and JavaScript realm. With its two static properties `Window` and `Document`, you can access most of the JavaScript and HTML elements of the page hosting the Silverlight application.

▶ Remember how we saw (in Chapter 8) that a global variable is actually a property of the global object? And that the global object is the `Window`? Well, here is a practical use for this knowledge: We access the global variable `jsDotNetInstance` by using the method `GetProperty` on the `Window`!

▶ Finally, calling the `Invoke` method on any `ScriptObject` will try to call the corresponding JavaScript method. In our case, we call `Invoke` on the instance we just fetched. If you have a global method, you can `Invoke` it on the `HtmlPage.Window`!

▶ Even though our JavaScript method expects strings, we can pass it a `DateTime` object. The method `ToString` will automatically be called on this object. Since .NET types and JavaScript types are not equivalent, a *conversion* must take place. In Chapter 21, we talk more about type conversions and the `ScriptObject` type.

> **NOTE**
>
> `HtmlPage`.`Window` has three handy shortcuts: `Alert`, `Confirm`, and `Prompt`. They call the corresponding functions in JavaScript and can be really helpful when you're debugging your code!

After you made these changes, run the application and test it by clicking on the new button.

Calling .NET Methods from JavaScript

Now that we saw how to handle .NET events in JavaScript and to call JavaScript methods from .NET, the opposite way is straightforward: To call .NET methods from JavaScript code, simply use the following syntax:

```
[control].Content.[objectname].[methodname]([parameters]);
```

▶ [control] is the Silverlight control added in the HTML markup. You can get a reference to that using the `sender.getHost()` in the JavaScript function handling the `onload` event (as we did before).

▶ Another way to get a reference to the Silverlight control is to set an ID in the `object` tag:

```
<object data="data:application/x-silverlight,"
type="application/x-silverlight-2"
width="100%" height="100%"
id="SilverlightControl">
```

and then

```
var silverlightControl = document.getElementById("SilverlightControl");
silverlightControl.Content.Page.DoSomething();
```

▶ [objectname] is the name you gave when you used the method `HtmlPage`.`RegisterScriptableObject` in the .NET code.

▶ [methodname] is the name of the scriptable method you want to call.

▶ [parameters] is the list of parameters to be passed to the .NET method.

14

Adding a "Login" Dialog to the Thumbnails Application

Let's extend our Thumbnails application (we edited it last in Chapter 11, "Progressing with Animations") by adding a login dialog. We will ask the user to enter a username and password. For the moment, we handle the password in the web client, since we don't know how to communicate with the web server yet. Later, we implement server-side logic to handle the passwords.

> **WARNING**
>
> It is bad practice to store passwords on the client. We do this here as an example only, but we will change this later!

Extending the User Object

Remember that we created a User class before? We will extend it with the needed functionality in this section. Again, it is nice to work with objects, as the changes will be limited to a couple of classes only.

User Properties

Let's extend our User class with two additional properties: A user name and a password.

1. Open the Thumbnails application in Visual Studio.

2. Open the file Data/User.cs and add two properties as in Listing 14.11:

LISTING 14.11   Two New Properties

```
public string Name
{
  get;
  internal set;
}
public string Password
{
  get;
  internal set;
}
```

The property LastVisit remains unchanged.

Serializing

The basic infrastructure we need to save the data to the data file is available already and must merely be extended. As mentioned previously, the DataFile class must not be modified at all, because the User class is responsible for delivering a string representing itself.

LISTING 14.12 Overriden Method ToString

```
public override string ToString()
{
  string result = Name + "\t" + Password + "\t";
  if (LastVisit != null)
  {
    result += LastVisit.ToString();
  }
  return result;
}
```

The modified ToString method creates a string with the user's name, a tab, the password, another tab, and finally the date and time of the last visit. To make sure that you didn't make a typo, build the application but don't try to run it yet.

TIP

C#, like other programming languages, defines a number of special characters. These start with a "backslash," used to signify that this is not a character like all the others. Then follows the character code itself. For example, "\t" represents a tabulator, "\n" represents a new line, and so on.

Constructing the Object

We also need to modify the constructors to fit with the new property and the new data format. After you copy the updated code in Listing 14.13, build your application again (this is something you should do often).

LISTING 14.13 Constructors of User Class

```
 1  public User()
 2  {
 3    Name = "";
 4    Password = "";
 5    LastVisit = null;
 6  }
 7  public User(string line)
 8  {
 9    try
10    {
11      char[] splitCharacters = new char[1] { '\t' };
12      string[] elements = line.Split(splitCharacters);
13      Name = elements[0];
14      Password = elements[1];
15      LastVisit = DateTime.Parse(elements[2]);
16    }
```

LISTING 14.13   Continued

```
17    catch (ArgumentNullException)
18    {
19      LastVisit = null;
20    }
21    catch (FormatException)
22    {
23      LastVisit = null;
24    }
25  }
```

▶ The default constructor (lines 1 to 6) simply initializes the properties Name and Password to an empty string.

▶ The second constructor (lines 7 to 25) *splits* the line, cutting it at every tab character (Line 12). The syntax of the Split method is a little complex:

  ▶ The only parameter of the Split method is an array of characters. The input string will be cut every time one of these characters is found. In our case, we need only one "cutting" character: the Tab character '\t'. This is the array we construct at line 11.

  ▶ The Split method returns an array of strings. For example, if the input string is Laurent\tHelloWorld\t12.02.2008 21:47:05, then the first cell of the array will contain Laurent, the second cell HelloWorld, and the third cell 12.02.2008 21:47:05.

▶ In lines 13 to 15, we assign the elements of the split string to the Name, Password, and LastVisit properties.

Comparing Two Users

We want to be able to compare one User instance with another User instance. We saw earlier that the operator == does exactly this. But this operator is not defined for the User class. We add this functionality to our class now.

The operator == is defined in the object class. It means that you can always compare two objects, whatever their type is. However, the equality operator defined in the object class is not sufficient for our needs and we must redefine it. In the User class, add the code in Listing 14.14:

LISTING 14.14   Redefining the Equality Operators

```
public static bool operator ==(User user1, User user2)
{
  if (object.Equals(user1, null))
  {
    return (object.Equals(user2, null));
```

LISTING 14.14   Continued

```
  }
  if (object.Equals(user2, null))
  {
    return (object.Equals(user1, null));
  }

  return (user1.Name == user2.Name
    && user1.Password == user2.Password);
}
public static bool operator !=(User user1, User user2)
{
  return !(user1 == user2);
}
```

▶ The keyword `operator` defines a new meaning for a given operator. In our case, we redefine the equality operator == and the inequality operator !=. These two should always be defined as a pair (it makes no sense to have equality without inequality). Our definition of equality is: If a `User`'s `Name` and `Password` are equal to another `User`'s `Name` and `Password`, then both `Users` are considered equals.

▶ We handle explicitly the case where one (or both) of the parameters is `null`. This allows us to use the == operator even if one of the operands is null, which is very handy.

If you compile this code now, you see two warnings in the Output tab of Visual Studio.

▶ `'Thumbnails.Data.User' defines operator == or operator != but does not override Object.Equals(object o)`

▶ `'Thumbnails.Data.User' defines operator == or operator != but does not override Object.GetHashCode()`

Should the Output tab be hidden, you can display it by selecting View, Output from the menu. You might need to scroll up a little in this panel to see the warnings I am talking about.

Warnings are not as critical as errors, and the application may run even if you don't correct your code to remove them. However, it is good practice to take care of all warnings before releasing your application. In this case, it is easy enough. Simply add the following two methods to the `User` class (Listing 14.15):

LISTING 14.15   Methods `Equals` and `GetHashCode`

```
public override bool Equals(object obj)
{
  return (this == (User) obj);
}
public override int GetHashCode()
{
  return Name.GetHashCode();
}
```

▶ The first overriden method `Equals` has the same functionality as the equality operator. It is defined by the `object` class (the basis class for all .NET objects). To suppress
the warning, we compare `this` (the current instance) to the object passed as a parameter by using our redefined `==` operator.

▶ The method `GetHashCode` is used by certain collections (`Hashtable`, `Dictionary`) that
use specific algorithms to sort and retrieve items. Since a username must be unique,
we decide that the `User`'s hash code is the same as the `Name`'s hash code.

If you compile the application now, you'll see that the two warnings are gone.

Handling Multiple Users

Our application will handle multiple users now, so we need to modify the `DataFile` class
accordingly with the following steps:

1. Open the file DataFile.cs.

2. To avoid conflicts with the previous data file (which used a different format), we
    will use a different file name:

    ```
    private const string DATA_FILE_NAME = "ThumbnailsData.2.txt";
    ```

3. Add an attribute to store the list of all users. To allow retrieving a user easily, we
    store them in a `Dictionary` that you declare below the line we just added.

    ```
    private Dictionary<string, User> _users;
    ```

A `Dictionary` (like a `List`) is a generic class containing a collection of items. However, a
`Dictionary` also contains a key for each item and allows retrieving the corresponding item
easily.

Because it is a generic class, you must specify the type of the key (`string`) and the type of
the item (`User`). We will talk about generics in Chapter 20, "Taking Silverlight 2 One Step
Further."

Loading the Users

Modify the method `LoadUser` as in Listing 14.16. Note that we renamed it to `LoadUsers` (plural). Instead of loading and returning a single user, it will load all the users and store them in the _users `Dictionary`. A new `User` is created and added to the list every time a line is read from the data file (using a do...while loop).

LISTING 14.16   Methods `LoadUsers`

```
internal void LoadUsers()
{
  _users = new Dictionary<string, User>();

  using (IsolatedStorageFile store
    = IsolatedStorageFile.GetUserStoreForApplication())
  {
    if (store.FileExists(DATA_FILE_NAME))
    {
      using (IsolatedStorageFileStream streamRead
        = store.OpenFile(DATA_FILE_NAME, FileMode.Open))
      {
        using (StreamReader reader = new StreamReader(streamRead))
        {
          string line;
          do
          {
            line = reader.ReadLine();
            if (line != null)
            {
              User newUser = new User(line);
              _users.Add(newUser.Name, newUser);
            }
          }
          while (line != null);
        }
      }
    }
  }
}
```

Saving the Users

Rename `SaveUser` in `SaveUsers` and modify it as in Listing 14.17. Here too, we must work with the `Dictionary` of users instead of a single `User` instance.

LISTING 14.17   Methods SaveUsers

```
internal void SaveUsers()
{
  using (IsolatedStorageFile store
    = IsolatedStorageFile.GetUserStoreForApplication())
  {
    using (IsolatedStorageFileStream streamWrite
      = store.OpenFile(DATA_FILE_NAME, FileMode.OpenOrCreate))
    {
      using (StreamWriter writer = new StreamWriter(streamWrite))
      {
        foreach (User user in _users.Values)
        {
          writer.WriteLine(user.ToString());
        }
      }
    }
  }
}
```

The `Dictionary` class contains two interesting properties: `Keys` contains all the keys for the items stored in the `Dictionary`, and `Values` contains all the items. Our `foreach` loop wants to access all the items and must therefore use the `Values` property.

Note that if you compile the application now, you will get errors because we renamed the methods `LoadUser` and `SaveUser`. We will take care of this in a moment.

Adding a New User

An important new functionality in our Thumbnails application is adding new users to the "database." The `DataFile` class will support this feature.

A new method `AddUser` is added to the `DataFile` class (Listing 14.18):

LISTING 14.18   Method AddUser

```
internal void AddUser(User newUser)
{
  if (newUser.Name == null
    || newUser.Name.Length == 0)
  {
    throw new Exception("Name may not be empty");
  }
  if (_users.ContainsKey(newUser.Name))
  {
    throw new Exception("This name already exists");
  }
```

LISTING 14.18   Continued

```
_users.Add(newUser.Name, newUser);
SaveUsers();
}
```

> ▶ If the name is empty or if it is already taken, the method throws an exception with an error message.

> ▶ If the new user is valid, it is added to the Dictionary.

> ▶ Eventually, the users are saved by a call to the SaveUsers method.

Validating a User's Password

The DataFile class must also check whether a given user/password combination is valid. A new method ValidateUser takes care of this (Listing 14.19). It takes a user as input and returns true if the name/password combination exists in the data file.

LISTING 14.19   Methods ValidateUser

```
1   internal bool ValidateUser(User inputUser)
2   {
3     if (inputUser == null)
4     {
5       // Refuse to validate null users
6       return false;
7     }
8     User existingUser = GetUser(inputUser.Name);
9     return (existingUser == inputUser);
10  }
```

> ▶ On line 9, we use the new == operator we created previously in the User class.

> ▶ If equality is found, the method returns true.

> ▶ Note that if a user is null, we simply return false. This is a way to protect the method from errors.

Getting a Saved User

The DataFile class's last task is to get a saved User according to its name. We need the saved User instance to read the LastVisit property, and to set the user interface accordingly.

The method GetUser (in Listing 14.20) checks whether the name passed as parameter exists in the collection. If it does, the corresponding User instance is returned.

LISTING 14.20   Methods GetUser

```
internal User GetUser(string name)
{
  if (_users.ContainsKey(name))
  {
    return _users[name];
  }
  else
  {
    return null;
  }
}
```

Modifying the Page Class

Now we will modify the Page class and make our application "buildable" again with the following steps:

1. Open the file Page.xaml.cs.

2. Add a private attribute in the class Page. It stores an instance of the class DataFile, which will be used throughout the application's runtime.

   ```
   private DataFile _dataFile;
   ```

3. In the Page constructor, remove the code starting with DataFile dataFile = new DataFile(); and ending with dataFile.SaveUser(user);

4. Instead, use the following code:

   ```
   _dataFile = new DataFile();
   _dataFile.LoadUsers();
   ```

As a consequence of these changes, LastVisitTextBlock will not display anything until a user logs in. The application can be compiled again though, so you can make sure that you didn't make mistakes when typing the code.

Since the Page is the "gateway" between JavaScript and .NET, we need to add two methods that JavaScript will call when an action in .NET needs to be performed.

1. To handle adding new users to the database, add the method in Listing 14.21 to the Page class:

LISTING 14.21   Method AddUser in Page Class

```
[ScriptableMember]
public string AddUser(string name, string password)
{
  try
```

LISTING 14.21   Continued

```
  {
    User newUser = new User();
    newUser.Name = name;
    newUser.Password = password;
    newUser.SetLastVisit();
    _dataFile.AddUser(newUser);
  }
  catch (Exception ex)
  {
    return ex.Message;
  }

  LastVisitTextBlock.Text = "(" + name + ", this is your first visit)";
  return null; // success
}
```

▶ It creates a new user, sets all its properties, and attempts to add it to the DataFile class.

▶ If this fails (for example, if the user name is taken already), an exception is caught, and the error message (created by the DataFile class) is returned to JavaScript.

▶ If it succeeds, LastVisitTextBlock displays a message, and null is returned to JavaScript.

2. In the page, we need to validate a name and a password passed from JavaScript. Add the method in Listing 14.22 to the Page class:

LISTING 14.22   Method ValidateUser in Page Class

```
[ScriptableMember]
public string ValidateUser(string name, string password)
{
  User inputUser = new User();
  inputUser.Name = name;
  inputUser.Password = password;
  if (_dataFile.ValidateUser(inputUser))
  {
    User savedUser = _dataFile.GetUser(name);
    LastVisitTextBlock.Text = "(" + name + ", your last visit was: "
      + savedUser.LastVisit.Value.ToShortDateString()
      + " " + savedUser.LastVisit.Value.ToLongTimeString() + ")";
    savedUser.SetLastVisit();
    _dataFile.SaveUsers();
```

LISTING 14.22   Continued

```
    return null; // success
  }
  else
  {
    return "Invalid user/password combination";
  }
}
```

- ▶ A test User is created and its Name and Password are set according to the user input.

- ▶ The DataFile's method ValidateUser is called.

- ▶ If the user name and password are found in the data file, the method returns true and the corresponding user can be fetched.

- ▶ The LastVisitTextBlock is set according to the saved user. Then the saved User's LastVisit property is updated.

- ▶ If on the other hand the DataFile's method ValidateUser returns false, an error message is displayed.

Here too, you can compile the application and even run it. No error should occur, even though the login is not functional yet.

Adding a "Login" Label

We now modify the XAML user interface to add a "login" link. When the label is clicked, the Silverlight application raises an event. Follow the steps:

1. Open the file Page.xaml and scroll down until you find a TextBlock named LastVisitTextBlock.

2. Remove the TextBlock and replace it with the markup in Listing 14.23. We add a control named HyperlinkButton, which looks like a hyperlink and has a Click event just like a button. Because of the StackPanel, the Login hyperlink will always appear neatly next to the LastVisitTextBlock, whatever the length of that TextBlock is.

LISTING 14.23   TextBlock and HyperlinkButton

```
<StackPanel Orientation="Horizontal">
  <TextBlock x:Name="LastVisitTextBlock"
    Margin="10,10,0,10" FontSize="14"
    VerticalAlignment="Bottom"/>

  <HyperlinkButton Content="(login)"
    x:Name="LoginLink" Margin="10,10,0,10"
```

LISTING 14.23   Continued

```
   Click="LoginLink_Click" FontSize="14"
   VerticalAlignment="Bottom" />
</StackPanel>
```

3. In Page.xaml.cs add the following event in the Page class. We don't need any special information for this event, so we use the generic EventHandler delegate. Also, the event is made scriptable because JavaScript must subscribe to it:

```
[ScriptableMember]
public event EventHandler LoginClicked;
```

4. Still in the Page class, add a method (Listing 14.24) to raise the LoginClicked event (for example under the method ValidateUser that we added before):

LISTING 14.24   Method OnLoginClicked

```
public void OnLoginClicked(EventArgs e)
{
  if (LoginClicked != null)
  {
    LoginClicked(this, e);
  }
}
```

5. Always in the Page class, handle the MouseLeftButtonDown event of the "login" TextBlock (Listing 14.25):

LISTING 14.25   Event Handler LoginLink_Click

```
private void LoginLink_Click(object sender, RoutedEventArgs e)
{
  EventArgs args = new EventArgs();
  OnLoginClicked(args);
}
```

6. Finally, we need to register the Page class with the web application. Add the following code in the Page constructor, under the call to _dataFile.LoadUsers():

```
HtmlPage.RegisterScriptableObject("Page", this);
```

Let's summarize shortly:

▶ When the user clicks the "login" HyperlinkButton, the method OnLoginClicked is called.

- ▶ If any object (including the JavaScript application) registered for this event, it will be raised.

- ▶ No additional information is passed to the event subscriber: The only information is that the link has been clicked.

Adding a Web Project

So far, we have always executed our Thumbnails application with the default HTML test page. In Chapter 9, we saw how to create a Silverlight application with a website to test it. Now we add a new website next to an existing Silverlight application with the following steps:

1. Select the menu File, Add, New Web Site.

2. Make sure that ASP.NET Web Site is selected, and use the name Thumbnails.Web. This new folder should be placed in the same folder as the file Thumbnails.sln and the Thumbnails folder with the Silverlight application. Then click OK.

> **WARNING**
>
> Be careful when you select the new website location. The website can (in theory) be placed anywhere on your hard disk, but it makes sense to group everything together, to make it easier to manage.

This creates a new project in the same Solution as the Silverlight application. Remember that this project will run on the web server, while the Silverlight application will run on the web client!!

Now we add a link to the Silverlight application, so that our website can deliver the Silverlight content to the web client when needed.

1. Right-click on the project you just added. Select Property Pages.

2. In the Property Pages dialog, select Silverlight Applications and click on the Add button.

3. Select Use an Existing Silverlight Project in the Solution and make sure that the Thumbnails project is chosen. You can leave all the other options at their default. Then close both dialogs.

4. In the Solution Explorer, rename the file ThumbnailsTestPage.html to index.html. This will be the file we work in for now.

Checking the Media Files' Build Action

We need to make sure that the media elements (images and videos) are copied to the website together with the Silverlight application. For the moment, the media elements belong to the Thumbnails project. This is not ideal, because we cannot easily add media elements after the application has been deployed to the web server. We will correct this later, in Chapter 19, "Creating User Controls and Custom Controls."

You can control what the compiler does with the files by setting the Build Action property.

1. In Studio, click on the image pic1.png and press F4. This opens the Properties dialog.

2. Make sure that the Build Action is set to Resource (it should be the case already). Also, the Copy to Output Directory property should be set to Do Not Copy.

The following values are available:

▶ None: No action is taken for this element. It will not be touched by the compiler.

▶ Content: The element will be copied to the output directory (for example bin/Debug). Note that this value depends on the value of the Copy to Output Directory property, which should be set to Copy if Newer (or Copy Always).

▶ Resource: The element will be embedded into the DLL.

There are other possible values for Build Action, but these three are the ones we use in Silverlight for elements that are referenced by `Image`, `MediaElement` or such controls.

We just saw that the images' Build Action is set to Resource. It means that they will be copied into the Thumbnails DLL, and will automatically be available on the web server too.

The movie's Build Action, however, is set to Content. The movie is available into the bin/Debug directory (you can see it there) but will not be copied to the web server automatically. To solve this, you can either copy the file mov1.wmv to the folder ClientBin in the website Thumbnails.Web, or you can change the file's Build Action to Resource (and handle it the same way as the images).

Adding the HTML Login Dialog

In this book we really work with a number of different technologies. In fact, this is to be expected in a heterogeneous environment like the Web. After creating Silverlight, JavaScript, and CSS code, let's do a little HTML with the following steps:

1. Open the file index.html and add the HTML markup in Listing 14.26 under the `silverlightControlHost div` element. We use the `LoginDialogStatus` element to display messages to the user in case of error. For the moment, this line displays nothing.

LISTING 14.26   HTML Login Dialog

```
<div id="LoginDialog">
  <form action="index.html">
    <input type="text" id="NameTextBox" />
    (user name)<br />
    <input type="password" id="PasswordTextBox" />
    (password)<br />
    <input type="button" class="button" value="submit"
           onclick="thumbnails.handleSubmitClicked();" />
    <input type="button" class="button" value="new user"
           onclick="thumbnails.handleNewUserClicked();" />
    <input type="button" class="button" value="cancel"
           onclick="thumbnails.handleCancelClicked();" />
  </form>
  <div id="LoginDialogStatus"></div>
</div>
```

2. We need CSS to make this HTML element look nicer. In the `head` section, under the `#silverlightControlHost` CSS style, add the CSS code in Listing 14.27:

LISTING 14.27   CSS Rules

```
#LoginDialog
{
  position: absolute;
  top: 20em;
  left: 3em;
  padding: 1em;
  background-color: #6699FF;
  font-family: Sans-Serif;
  border: solid 2px black;
  display: none;
}
.button
{
  width: 6em;
  margin: 1em 0.5em 0 0;
}
```

These changes add an HTML login dialog positioned on top of the Silverlight application. For the moment, however, the dialog is hidden (`display: none`). We now use JavaScript to show the dialog when the "login" label is clicked in XAML.

Blending the Silverlight Application with HTML

Remember the `windowless` attribute from Chapter 7, "Deploying to a Web Page." It specifies how the Silverlight "real estate" interacts with the HTML page. If you set it to `false` (that's the default value), the Silverlight content appears on top of the HTML content in all circumstances.

In our case, we want to set it to `true` to allow the login dialog to be displayed on top of the thumbnails gallery.

1. In index.html, in the `object` tag, add the `windowless` parameter and set it to `true`.

```
<param name="windowless" value="true" />
```

2. While we are at it, let's set the Silverlight application's background to `Transparent`. This allows it to "blend" even better with the HTML page.

```
<param name="background" value="Transparent" />
```

Catching the .NET Event

As we saw previously, catching a .NET event involves a few modifications in the JavaScript application. Use the following steps:

1. Add a new JavaScript file to the Thumbnails.Web website (right-click on the Project, then choose Add New Item and choose a JScript file). Name this file Thumbnails.js.

2. Add a constructor for the `Thumbnails` object. This constructor accepts a reference to the `Page` element (this is the Silverlight page we registered earlier). It gets references to some HTML elements for later. Finally, we register for the `LoginClicked` event that the Silverlight application raises when the corresponding `HyperlinkButton` is clicked (Listing 14.28).

LISTING 14.28   Thumbnails Constructor

```
Thumbnails = function(page)
{
  this._loginDialog
    = document.getElementById("LoginDialog");
  this._nameTextBox
    = document.getElementById("NameTextBox");
  this._passwordTextBox
    = document.getElementById("PasswordTextBox");
  this._loginDialogStatus
    = document.getElementById("LoginDialogStatus");

  this._page = page;
  this._page.LoginClicked
    = Thumbnails.createDelegate(this, this.handleLoginClicked);
}
```

14

3. The famous method `createDelegate` also needs to be added, below the constructor (Listing 14.29):

LISTING 14.29   Method `createDelegate`

```
Thumbnails.createDelegate = function(instance, method)
{
  return function()
  {
    return method.apply(instance, arguments);
  }
}
```

4. Define a new prototype for the Thumbnails object as in Listing 14.30.

LISTING 14.30   `Thumbnails` Prototype

```
Thumbnails.prototype =
{
  handleLoginClicked : function()
  {
    this._loginDialog.style.display = "block";
  },
  handleCancelClicked : function()
  {
    this.cancel();
  },
  handleSubmitClicked : function()
  {
  },
  handleNewUserClicked : function()
  {
  },
  checkErrorMessage : function(errorMessage)
  {
    if (errorMessage == null)
    {
      // success
      this.cancel();
    }
    else
    {
      this._loginDialogStatus.innerHTML = errorMessage;
    }
  },
```

LISTING 14.30   Continued

```
cancel : function()
{
  this._loginDialog.style.display = "none";
  this._nameTextBox.value = "";
  this._passwordTextBox.value = "";
  this._loginDialogStatus.innerHTML = "";
}
}
```

▶ handleLoginClicked is the event handler for the LoginClicked event coming from Silverlight. It uses the login dialog's CSS style to display it.

▶ handleCancelClicked is handling the Cancel button. It simply calls the cancel method.

▶ handleSubmitClicked and handleNewUserClicked will be implemented in just a minute and will handle the events raised by both HTML buttons in the Login dialog.

▶ checkErrorMessage is a utility that accepts a string as a parameter. If the string is null (meaning that there are no errors), the method cancel is called. If there is an error message, however, the message is displayed in the status line.

▶ cancel is a utility method, called by the handleCancelClicked event handler and by the checkErrorMessage method. It hides the login dialog and resets its state.

Wiring Up the Scripts

To get the JavaScript to work, we need to add the file Thumbnails.js to the page index.html. Then, we "wire" the code together with the following steps.

1. In index.html, before the existing script block, include the file Thumbnails.js.

```
<script type="text/javascript" src="Thumbnails.js"></script>
```

2. Add the following global variable and event handler to the existing script block (below onSilverlightError):

```
var thumbnails;
function onSilverlightLoaded(sender, args)
{
  thumbnails = new Thumbnails(sender.getHost().Content.Page);
}
```

3. "Wire" the event handler we just declared to the `onload` event of the Silverlight application:

```
<param name="onload" value="onSilverlightLoaded" />
```

At this stage, we can test the application. As we did earlier (with the JavaScriptDotNet application), set the project Thumbnails.Web as StartUp Project and the page index.html as StartUp Page. Then press Ctrl+F5. In the web page, click on the login `HyperlinkButton` (see Figure 14.2).

FIGURE 14.2   HTML login dialog on top of Silverlight application

Handling the HTML Events

The last remaining task is to "fill" the JavaScript methods `handleSubmitClicked` and `handleNewUserClicked` and to call the corresponding .NET methods in the `Page` class with the following steps:

1. In Thumbnails.js, replace the existing `handleSubmitClicked` method with the code in Listing 14.31:

LISTING 14.31   Event Handler `handleSubmitClicked`

```
handleSubmitClicked : function()
{
  var name = this._nameTextBox.value;
  var password = this._passwordTextBox.value;

  var errorMessage
    = this._page.ValidateUser(name, password);

  this.checkErrorMessage(errorMessage);
},
```

▶ The name and password are read from the HTML form.

▶ The .NET method `ValidateUser` is called. The returned error message is saved.

▶ The JavaScript method `checkErrorMessage` is called. If there were no errors, the login dialog will be closed.

2. Replace the method `handleNewUserClicked` with the code in Listing 14.32:

LISTING 14.32   Event Handler `handleNewUserClicked`

```
handleNewUserClicked : function()
{
  var name = this._nameTextBox.value;
  var password = this._passwordTextBox.value;

  var errorMessage
    = this._page.AddUser(name, password);

  this.checkErrorMessage(errorMessage);
},
```

▶ Here too, the name and password are read from the HTML form.

▶ The .NET method `AddUser` is called, and the returned error message is saved.

▶ The JavaScript method `checkErrorMessage` takes care of the rest.

Test the application now: Press Ctrl+F5 to run it, and then press the login link. In the dialog, enter your name and password, and play with the Submit and New user button to see how the application reacts.

Summary

In this chapter we demonstrated how to enable .NET to JavaScript and JavaScript to .NET communication. We also honed our .NET skills and learned a great deal about organizing an application in objects, overloading operators, raising and handling events, serializing and deserializing objects, and interacting with the web page.

CHAPTER 15

Digging into Silverlight Elements

Silverlight not only delivers a rich programming framework, it also provides a collection of panels and controls, ranging from basic (`Canvas`, `TextBlock`) to complex (`DataGrid`, `MultiScaleImage`). Understanding how these controls work, and how they relate to each other is impor-tant when you must choose the best control for the task.

With new controls appearing in every new release of the Silverlight framework, it is not possible to give a detailed explanation of each of these. This chapter and the next give you a good overview of the most common controls (and of a couple of advanced ones).

At the time of writing, Microsoft is working on a new set of new controls such as Charts, WrapPanel, DockPanel, ViewBox, TreeView, Expander and more. These controls will be published in a different release model, comparable to the ASP.NET AJAX controls set on CodePlex (www.codeplex.com). More information about these controls will be posted at http://blog.galasoft.ch where I will post demos and tutorials when available.

Exploring the Class Hierarchy

If you check the documentation (we downloaded and installed it in Chapter 1, "Introducing Silverlight,"), you'll see that a class (for example `TextBlock`) has a parent class, and that this parent class also has a parent class, and so on. Understanding this *inheritance hierarchy* is a good way to get more familiar with the Silverlight controls.

> **NOTE**
>
> As we saw before, the inheritance hierarchy can be found at the bottom of the documentation page titled "TextBlock Class." Use the Search tab to find this page.

All the classes described in this section are *abstract* (with the notable exception of `Object`). This means that you cannot directly use them. You cannot write, for example:

```
DependencyObject myObject = new DependencyObject(); // Doesn't compile
UIElement myElement = new UIElement(); // Doesn't compile
```

These classes are only used as a basis class for the framework. One might wonder where this hierarchy comes from, and why we have `UIElement` and `FrameworkElement`, instead of having only one class fulfilling both roles. In fact, don't forget that Silverlight has a "big sister" named Windows Presentation Foundation (WPF). Silverlight is (more or less) a subset of WPF, and the class hierarchy is also the same in both frameworks.

Exploring the `Object`

In the .NET framework, everything is an `Object`. This class contains a set of basic methods that every object ever instantiated automatically inherits. Note that `System.Object` and `object` are both exactly equivalent (as we saw before with `System.String` and `string`).

Your new classes will probably need to *override* the `Object`'s methods. We saw that earlier when we overrode the `ToString` method (in Chapter 10, "Progressing with .NET").

Exploring the `DependencyObject`

This next class in the hierarchy is an important basic class for Silverlight elements. `DependencyObject` is the building block for the whole animation system and for data binding (we talk about that in a few chapters), and a parent class for most of the objects delivered in the Silverlight framework. To put it bluntly, without `DependencyObject`, Silverlight (and WPF) would simply not work.

`DependencyProperty`

If `DependencyObject` is a building block, then `DependencyProperty` is the mortar between the blocks, holding Silverlight together.

The `DependencyProperty` system was invented for Windows Presentation Foundation and is also an important part of Silverlight. When you use a `Timeline` to animate a property, that's a `DependencyProperty`. When you *data bind* two properties together, these are (mostly) `DependencyProperties`. When you define a style and resources for a control (we talk more about this in Chapter 17, "Using Resources, Styling, and Templating,") you use `DependencyProperties`.

> **NOTE**
>
> You can also add custom `DependencyProperties` to your own controls, as we will do in Chapter 19, "Creating User Controls and Custom Controls," thus including them in the `DependencyProperty` system.

Exploring the `UIElement`

With `UIElement`, we add graphics capabilities to our types, for example, finding out which object is currently getting the mouse input and handling some of the events triggered by a user when he enters data. It is the basis class for all the elements involved in a user interface (that's what UI stands for).

This class is also responsible for various layout operations, such as calculating its own size (and its children's sizes too), and arranging them on the screen. While most of the derived classes *override* these functions and define their own, UIElement is the basis for *measuring* and *arranging*.

Remember in Chapter 6, "Blending a Little More," when we played with an element's opacity and the opacity mask? That's also one of the roles of the UIElement class.

Exploring the FrameworkElement

As we navigate down the family tree, the classes become more and more specialized. FrameworkElement is responsible for extending the layout capabilities, for watching an element's life time, and for providing a support for data binding (which we study in Chapter 18, "Data Binding and Using Data Controls").

FrameworkElement also defines properties such as Width, Height, ActualWidth, ActualHeight, alignment properties, margins, style, and many others. All these properties are defined as DependencyProperties, meaning that you can animate them, reference them in styles, and data bind them.

Choosing XAML or Code-Behind

Let's take a moment to understand (or remember) the relationship between XAML and the code-behind.

XAML is, in fact, a *serialization language*. We talked about serialization already, and explained that this is a mechanism used to save an object's state to a file, for example. We did the same thing in our Thumbnails application, to *serialize* a User to a file in the isolated storage.

XAML is no different. It is a representation of .NET objects. These objects are, in the case of Silverlight, user interface objects. But XAML can also be used to describe any type of object, as we see when we talk about resources.

In fact, XAML is not directly linked to Silverlight. It is also used in WPF and in a technology having no ties to the user interface, called Windows Workflow Foundation. In your own applications, you can also use the XamlReader class to dynamically load fragments of XAML markup stored in a file or in a string.

The consequence of all this is that *anything you can do in XAML can also be done in code-behind*. For example, the markup in Listing 15.1 and the code in Listing 15.2 are exactly equivalent and both create the result shown in Figure 15.1. The examples in this chapter are displayed in XAML and in C#. You can choose which one you want to test. To try these examples, create a new Silverlight application and enter the markup or the code as follows.

▶ The XAML markup should be placed within the `UserControl` tag.

▶ The C# code should be placed in the `Page` constructor, right after the call to the method `InitializeComponent`.

▶ To make it more interesting, remove the `Width` and `Height` attributes from the `UserControl` tag in Page.xaml. This way, the Silverlight application will take the whole space, and you can resize it, observing the effect on the layout.

LISTING 15.1   XAML Elements

```xml
<Grid x:Name="LayoutRoot" Background="Red">
  <Grid.RowDefinitions>
    <RowDefinition Height="Auto"/>
    <RowDefinition />
    <RowDefinition Height="100" />
  </Grid.RowDefinitions>

  <TextBlock Text="Hello world" Margin="10,5,5,5" />

  <Ellipse Grid.Row="1">
    <Ellipse.Fill>
      <LinearGradientBrush StartPoint="0,0" EndPoint="1,1">
        <GradientStop Offset="0" Color="Purple" />
        <GradientStop Offset="1" Color="Yellow" />
      </LinearGradientBrush>
    </Ellipse.Fill>
  </Ellipse>

  <StackPanel Orientation="Horizontal" Grid.Row="2">
    <Button Margin="30" Width="80" Content="Click me" />
    <CheckBox Content="Check me" />
  </StackPanel>

</Grid>
```

LISTING 15.2   C# Elements

```csharp
Grid LayoutRoot = new Grid();
LayoutRoot.Background = new SolidColorBrush(Colors.Red);

RowDefinition row1 = new RowDefinition();
```

LISTING 15.2   Continued

```
row1.Height = GridLength.Auto;
RowDefinition row2 = new RowDefinition();
RowDefinition row3 = new RowDefinition();
row3.Height = new GridLength(100);
LayoutRoot.RowDefinitions.Add(row1);
LayoutRoot.RowDefinitions.Add(row2);
LayoutRoot.RowDefinitions.Add(row3);

TextBlock title = new TextBlock();
title.Text = "Hello world";
title.Margin = new Thickness(10, 5, 5, 5);
LayoutRoot.Children.Add(title);

Ellipse ellipse = new Ellipse();
Grid.SetRow(ellipse, 1);

LinearGradientBrush brush = new LinearGradientBrush();
brush.StartPoint = new Point(0, 0);
brush.EndPoint = new Point(1, 1);
GradientStop stop1 = new GradientStop();
stop1.Offset = 0;
stop1.Color = Colors.Purple;
GradientStop stop2 = new GradientStop();
stop2.Offset = 1;
stop2.Color = Colors.Yellow;
brush.GradientStops.Add(stop1);
brush.GradientStops.Add(stop2);

ellipse.Fill = brush;
LayoutRoot.Children.Add(ellipse);

StackPanel panel = new StackPanel();
panel.Orientation = Orientation.Horizontal;
Grid.SetRow(panel, 2);
LayoutRoot.Children.Add(panel);

Button button = new Button();
button.Margin = new Thickness(30);
button.Width = 80;
button.Content = "Click me";
panel.Children.Add(button);

CheckBox checkBox = new CheckBox();
checkBox.Content = "Check me";
```

LISTING 15.2   Continued

```
panel.Children.Add(checkBox);

this.Content = LayoutRoot;
```

What do we learn from Listings 15.1 and 15.2?

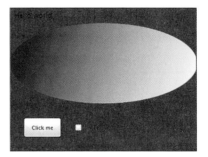

- ▶ It usually takes more lines to create a scene in code-behind than in XAML.

- ▶ XAML uses many converters (we talked about that already). For example, Background="Red" will convert Red into Colors.Red and then into a SolidColorBrush.

FIGURE 15.1   Silverlight scene

- ▶ Many operations are implicit in XAML, but they must be explicit in code-behind. For example, adding an element to a Grid in XAML is simple, just enclose the element between the <Grid> opening tag and the </Grid> closing tag. In C#, you must explicitly add the element to the Children collection.

But most important, the biggest difference is that XAML is well suited for tools such as Expression Blend. You will find yourself working in XAML sometimes, in code other times, and also in Expression Blend! The important thing to remember is that the result is equivalent.

Although it is true that you can do in code everything that you do in XAML, the contrary is not true. There are a few operations that you can do only in code. For example, data binding converters or event handlers can only be written in code-behind, not in XAML.

Packing and Laying out with Panels

Directly under FrameworkElement in the class hierarchy, we find another abstract class named System.Windows.Controls.Panel. This important class is responsible for grouping children, measuring them, and arranging them on the screen. This allows defining new ways to organize the children on the screen, with creativity as your only limit.

In addition to being able to create your own Panel, the Silverlight framework also contains enough of them for most situations. Let's talk about them.

Composing Elements

When we started playing with XAML in Chapter 2, "Understanding XAML," we saw an important feature of Silverlight: Since a `Panel` can contain `UIElements`, and since a `Panel` is itself a `UIElement`, it means that a `Panel` can contain other `Panels` too. This allows the developer to store a `StackPanel` in a cell of a `Grid` and to store a `Button` next to a `Border` next to a `Canvas` inside this `StackPanel`. You can compose and arrange elements in any way you want.

Discovering the `Canvas`

`Canvas` is the simplest panel there is. It doesn't do much: Its children are positioned using the `Canvas.Top` and `Canvas.Left` attached properties. If the `Canvas` is resized, the children are not repositioned. Because it is simple, it was also the only panel available in Silverlight V1.

To add a control to a `Canvas` is simple, but every layout operation must be implemented explicitly. For example (see Table 15.1):

TABLE 15.1   Canvas in XAML and in Code

``
<Canvas x:Name="LayoutRoot"
        Background="Orange">
  <Button Canvas.Top="10"
    Canvas.Left="10"
    x:Name="MyButton"
    Height="30"
    Content="No layout there, mate" />
</Canvas>
``
	``
	Canvas LayoutRoot = new Canvas();
	LayoutRoot.Background
	  = new SolidColorBrush(Colors.Orange);
	Button MyButton = new Button();
	Canvas.SetTop(MyButton, 10);
	Canvas.SetLeft(MyButton, 10);
	MyButton.Height = 30;
	MyButton.Content
	  = "No layout there, mate";
	LayoutRoot.Children.Add(MyButton);
	this.Content = LayoutRoot;
	``

Enter the C# code in the `Page` constructor first and run the application. Then remove it, enter the XAML markup in Page.xaml and run the application again. You'll see that the orange `Canvas` fills the whole space (because its `Height` and `Width` properties are not set, and take the default value `Auto`). The button automatically sizes to display the whole content, but not more and not less. If you resize the browser window, the button doesn't change its size.

There is a way to detect whether a `Canvas` (or any panel) changes its size, with the following steps:

1. Modify the XAML markup of the `Canvas` in Table 15.1 by adding the `SizeChanged` event.

```
<Canvas x:Name="LayoutRoot"
        Background="Orange"
        SizeChanged="LayoutRoot_SizeChanged">
```

2. In the file Page.xaml.cs, handle the event and set the `Button`'s size according to the panel's size.

```
private void LayoutRoot_SizeChanged(object sender, SizeChangedEventArgs e)
{
    Panel senderAsPanel = sender as Panel;
    MyButton.Width = senderAsPanel.ActualWidth - 20;
}
```

3. Run the application and resize the web browser's window. The button's width will also get resized. Using this mechanism, you can calculate the layout of a `Canvas`' children if needed (but honestly, it's easier to use a `Grid`...)

We use `ActualWidth` instead of `Width`. Since we didn't set the `Canvas`'s `Width` property (because we want it to occupy the whole space), trying to read this property returns the value NaN (Not a Number). Any mathematical operation on NaN results in an error. On the other hand, `ActualWidth` is always set to a numeric value.

Using a `Canvas` to Drag an Element

With the possibility to position its children in an absolute way using the `Canvas.Left` and `Canvas.Top` properties, the `Canvas` is great when you must move an element on the screen, for example with the following steps:

1. Create a new Silverlight application in Visual Studio and name it CanvasDrag.

2. Create a XAML scene within the `UserControl` in the file Page.xaml as in Listing 15.3:

LISTING 15.3   XAML Scene for Dragging

```
<Grid x:Name="LayoutRoot" Background="Red"
      MouseMove="LayoutRoot_MouseMove"
      MouseLeave="LayoutRoot_MouseLeave">
  <Grid.ColumnDefinitions>
    <ColumnDefinition />
    <ColumnDefinition />
  </Grid.ColumnDefinitions>

  <Button Grid.Column="1" Height="30" Margin="10,0,10,0"
```

LISTING 15.3   Continued

```
        Content="Click me"/>

  <Canvas x:Name="DragCanvas" Width="0" Height="0"
        HorizontalAlignment="Left" VerticalAlignment="Top">
    <Rectangle Width="30" Height="30" x:Name="MyRectangle"
            Fill="Orange"
            MouseLeftButtonDown="MyRectangle_MouseLeftButtonDown"
            MouseLeftButtonUp="MyRectangle_MouseLeftButtonUp"/>
  </Canvas>
</Grid>
```

▶ Notice how the Canvas is placed in the Grid, on top of the button (because it's the last element added to the Grid). It has a Width and Height of 0×0 pixels. Even though the Canvas is dimensionless, its children will be drawn on the screen, because the Canvas doesn't do any layout and doesn't care whether its children are inside or outside.

▶ Since the Canvas alignment is Left and Top, the reference point will always be the top-left corner of the Grid. Perfect for what we need to do.

3. Implement the event handlers below the Page constructor as in Listing 15.4:

LISTING 15.4   Code-behind for Dragging

```
1  private UIElement _draggedElement;
2  private Point _lastMousePosition;
3
4  private void MyRectangle_MouseLeftButtonDown(object sender,
5    MouseButtonEventArgs e)
6  {
7    _draggedElement = sender as UIElement;
8    _lastMousePosition = e.GetPosition(DragCanvas);
9  }
10
11 private void LayoutRoot_MouseMove(object sender,
12   MouseEventArgs e)
13 {
14   if (_draggedElement != null)
15   {
16     Point newPosition = e.GetPosition(DragCanvas);
17     double offsetX = newPosition.X - _lastMousePosition.X;
18     double offsetY = newPosition.Y - _lastMousePosition.Y;
19
20     Canvas.SetTop(_draggedElement,
```

LISTING 15.4   Continued

```
21        Canvas.GetTop(_draggedElement) + offsetY);
22      Canvas.SetLeft(_draggedElement,
23        Canvas.GetLeft(_draggedElement) + offsetX);
24      _lastMousePosition = newPosition;
25    }
26  }
27
28  private void MyRectangle_MouseLeftButtonUp(object sender,
29    MouseButtonEventArgs e)
30  {
31    _draggedElement = null;
32  }
33
34  private void LayoutRoot_MouseLeave(object sender,
35    MouseEventArgs e)
36  {
37    _draggedElement = null;
38  }
```

▶ Lines 1 and 2 define private attributes to store the element being dragged (the rectangle) and the last-known position of the mouse.

▶ Lines 4 to 9 handle the event raised when the mouse button is pushed down on the rectangle: It saves the sender (which tells the application that the element is being dragged), and also saves the mouse position (relative to the Canvas).

▶ Lines 11 to 26 handle the event raised whenever the mouse moves within the Grid LayoutRoot.

  ▶ First we check whether the dragged element is null. If it is, the application doesn't need to do anything (it means the orange rectangle has not been clicked).

  ▶ If the dragged element is not null, we must indeed drag it. We need the current mouse position. Then we calculate how much the mouse moved since last time we saved its position. This is offsetX and offsetY.

  ▶ Knowing how much the mouse moved, we can set the rectangle's new position. Finally we save the mouse position again as the last known one.

▶ Lines 28 to 32 handle the event raised when the mouse is lifted up from the rectangle. In that case, we simply set the _draggedElement back to null. This way we tell the application that it doesn't need to drag anything anymore.

▶ Finally, lines 34 to 38 handle the event raised when the mouse gets out of the main Grid. In that case, we also stop dragging the rectangle.

Run the application, then click on the small orange square and drag it on the screen. Because the Canvas is set to 0x0 pixels, it doesn't block the clicks to the button (the button doesn't have an event handler, but you'll see its appearance change when you pass the mouse over it or click on it).

There are other ways to drag an element, for example using its Margin if it is in a Grid. But using a Canvas is easy and straightforward. Generally, a Canvas is good whenever you need an absolute positioning of an element. Instead of using a rectangle, the element of choice for drag functionality is called the Thumb control. We study this control in Chapter 16, "Digging Deeper into Silverlight Elements."

Stacking Elements in a StackPanel

Another simple panel is called the StackPanel. As the name shows, it is used to stack elements one below the other (if the orientation is vertical, which is the default) or next to the other (if the orientation is horizontal) as seen in Table 15.2. Here too, you can copy either the markup in Page.xaml, or the C# code in the Page constructor and run it.

TABLE 15.2   StackPanel in XAML and in Code

```
<StackPanel x:Name="LayoutRoot"
        Orientation="Horizontal"
        Height="60">
  <Button Content="Button1"
        Margin="10" Width="80" />
  <Button Content="Button2"
        Margin="10" Width="80" />
</StackPanel>
```

```
StackPanel LayoutRoot
  = new StackPanel();
LayoutRoot.Orientation =
  Orientation.Horizontal;
LayoutRoot.Height = 60;
Button button1 = new Button();
button1.Content = "Button1";
button1.Margin = new Thickness(10);
button1.Width = 80;
Button button2 = new Button();
button2.Content = "Button2";
button2.Margin = new Thickness(10);
button2.Width = 80;

LayoutRoot.Children.Add(button1);
LayoutRoot.Children.Add(button2);
this.Content = LayoutRoot;
```

Using a StackPanel for "Flow Layout"

StackPanels are great when you want to position elements, but you don't know yet how many you will have, or what their size is going to be at runtime. For example, let's imagine an application where each button represents one word of a sentence. Whatever the sentence, and whatever the language, the layout will always flow as shown in Listing 15.5. Copy this code in a new Silverlight application, in the Page constructor (under the call to InitializeComponent) and run the application.

LISTING 15.5   Flow Layout with StackPanel

```
List<string> sentences = new List<string>();
sentences.Add("The quick brown fox jumps over the lazy dog");
sentences.Add("Le renard brun et rapide saute par dessus le chien paresseux");

StackPanel LayoutRoot = new StackPanel();
this.Content = LayoutRoot;

foreach (string sentence in sentences)
{
  StackPanel panel = new StackPanel();
  panel.Margin = new Thickness(10);
  panel.Orientation = Orientation.Horizontal;
  string[] words = sentence.Split(new char[] { ' ' });
  foreach (string word in words)
  {
    Button button = new Button();
    button.Content = word;
    panel.Children.Add(button);
  }
  LayoutRoot.Children.Add(panel);
}
this.Content = LayoutRoot;
```

With this code, you don't need to worry about calculating the number of buttons, or the buttons' width. They will be stacked nicely next to each other (see Figure 15.2).

FIGURE 15.2   The quick brown fox

Using a Grid to Align Elements

The Grid is without a doubt the most powerful panel available in Silverlight. It is flexible, yet easy to use. The most powerful feature is that you can combine Grids to build very complex layouts.

Another great thing with `Grids` is that they will resize their children if needed. That makes it a perfect container when you need to arrange elements on a surface of varying size.

Do not be afraid to use `Grids` (or any panel) even to arrange elements on small surfaces. We see later that a `Button`, for example, can have a `Grid` as its *Content*. This allows creating complex layouts even on small controls.

Before you start adding elements to a `Grid`, you need to specify its layout. This is done with the `Grid.RowDefinitions` and `Grid.ColumnDefinitions` collections as shown in Table 15.3.

> **TIP**
>
> Designing a `Grid` is easier in Expression Blend. We saw how to do this in Chapter 5, "Using Media." As usual, everything you do in Blend can be done by typing XAML, but it's a bit easier in Blend.
>
> Also, remember that in Expression Blend, you can easily switch from one type of panel to another. To do this, you can right-click on a panel in the Objects and Timeline category, and select Change Layout Type from the context menu.

TABLE 15.3   Grid Layout in XAML and in Code

```
<Grid x:Name="LayoutRoot">
  <Grid.ColumnDefinitions>
    <ColumnDefinition Width="0.4*" />
    <ColumnDefinition Width="65" />
    <ColumnDefinition Width="0.6*" />
  </Grid.ColumnDefinitions>

  <Grid.RowDefinitions>
    <RowDefinition Height="25" />
    <RowDefinition Height="*" />
    <RowDefinition Height="*" />
    <RowDefinition Height="Auto" />
  </Grid.RowDefinitions>
</Grid>
```

```
Grid LayoutRoot = new Grid();
this.Content = LayoutRoot;

ColumnDefinition col1
  = new ColumnDefinition();
col1.Width = new GridLength(0.4,
  GridUnitType.Star);
LayoutRoot.ColumnDefinitions.Add(col1);
ColumnDefinition col2
  = new ColumnDefinition();
col2.Width = new GridLength(65);
LayoutRoot.ColumnDefinitions.Add(col2);
ColumnDefinition col3
  = new ColumnDefinition();
col3.Width = new GridLength(0.6,
  GridUnitType.Star);
LayoutRoot.ColumnDefinitions.Add(col3);

RowDefinition row1
  = new RowDefinition();
row1.Height = new GridLength(25);
LayoutRoot.RowDefinitions.Add(row1);
RowDefinition row2
  = new RowDefinition();
row2.Height = new GridLength(1,
  GridUnitType.Star);
LayoutRoot.RowDefinitions.Add(row2);
```

15

TABLE 15.3   Continued

```
                                      RowDefinition row3
                                        = new RowDefinition();
                                      row3.Height = new GridLength(1,
                                        GridUnitType.Star);
                                      LayoutRoot.RowDefinitions.Add(row3);
                                      RowDefinition row4
                                        = new RowDefinition();
                                      row4.Height = new GridLength(1,
                                        GridUnitType.Auto);
                                      LayoutRoot.RowDefinitions.Add(row4);
```

A `ColumnDefinition`'s `Width` and a `RowDefinition`'s `Height` are of type `GridLength`. You can give them one of three possible values in XAML (for the C# equivalent, refer to Table 15.3):

▶ A number of pixels, making this a fixed-size column or row.

▶ The word `Auto`: The column or row automatically adapts its size to the size of the content.

▶ A fraction of a "star," for example 0.6*. This means "60% of the rest of the space after all other columns (or rows) have been computed."

For instance, let's imagine that the grid in the preceding code has a height of 400 pixels and a width of 600 pixels.

▶ The first row has a fixed height of 25 pixels.

▶ The last row has a height of `Auto` so it will adapt its height to the content. If its content is a `StackPanel` with a height of 75 pixels, then that will be the height of the row too.

▶ The second and third rows have a height of "1 star," so each of them will take a height of (400 − 25 − 75) / 2 = 150 pixels.

For the columns, the same calculation goes:

▶ The second column has a fixed `Width` of 65 pixels.

▶ The first column has a `Width` of 0.4*, so it will get 40% of the remaining space, which is (600 − 65) * 0.4 = 214 pixels.

▶ As for the second column, it gets (600 − 65) * 0.6 = 321 pixels.

Adding Elements to a `Grid` in Code-Behind

The elements can as usual be created and added to the `Grid` in code-behind. To set attached properties in C#, use the method `Grid.SetXXX`. For example, Listing 15.7 shows how the red `Ellipse` from Listing 15.6 can be added to the `Grid` in C#:

LISTING 15.7   Adding Elements to a `Grid` in Code

```
Ellipse ellipse = new Ellipse();

Grid.SetColumn(ellipse, 1);
Grid.SetColumnSpan(ellipse, 2);
Grid.SetRow(ellipse, 2);

ellipse.Fill = new SolidColorBrush(Colors.Red);
ellipse.Margin = new Thickness(20);
LayoutRoot.Children.Add(ellipse);
```

Scrolling and Bordering

Two additional containers can be used in Silverlight to enclose elements. Both of them can contain only one child (as you guessed, these two are not panels!). Since this only child may be a panel, you can end up creating the desired layout anyway.

Using a `ScrollViewer` to Scroll Big Areas

We used a `ScrollViewer` already in Chapter 6 and also in our Thumbnails application. The purpose of this container is to provide scrollbars so that the element inside the `ScrollViewer` can be bigger than the `ScrollViewer` itself.

Using a `ScrollViewer` in XAML is straightforward as shown in Listing 15.8:

> **NOTE**
>
> `ScrollViewer` is not a panel. Instead, it is a `ContentControl`, a class deriving from `Control`, which itself derives from `FrameworkElement`.
>
> `ContentControls` are a special type of control with a property named `Content`. This property, of type object, can contain anything (as long as the Silverlight framework knows how to render it). Typically, it can be a panel, another control, a string, an image, and so on.

LISTING 15.8   `ScrollViewer` in XAML

```
<ScrollViewer Width="500"
  ScrollViewer.HorizontalScrollBarVisibility="Auto"
  ScrollViewer.VerticalScrollBarVisibility="Disabled">
  <Grid x:Name="LayoutRoot"
        Width="1000">
    <!-- ... -->
  </Grid>
</ScrollViewer>
```

Or in C# (Listing 15.9):

LISTING 15.9   ScrollViewer in Code

```
ScrollViewer scrollViewer = new ScrollViewer();
scrollViewer.Width = 500;
ScrollViewer.SetHorizontalScrollBarVisibility(scrollViewer,
  ScrollBarVisibility.Auto);
ScrollViewer.SetVerticalScrollBarVisibility(scrollViewer,
  ScrollBarVisibility.Disabled);

Grid LayoutRoot = new Grid();
LayoutRoot.Width = 1000;
scrollViewer.Content = LayoutRoot;

this.Content = scrollViewer;
```

You can control the way the scrollbars are displayed with the attached properties
ScrollViewer.HorizontalScrollBarVisibility and
ScrollViewer.VerticalScrollBarVisibility.

▶ Auto—The scrollbar will only be displayed if needed. If the ScrollViewer becomes
  smaller than its content, then the scrollbar will appear.

▶ Disabled—The scrollbar will never appear. This can be useful if you want only the
  vertical scrollbar but not the horizontal one, for example.

▶ Hidden—Here too, the scrollbar will never appear. We will talk about the difference
  between Disabled and Hidden in just a minute.

▶ Visible—The scrollbar will always be displayed, even if it is not needed.

Disabling or Hiding a ScrollBar

A ScrollBar can be Hidden or Disabled. There are a couple of subtle differences between
both these settings. The most important one is that when the scrollbar is Hidden, even if it
doesn't appear, the content can still be scrolled programmatically using the methods
ScrollToVerticalOffset and ScrollToHorizontalOffset.

In practice, you will mostly use the Disabled setting, but Hidden can be useful if you want
to implement your own scrolling mechanism.

Surrounding an Element with a Border

Here is another container used to enclose an element and add some functionality: The
Border element. Its purpose is to surround an element (typically a panel) with a border.

`Border` is not a panel. In fact, `Border` derives directly from `FrameworkElement`. It is not a `ContentControl` either (unlike `ScrollViewer`). The `Border` doesn't have a `Content` property; it has a `Child` property instead. Table 15.4 shows the markup and C# code for a `Border` and its properties. As usual, you can create a new Silverlight application and try this markup (in Page.xaml) or the C# code (in the `Page` constructor).

▶ To set the color of the `Border`, use the `BorderBrush` property. Note that as usual in Silverlight, this is a brush, so you can use a `SolidColorBrush`, but you can also use a gradient brush, an image brush, a video brush, or any kind of brush.

▶ Use the `BorderThickness` property to specify how thick the `Border` must be. Since this property is of type `Thickness` (like the `Margin` property), you can set a different value for left, top, right, and bottom.

▶ You can round each corner separately using the `CornerRadius` property. Note that `CornerRadius` can be tricky. If you round a `Border`'s corners too much, the element it contains might overflow the `Border` as shown in Figure 15.5. To avoid this, you can set a smaller corner radius or use some padding (see the C# code in Table 15.4).

▶ Also very useful, a `Border` has a `Padding` property. Also defined as a `Thickness`, you can use it to set the spacing between the border and its content.

TABLE 15.4   Border in XAML and in Code

```
<Border Margin="10"
        BorderBrush="Blue"
        BorderThickness="5,2,5,2"
        CornerRadius="10,10,20,20"
        Padding="8,5,8,15"
        Background="Red">
  <Grid x:Name="LayoutRoot"
        Background="Red" />
</Border>
```

```
Border myBorder = new Border();
myBorder.Margin = new Thickness(10);
myBorder.BorderBrush
  = new SolidColorBrush(Colors.Blue);
myBorder.BorderThickness
  = new Thickness(5,2,5,2);
myBorder.CornerRadius
  = new CornerRadius(20,20,40,40);

// Avoid Grid overflow
myBorder.Padding
  = new Thickness(8,5,8,15);
myBorder.Background
  = new SolidColorBrush(Colors.Red);

Grid LayoutRoot = new Grid();
LayoutRoot.Background
  = new SolidColorBrush(Colors.Red);
myBorder.Child = LayoutRoot;

this.Content = myBorder;
```

FIGURE 15.5   Grid overflowing a Border (and the cure)

Using Pop-Ups

The last container we will study in this chapter is the Popup. As the name suggests, it is a control that pops up. It is handy when you need to display a dialog of some kind, for example, the settings for an application.

Like Border, Popup is not a panel, and not a ContentControl either, but derives directly from FrameworkElement, and uses the Child property to set its content as shown in Table 15.5.

TABLE 15.5   Popup in XAML and in Code

```
<Popup IsOpen="True"               Popup popup = new Popup();
     VerticalOffset="20"           popup.VerticalOffset = 20;
     HorizontalOffset="20">        popup.HorizontalOffset = 20;
  <Border Height="200"             popup.IsOpen = true;
       Width="200"                 Border border = new Border();
       Background="White"          border.Width = 200;
       BorderBrush="Black"         border.Height = 200;
       BorderThickness="2" />      border.Background
</Popup>                               = new SolidColorBrush(Colors.White);
                                   border.BorderBrush
                                       = new SolidColorBrush(Colors.Black);
                                   border.BorderThickness
                                     = new Thickness(2);

                                   popup.Child = border;
                                   this.Content = popup;
```

▶ To open the Popup, use the property IsOpen and set it to True.

▶ The Popup is placed on the screen using the properties VerticalOffset and HorizontalOffset. These values are relative to the top-left corner of the Silverlight application.

▶ Popups don't have any graphic attributes. A Popup without any content will remain invisible. This is why they will typically have a Border as their Child. The Border will have its Background, BorderBrush, and BorderThickness set.

▶ Even though the properties `Height`, `Width`, `VerticalAlignment`, and `HorizontalAlignment` can be set on a `Popup`, they don't currently have any effect. The only way to position a `Popup` is by using the `VerticalOffset` and `HorizontalOffset` properties.

> **NOTE**
>
> If you worked in Windows Presentation Foundation already, you will notice one big difference between WPF `Popups` and Silverlight `Popups`: In Silverlight the `Popup` can never exit the boundaries of the application. Having a "floating `Popup`" in a web application would be a security hazard.

Drawing Shapes

We already talked about shapes earlier in this book, and there is not too much to add. Shapes belong to the namespace `System.Windows.Shapes`. Their basis class is abstract, and it is named `Shape` (logically).

Since a `Shape` derives from `FrameworkElement`, it can be handled in many ways like a control. It can be animated, it can be placed in a panel, and you can also use data binding. Through their common basis class, all shapes share properties such as the following:

▶ The `Fill` property (a brush used for the `Shape`'s background)

▶ The `Stroke` (also a brush used for the external line of the `Shape`)

▶ The `StrokeThickness` (defining how thick the `Stroke` will be)

▶ Other properties used to specify the "fine look" of the shape, such as dashes, the way the strokes join, and so on.

A `Shape` can also raise events, for example, when the mouse is clicked on it (`MouseLeftButtonDown` event), or other events to collect user input and enhance your application.

There are multiple types of shapes: We already encountered the most basic ones: `Rectangle`, `Ellipse`, and `Line`. Other more complex shapes can also be used:

▶ `Polygon` is a group of connected straight lines, defined by a collection of `Points`. The shape will always be closed.

▶ `Polyline` is also a group of connected straight lines, similar to a `Polygon` except that the shape is not necessarily closed. If you want the `Polyline` to be closed, you must set the last `Point` of the collection to the same value as the first `Point`.

▶ `Path` is the Ferrari of the shapes! It can be pretty much anything, straight lines and curves. It can be closed or open, filled or not. Its shape is defined by the `Data` property.

The Data Property

To define a Path, you have to specify its Data property. This property can take either a geometry object, such as EllipseGeometry, RectangleGeometry, LineGeometry, or a group of simple geometries to form complex shapes. It can also be specified using a complex language called the Path Mini-Language.

It is outside the scope of this book to explore Paths more. Often, Paths are created with a drawing tool such as Microsoft Expression Design. For more information about shapes, Paths, and the Path Mini-Language, refer to the documentation in the SDK, or online. Note also that the shapes are the same as those used in Windows Presentation Foundation. More information can be found in books or web pages about this technology too.

Listing 15.10 and Figure 15.6 show multiple shapes on a Canvas. You can test this by creating a new Silverlight application and replace the LayoutRoot in the Page.xaml with this markup.

LISTING 15.10   Shapes

```
<Canvas Background="#FFFFFFFF" Width="400" Height="300">

  <Polygon Points="10,10 100,100 30,100"
           Stroke="Red" StrokeThickness="4"
           Fill="Blue" Canvas.Top="10" Canvas.Left="10" />

  <Polyline Points="10,10 100,100 30,100"
            Stroke="Red" StrokeThickness="4"
            Fill="Green" Canvas.Left="134" Canvas.Top="10" />

  <Path Height="135" Width="235"
        Canvas.Left="153" Canvas.Top="142"
        Data="M2,2 C151.34538,-58.838524
              238,-56.998932 235,2
              L235,88 C229.7094,37.716103
              148.02191,10.250371 2,2 z"
        Fill="Yellow" Stretch="Fill"
        Stroke="Red" StrokeThickness="4" />

  <Rectangle Height="49" Width="109"
             Canvas.Left="25" Canvas.Top="155"
             Fill="Blue" Stroke="Red"
             StrokeThickness="4"/>

  <Line X1="10" Y1="100" X2="80" Y2="30"
```

LISTING 15.10   Continued

```
        Stroke="Red" StrokeThickness="10"
        Canvas.Top="-16" Canvas.Left="238" />

  <Line X1="10" Y1="100" X2="80" Y2="30"
        Stroke="Red" StrokeThickness="10"
        StrokeDashArray="2 2" StrokeDashCap="Round"
        Canvas.Left="257" />

  <Line X1="10" Y1="100" X2="80" Y2="30"
        Stroke="Red" StrokeThickness="10"
        StrokeDashArray="3 3" StrokeDashCap="Triangle"
        Canvas.Left="276" Canvas.Top="17" />

  <Ellipse Height="54" Width="282"
           Canvas.Left="40" Canvas.Top="223"
           Fill="Green" Stroke="#FFFF0000" StrokeThickness="4" />
</Canvas>
```

FIGURE 15.6   Various types of shapes on a Canvas

Summary

After using many of Silverlight's elements in previous chapters, we got a much closer look at some of them in this chapter. Using `Grids`, `StackPanel`, or even the simple `Canvas`, adding `ScrollViewers` and `Borders`, you can create elaborate layouts for your Silverlight application. Adding shapes, you can give freedom to your artistic side and make your application look beautiful.

In Chapter 16 we continue our exploration and spend more time with Silverlight controls.

Digging Deeper into Silverlight Elements

Let's continue our exploration of Silverlight elements. After discovering the features of panels and shapes, we now talk about controls.

When Silverlight 1 was released, it didn't include any controls except the most simple one: TextBlock. To build a Button or any other interactive control, you had to use shapes and handle the mouse events. This is the reason why Silverlight video players shipped with Expression Blend are not using any controls (except, yes, TextBlock).

With Silverlight 2, on the other hand, we get a wealth of controls. Some are basic building blocks for your application, but others are sophisticated. This chapter is not a reference, so not all the properties, events, and methods are explained in detail. The SDK documentation will help you there. This chapter gives you a good insight on most of the controls included in Silverlight 2.

Understanding the Control **Class**

The Control class derives directly from FrameworkElement, which ensures a nice transition from the previous chapter! In addition to visual states and templates, a Control has a set of methods that will apply to all its descendants:

▶ A Control can be "focused," which means that it gets the keyboard's attention.

  ▶ Typically, the focus is being passed to a Control by pressing the Tab key, but you can also give the focus programmatically by using the Focus method.

▶ You can find out whether a `Control` has the focus by using the `IsFocused` property.

▶ You can also specify in which order the controls will get the focus by using the `IsTabStop` and the `TabIndex` properties.

▶ A `Control`'s look can be modified by using a set of properties such as `Background`, `BorderBrush`, `BorderThickness`, and all the font properties (we'll talk more about them in just a minute).

▶ A `Control`'s content can be aligned using the `HorizontalContentAlignment` (see Figure 16.1) and `VerticalContentAlignment` properties. These properties can take the value `Left`, `Center`, `Right`, or `Stretch` (meaning that the content will occupy the whole space within the control).

FIGURE 16.1   `HorizontalContentAlignment`

▶ A `Control`'s appearance can be totally changed using a template and a collection of states. The class has a set of methods to help you in handling those. We describe this in Chapter 17, "Using Resources, Styling and Templating" and also Chapter 19, "Creating User Controls and Custom Controls."

Enabling and Disabling Controls

Depending on the state of your application, it can be necessary to *disable* some of the controls. For example, if your application displays a collection of pictures, the button Next Picture shouldn't be active when the last picture is displayed.

Some controls (but not all) have a property named `IsEnabled`. Its default value is `true`. By setting it to `false`, you prevent any activation of the control by the user. A slightly different style is used when the control is disabled, to inform the user (see Figure 16.2).

FIGURE 16.2   Enabled and disabled `Button` and `CheckBox`

Styling and Templating Controls

One fascinating feature of Silverlight (and Windows Presentation Foundation) is the ability to modify a control's appearance without changing its functionality. This is done using a combination of *styles* and *templates*. We talk about this in Chapters 17 and 19, but as a preparation, take a look at Corrina Barber's control templates for Silverlight at http://blogs.msdn.com/corrinab/archive/2008/06/16/8602865.aspx.

By redrawing the controls, but keeping their core functionality untouched, it is possible to create *skins* for your application—that is, a set of styles and templates that redefine the looks of your application (see Figure 16.3).

FIGURE 16.3   Flat skin and Red skin

About Fonts

The default font for all controls is called Portable User Interface. It is in fact a composite font based on the Lucida font, and on other East Asian fonts. You can set any of the following fonts, and they will automatically be supported by Silverlight: Arial, Comic Sans MS, Courier New, Georgia, Lucida, Times New Roman, Trebuchet MS, Verdana and Webdings.

If you want another font, you must include it in the XAP file for download. We see how to do that in Chapter 17.

> **TIP**
>
> The SDK documentation we installed in Chapter 1, "Introducing Silverlight," contains a wealth of information about TextBlocks, text, and fonts. Search for "Text and Fonts (Silverlight 2)."

Discovering Basic Controls

Let's talk shortly about the most basic Silverlight controls. We actually used some of them in previous chapters, so we are already familiar with some of their features.

Presenting and Inputting Text

The most basic interaction between an application and the user is text. The application will *output* information, and the user will *input* data if needed. This section talks about these controls that may seem basic at first, but are in fact quite sophisticated.

TextBlock

`TextBlock` is the most basic of all controls and fulfills only one goal: presenting text to the user. Note that even this simple control can display complex content: By adding *inline elements* such as instances of `Run` or `LineBreak`, you can structure your text. Each `Run` instance can have a different font setting! We test this with the code in Table 16.1. You can copy the markup inside the `LayoutRoot` `Grid`, or copy the C# code inside the `Page` constructor, after the call to `InitializeComponent`, and run the application.

TABLE 16.1   TextBlock in XAML and in Code

```
<TextBlock FontSize="32">
  <Run Text="The quick "
       FontStyle="Italic" />
  <Run Text="brown fox "
```

```
TextBlock textBlock = new TextBlock();
textBlock.FontSize = 32;
Run run1 = new Run();
run1.Text = "The quick ";
```

TABLE 16.1   Continued

```
     FontFamily="Courier New"          run1.FontStyle = FontStyles.Italic;
     FontWeight="Bold" />              textBlock.Inlines.Add(run1);
 <LineBreak />
 <Run Text="jumps over the lazy dog"  Run run2 = new Run();
     Foreground="#FFFF0000"            run2.Text = "brown fox ";
     FontFamily="Comic Sans MS"        run2.FontFamily
     FontSize="14" />                    = new FontFamily("Courier New");
</TextBlock>                           run2.FontWeight = FontWeights.Bold;
                                       textBlock.Inlines.Add(run2);

                                       textBlock.Inlines.Add(
                                         new LineBreak());

                                       Run run3 = new Run();
                                       run3.Text = "jumps over the lazy dog";
                                       run3.Foreground
                                         = new SolidColorBrush(Colors.Red);
                                       run3.FontFamily
                                         = new FontFamily("Comic Sans MS");
                                       run3.FontSize = 14;
                                       textBlock.Inlines.Add(run3);
                                       this.Content = textBlock;
```

If you want your TextBlock to automatically wrap when its container becomes too small, set the property TextWrapping to Wrap. Note that even though the default value for this property is NoWrap, Expression Blend automatically sets it to Wrap when you add a new TextBlock.

TextBox
The TextBox is used whenever the user must enter text into the application. Note that unlike HTML, there is only one control for that purpose, but it can accept multiline input (like the HTML textarea control) by using the AcceptsReturn property.

▶ In multiline mode, it might make sense to display scrollbars. These are controlled by the two properties HorizontalScrollBarVisibility and VerticalScrollBarVisibility, which we know from our study of the ScrollViewer in Chapter 15, "Digging into Silverlight Elements."

▶ Other properties that we studied for the `TextBlock` also apply here, for example, `TextWrapping`, `FontFamily`, `FontSize`, `FontWeight`, and so on.

▶ The property `IsReadOnly` is useful if you want to allow the application's user to copy some text, but not to modify it.

▶ To find out which text the user selected, use the properties `SelectionStart` and `SelectionLength` in code. These two indexes can be used together with the method `Substring` on the `Text` property of the `TextBox`.

```
string selectedText = textBox.Text.Substring(textBox.SelectionStart,
    textBox.SelectionLength);
```

Discovering the `ButtonBase`

What do a `Button`, `Checkbox`, and `RadioButton` have in common? When you click on them something happens. This is enough to make them share a base class: the `ButtonBase`.

▶ This class defines one important event: the `Click` event. By handling this event, you define what the reaction of the application must be.

▶ `ButtonBase` derives from `ContentControl`. All subclasses get a `Content` property that is of type `object`. You can store anything in the `Content` property, for example, a `string` (which will become the text of the control), but also an image, any control, or even a panel containing other controls.

▶ You can use the property `ClickMode` to define when the `Click` event must be raised: `Press` raises the event when the mouse is pressed down, `Release` when it is not pressed anymore, and `Hover` when the mouse just passes over the control.

▶ Other properties help you to find out what the state of the button is—for example, `IsFocused`, `IsPressed`, `IsMouseOver`. Like all the properties starting with the `Is` prefix, these are boolean values.

> **WARNING**
>
> You won't find these "Is" properties in the XAML editor. Why not? They are read-only, and cannot be set! You can only access them from the code-behind.

Button, HyperlinkButton, RepeatButton, and ToggleButton

Let's talk about four important controls deriving from `ButtonBase` and thus sharing its functionality:

▶ A `Button` is pretty obvious. Click it and something happens. To specify what, handle the `Click` event. It's as simple as can be.

▶ The `HyperlinkButton` looks just like an HTML hyperlink. You can also simulate this by using a `TextBlock` and handling its events. However, using the `HyperlinkButton` is actually a clever move. Since it's a `Control`, it has states (`MouseOver`, `Unfocused`, `Focused`, `Pressed`, and so on) for which you can easily create a different look and feel, for example, in Blend. We talk about that in later chapters.

▶ A `RepeatButton` also has a `Click` event. The difference is that, if the user holds down the mouse button, the `Click` event will be raised again in a rapid succession until the mouse button is released.

You can control the timing with the `Delay` (milliseconds before rapid succession starts) and the `Interval` property (milliseconds between two `Click` events).

▶ Finally, a `ToggleButton` is a button that switches between two states (toggled or untoggled) when you press it. The visual aspect of the button changes to notify the user. The state of the control is saved in the `IsChecked` property.

In fact, the `ToggleButton` has a 3rd state. If you look at the `ToggleButton` class in the SDK documentation, you will see that the property `IsChecked` is a nullable boolean (we talked about them briefly in Chapter 10, "Progressing with .NET"). It means that this value can be `true`, `false` or `null`. In that last case, the `ToggleButton` is said to be in indeterminate state.

CheckBox **and** RadioButton

`CheckBox` and `RadioButton` are derived from `ToggleButton`. Since these controls all switch between a toggled and untoggled state (and don't forget the indeterminate state), and since the only difference between the states is really just a matter of graphics design, it makes sense to reuse the capabilities of the `ToggleButton`.

▶ A `CheckBox` is really just a `ToggleButton`. It adds strictly no functionality; it just looks different.

▶ A `RadioButton` is similar to a `CheckBox`. There is one big difference though: The `GroupName` property. Setting this property adds the `RadioButton` to a group. Only one button in each group can be checked. Note that the buttons of the same group are mutually exclusive wherever they are placed in the user control. They don't need to be all in the same panel, for example.

Scrolling and Dragging

Besides reading and inputting text, and clicking on elements, the user needs to move things around. Let's see how controls can help you there.

Scrollbar **and** Slider

These two controls are derived from another class named `RangeBase`. Since `RangeBase` itself derives from `Control`, the `Scrollbar` and the `Slider` controls have all the properties we discussed previously. In addition, the `RangeBase` class defines properties to help these controls fulfill their tasks.

▶ The controls deriving from `RangeBase` can have a `Value` comprised between a `Minimum` and a `Maximum`.

▶ The `LargeChange` and `SmallChange` properties define by how much the `Value` changes when corresponding areas of the control are pressed (see Figure 16.4).

▶ Both the `Slider` and the `Scrollbar` can also be used vertically. This is controlled by the `Orientation` property. Note, however, that this property is not available on the `RangeBase` basis class.

▶ The `Slider` has an additional property named `IsDirectionReversed`. By default, when the `Slider` is dragged to the right (or down, if it is vertical), the `Value` is increased.

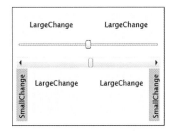

FIGURE 16.4   `Slider` and `ScrollBar`, `LargeChange` and `SmallChange`

If you set this property to `true`, the `Value` will be increased in the other direction.

Understanding Value Coercion

When any object has a `Value` comprised between a `Maximum` and a `Minimum`, the developer needs to think of the following issues:

▶ What happens when the `Minimum` is set to a number higher than the current `Value`?

▶ What happens when the `Minimum` is set to a number higher than the current `Maximum`?

In the `Scrollbar` and `Slider` controls, Silverlight uses *coercion* to handle these issues. Let's imagine a scenario:

1. `Minimum` is set to 0, `Value` to 5, `Maximum` to 10.

2. The application sets `Minimum` to 20.

3. Automatically, `Value` and `Maximum` are set to 20, to comply with the ground rule *Value and Maximum may not be smaller than Minimum*.

4. In a second operation, the application attempts to set `Maximum` to 15. This is hurting the ground rule, so the actual value remains set to 20.

5. Later, the application sets `Minimum` to 8.

6. The framework *remembers* that `Maximum` should be set to 15. This doesn't hurt the ground rule anymore, so the framework allows it.

7. The framework *remembers* that Value was set to 5 before. This still hurts the ground rule, however, so Value is set to 8.

Using coercion to force an application to respect a set of ground rules ensures that the properties can be set in any order. This is one of the important conditions to enable XAML to work: The properties of a control can be set in any order, and yet the rules are ensured.

Thumb

The Scrollbar and the Slider we just saw have a middle part that the user can *drag* on either side. This functionality is implemented by a Thumb control.

Deriving directly from Control, the Thumb class is placed into the namespace System.Windows.Controls.Primitives. Even though you can use a Thumb directly in your application, it is typically used as a *part* of other controls (such as the Scrollbar). This is typical from Silverlight, where we speak of the *parts and states* model.

To drag a Thumb control, you must handle its DragDelta event. You can reposition the Thumb using the Canvas.Top and Canvas.Left properties (if the parent is a Canvas), or using the Margin property (on a Grid).

To test this, create a new application and copy the markup in Listing 16.1 into Page.xaml, replacing the existing LayoutRoot Grid.

LISTING 16.1   Dragging a Thumb, XAML Markup

```
<Grid x:Name="LayoutRoot" Background="White">
  <Grid.RowDefinitions>
    <RowDefinition Height="*" />
    <RowDefinition Height="25" />
  </Grid.RowDefinitions>

  <Thumb x:Name="MyThumb" Width="50" Height="50"
         DragStarted="MyThumb_DragStarted"
         DragDelta="MyThumb_DragDelta"
         DragCompleted="MyThumb_DragCompleted"
         HorizontalAlignment="Left" VerticalAlignment="Top" />

  <TextBlock Grid.Row="1">
    <Run Text="Events: " />
    <Run x:Name="EventRun" FontStyle="Italic"/>
  </TextBlock>
</Grid>
```

Then copy the code in Listing 16.2 into the Page class, in Page.xaml.cs. Once this is done, build and run the application (you will have to add a using directive) and drag the Thumb control around using the mouse.

LISTING 16.2   Dragging a Thumb, C# Code

```
private void MyThumb_DragStarted(object sender, DragStartedEventArgs e)
{
  EventRun.Text = "DragStarted";
}
private void MyThumb_DragDelta(object sender, DragDeltaEventArgs e)
{
  EventRun.Text = "DragDelta";
  double marginLeft = MyThumb.Margin.Left;
  double marginTop = MyThumb.Margin.Top;
  MyThumb.Margin = new Thickness(marginLeft + e.HorizontalChange,
    marginTop + e.VerticalChange, 0, 0);
}
private void MyThumb_DragCompleted(object sender, DragCompletedEventArgs e)
{
  EventRun.Text = "DragCompleted";
}
```

Adding the System.Windows.Controls Assembly

Some of the new controls in Silverlight 2 are defined in an external assembly named System.Windows.Controls. This assembly can be added manually to the Silverlight application using the following steps.

1. In Visual Studio, right-click on the Silverlight project and choose Add Reference... from the context menu.

2. In the Add Reference dialog, on the .NET tab, select the assembly System.Windows.Controls and click OK.

3. Inside the XAML file where you want to use the control, add an XML namespace to the UserControl tag, for example:

```
<UserControl x:Class="SilverlightApplication2.Page"
  xmlns="http://schemas.microsoft.com/winfx/2006/xaml/presentation"
  xmlns:x="http://schemas.microsoft.com/winfx/2006/xaml"
  xmlns:controls="clr-namespace:System.Windows.Controls;assembly=System.Win-
dows.Controls"
  Width="400" Height="300">
```

The controls prefix you added in step 3 must be used when you reference the control located in System.Windows.Controls.dll. We will use this assembly a few times in the course of this chapter.

Alternatively, you can drag and drop the UI element from the Visual Studio toolbox on the XAML markup, at the position where you want to include the element. This will automatically take care of steps 1 to 3 above.

Note that you can find in the SDK documentation in which assembly each control is placed. For example, this information is available on top of the GridSplitter class page.

GridSplitter
When a Grid has multiple rows (or columns) you would often like to be able to resize them. It's easy with a GridSplitter (see Figure 16.5). You can test it yourself by copying the markup in Listing 16.3 in a new Silverlight application's Page.xaml and running the application.

FIGURE 16.5   Grid with a GridSplitter

LISTING 16.3   Using a GridSplitter

```
<Grid x:Name="LayoutRoot"
      Background="White">

  <Grid.RowDefinitions>
    <RowDefinition Height="*" />
    <RowDefinition Height="10" />
    <RowDefinition Height="*" />
  </Grid.RowDefinitions>

  <Rectangle Fill="Orange" />
  <controls:GridSplitter Grid.Row="1" Height="Auto" Width="Auto"
                         HorizontalAlignment="Stretch" />
  <Rectangle Fill="Yellow" Grid.Row="2" />
</Grid>
```

The easiest way to use a GridSplitter is to dedicate a whole Grid cell (or Row, or Column) to it, and to set its dimension so that it is clear in which direction the other cells should be resized. Note, however, that it is also possible to place the GridSplitter in a cell shared by other elements. In that case, the direction in which the GridSplitter acts is determined by its size, its alignment, and so on. For more information about the GridSplitter and its features, check the SDK documentation.

Presenting Media

We studied the two media controls Image and MediaElement in detail in Chapter 5, "Using Media," and later chapters. One interesting thing to note is that, even though Image and MediaElement are placed in the namespace System.Windows.Controls, they are not actually deriving from Control. In fact, they derive directly from FrameworkElement. This means that they don't enjoy the added functionality that we described earlier in this chapter.

But in fact, it doesn't matter. Since Image and MediaElement can be placed within a Control (for example a Button), and since the Button's template can be modified at will (for example so that only the `Image` appears), you can also tab through the "image buttons," check when they get the focus, execute a `Click` event, and so on. We'll talk about templates soon.

Picking Dates with Calendar and DatePicker

The purpose of these two controls is specialized and easy to understand: They help pick a date.

Using the Calendar

The `Calendar` displays the current date in a month view. The user can select a date that the application can read and use. Note that the Calendar control is included in the assembly System.Windows.Controls.dll we discussed earlier. This assembly must be referenced, as explained in the section "Adding the System.Windows.Controls Assembly" in this chapter.

▶ The `Calendar` control can display various modes. Use the `DisplayMode` property. When the `Calendar` is displayed, the user can switch from `Month` to `Year`, and from `Year` to `Decade` by clicking on the `Calendar`'s title (see Figure 16.6). The opposite way goes by a click on a year, then on a month.

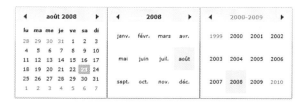

FIGURE 16.6   Calendar with DisplayMode Month, Year, and Decade

▶ The range of dates displayed by the `Calendar` is set by the properties `DisplayDateStart` and `DisplayDateEnd`.

▶ The date currently displayed in the `Calendar` can be set or read with the property `DisplayDate`. Note that an error occurs if `DisplayDate` is not included between `DisplayDateStart` and `DisplayDateEnd`.

▶ The property `FirstDayOfWeek` tells the `Calendar` when the week starts for the current user (depending on its regional settings).

▶ The mode of selection can also be customized using the `SelectionMode`. The possible values are

　　▶ None—No date can be selected.

　　▶ SingleDate—This is the default. Only one date can be selected and is stored in the `SelectedDate` property.

- ▶ SingleRange—A period of time between two dates is selected. The chosen dates are stored in the property SelectedDates (with an "s").

- ▶ MultipleRange—Multiple periods of time are selected. Here too, the SelectedDates property stores the chosen dates.

▶ Note that the property SelectedDate can also be used to set the Calendar to a different date, for example, when you initialize it. It must be included between DisplayDateStart and DisplayDateEnd. It may not be one of the dates into the BlackoutDate collection (see the last item in this list).

▶ If you don't want today's date (or month or year) to be highlighted, set the property IsTodayHighlighted to false.

▶ You can add dates to the BlackoutDates collection. All the dates within this collection will be displayed disabled in the Calendar.

▶ The Calendar control is automatically *localized*, that is, adapted to the user's regional settings. In Figure 16.6, notice how the names of days and months are in French.

WARNING

There are two Calendar classes in Silverlight. One is the control that we discussed in this section. The other (System.Globalization.Calendar) is a helper class to help you handle dates, weeks, months, and so on. Don't confuse them when you check the documentation.

Using the DatePicker

A Calendar all alone can be useful, but in some case what you really need is a DatePicker—a control that uses a Calendar to pick a date and display it (see Figure 16.7). This control is also included in the System.Windows. Controls assembly. Refer to the section titled "Adding the System.Windows. Controls Assembly" in this chapter for

FIGURE 16.7   DatePicker in closed and open state

more information about adding a reference to this assembly to your application.

▶ Most of the DatePicker's properties are actually mapped to the Calendar properties. We saw them all in the previous section.

▶ In addition, you can control the DatePicker popup with the property IsDropDownOpen. By setting it to true, you can force the Calendar to open programmatically.

Catching Errors

Since the `DatePicker` has a `TextBox`, the user can enter any text she wants, and the `DatePicker` will attempt to convert it into a valid `DateTime`. This is not always possible: The user may type meaningless text, enter a typo, or use a format that is not recognized.

The default behavior when an error occurs is that the previous valid date will simply be displayed again. You can change this by handling the `DateValidationError` event. To test this, create a new Silverlight application and enter the markup in Listing 16.4 in the Page.xaml.

LISTING 16.4   Using a `DatePicker` and Catching Errors, XAML Markup

```
<StackPanel x:Name="LayoutRoot" Background="White">
  <controls:DatePicker Width="200" Margin="10"
    DateValidationError="DatePicker_DateValidationError"
    HorizontalAlignment="Center" />
  <TextBlock x:Name="ErrorDisplay"
            Foreground="Red" Margin="10"
            HorizontalAlignment="Center"/>
</StackPanel>
```

Then, open Page.xaml.cs and implement the event handler in the `Page` class (see Listing 16.5):

LISTING 16.5   Using a `DatePicker` and Catching Errors, C# Code

```
private void DatePicker_DateValidationError(object sender,
  DatePickerDateValidationErrorEventArgs e)
{
  ErrorDisplay.Text = "This is not a valid date: " + e.Text;
  //e.ThrowException = true;
}
```

By setting the property `e.ThrowException` to true, you raise an `Exception` (an error) in the application. If you don't handle this error somewhere in the application, it will crash. By default, the error will not be raised. We will talk about `Exceptions` and how to handle them in Chapter 23, "Placing Cross-domain Requests and Handling Exceptions."

Writing with Ink

The `InkPresenter` control allows you to draw strokes on a surface. This element derives from `Canvas` (so it's not a control, but a panel). You can set its `Background`, its size (or leave it to `Auto` if you want it to fill the whole surface), and so on. What's special about the `InkPresenter` is that it contains a collection of `Stroke` elements. Each one is a tiny graphic element drawn on the `InkPresenter`. When it is created, you can specify its color, `Width`, and `Height`. Each `Stroke` contains a collection of `StylusPoint` elements.

> **WARNING**
>
> If you check the documentation, you'll see that StylusPoint is not a class, but a structure. In .NET, a structure is a kind of lightweight class.

With today's input devices becoming more sophisticated, such as tablet devices, tablet PCs with touch screens, and the multi touch screens such as the Surface computer made by Microsoft, alternative user interfaces will become more and more popular. The `InkPresenter` plays an important role in this new landscape.

Making a Simple Drawing Application

We are going to use the knowledge gained in this chapter and in Chapter 15 to build a small but interesting application that allows the user to draw on the computer screen. The functionality of the application is basic: The user can choose a pen color and size, and then draw on the `InkPresenter`.

Preparing the Scene

Let's create a scene in XAML for our application with the following steps:

1. Create a new Silverlight application in Visual Studio named SilverlightDraw. Then open the Page.xaml and set the `Grid` LayoutRoot as in Listing 16.6:

LISTING 16.6   SilverlightDraw, Setting the Scene

```
<Grid x:Name="LayoutRoot" Background="#FFFEFE00"
      MouseLeave="LayoutRoot_MouseLeave">
  <InkPresenter x:Name="MyInkPresenter" Background="#FFFFCF77" Cursor="Stylus"
              MouseLeftButtonDown="InkPresenter_MouseLeftButtonDown"
              MouseMove="InkPresenter_MouseMove"
              MouseLeftButtonUp="InkPresenter_MouseLeftButtonUp" />
</Grid>
```

   ▶ Notice the mouse events that we will handle in code later.

   ▶ We set the `Cursor` property to `Stylus`. This gives the cursor the shape of a dot, with which it is easier to draw.

2. Now create a settings section, in the form of a `Popup` containing `Sliders`. First create the `Popup` below the `InkPresenter`, and position it as in Listing 16.7. Copy this markup inside the LayoutRoot `Grid`.

LISTING 16.7   Settings Popup

```
<Popup x:Name="SettingsPopup"
       HorizontalOffset="10" VerticalOffset="10">
</Popup>
```

3. Within the `Popup`, we need a `Border` to serve as a visual background for the settings controls. This `Border` will host a `Grid` for the layout (Listing 16.8).

LISTING 16.8   Settings Border and Grid

```
<Border BorderBrush="#FF000000" BorderThickness="2,2,2,2"
        Width="180" Height="200">
  <Grid>
    <Grid.RowDefinitions>
      <RowDefinition Height="*" />
      <RowDefinition Height="*" />
      <RowDefinition Height="*" />
      <RowDefinition Height="*" />
    </Grid.RowDefinitions>
    <Grid.ColumnDefinitions>
      <ColumnDefinition Width="0.3*" />
      <ColumnDefinition Width="0.7*" />
    </Grid.ColumnDefinitions>
  </Grid>
</Border>
```

Notice that the `Border` doesn't have its `Background` property set. If we leave it like this, it will be transparent. However, we set the `Background` in code-behind to add a nice effect when we set the stroke's color.

4. Within the `Grid` located inside the `Border`, copy the two controls in Listing 16.9. In addition to a label marked "R" for red, we place a `Slider` control going from 0 (the default value) to 255 (the decimal value for $FF_{[16]}$).

LISTING 16.9   Color Slider

```
<TextBlock Text="R:" Margin="0,0,5,0" Grid.Row="0"
           HorizontalAlignment="Right" VerticalAlignment="Center" />
<Slider x:Name="ColorRSlider"
        LargeChange="10" SmallChange="1"
        Maximum="255" Value="255"
        ValueChanged="ColorSlider_ValueChanged"
        Margin="0,0,5,0" Grid.Column="1" Grid.Row="0" />
```

16

5. Copy the same markup again, but this time change the text to G: (for green). Set the Grid.Row property to 1 for both the TextBlock and the Slider. Name the Slider ColorGSlider.

6. Finally, copy the same markup a third time, this time for B: (blue) and set Grid.Row to 2 for both controls. Name the Slider ColorBSlider. Notice that all three Sliders (R, G, and B) use the same event handler named ColorSlider_ValueChanged:.

7. We need a last Slider for the Stroke's Width and Height. We use only one Slider for both dimensions to keep it simple (Listing 16.10).

LISTING 16.10   Size Slider

```
<TextBlock Text="Size:" Margin="0,0,5,0" Grid.Row="3"
          HorizontalAlignment="Right"
          VerticalAlignment="Center" />
<Slider x:Name="SizeSlider"
        LargeChange="2" SmallChange="1"
        Minimum="2" Maximum="20" Value="2"
        ValueChanged="SizeSlider_ValueChanged"
        Margin="0,0,5,0" Grid.Column="1" Grid.Row="3" />
```

8. The last control we need is a Button to show the settings Popup on the screen. Place the markup in Listing 16.11 outside the Popup control, but still inside the Grid LayoutRoot.

LISTING 16.11   Settings Button

```
<Button x:Name="SettingsButton" Height="30" Width="30"
        HorizontalAlignment="Left" VerticalAlignment="Top"
        Margin="10,10,0,0" Cursor="Hand"
        Click="SettingsButton_Click" />
```

9. Before we start writing C# code, remove the Height and Width properties on the top UserControl, to make the application fill the whole space.

Handling the Events

If you run the application at this stage, the initial animation (Figure 7.5) will never disappear and you get an error on the web page. Depending on the web browser you use and on your settings, the error might appear as a yellow warning sign in the bottom left corner on the web browser (Internet Explorer). By clicking on this sign, you get more information.

In Firefox, the error is more difficult to find: You need to display the JavaScript console by typing the text `javascript:` (including the colon) in the browser's location bar, and click enter.

The cause of the error is that the XAML markup references event handlers that don't exist in code yet. We will implement them now.

Drawing a New Stroke

First we will let the user draw on the presenter, which is the main purpose of the application, with the following steps:

1. Open Page.xaml.cs and a private attribute to the `Page` class:

   ```
   private Stroke _currentStroke = null;
   ```

2. In the `Page` constructor, below the call to `InitializeComponent`, add the initialization code in Listing 16.12:

LISTING 16.12   Initialization Code

```
Color strokeColor = GetColor();
SettingsButton.Background = new SolidColorBrush(strokeColor);
(SettingsPopup.Child as Border).Background = SettingsButton.Background;
```

> ▶ This code uses a private method named `GetColor` (we define it later) to get the color corresponding to the three color `Sliders`.

> ▶ We then use this color as the `Background` of the `SettingsButton` (in the top-left corner) and of the `SettingsPopup`.

3. The private method `GetColor` is getting the values of the three `Sliders`, and using it to build a new `Color` and to return it. Note that we fix the Alpha channel to 255 (fully opaque). Copy the code in Listing 16.13 in the `Page` class, under the `Page` constructor. To make sure that there are no mistakes, you can build the application, but don't run it yet.

LISTING 16.13   Method GetColor

```
private Color GetColor()
{
  if (ColorRSlider == null
    || ColorGSlider == null
    || ColorBSlider == null)
  {
    return Colors.Black;
  }

  Color strokeColor = Color.FromArgb(255,
    (byte) ColorRSlider.Value,
```

16

LISTING 16.13   Continued

```
    (byte) ColorGSlider.Value,
    (byte) ColorBSlider.Value);
  return strokeColor;
}
```

4. Let's now handle what happens when the mouse is pressed down on the `InkPresenter`. Copy Listing 16.14 in the `Page` class, after the code we entered in step 3. Here too, you should be able to build the application.

LISTING 16.14   Event Handler InkPresenter_MouseLeftButtonDown

```
 1  private void InkPresenter_MouseLeftButtonDown(object sender,
 2    MouseButtonEventArgs e)
 3  {
 4    SettingsPopup.IsOpen = false;
 5    _currentStroke = new Stroke(e.StylusDevice.GetStylusPoints(MyInkPresenter));
 6    _currentStroke.DrawingAttributes = new DrawingAttributes();
 7
 8    Color strokeColor = GetColor();
 9    _currentStroke.DrawingAttributes.Color = strokeColor;
10    _currentStroke.DrawingAttributes.OutlineColor = strokeColor;
11
12    _currentStroke.DrawingAttributes.Height =
13      _currentStroke.DrawingAttributes.Width = SizeSlider.Value;
14    MyInkPresenter.Strokes.Add(_currentStroke);
15  }
```

▶ On line 4, we close the `SettingsPopup` every time the mouse is clicked. Note that most of the time, this is not necessary because it will already be closed. However, this simple operation makes it unnecessary to check every time whether the `Popup` is open or not.

▶ Line 5 creates a new `Stroke` instance, adds the current `StylusPoints` to it and saves it in the private attribute we declared in step 1. Then we create its `DrawingAttributes` on line 6.

▶ On lines 8 to 10, we get the color corresponding to the three `Sliders`, and we set the `Stroke`'s color. Note that each `Stroke` can have a different outline color. In our case we set both to the same value.

> **N O T E**
>
> The fact that each `MouseEventArgs` (and thus `MouseButtonEventArgs`) contains information about the `StylusDevice` is the key to having an `InkPresenter` work correctly. It shows that ink technology is an intrinsic part of the Silverlight technology.

> ▶ On lines 12 and 13 we set the Height and Width of the Stroke to the value of the SizeSlider.

> ▶ Finally we add the new Stroke to the InkPresenter (line 14).

5. We must now handle what happens when the mouse moves. It's in fact easy: Since we get a MouseEventArgs parameter and since we saw that it contains information about the StylusDevice, we can simply add this to the current Stroke. Note that this is only done if the mouse is pressed, which is made evident by the value of the _currentStroke attribute as shown in Listing 16.15. Add this code below the method we implemented in step 4.

LISTING 16.15   Event Handler InkPresenter_MouseMove

```
private void InkPresenter_MouseMove(object sender,
  MouseEventArgs e)
{
  if (_currentStroke != null)
  {
    _currentStroke.StylusPoints.Add(e.StylusDevice.GetStylusPoints
➥(MyInkPresenter));
  }
}
```

6. We must end drawing sometimes: When the mouse button is not pressed anymore, or when the mouse cursor leaves the Grid, we set the Stroke to null, which ends the action of the MouseMove event handler. The code in Listing 16.16 comes below the method we implemented in step 5.

LISTING 16.16   Event Handlers InkPresenter_MouseLeftButtonUp and LayoutRoot_MouseLeave

```
private void InkPresenter_MouseLeftButtonUp(object sender, MouseButtonEventArgs e)
{
  _currentStroke = null;
}
private void LayoutRoot_MouseLeave(object sender, MouseEventArgs e)
{
  _currentStroke = null;
}
```

The current Stroke has already been added to the InkPresenter, so any change made to it is saved in memory already. When you work with objects in C#, you work with references to them. There may be multiple references to the same object in memory. Working with

the same object from multiple "clients" (adding points to the Stroke, drawing the same
Stroke on the screen) is an illustration of the advantages of object-oriented programming.

Handling the Settings

We still have three events to handle with the following steps:

1. First open the SettingsPopup when the SettingsButton is clicked. The code in
   Listing 16.17 comes inside the Page class:

LISTING 16.17   Event Handler SettingsButton_Click

```
private void SettingsButton_Click(object sender,
  RoutedEventArgs e)
{
  SettingsPopup.IsOpen = true;
}
```

2. Handle what happens when the user moves the slider's cursors. Remember that all
   three color sliders use the same event handler in Listing 16.18, to be copied inside
   the Page class.

LISTING 16.18   Event Handler ColorSlider_ValueChanged

```
private void ColorSlider_ValueChanged(object sender,
  RoutedPropertyChangedEventArgs<double> e)
{
  if (SettingsButton == null ¦¦ SettingsPopup == null)
  {
    return;
  }
  Color strokeColor = GetColor();
  SettingsButton.Background = new SolidColorBrush(strokeColor);
  (SettingsPopup.Child as Border).Background = SettingsButton.Background;
}
```

▶ This handler checks whether the UI elements are already created (if not, their
  value is null and we exit without doing anything). This is needed, because the
  Silverlight framework calls this event handler as soon as the Sliders are
  created. However, the rest of the UI may not be ready yet.

▶ Then we use the method GetColor to calculate the current color, and we set
  the button's background as well as the Popup's border's Background to this new
  color. This gives the user feedback about the color he picks.

3. The last Slider sets the size of the Stroke. Here too, we check whether the UI is
   ready, and then we act on the Popup's border's thickness for feedback. This is Listing
   16.19, to be copied at the end of the Page class.

LISTING 16.19   Event Handler SizeSlider_ValueChanged

```
private void SizeSlider_ValueChanged(object sender,
  RoutedPropertyChangedEventArgs<double> e)
{
  if (SettingsPopup == null)
  {
    return;
  }
  Thickness borderSize = new Thickness(SizeSlider.Value);
  (SettingsPopup.Child as Border).BorderThickness = borderSize;
}
```

Setting the Popup's border's attributes like that is dangerous. What happens if the designer decides to change the way the UI is built and removes the Border, or adds something between the Border and the Popup? The code will fail with an error!! In Chapter 18, "Data Binding and Using Data Controls," we see a much better way to handle this scenario! This is why you should save this application somewhere, and we will reopen it in two chapters.

Running the Application

That's it; we're done. Run the application from Visual Studio, and see how you can now draw on the screen (Figure 16.8, with a drawing courtesy of the artist Gigi Lee!). This application is basic, and already we get ideas on how to make it better: An Undo operation is really needed, setting the InkPresenter's background color would be nice, using a color picker instead of the three Sliders would make it easier to choose a color, and so on. Maybe you also have your own improvements you want to add. Don't hesitate!

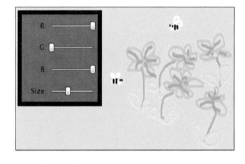

FIGURE 16.8   Silverlight Draw application

Presenting Data with ItemsControls

Often in an application, you need to present data to the user, but you don't know exactly how many data items you will get. For example, you place a request with Flickr for images tagged with the word "Silverlight." The service can send 0, 1, 100, or more items as a response. Also, there are multiple data sources. We mentioned XML data already. There are also services, databases, files, objects collections, and so on.

The best way to display a variable number of data items is to use a control derived from ItemsControl. A couple of them are included in Silverlight 2, such as the ListBox that we study in Chapter 18. In this section, we talk about another class deriving from ItemsControl.

Using the `TabControl`

A `TabControl` doesn't look anything like a `ListBox`, but both display a variable collection of items. For the `TabControl`, the items are of type `TabItem`.

That a `TabControl` and a `ListBox` share functionality but look completely different is another example of the separation of appearance and functionality, one of the core principles of Silverlight.

Note that a `TabItem` is not a panel but a `ContentControl`. To set a `TabItem`'s content, simply set its `Content` property. The content may, as usual, be anything, including a panel with multiple children. The markup in Table 16.2 can be copied into a new Silverlight application, into the `LayoutRoot` in the Page.xaml file. Or you can copy the C# code in the Page constructor in Page.xaml.cs. Then run the application. This control is also included in the System.Windows.Controls assembly that must be added manually to the Silverlight application, as explained earlier in this chapter.

TABLE 16.2   TabControl in XAML and in Code

```
<controls:TabControl>                    TabControl tabControl
  <controls:TabItem Header="Oranges">       = new TabControl();
    <Grid Background="Orange">
      <!--...-->                           TabItem tab1 = new TabItem();
    </Grid>                                tab1.Header = "Oranges";
  </controls:TabItem>                      Grid orangePanel = new Grid();
                                           orangePanel.Background
  <controls:TabItem                          = new SolidColorBrush(Colors.Orange);
    Header="Red roses">                    tab1.Content = orangePanel;
    <StackPanel Background="Red">          tabControl.Items.Add(tab1);
      <!--...-->
    </StackPanel>                          TabItem tab2 = new TabItem();
  </controls:TabItem>                      tab2.Header = "Red roses";
</controls:TabControl>                     StackPanel redPanel = new StackPanel();
                                           redPanel.Background
                                             = new SolidColorBrush(Colors.Red);
                                           tab2.Content = redPanel;
                                           tabControl.Items.Add(tab2);
                                           this.Content = tabControl;
```

▶ The `TabItems` are added to the `TabControl`'s `Items` collection. This is typical of a class deriving from `ItemsControl`.

▶ To set on which side the tabs will be placed, use the property `TabStripPlacement`. It can take the value `Dock.Left`, `Dock.Top`, `Dock.Right`, or `Dock.Bottom` (see Figure 16.9). The default is `Dock.Top`.

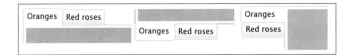

FIGURE 16.9   TabStripPlacement Dock.Top, Dock.Bottom, and Dock.Left

▶ To be notified when a tab is selected by the user, you can handle the SelectionChanged event.

▶ The selected tab can be found in different ways:

   ▶ The SelectedItem property contains a reference to the selected TabItem.

   ▶ The SelectedContent property returns the content included in the selected TabItem.

   ▶ Finally, the SelectedIndex property returns the index of the selected TabItem in the Items collection.

The Items of an ItemsControl can either be set explicitly as we just did in Table 16.2, or they can be data bound as we see in Chapter 18. For a TabControl, typically, the number of TabItems is set when the application starts and doesn't change. But having the possibility to data bind the TabItems to a collection of data objects can be useful in some circumstances.

Deep Zooming Your Image Collection

We talked about DeepZoom shortly in Chapter 1, and you probably took a look at the excellent application made by Vertigo for the Hard Rock Café memorabilia at www.hardrock.com/memorabilia.

How Does It Work?

DeepZoom uses a pyramid of pictures of different sizes. All the pictures in the pyramid are based on the same high-resolution picture, the one you want to "deep zoom" in.

At runtime, the DeepZoom control (named a MultiScaleImage) loads the pictures in the pyramid according to the level of zoom applied by the user. Thanks to .NET's power of calculation, the transition between the images is usually smooth.

Creating a DeepZoom Image Pyramid

Creating a DeepZoom control is easy thanks to the DeepZoom Composer. This application takes an image (or a collection of images) as input and processes them to create an image pyramid as shown in Figure 16.10. Note that for each image processed, the image pyramid starts with an image of 1×1 pixels and ends with the size of the original image. You can create an image pyramid with the following steps.

FIGURE 16.10   Image pyramid

1. Download and install DeepZoom Composer, available at http://silverlight.net/GetStarted. Click on the link labeled "Install Deep Zoom Composer."

2. Start the Composer and create a new project.

3. You are now in the *Import* phase. Click on the Add Image button. You can choose one or multiple images as you want. Note that after the images are imported, you cannot edit them. You must do this before you load the images in the DeepZoom Composer.

4. Click on the Compose button on top of the Composer window.

5. Drag and drop the images you want to use on the workspace. You can either use one image only, or multiple ones. The DeepZoom Composer helps you to align the pictures, resize them, and arrange them on the workspace.

6. Click on the Export button on top of the window.

7. Select the Silverlight Export tab, then enter a name and an export location.

8. You can export the images as a *Composition* (only one big image will be created) or as a *Collection* (each image remains independent). For now, choose the Collection option. You can also select the output format (PNG or JPG).

9. In the Output Type section, select to export the images and a Silverlight project.

10. Click Export.

After processing the images, DeepZoom Composer gives you a choice, as shown in Figure 16.11.

FIGURE 16.11   Deep Zoom Composer after processing

▶ Preview in Browser starts your favorite web client and displays the DeepZoom image for you. In fact, a Silverlight application has automatically been created and is now displayed. Use the mouse wheel to zoom in and out smoothly, clicking on one point of the picture to zoom in. You can also use your mouse to move the pictures around. Notice how smooth the movement is.

▶ View Image Folder shows the folder containing the image pyramid. You can explore the folders to see how the DeepZoom Composer cut the pictures to create the pyramid.

▶ View Project Folder displays the Visual Studio (or Blend) project location. You can open the SLN file in Studio or in Blend to modify the Silverlight application.

▶ Learn More opens the Expression team blog.

The `MultiScaleImage` **Control**

The DeepZoom functionality is packed into a control named `MultiScaleImage` deriving from `FrameworkElement`. This is where the magic happens. This control has one property, `Source`, that must be set to the XML file dzc_output.xml generated by the DeepZoom composer.

This XML file is located in the folder that you open when you click View Image Folder. If you choose the option to export a Silverlight project, the Composer automatically creates a web application too and places the generated images, the XAP file, and an HTML test page in the web application's ClientBin folder.

It is outside the scope for this book to examine DeepZoom further, but to see a nice example of how one or multiple `MultiScaleImage` controls can enhance your web page, take a look at Jose Fajardo's interview at http://delicategeniusblog.com/?p=692.

> **NOTE**
>
> The `MultiScaleImage` does not handle mouse input, but it exposes methods to make it easier. When the Silverlight project is created, the Composer adds a C# class named MouseWheelHelper.cs. In addition, the file Page.xaml.cs has generated code that controls the `MultiScaleImage` according to the mouse input. You can of course modify the application to add your own functionality.

16

Summary

In this chapter, we met many new controls and consolidated our knowledge about others that we had met before. But in truth, to really know the controls you must use them in an application (or two or three) and also browse through the documentation. Also, don't hesitate to look for answers online when you encounter a specific issue, or to find samples.

In later chapters, we continue to use controls in our applications. We also learn how to use styles and templates to change the controls' appearance, and spend more time with data controls. Finally, we see how to combine controls and other `FrameworkElements` to create custom controls.

CHAPTER 17

Using Resources, Styling, and Templating

Silverlight was developed from the start with the need to have a clean separation of an application's behavior and appearance in mind. As in HTML (with the Cascaded Style Sheets), the many advantages of storing a control's look and feel in a different place than its functionality are clear.

However, Silverlight goes a couple of steps further than CSS:

▶ You can *style* a control (that is, create a set of properties that you store in a `Style` object, and that you can easily modify to change the application's looks).

▶ But you can also change the shape and looks of the control entirely by redefining its *template*.

▶ Thanks to the separation, you can let designers and developers work on the same application at the same time and minimize the process of merging the changes.

▶ By creating sets of styles and templates, you can create new skins for an application even after it has been released without touching its behavior.

This separation (proven first in Windows Presentation Foundation) brings the collaboration between graphics designers and software developers to a new level. With new iterative workflows, you can let graphics designers create a professional appearance for your application. Using Blend, they can work on the XAML markup and not just on static pictures anymore. In the meantime, developers can concentrate on what they do best—creating software architecture, software design, and, well, software code for the application.

Storing Items in Collections

Remember when we stored storyboards within the `UserControl.Resources`? This property is a `ResourceDictionary`. `Arrays`, `Collections`, and `Dictionaries` play a big role in any programming framework. Programmers need them to store objects, iterate through them, sort them, and so on.

But how do we know what functionalities a collection fulfils? Let's take a look in the SDK documentation at the `ResourceDictionary` class. We see that the class is declared as follows:

```
public class ResourceDictionary : DependencyObject,
  IDictionary<Object, Object>,
  ICollection<KeyValuePair<Object, Object>>,
  IEnumerable<KeyValuePair<Object, Object>>,
  IEnumerable
```

First, notice that the `ResourceDictionary` is a `DependencyObject`, but that's not surprising, seeing as many objects in Silverlight derive from this class. More interesting is what comes next.

Implementing Interfaces

In .NET we use *interfaces* to create a definition for functionality. It's like a contract between the person who implements a class and the person who uses it. The `ResourceDictionary` shown previously *implements* the interfaces `IDictionary`, `ICollection`, and two kinds of `IEnumerable`. For users of this class, it means that we know which methods the developers implemented and which functionality is fulfilled.

Earlier in this book, we talked about abstract classes, and we said that they cannot be instantiated. This is because some of their methods are not implemented (they are *abstract*). An object can derive from an abstract class, but it needs to *implement* the abstract methods explicitly. Similarly, an object needs to implement all the methods defined by the Interface. Interfaces do not have any implementation. They only define abstract methods, methods that an object needs to implement. This is why we don't say that an object derives from an interface. Instead, we say that an object *implements* an interface.

By convention, all the Interfaces in the .NET framework start with the capital letter I. This is to make it easy to recognize them. If you create an Interface yourself some day, it is recommended to follow this guideline.

In .NET, an object can *derive* from one parent class only (abstract or not), but it can *implement* as many interfaces as it needs.

▶ IDictionary—Stores items according to a key and provides methods to retrieve an item. There are also helper methods and properties to check if a Dictionary contains an item or a key, to add and remove items, to clear the collection, to know how many items there are, and so on.

▶ ICollection—Also stores items, but not according to a key. Implementing both ICollection and IDictionary allows the ResourceDictionary to provide access to the items by key or by index.

```
<UserControl.Resources>
  <Storyboard x:Key="MyStoryboard">
    <!--...-->
  </Storyboard>
</UserControl.Resources>
```

with

```
Storyboard myStoryboard = Resources["MyStoryboard"] as Storyboard;
```

or

```
Storyboard myStoryboard = Resources[0] as Storyboard;
```

▶ IEnumerable—Defines methods to iterate through the items. Thanks to IEnumerable, we can loop through all the resources if we want.

As we said earlier, a ResourceDictionary can store anything. This is why the Value is stored as Object, and why it's necessary to cast it to the desired type when you retrieve the item from the dictionary.

The notation IDictionary<Object, Object> means that the ResourceDictionary is implemented as a *generic* collection. We talk about generics in Chapter 20, "Taking Silverlight 2 One Step Further." For now, let's just say that the Value stored in a ResourceDictionary and the Key referencing it are of type Object, so in fact they can be anything. Often, however, we use a String as Key.

Using ResourceDictionaries **in Silverlight**

By studying which interfaces the ResourceDictionary implements, we learn a great deal about this class. We know that

▶ A ResourceDictionary can store any Object.

▶ You can loop through all the items, for example using a foreach loop.

▶ Each item stored must have a unique key.

▶ You can access the items using their key or (if you know which position they have in the dictionary) using their index.

> **WARNING**
>
> Accessing resources by index is not a good idea if you can avoid it. It's easy to make mistakes—for example, forgetting to update the index in the accessing method when you restructure your resources.

Storing Resources

The `Resources` property is defined on the class `FrameworkElement`, so each class deriving from it can store resources.

In XAML you store resources in an element using Listing 17.1:

LISTING 17.1   Defining Resources in XAML

```
<UserControl.Resources>
  <LinearGradientBrush x:Key="BackgroundBrush">
    <GradientStop Offset="0" Color="Yellow" />
    <GradientStop Offset="1" Color="Red" />
  </LinearGradientBrush>
</UserControl.Resources>

<Grid x:Name="LayoutRoot">
  <Grid.Resources>
    <SolidColorBrush x:Key="MyBrush2" Color="Green" />
  </Grid.Resources>
</Grid>
```

The same in C# would be (see Listing 17.2):

LISTING 17.2   Defining Resources in C#

```
LinearGradientBrush brush1 = new LinearGradientBrush();
GradientStop stop1 = new GradientStop();
stop1.Offset = 0;
stop1.Color = Colors.Yellow;
brush1.GradientStops.Add(stop1);
GradientStop stop2 = new GradientStop();
stop2.Offset = 0;
stop2.Color = Colors.Red;
brush1.GradientStops.Add(stop2);
this.Resources.Add("BackgroundBrush", brush1);

SolidColorBrush brush2 = new SolidColorBrush();
brush2.Color = Colors.Green;
LayoutRoot.Resources.Add("MyBrush2", brush2);
```

Using Resources in Code-Behind

Once resources have been stored, you can access them in .NET through the `Resources` property. You can only access resources stored in XAML markup after the method `InitializeComponent` has been executed. This method *parses* the XAML markup and creates the objects in memory, for example in Listing 17.3.

LISTING 17.3   Using a Resource in Code

```
public Page()
{
  InitializeComponent();

  Rectangle rectangle = new Rectangle();
  Brush brush = this.Resources["BackgroundBrush"] as Brush;
  if (brush != null)
  {
    rectangle.Fill = brush;
  }

  LayoutRoot.Children.Add(rectangle);
}
```

What's the Point Anyway?

So why do we want to store a brush in resources when we could have built it just as well in code? The answer is that we want separation of behavior and presentation. The code-behind defines the behavior. The XAML markup defines the presentation. And using resources in XAML creates an even neater separation. Simply by setting `BackgroundBrush` to a different brush in the XAML resources, you change the look of your application without having to touch the code-behind.

> **WARNING**
>
> Windows Presentation Foundation, which is Silverlight's "big sister," allows storing resources in external files and even external assemblies. This creates an even better separation.
>
> This is not possible in Silverlight yet, however, and all the resources must be stored in the same XAML file as the controls using them, or in the global file App.xaml.

Using Resources in XAML

You can also use resources in XAML directly. In fact, it is common to do so! This is made possible by something called the `StaticResource` markup extension.

Markup Extensions

These extensions are used to add functionality to the XAML markup. Silverlight has four of them built in:

- ▶ `StaticResource`—Used to refer to a resource stored in the same XAML file or in App.xaml

- ▶ `Binding`—Used in data binding, and which we study in Chapter 18, "Data Binding and Using Data Controls"

- ▶ `TemplateBinding`—Used in the creation of templates, which we learn about later in this chapter

- ▶ `x:Null`—Used when you need to set a property to `null` in XAML

Markup extensions in XAML are used within curly brackets:

```
<Rectangle Fill="{StaticResource MyBrush}" Height="20"/>
```

Walking the Tree

The `StaticResource` markup extension has a neat feature: It walks the tree of elements trying to find the right resource. For example, the XAML markup in Listing 17.4 works:

LISTING 17.4   Walking the Tree

```
<Grid x:Name="LayoutRoot">
  <Grid.Resources>
    <SolidColorBrush x:Key="BackgroundBrush" Color="Red" />
  </Grid.Resources>

  <StackPanel>
    <StackPanel.Resources>
      <SolidColorBrush x:Key="ForegroundBrush" Color="Blue" />
    </StackPanel.Resources>

    <TextBox Text="Hello"
             Foreground="{StaticResource ForegroundBrush}"
             Background="{StaticResource BackgroundBrush}" />
  </StackPanel>
</Grid>
```

Even though the `ForegroundBrush` is defined in the `TextBox`'s parent, and the `BackgroundBrush` in its parent's parent, the brushes are found because of the "tree walking." Note however that the tree can only be walked upwards, not downwards. The `StaticResource` markup extension cannot use forward references. For example, trying to run the markup in Listing 17.5 causes an exception to be thrown. The issue is that when the `StaticResource` is used, the corresponding resource has not been parsed yet by the XAML parser.

LISTING 17.5   Undefined Resource

```
<TextBox Text="Hello"
        Foreground="{StaticResource MyOwnBrush}">
  <TextBox.Resources>
    <SolidColorBrush x:Key="MyOwnBrush" Color="Orange" />
  </TextBox.Resources>
</TextBox>
```

To solve this problem, you can use the syntax in Listing 17.6:

LISTING 17.6   Correcting the Error

```
<TextBox Text="Hello">
  <TextBox.Resources>
    <SolidColorBrush x:Key="MyOwnBrush" Color="Orange" />
  </TextBox.Resources>
  <TextBox.Foreground>
    <StaticResource ResourceKey="MyOwnBrush"/>
  </TextBox.Foreground>
</TextBox>
```

For the moment there is no equivalent to `StaticResource` and its "tree-walking" in code-behind in Silverlight. Only the local resources of an element can be read using the element's `Resources` property. However, implementing the equivalent of the `TryFindResource` method (existing in Windows Presentation Foundation) is not difficult. We see how to do this in Chapter 24, "Silverlight: Continuing the Journey."

Storing Resources in App.xaml

The `StaticResource` extension also allows finding resources stored in the App.xaml file. On parsing, these resources are added to the `Application` object `App.Current`, which we discuss in more detail in Chapter 20.

In App.xaml:

```
<Application.Resources>
  <SolidColorBrush x:Key="MyBrushInApp" Color="Turquoise" />
</Application.Resources>
```

In Page.xaml:

```
<StackPanel x:Name="MyStackPanel"
```

17

```
            Background="{StaticResource MyBrushInApp}">
   <!--.....-->
</StackPanel>
```

or in Page.xaml.cs:

```
Brush brushInApp
  = App.Current.Resources["MyBrushInApp"] as Brush;
MyStackPanel.Background = brushInApp;
```

Storing resources in App.xaml creates a good separation of behavior and presentation. However, be careful not to put everything in there. Making all resources global throughout the application creates an impact on performances (because all the resources will be created in memory) and makes it difficult to create a key for these resources (because the scope is now global).

The best practice is to use a wise compromise of global resources (for example, brushes used throughout the application) and local ones (for resources used more rarely).

Styling a Control

A `Style` is nothing but a collection of *property setters* for a control. Every property of a `FrameworkElement` (as long as it is a `DependencyProperty`) can be set through a `Style`.

> **NOTE**
>
> Since not all properties of a control are used for look and feel only, you can in fact set more than "just" the looks of a control using a `Style`. For example, the property `DataContext` (used in data binding as we see in Chapter 18) or the `Content` of a `Button`.

Creating a `Style`

A `Style` is a class like any other (it's `System.Windows.Style`). The typical way to define a new style is to create it in resources (for example Listing 17.7) and refer to it using the `StaticResource` markup extension discussed earlier.

LISTING 17.7   Defining a `Style` in XAML

```
<StackPanel.Resources>
  <Style TargetType="Button"
        x:Key="ButtonStyle">
    <Setter Property="Background">
      <Setter.Value>
        <LinearGradientBrush>
          <GradientStop Offset="0" Color="Yellow"/>
          <GradientStop Offset="1" Color="Red" />
        </LinearGradientBrush>
      </Setter.Value>
    </Setter>
    <Setter Property="Foreground" Value="Orange" />
```

LISTING 17.7   Continued

```
    <Setter Property="Width" Value="80" />
    <Setter Property="Height" Value="30" />
  </Style>
</StackPanel.Resources>
```

- ▶ Set the `TargetType` to the type of the control for which the style is created. You can also use a parent type of this control. For example, a `CheckBox` and a `Button` can both use a `Style` defined for the `ButtonBase` type.

- ▶ Use a collection of `Setters`. For each `Setter`, define the `Property`, and the `Value` for that `Property`.

- ▶ Using the expanded property syntax discussed in Chapter 2, "Understanding XAML," you can set the `Value` property to complex content, for example, a `LinearGradientBrush`.

Using a `Style`

Using a `Style` in XAML is easy: It's just like using any other kind of resource.

```
<Button Content="Style me"
        Style="{StaticResource ButtonStyle}" />
```

In C# too, setting a Style is no different than setting any other kind of property.

```
Style style = LayoutRoot.Resources["ButtonStyle"] as Style;
MyButton.Style = style;
```

Note however that unlike in Windows Presentation Foundation, a `Style` can be set only once on a control. You cannot switch styles at runtime.

Deciding which property of a control should be set in a `Style` can be tricky. In general, place in the `Style` the properties that you want a designer to take care of (such as all the brushes, the control's size, location, alignment, and so on), and keep on the control the properties that define the behavior of the control (such as all the event handlers, and so on).

Priority of Property Setters

Since each property can be set directly on a control or through a `Style`, a priority system must be established. In Silverlight, setting a property directly on a control has priority over the value set by a `Style`. This means that if you want to change a control's appearance at runtime, you can do so by addressing the control's properties directly. For example if you use a `Style` setting a red `Background` on a `Button`, but change this color at runtime to blue, the `Button` will end up being blue.

```
<Style TargetType="Button" x:Key="Style1">
  <Setter Property="Background" Value="Red" />
  <Setter Property="Foreground" Value="Orange" />
</Style>
```

with

```
<Button Content="Style me" x:Name="MyButton1"
        Style="{StaticResource Style1}"
        Click="MyButton_Click" />
```

and

```
private void MyButton_Click(object sender, RoutedEventArgs e)
{
  (sender as Button).Background = new SolidColorBrush(Colors.Blue);
}
```

Similarly, this markup creates a purple button:

```
<Button Content="Style me too" x:Name="MyButton2"
        Background="Purple"
        Style="{StaticResource Style1}"
        Click="MyButton_Click" />
```

The `Button` appears purple because the property `Background` is set both in the `Style` and on the control directly. The direct property wins! The property `Foreground` defined in the `Style` is used by both buttons however.

Creating a `Style` in Blend

Expression Blend provides a great help when handling styles, for example with the following steps:

1. Create a new Silverlight application in Blend.

2. Add a control to the LayoutRoot, for example, a `Button`.

3. Select Object, Edit Style from the menu.

4. You have two active choices:

   ▶ Edit a Copy...—Places a copy of the default style in the resources. Each control comes with a default style that will be used when nothing else is specified. This command creates a local copy of this default `Style` that you can modify. If you use this command, you will notice that the `Template` property is set too. We talk about templates later in this chapter.

▶ Create Empty...—Provides you with a brand new `Style` where you can set all the properties you need. This is the option we will work with for the moment.

5. In the Create Style Resource dialog shown in Figure 17.1, enter a name for the new `Style`, and set whether it should be created in the Application (App.xaml) or in the current document. Note that you can choose to create the control in the `Button` itself or in the `UserControl`. Choose the `UserControl` if you intend to reuse this `Style` in other controls as well.

FIGURE 17.1   The Create Style Resource dialog

6. Blend now shows the `Style` in the Objects and Timeline category (see Figure 17.2). This means that any property you set now is going to be set in the `Style`, and not directly in the control.

FIGURE 17.2   Objects and Timeline category for a `Style`

7. Using the Properties panel, set the `Style` properties. For example, set the `Foreground` color to red.

8. When you're finished, set Blend's scope back to the `UserControl` by clicking on the button to the left of ButtonStyle1 in Figure 17.2. Blend added the `Style` property to the `Button` with a `StaticResource`.

9. With the `Button` selected, check the Properties panel again. Notice that the `Foreground` property is set to red, but the small square next to the property name is not white. This is because the property is not set locally on the control, but externally in a `Style`. The Properties panel helps you to understand how a control's look and feel is built, with a combination of local properties and `Style` properties.

Editing a `Style` in Blend

When a control uses a `Style`, Blend can edit it. Follow the steps:

1. Click on the `Button` for which we just created a `Style` in the preceding section.

2. From the menu select Object, Edit Style, Edit `Style` (the one that was disabled before).

3. Blend's scope is set to the `Style` again.

17

You can also switch back to the selected control's `Style` easily by clicking on the painter's palette in the crumb bar, right under the Design panel's title (see Figure 17.3).

FIGURE 17.3   Crumb bar

Styling the Thumbnails Application

We are going to use the knowledge we acquired so far to create styles in our Thumbnails application. This will make it easier to change the application's look and feel. In addition, we will see how to embed fonts in our application to make this font available on the client computer, even if it is not installed there.

Styling the `TextBlocks`

After opening the Thumbnails application in Blend (the one we edited last in Chapter 14, "Letting .NET and JavaScript Talk"), follow the steps:

1. If needed, make sure that the web project Thumbnails.Web is set as a startup project. It should appear in bold in the Project panel. You can change this by right-clicking on the project and selecting Startup Project. Then right click on index.html and select Startup.

2. Open the file Page.xaml and select the second `TextBlock` in the Objects and Timeline category—the one saying "Have some fun."

3. Reset its look and feel to the default in the Properties panel. Remember everything you set back to default, because we will set these properties in the `Style` in a moment. The properties to reset are `TextWrapping`, `Margin`, `FontFamily`, and `FontSize` (these are combo boxes in the Text category) and the Bold `FontWeight`. We don't reset the properties `Foreground` and `Text` because they are not supposed to be modified by the designers.

> **TIP**
>
> To reset a property in Blend, click on the white square button next to it and select Reset.

4. From the menu select Object, Edit Style, Create Empty and create a new style in the `UserControl`. Name it TitleTextBlockStyle.

5. Set all the properties we just reset to their previous values. The difference is that now they are set in the `Style`! Reminder: We had the `TextWrapping` set to Wrap, the left and right `Margin` set to 10, the `FontFamily` set to Arial, `FontSize` to 48, and the `FontWeight` was Bold.

Yeah, I know, it's annoying. It's a repetitive task. This is why you should remember to create the `Styles` early when you design the UI, instead of setting the properties locally and creating styles afterward.

Now that we have created a new `Style`, we want to reuse it for the second `TextBlock`. It makes sense, because both look the same (with the exception of their `Foreground` brush).

1. Set the scope back to the `UserControl` and select the first `TextBlock` in the title.

2. Select the `Style` property (if needed, search for it using the Search text box on top of the Properties panel).

3. Using the small square button on the right of the Style text box, select Local Resource and use the style we just created (see Figure 17.4).

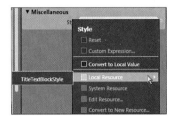

4. The properties are still set locally, so with the scope set to the `UserControl`, you'll see that small white square next to them. Again,

FIGURE 17.4   Selecting a local resource

reset them to their default value. Notice how the value doesn't change, but the small square becomes colorless, indicating that the value is now set through the style.

Styling the Thumbnails

We now create styles for the `MediaElements` and `Images` inside the `ScrollViewer`. This allows graphics designers to easily change the look and feel of the application. Follow these steps:

1. Expand the `ScrollViewer` and the `StackPanel` in the Objects and Timeline category.

2. Select the first `Grid` and reset the `Margin` property.

3. Create a `Style` for the `Grid`. Name it ThumbnailGridStyle and place it in the `UserControl`.

4. Use this `Style` to set the `Margin` property: Left = Right = 10, Top = Bottom = 5. Also set the `Cursor` to Hand.

5. Set the scope back to the `UserControl`. Select the first `Border` within the `Grid` and reset the `BorderThickness` and the `BorderBrush`.

6. Create a `Style` for the `Border`. Name it ThumbnailBorderStyle.

7. In the `Style`, set the `BorderThickness` to 2,2,2,2 and the `BorderBrush` to #FFA9A899 and set the scope back to the `UserControl`.

Now that we have created `Styles`, we can reuse them for all the other thumbnails. For each thumbnail, reset the properties we created in the corresponding `Style` for the `Grid` and the first `Border`. Then assign the `Style` property of each of these elements.

To make this less repetitive, you can multi select elements in the Objects and Timeline category. Click on the elements while holding down the Ctrl key.

Moving Resources in Blend

Just for the sake of the demonstration, let's move the Styles we just created from the UserControl into App.xaml. This is easy with Blend with the following steps:

1. With Page.xaml open in Blend, select the Resources panel.

2. Expand the TopUserControl. You will see that it contains three Styles—the three that we just created (see Figure 17.5).

3. Select the first Style and drag it to the App.xaml.

4. Repeat the operation for all three Styles.

FIGURE 17.5   Resources panel

If you check the XAML markup now, you'll see that the Styles have effectively been moved from one file to the other. Don't forget to save!

If you double-click on one of the resources, Blend will display it in the Design panel (if it can represent it). This gives you another entry point to modify a Style.

The Resources panel is useful when you have a lot of resources in your application. It can edit brushes, help you to visualize icons, and enable you to reorder resources or move them like we just did.

Embedding Fonts in the Application

The problem with fonts is that you're never sure if they are available on the target client. This is why CSS has a *fallback* strategy, where you can select multiple fonts ranging from specific fonts (which might not be available) to more generic fonts (which are certainly there).

Another strategy is to make sure that the font is available to the application, by *deploying* it. You can embed a font in a Silverlight application using Blend or using Visual Studio.

Embedding a Font in Blend

Expression Blend offers an elegant way to solve the problem of font availability. Not only is the functionality easy to use, thanks to a font manager dialog, but also Blend will analyze your application's needs and extract a subset of the font needed for the application to run. Follow the steps:

1. In Expression Blend, open the file Page.xaml of the Thumbnails application.

2. Select either one of the title `TextBlocks`. Then choose Object, Edit Style, Edit Style from the menu.

3. In the Properties panel, in the Text category, select the font that you want to use. The combo box displays all the fonts installed on your PC. Some fonts have small icons next to their name (see Figure 17.6). A small Silverlight logo near a capital A means that the font is available in the default Silverlight installation. In that case, you don't need to worry about embedding the font. Select a font that is not a Silverlight default (in our example, we choose the Algerian font).

FIGURE 17.6   Fonts available in the application and in Silverlight

4. If Blend displays an error, build the application. The error should disappear and you should be able to see the `TextBlock` with the new font applied. Notice however that Blend displays a warning in the Results panel, telling you that you should embed the font in the application.

5. In the Text category of the Properties panel, check the Embed check box. Then, build the application. The font now appears in the combo box with a small window next to the capital A, meaning that the font is embedded.

6. If the `TextBlock`'s content never changes during the course of the application (this is our case), you can select Static from the Subset selection combo box, at the right of the Embed check box. In that case, Blend will only embed the characters that the element needs. If the `TextBlock`'s content may change during runtime, you should select Dynamic instead.

7. In the Project panel, you'll see that Blend created a new folder named Fonts. The font file is included in this folder. This file is included inside the Thumbnails.dll when you build, and made available to the application on every platform.

8. To have more control on the embedded subset, open the Font manager with the menu Tools, Font Manager (see Figure 17.7). This dialog offers a very flexible way to embed exactly the subset that your application needs.

9. Check the XAML markup for the `Style` in App.xaml. You'll see that Blend set the `FontFamily` value to `./Fonts/Fonts.zip#[FontName]`. This syntax tells Silverlight where to find the font subset.

FIGURE 17.7   Font manager dialog

When you open a Silverlight project with an embedded font in Visual Studio, you may see a security warning. This is because Blend adds a custom step to the build process, to extract and embed the necessary glyphs. You can safely dismiss this warning.

WARNING

Some fonts are subjected to copyright, and you may not redistribute them freely. You must check if the font is free of rights before you embed it in your application!

Embedding a Font in Visual Studio

Embedding a font in Visual Studio requires a little more manual work, and you cannot choose a subset. Follow the steps:

1. Locate the Fonts folder on your PC. It is located in your Windows folder (depending on your configuration, it can be C:\Windows\Fonts, or C:\WINNT\Fonts).

2. Copy the Font file(s) (for example, Algerian) that you want to add to your application. For some fonts, a separate file is available for Bold, Italic, or Bold Italic. If you want to use these variations of a font, you must copy the files too.

3. Paste the Font files in a temporary folder, for example, C:\temp.

4. From the temporary folder, drag and drop the Font files to the Thumbnails project in Studio.

5. We must now make sure that the compiler embeds the fonts inside the application. To do this, select the Font file, display the Properties panel (F4), and set the Build Action to Resource.

6. In the XAML markup, change the `FontFamily` to `./[FONTFILE].TTF#[FontName]`. Replace the `[FONTFILE]` with the Font file name, and `[FontName]` with the Font name that you want to use.

To find out the exact font name, double-click the TTF file in Windows Explorer. This opens an information view about the font. The Font Name is in the window's title. Note that some font names have a (TrueType) or (OpenType) suffix, which should not be copied to the XAML `FontFamily` property.

Templating the Lookless Control

Pushing the separation of behavior and presentation much further, the teams who built Windows Presentation Foundation and Silverlight decided to completely change the way that controls are handled by the framework. Until now, a control pretty much always looked the same. Take a check box in HTML, WinForms, and MFC, for example, it's always the same check box. There isn't much room for fantasy here.

With these two new frameworks, however, we know what the control *does*, but we can rework the way it *looks* from scratch. We can make a check box look like anything with two states. The *states* of the control and its *events* define the behavior of the control. But the check box in Silverlight doesn't have a *look*. We call this the *lookless control*!

But the Control Has a Look!

Yes it does. But only because the makers of Silverlight added a *default template* that the check box will use if nothing else is specified. In fact, you can see how the default template looks in Blend with the following steps:

1. Open a new Silverlight application in Blend and add a check box to LayoutRoot.

2. With the check box selected, choose Object, Edit Control Parts (Template), Edit a Copy... from the menu and place the copy of the default style in the `UserControl`.

> **NOTE**
>
> In Silverlight, the `Template` is always set through the `Style`, so if you create a copy of the default style as we did before, you will also see the `Template`. In WPF, this is slightly different (but that's another story). It is good practice to always set the `Template` through a `Style` anyway.

3. In the Objects and Timeline category, you see how a check box is built in Silverlight when nothing else is specified. A `Grid`, a number of `Rectangles`, a `Path` (that's the small "tick" sign that you get when the check box is checked), and something called the `ContentPresenter`, which we discuss in a minute.

4. Notice how the "tick" (called CheckIcon) is invisible. If you look at it in the Properties panel, you'll see that its `Opacity` is 0%. The default state for the check box is unchecked, so the "tick" should be invisible.

Editing the Template

Since we can get a copy of the default template in Blend, we can also edit it, with the following steps:

1. In the check box template that we opened in the preceding section, select the CheckIcon and in the Properties panel, set its `Fill` to #FFA50C0C.

2. Save everything and run the application. Check the check box and see how it's now dark red.

Let's make it a little more interesting. Since we saw that the control's look is mostly made by a bunch of `Rectangles`, and we know that we can convert a `Rectangle` to a `Path`, and then use the Pen tool to modify this `Path`, why should we stop?

1. In the Objects and Timeline category, expand the `Grid` under the `Template`. This `Grid` has another `Grid` as first child. Select that inner `Grid` and set its `Width` and `Height` to 16 pixels.

2. Select the `Rectangle` named BoxMiddle and delete it. Then do the same for the one called ContentFocusVisualElement.

3. Select the `Rectangle` named Background and set its properties `RadiusX` and `RadiusY` to 0.

4. Convert the Background into a `Path` by selecting Object, Path, Convert to Path from the menu.

5. Select the Pen tool in the toolbar and modify the `Path` to make it look like a star (see Figure 17.8). Remember what we learned in Chapter 6, "Blending a Little More." You can also change other properties such as a `RotateTransform`, and so on.

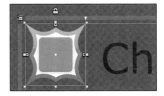

FIGURE 17.8   Modifying a `CheckBox`'s template

Modifying the States

We mentioned already that Silverlight uses a concept called "parts and states" to create a control's look and feel. The meaning of "parts" is clear: It's everything that composes a template. In the check box example, we saw what the check box is made of. Probably the most important part is the CheckIcon, because it gives its true meaning to the check box.

> **TIP**
>
> To make it easier to concentrate on Background only, you can hide the other elements by using the small Eye icon next to their name in the Objects and Timeline category. Don't forget to check often whether your changes play well with the rest of the control! You can also zoom in to make it easier to work.

Let's now see how to change the way the control looks when it is checked. We do this by editing the control's states.

Each control defines a number of states that it can have. In Chapter 19, "Creating User Controls and Custom Controls," we learn how to specify this for our own controls, but for the moment, let's just review the states that the `CheckBox` can have. Observe the category located above the Objects and Timeline category in the Interaction panel: That's the States category where the control's states and the transitions are defined (see Figure 17.9).

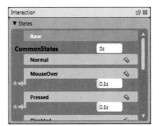

FIGURE 17.9   States category

1. Scroll down a little and find the states called Checked, Unchecked, and Indeterminate.

2. Click on the Checked state. This shows you how the control looks in that state. Note also that Expression Blend is now in State recording mode. That should remind you of the Timeline recording mode that we used when we created animations in Blend.

3. In the Properties panel, use the `ScaleTransform` section in the Properties panel to make the CheckIcon look three times as wide and twice as high. Set the `RenderTransformOrigin` to 0.5,1 so that the `Path` grows relatively to its bottom-center point. You can also move the `Path` a little to the right to position it more neatly.

Now we set the transition between the Unchecked and Checked states. It would be nice to have a smooth transition. Since the Unchecked state has no transform and an `Opacity` of 0%, and the Checked state has a transform and an `Opacity` of 100%, we specify how long it should take to make the change.

1. Click on the Unchecked state now, and then on the small arrow with a plus sign on the right. You can now select the transition that you want to edit. Choose the Unchecked to Checked transition (see Figure 17.10).

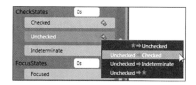

FIGURE 17.10   Adding a transition

2. Decide how long you want this transition to last, for example, 0.5 seconds. Enter this value in the text box with the Transition duration ToolTip.

3. Run the application by pressing F5 and check the check box. The control's look and feel is now different from a default check box, but its behavior didn't change at all.

Editing a template can take a lot of time and requires a lot of artistic talent. Typically, a graphics designer will be in charge of making these changes. As mentioned previously, Silverlight (and WPF before that) introduces new workflows and new roles to make your applications look professional and neat.

Binding the `Template` to the `Control`

One thing is annoying: The `Rectangle` named BoxMiddleBackground is blue. It would be nice if we could change this color easily, without having to edit the template every time. Since the `CheckBox` control is a `Control`, it has a `Background` property. Why not simply set the `Background` on the `CheckBox` control, and propagate this change within the template?

In fact, that's exactly what happens, thanks to something called a *TemplateBinding*. We talk about bindings in Chapter 18, but let's take a moment to understand the `TemplateBinding` here with the following steps:

1. In Blend, make sure that the State recording mode is switched off, and select the BoxMiddleBackground in the Objects and Timeline category.

2. In the Properties panel, notice how the small square next to the `Fill` property is orange. This means that its value is set through a binding.

3. Click on this small orange square and select Template Binding from the context menu. The value is set to Background (see Figure 17.11).

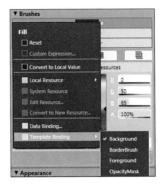

FIGURE 17.11   Template Binding

   ▶ To offer this dialog, Blend looks at the `TargetType` of the `Template` that we are currently editing.

   ▶ Since it's a `CheckBox`, it looks at what properties of the `CheckBox` are of the same type as the `Fill` property of the `Path`. We know that `Fill` is a `Brush`, so Blend shows all the `CheckBox`'s properties that are of type `Brush`.

   ▶ The `TemplateBinding` is set to Background. This means that when the `CheckBox`'s Background property is set, the `Brush` will be used to fill the rectangle in the template.

This also explains why the Background rectangle is blue: This is the default brush for a `ButtonBase` control. It's the color that will be used on a `Button` control, for example, when you don't set its `Background` to anything else. And we know that a `CheckBox` derives from `ButtonBase`...

4. To try this out, exit the template editing mode by giving the scope back to the `UserControl` (that's the button with an arrow pointing up, located on the left of the CheckBoxStyle1 title in the Objects and Timeline category). From the template editor, you must click twice, once to set the scope to the `Style` containing the template, and once more to set the scope to the `UserControl`.

5. Select the `CheckBox` and set its `Background` property to a light yellow (see Figure 17.12). There is also a Template Binding between the `Stroke` of the Background `Path` and the check box's `BorderBrush`, so try and set this property to #FFA50C0C. Then run the application.

FIGURE 17.12   Check boxes with a new look and feel

Presenting Content

The last thing we need to understand in our template is how content is displayed. We mentioned the `ContentPresenter`, which is included in the `CheckBox` template. This control's only functionality is to display whatever is included in the content property.

We talked about this property in Chapter 2, and also when we studied `ContentControls` earlier. The content property is any property of a control that the developer marked as the default property for that control. For a `ContentControl` (of which `ButtonBase` and thus `CheckBox` derives), the property is also named `Content`, which is a little bit confusing.

When you want the `Content` of a control to be displayed within the `Template`, the easiest way is to use a `ContentPresenter`. In the `CheckBox` template, you will find this control under the name contentPresenter. The XAML markup looks like Listing 17.8:

LISTING 17.8   ContentPresenter for a CheckBox

```
<ContentPresenter HorizontalAlignment="{TemplateBinding HorizontalContentAlignment}"
Margin="{TemplateBinding Padding}" x:Name="contentPresenter"
VerticalAlignment="{TemplateBinding VerticalContentAlignment}" Grid.Column="1"
Content="{TemplateBinding Content}" ContentTemplate="{TemplateBinding ContentTem-
➥plate}"/>
```

Notice all the properties with a `TemplateBinding`. You can set all these properties on the `CheckBox` directly, and they will be applied to the `Template`.

By modifying the `ContentPresenter`'s properties—for example, alignment, position within the `Grid`, and so on, you will modify how the `CheckBox` looks. For example, you could put the `ContentPresenter` inside a `Border`, and this `Border` would always be drawn around the content.

Since `ContentPresenter` can display any content, you can set the `CheckBox`'s content to anything, such as an `Image`, a `MediaElement`, another `Control`, and so on. There are no limits!

Summary

This chapter put a lot of emphasis on the separation of behavior and presentation. This principle exists in HTML with CSS and is important in Silverlight, where it has been developed even further. It's important to understand this well, because the way you structure your application, the workflow within the project—especially between designers and developers, and eventually the way your application looks are strongly influenced by this concept.

Using resources, and especially styles and templates, you have a great way to organize your code, to reuse code at multiple places, and eventually to make your application look just like you want it to look.

For further discussions and examples of this subject, check Chapter 19, where we design a couple of controls ourselves. But first, we have a big step in front of us: data binding!

CHAPTER 18

Data Binding and Using Data Controls

Data binding was not invented for Windows Presentation Foundation or Silverlight. In technologies such as ASP.NET, you can already bind a data control to a data source. However, data binding was reserved for data controls only. In Silverlight, you can data bind almost any property to any other property.

When a property is data bound to another property (and when certain conditions are met—we'll talk about that soon), the value of the two properties will be kept in sync. The neat thing is that you can bind many different types together. For example, you can bind all the Background and Fill properties of various controls and shapes together, so that when one is modified in code, the others will automatically change too!

In the second half of the chapter, we talk about two data controls used to display a variable number of items: the ListBox and the DataGrid.

Understanding Data Binding

To understand data binding and how it works, probably the best way is to use it in an example. Maybe you remember that in Chapter 16 "Digging Deeper into Silverlight Elements," we built a small drawing application named SilverlightDraw. We used events to set the visual appearance of the SettingsPopUp, for example when a Slider responsible for the Stroke thickness is moved. We also said that it is not the best way to do things, because of the strong dependency it introduces between the UI and the software logic. In this section, we will use a data binding to decouple them.

Creating a Data Object

The first step is to create a data object to store the values of the settings, with the following steps:

1. Start Visual Studio and reopen the SilverlightDraw application that we created in Chapter 16.

2. Right-click on the SilverlightDraw project in the Solution Explorer and choose Add, New Folder. Name this folder Data.

3. Right-click on the new folder and choose Add, Class. Name the new class Settings.cs.

4. Change the Settings class as in Listing 18.1:

LISTING 18.1   Settings Class

```
 1  public class Settings : INotifyPropertyChanged
 2  {
 3    #region INotifyPropertyChanged Members
 4    public event PropertyChangedEventHandler PropertyChanged;
 5    #endregion
 6
 7    private void OnPropertyChanged(string propertyName)
 8    {
 9      if (PropertyChanged != null)
10      {
11        PropertyChangedEventArgs args
12          = new PropertyChangedEventArgs(propertyName);
13        PropertyChanged(this, args);
14      }
15    }
16
17    private double _strokeThickness = 2.0;
18    public double StrokeThickness
19    {
20      get { return _strokeThickness; }
21      set
22      {
23        _strokeThickness = value;
24        OnPropertyChanged("StrokeThickness");
25      }
26    }
27  }
```

▶ On line 1, we declare that the new class `Settings` *implements* the interface called `INotifyPropertyChanged`. You have to add a `using` directive to enjoy the benefits of this interface.

▶ This interface is crucial to the whole data binding mechanism in Silverlight. It specifies just one member: The `PropertyChanged` event, declared on line 4. Note that interfaces can have any number of properties, events, methods, and so on. To fulfill its task, `INotifyPropertyChanged` just needs that event to be raised whenever one of the properties of the object is modified.

▶ On lines 7 to 15, we declare a helper method `OnPropertyChanged`. When it is called, it checks whether anyone subscribed to the event (line 9) and if that is the case, it creates a new instance of `PropertyChangedEventArgs` according to the parameter `propertyName` and raises the event. This way, all subscribers will be notified that something happened.

▶ On lines 17 to 26, we declare a property that will host the value of the `StrokeThickness`. This is a `double` value, like the property of the `Stroke` object that it will represent.

▶ On line 24, whenever the value of `StrokeThickness` is set, we call our helper method with the name of the `StrokeThickness` property as a parameter.

> **TIP**
>
> When you enter the interface name `INotifyPropertyChanged`, you'll notice the small red "underline" sign mentioned in Chapter 10, "Progressing with .NET." Press Shift+Alt+F10 to add a `using` directive with the corresponding namespace. Then, you'll see another small blue "underline" sign. Press Shift+Alt+F10 again to *implement* the interface. This enters the code you need to fulfill the "contract" that the interface represents.

At this point, build the application to make sure that you didn't make any typos. Our data object is ready already. That was not so terrible, was it?

Creating the Data Object in Resources

We need to place an instance of the new `Settings` object in the page's resources. This makes it available to both the XAML markup and the code-behind. By doing so, we make sure that all the code uses the same instance! This is important, because if one of the application's elements modifies a value, we want to make sure that all the other elements are notified of the change. Use the following steps:

1. In Page.xaml, add a new XML namespace `xmlns:data` to the `UserControl` tag as in Listing 18.2. As a reminder, the prefix `data` could actually be any word. This is just a way for us to remember which prefix corresponds to which namespace.

18

LISTING 18.2   Adding a Namespace

```
<UserControl x:Class="SilverlightDraw.Page"
  xmlns="http://schemas.microsoft.com/winfx/2006/xaml/presentation"
  xmlns:x="http://schemas.microsoft.com/winfx/2006/xaml"
  xmlns:data="clr-namespace:SilverlightDraw.Data">
```

2. Add an instance of the `Settings` class to the UserControl's resources as in Listing 18.3. Here, too, we can use any key for this instance. The only rule is that it must be unique within an object's resources.

LISTING 18.3   Settings in Resources

```
<UserControl.Resources>
  <data:Settings x:Key="Settings" />
</UserControl.Resources>
```

Remember when we talked about resources in Chapter 17, "Using Resources, Styling, and Templating"? We mentioned that you can add any object to a `ResourceDictionary`. This is just what we did here. The object `Settings` is a custom .NET object, and by adding it to the resources, we store it in a way that makes it easy to use in XAML and in code-behind.

Writing to the Data Object with a Binding

We now write to the `Settings` instance when the `SizeSlider` moves. Remember that for the moment, we do this in an event handler. This creates a tight connection between the XAML UI and the code-behind, which is annoying. If a graphics designer changes the UI and replaces the `Slider` with another control, a change is needed in the code-behind.

With a binding, on the other hand, the XAML can directly write (and read) to (and from) the data object. The coupling is looser, cleaner, and easier to modify if needed. Implement the following steps:

1. In the Page.xaml.cs, remove the whole event handler called `SizeSlider_ValueChanged`. We don't need that code anymore.

2. Change the `SizeSlider` in Page.xaml as in Listing 18.4:

LISTING 18.4   New `SizeSlider`

```
<Slider x:Name="SizeSlider"
  LargeChange="2" SmallChange="1"
  Minimum="2" Maximum="20"
  Value="{Binding Source={StaticResource Settings},
              Path=StrokeThickness,
              Mode=TwoWay}"
  Margin="0,0,5,0" Grid.Column="1" Grid.Row="3" />
```

▶ We removed the event handler for `ValueChanged` and modified the `Value` property. Instead of setting the initial value to "2" as before, we *bind* the value to the `StrokeThickness` property of the `Settings` instance.

▶ A `Binding` in XAML is a markup extension (like `StaticResource`). Like this other extension that we studied in Chapter 17, we use the `Binding` extension with curly brackets {}. We set the `Binding` properties such as `Source`, `Path`, and `Mode` using a simple `Name=Value` syntax.

▶ Note how we get the `Settings` instance from the resources using the `StaticResource` markup extension that we studied in Chapter 17. A markup extension (`StaticResource`) can be nested into another markup extension (`Binding`).

▶ We set the binding to `TwoWay`. We explain later in the "Digging in the Binding Class" section what the different values are for the `Mode` property.

▶ Since both the `Value` property on the `Slider` and the `StrokeThickness` property in the `Settings` are `double`, we don't need any type conversion.

At this point, our `Slider` is writing to the `Settings` instance, but this is not very spectacular. If you run the application and move the `SizeSlider`, nothing happens (in fact, the `Settings` instance gets updated, but nothing *visual* happens).

Getting Notified, Finding Binding Errors

Let's now bind the `Border` thickness to the same `Settings` instance so that its visual aspect changes accordingly, with the following steps:

1. Modify the opening `Border` tag within the `SettingsPopup` as in Listing 18.5:

LISTING 18.5   Updated `Border`

```
<Border BorderBrush="#FF000000"
        BorderThickness="{Binding Source={StaticResource Settings},
                          Path=StrokeThickness}"
        Width="180"
        Height="200">
```

2. Run the application in debug mode by pressing the F5 key in Visual Studio.

3. Display the Output tab (if needed, open it by selecting View, Output from the menu).

You should see a `System.Windows.Data Error` telling you that the `Double` value couldn't be converted to a `Thickness`.

The problem here is that the `Slider` value is a `Double`. However, we want to use that value on a `Thickness` object. While Silverlight can implicitly convert some values to other types, it notifies you here that it doesn't know how to convert the `StrokeThickness` value.

18

A binding error can be difficult to find, because it will not crash the application. The symptom is that the desired functionality just doesn't work. In this case, if you run the application, the Border is just invisible. Move the Slider, and nothing happens.

Converting Values in Bindings

We need to *convert* the double value into a Thickness. That's the job of a binding converter.

1. In Visual Studio, right-click on the Data folder in the Solution Explorer, and choose Add Class. Name this new class DoubleToThicknessConverter.

2. In the class file, change the class declaration as in Listing 18.6. The empty class implementation is created when you enter the IValueConverter interface declaration and then press Shift+Alt+F10 twice just as we did before with the INotifyPropertyChanged interface. Then modify the method Convert and ConvertBack. After entering this code, you can build the application to check if everything is OK.

LISTING 18.6   DoubleToThicknessConverter Class

```
public class DoubleToThicknessConverter : IValueConverter
{
  #region IValueConverter Members

  public object Convert(object value, Type targetType,
    object parameter, System.Globalization.CultureInfo culture)
  {
    return new Thickness((double) value);
  }

  public object ConvertBack(object value, Type targetType,
    object parameter, System.Globalization.CultureInfo culture)
  {
    return ((Thickness) value).Top;
  }

  #endregion
}
```

We just create a new Thickness instance, where all the four sides (left, top, right, and bottom) have the same size. As for ConvertBack, since we always deal with Thickness objects that have their four dimensions set to the same value, it is easy to implement this method.

> **NOTE**
>
> The ConvertBack method is used to change a double value (for example, Settings.StrokeThickness) into the Border's Thickness. Implementing the ConvertBack method is not strictly needed in our example, but it's good practice.

3. Add an instance of this new converter class in the `UserControl`'s resources in Page.xaml (Listing 18.7):

LISTING 18.7   `DoubleToThicknessConverter` in Resources

```
<UserControl.Resources>
  <data:Settings x:Key="Settings" />
  <data:DoubleToThicknessConverter x:Key="DoubleToThicknessConverter" />
</UserControl.Resources>
```

4. In the `SettingsPopup`, set the `Binding` to use this converter (Listing 18.8):

LISTING 18.8   Using the `DoubleToThicknessConverter`

```
<Border BorderBrush="#FF000000"
        BorderThickness="{Binding Source={StaticResource Settings},
          Path=StrokeThickness,
          Converter={StaticResource DoubleToThicknessConverter}}"
        Width="180"
        Height="200">
```

If you run the application now, you will see that the `Border`'s thickness in the settings popup changes when you move the `Slider`.

Digging in the `Binding` Class

Our SilverlightDraw application is now a mix of `Bindings` (the `StrokeThickness`) and event handlers. Binding the `Border`'s background color to the three "color `Sliders`" is possible but a little more complex. By using a binding instead of an event handler to modify the `Thickness` of the SettingsPopup `Border`, we decouple the XAML UI from the code-behind.

▶ If the UI designer decided to use another control to set the `Stroke` thickness (for example, a `TextBox` where the user can input a value), the developer doesn't need to change anything. The `Settings` class remains exactly the same.

▶ It is now easy to save the `Settings` class to a file, for example, by *serializing* it to XML. Using the `XmlSerializer` class, you can serialize any CLR object (well, almost any... but that's another story) to an XML file, for example, in the isolated storage. You can find more information about this in the SDK documentation.

The `Binding` class has the following properties:

▶ Source—We saw that property. It specifies where the property to bind to is located. This is typically a resource placed in a `ResourceDictionary`. In XAML, use the `StaticResource` markup extension to get the source.

▸ `Path`—This is the path to the property you want to data bind. Note the following:

   ▸ If you want to bind to the source object directly, you can omit the `Path` altogether. We create an example of this in Chapter 24, "Silverlight: Continuing the Journey."

   ▸ The `Path` may be complex. Remember when we talked about animations, and how we said that the `Storyboard`.`TargetProperty` can be complex to create? That's the same here. In Chapter 24, check the "Setting a Binding in Blend" section to see how Blend can assist you.

▸ `Mode`—Specifies in which direction the `Binding` acts. This can be

   ▸ `OneWay`—When the value changes in the source, the target will be notified. However, changes triggered by the target will not be passed back to the source. This is typically used when the target is immutable, for example, a `TextBlock`. That's also the default value.

   ▸ `TwoWay`—The target of the `Binding` may change the value, and the changes will be propagated to the source. For example, the target is a `TextBox` or a `Slider`, and the source should be notified when the value changes.

   ▸ `OneTime`—The value will be fetched only when the binding is created. Any subsequent changes will be ignored. This mode is good for properties that never get updated during the course of the runtime.

▸ `Converter`, `ConverterParameter`, `ConverterCulture`—These properties are used when a `Converter` must be used. We see examples of that in Chapter 24.

▸ `NotifyOnValidationError`, `ValidatesOnExceptions`—These two properties are used to specify the application's behavior when a value is updated by a `Binding`, but cannot be converted. Again, we see an example in Chapter 24.

When you check the documentation, note that there are two classes named `Binding` in the SDK documentation. The one that interests us is the `System.Windows.Data`.`Binding` class.

Setting the `DataContext`

Each `FrameworkElement` in Silverlight gets a `DataContext` property. This is a handy way to tell a `FrameworkElement` "every time that you use data, this is where you will find it." Another nice feature of `DataContext` is that it is propagated to the children of the `FrameworkElement`. This way, you can just set it once and simplify all your bindings' syntax. We call this the *explicit data context*. Let's demonstrate this with the following steps:

   1. In the SilverlightDraw application in Visual Studio, modify the SettingsPopup's markup to Listing 18.9:

LISTING 18.9   Setting the Data Context

```
<Popup x:Name="SettingsPopup"
       HorizontalOffset="10"
       VerticalOffset="10"
       DataContext="{StaticResource Settings}">
```

This sets the DataContext property for the Popup (and all its children) to the instance of Settings that we were using before.

2. As a consequence, we can now simplify our Binding expression and use the explicit data context instead as in Listing 18.10:

LISTING 18.10   Using the Explicit Data Context in the Border

```
<Border BorderBrush="#FF000000"
        BorderThickness="{Binding StrokeThickness,
          Converter={StaticResource DoubleToThicknessConverter}}"
        Width="180"
        Height="200">
```

When the Binding expression gets evaluated, the DataContext is evaluated, and since it is not set on the Border, the parent's DataContext is used.

3. For the Slider named SizeSlider, the markup becomes Listing 18.11:

LISTING 18.11   Using the Explicit Data Context in the Slider

```
<Slider x:Name="SizeSlider"
  LargeChange="2" SmallChange="1"
  Minimum="2" Maximum="20"
  Value="{Binding StrokeThickness, Mode=TwoWay}"
  Margin="0,0,5,0" Grid.Column="1" Grid.Row="3" />
```

The Path property is the Binding's default property. So you can omit it from the Binding declaration. It means that Path=StrokeThickness is equivalent to StrokeThickness.

As you can see, using the DataContext is a good way to simplify the Binding expressions. By setting the DataContext on a parent, you also set it on the children (unless of course a child explicitly set its own DataContext to something else.)

NOTE

You can explicitly set the Source property of a binding even when the DataContext is set to something else. The DataContext must be understood as a simpler way to specify the context of data operations for an element and its children.

18

Using Data Controls

In Chapter 17, we talked about a control that can display a collection of items: the TabControl. We also mentioned that this control derives from a basis control called the ItemsControl.

ItemsControls are great when it comes to displaying a variable number of items. In this section we learn how to use a ListBox (one of the controls derived from ItemsControl) and discuss another data control named the DataGrid.

Using a ListBox

ListBoxes are easy to use and are the logical choice when a list of items must be displayed quickly. Like every other Silverlight control, a ListBox can be customized by editing its control template if the need arises.

Creating the Data Items

Let's see how to use a ListBox with the following steps:

1. Create a Silverlight application in Visual Studio. Name it ColorChooser and select the option to generate a dynamically generated HTML test page.

2. In the ColorChooser project, add a new class and name it MyColor. The class declaration is rather simple, and has just three properties and one constructor. However, because we want to edit the Name and Timestamp properties later, we implement the INotifyPropertyChanged interface. Note that the MyBrush property is read-only. After you copy the code in Listing 18.12, build the application to check that everything is OK.

LISTING 18.12   Data Class MyColor

```
public class MyColor : INotifyPropertyChanged
{
  #region INotifyPropertyChanged Members
  public event PropertyChangedEventHandler PropertyChanged;
  #endregion

  public Brush MyBrush
  {
    get;
    private set;
  }

  private DateTime _timestamp = DateTime.Now;
  public DateTime Timestamp
  {
```

LISTING 18.12   Continued

```
    get { return _timestamp; }
    set
    {
      _timestamp = value;
      OnPropertyChanged(new PropertyChangedEventArgs("Timestamp"));
    }
  }

  private string _name;
  public string Name
  {
    get { return _name; }
    set
    {
      _name = value;
      OnPropertyChanged(new PropertyChangedEventArgs("Name"));
    }
  }

  public MyColor(string name, Brush brush)
  {
    Name = name;
    MyBrush = brush;
  }

  private void OnPropertyChanged(PropertyChangedEventArgs e)
  {
    if (PropertyChanged != null)
    {
      PropertyChanged(this, e);
    }
  }
}
```

3. Add another new class and name it ColorBrushes.

4. Edit the class declaration to make it derive from the ObservableCollection class.
Note that we use the *generics* notation to tell Silverlight that the collection contains
instances of the MyColor class. We talk about generics more in Chapter 20, "Taking
Silverlight 2 One Step Further."

```
public class ColorBrushes : ObservableCollection<MyColor>
```

> **NOTE**
>
> ObservableCollection is a wonderful class when you work with a variable number of items. Each time an item is added or removed (or if the sorting order changes), the collection raises events. When you use an ObservableCollection as the source of a binding, the ItemsControl automatically updates its view when such an event occurs.
>
> Deriving from ObservableCollection is an elegant way to create a new collection and possibly to extend it with custom properties. We could also have declared the collection as a *property* of the ColorBrushes class.

5. Initialize the ColorBrushes class with a collection of items. Add the code in Listing 18.13 in the class declaration. Note that these are test items only. Typically, a collection of items will be created outside of the collection class declaration. At this point, you can build the application again to check if all is fine.

LISTING 18.13   Initializing the ColorBrushes Class

```
 1  // Constructor
 2  public ColorBrushes()
 3  {
 4    Random random = new Random();
 5    for (int index = 0; index < 10; index++)
 6    {
 7      byte[] bytes1 = new byte[3];
 8      random.NextBytes(bytes1);
 9      Color color1 = Color.FromArgb(255, bytes1[0], bytes1[1], bytes1[2]);
10      byte[] bytes2 = new byte[3];
11      random.NextBytes(bytes2);
12      Color color2 = Color.FromArgb(255, bytes2[0], bytes2[1], bytes2[2]);
13
14      LinearGradientBrush brush = new LinearGradientBrush();
15      GradientStop stop1 = new GradientStop();
16      stop1.Offset = 0;
17      stop1.Color = color1;
18      brush.GradientStops.Add(stop1);
19      GradientStop stop2 = new GradientStop();
20      stop2.Offset = 1;
21      stop2.Color = color2;
22      brush.GradientStops.Add(stop2);
23
24      this.Add(new MyColor("Random" + this.Count, brush));
25    }
26  }
```

▶ On line 4, we create a new `Random` object.

▶ Line 7 allocates a new `byte` array with three cells.

▶ Line 8 fills the `byte` array with three random `bytes`, between 0 and 255.

▶ Line 9 creates a new `Color` with these random values. Note that the first value (the Alpha channel defining the `Color`'s opacity) is set to the maximum 255 (or FF). The result of this operation is a random color.

▶ We repeat the same operations on lines 10 to 12 to create a second random color.

▶ Lines 14 to 22 create a new `LinearGradientBrush` using the two random `Colors`.

▶ Line 24 creates a new `MyColor` instance and adds it to the collection. Since the `ColorBrushes` class derives from `ObservableCollection`, we can directly use the `Add` method on the `this` keyword.

6. Select File, Save All from the menu (or press Ctrl+Shift+S).

7. Open the Solution file in Expression Blend. If needed open the file Page.xaml and build the application.

8. In the Project panel, under Data, click on the +CLR Object button.

9. In the Add CLR Object Data Source dialog, select the `ColorBrushes` class and enter a name in Data Source Name, for example, MyColorBrushes. Then click OK.

This step adds an instance of `ColorBrushes` to the XAML resources. The selected data source also appears in the Data section (see Figure 18.1).

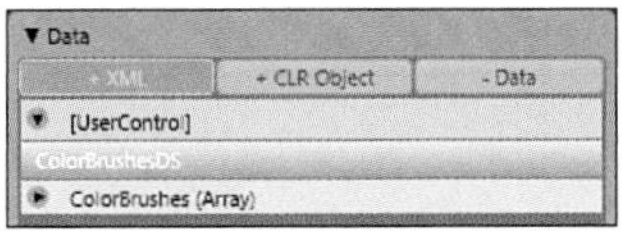

FIGURE 18.1   Data section with `ColorBrushes` instance

Adding a `ListBox`

Now that our ColorChooser application has (dummy) data ready, we can use this data in a control. Let's use a `ListBox` with the following steps:

1. If needed, set the LayoutRoot Grid in Grid Layout Mode (see Figure 5.7) and add a row on its bottom. Make the new row 60 pixels high.

WARNING

Even though the button +XML is there, it is not possible to work directly with XML data sources in Silverlight 2 (it is in WPF, though, and that's why the button exists in Blend). We see how to use XML data in Chapter 22, "Connecting to the Web."

2. In the toolbar, click and hold the `Button` tool and select a `ListBox` control. Add it to the `Grid`'s first row (the bigger one). Name the `ListBox` ColorsList.

3. Reset the `ListBox`'s `Width` and `Height` to Auto, and set its `Margin` to 10,10,10,10.

4. Select the `ListBox` and right-click on it; then select Bind ItemsSource to Data.

5. In the Create Data Binding dialog, select the instance of `ColorBrushes` that we added to the resources before. In the Fields panel, simply select the `ColorBrushes` instance. We don't bind to a property of this class, but to the whole collection. Then press Finish.

6. Run the application. The string ColorChooser.MyColor should be listed ten times in the `ListBox`.

> **NOTE**
>
> Remember the `IEnumerable` interface we saw in Chapter 17? You can use any class implementing `IEnumerable` as the `ItemsSource` of an `ItemsControl`. `ObservableCollection` is implementing this interface, so our `ColorBrushes` class (which derives from `ObservableCollection`) automatically does too.

Since we didn't specify yet how the `MyColor` instances should be displayed, Silverlight takes the easy way and simply calls the `ToString` method on each of the items. Because nothing else is specified (we didn't *override* the `ToString` method), it returns the type name.

Creating a `DataTemplate`
Now we specify how the `ListBox` should represent the data items with the following steps:

1. In Blend, right-click on the `ListBox`, and select Edit Other Templates, Edit Item Template, Create Empty.

2. Enter a name for the template, for example BrushTemplate and click OK. This creates the template in the resources of the `UserControl`. We could also have placed the template in the App.xaml, for example, if this template is reused throughout the application.

3. In the `DataTemplate`'s `Grid`, add an `Ellipse`.

4. Set the `Ellipse`'s `Width` to 100, its `Height` to 50, and reset its `HorizontalAlignment` and `VerticalAlignment` to Stretch.

5. Click on the small square next to the `Fill` property and select Data Binding.

6. In the Create Data Binding dialog, select the Explicit Data Context tab. Check the Use a Custom Path Expression box and enter MyBrush. Then click Finish and set the scope back to the `UserControl`.

Doing this creates a One Way `Binding` from the data item's property named `MyBrush` to the `Ellipse`'s `Fill` property. But why does it work? The reason is that the `ItemsControl` class (and all derived controls) will automatically set a row's *DataContext* to the corresponding data item in the `ItemsSource` collection. For instance, in our application, the third `Ellipse`'s `DataContext` will be set to the third instance of `MyColor` in the collection.

Because of this, even without setting the binding's `Source` explicitly, you can bind the `DataTemplate`'s elements to the data item's properties.

Run the application by pressing F5. You should see ten ellipses in the `ListBox` with random gradients (see Figure 18.2).

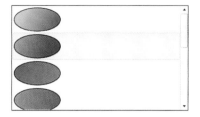

FIGURE 18.2   Random brushes in a `ListBox`

Taking a Look at the XAML

In this section, we worked in Blend, but as usual, everything we did can be done in XAML directly. Let's see what markup Blend created in Page.xaml (use the XAML tab in the Design panel).

▶ Blend created two resources in the `UserControl`'s resource dictionary:

▶ An instance of our `ColorBrushes` class as data source. Notice the attribute that Blend added: `d:IsDataSource` specifies that the resource should appear in the Data Source and Data Binding dialogs in Blend. This attribute has strictly no effect except in Blend.

```
<ColorChooser:ColorBrushes x:Key="MyColorBrushes"
                           d:IsDataSource="True" />
```

> **WARNING**
>
> If you want to add the `d:IsDataSource` attribute in XAML directly, you must also add the following namespaces to the `UserControl` tag:
>
> `xmlns:d=http://schemas.microsoft.com/expression/blend/2008`
>
> `xmlns:mchttp://schemas.openxmlformats.org/markup-compatibility/2006`
>
> `mc:Ignorable="d"`

18

▶ A `DataTemplate` was added with the key `BrushTemplate` (see Listing 18.14). This template contains a `Grid`, and the `Grid` contains an `Ellipse`. Notice how we bind the `Fill` property to the current item of the collection, using the explicit data context:

LISTING 18.14   `DataTemplate` for a Brush

```
<DataTemplate x:Key="BrushTemplate">
  <Grid>
    <Ellipse Fill="{Binding Path=MyBrush, Mode=OneWay}"
```

LISTING 18.14   Continued

```
                Stroke="#FF000000" Height="50" Width="100" />
  </Grid>
</DataTemplate>
```

▶ The `ListBox` itself contains two interesting attributes `ItemsSource` and `ItemTemplate` (Listing 18.15):

LISTING 18.15   ListBox Markup

```
<ListBox x:Name="ColorsList" Margin="10,10,10,10"
  ItemsSource="{Binding Mode=OneWay,
                    Source={StaticResource MyColorBrushes}}"
  ItemTemplate="{StaticResource BrushTemplate}" />
```

▶ The `ItemsSource` property (inherited from the `ItemsControl` parent class) is set to a `Binding` to the collection in the resources `MyColorBrushes`.

▶ The `ItemTemplate` property uses a `StaticResource` that points to the `DataTemplate` that was added in the `UserControl`'s resources.

In just a few lines of code, and with (or without) Blend's assistance, we were able to create a visual representation of a collection of data items. Data controls are powerful in Silverlight, especially thanks to the use of `DataTemplate`, which can be modified at will. There are no limits to your creativity.

Adding and Removing Items

We mentioned that the `ObservableCollection` automatically notifies the Silverlight framework when an item is added or removed (or when the sorting order is modified). Let's demonstrate with the following steps:

1. In Blend, in Page.xaml, add a `StackPanel` to the main `Grid`. Set the `StackPanel`'s `Row` to 1, reset the `Margin` to 0, reset the `Width` and `Height` to Auto, and reset the `HorizontalAlignment` and `VerticalAlignment` to Stretch. Set the `Orientation` to Horizontal.

2. Add four `TextBoxes` to the `StackPanel`. Set their names to A, R, G, and B. Set their `Width` to 30, `Height` to Auto, and `Margin` to 5,5,5,5. Set their `VerticalAlignment` to Center and delete the `Text` property.

3. Add two buttons to the `StackPanel`. Set both buttons' `Width` to 60, `Height` to Auto, and `Margin` to 10,10,0,10.

4. Set the first button's `Content` to Add and name it AddColorButton. For the second one, use Remove as `Content`, and RemoveColorButton as name.

5. Click on the small button with a lightning bolt on top of the Properties panel. Select the AddColorButton and double-click in the text box next to the `Click` event. This adds an event handler to the file Page.xaml.cs in Visual Studio.

6. Go back to Blend and do the same for the RemoveColorButton.

7. In Visual Studio, implement the event handlers as in Listing 18.16:

LISTING 18.16   Adding and Removing Items

```
private void AddColorButton_Click(object sender, RoutedEventArgs e)
{
  Color newColor = Color.FromArgb(byte.Parse(A.Text),
    byte.Parse(R.Text), byte.Parse(G.Text), byte.Parse(B.Text));
  SolidColorBrush newBrush = new SolidColorBrush(newColor);
  ColorBrushes collection = Resources["MyColorBrushes"] as ColorBrushes;
  MyColor newItem = new MyColor("Manual " + collection.Count, newBrush);
  collection.Add(newItem);
}
private void RemoveColorButton_Click(object sender, RoutedEventArgs e)
{
  MyColor selected = ColorsList.SelectedItem as MyColor;
  (Resources["MyColorBrushes"] as ColorBrushes).Remove(selected);
}
```

▶ The first event handler creates a new instance of the `MyColor` class based on the value of the `TextBoxes` and adds it to the collection. Since this is an `ObservableCollection`, the `ListBox` automatically displays a new item based on the `SolidColorBrush` we create here and on the `DataTemplate` we specified earlier.

▶ The second event handler checks which item is selected in the `ListBox`, and removes it from the collection. Here too, the `ListBox`'s view gets updated. Notice how handy it is to get access to the data item (the instance of `MyColor`) directly using the `SelectedItem` property!

8. Then add the initialization code in Listing 18.17 in the `Page` constructor. We initialize the four `TextBoxes` with the components of the purple color.

LISTING 18.17   Initializing the `TextBoxes`

```
public Page()
{
  InitializeComponent();
  Color initialColor = Colors.Purple;
  A.Text = initialColor.A.ToString();
  R.Text = initialColor.R.ToString();
```

18

LISTING 18.17   Continued

```
  G.Text = initialColor.G.ToString();
  B.Text = initialColor.B.ToString();
}
```

9. Now run the application and click on the Add button. You should see a new purple ellipse being added in the ListBox. Note that the new item gets added to the bottom of the ListBox, so you may have to scroll down to see it. In fact, the new item was added in the ObservableCollection, but through the binding and the data template, the new data item was "translated" visually. Similary, clicking the Remove button takes the selected item out of the ObservableCollection, and the ListBox is automatically updated.

Using the DataGrid

While the ListBox we saw earlier can display a collection of data items in a simple way (and even in a more complex way by changing the DataTemplate representing the data item), it is somehow limited. Fortunately, Silverlight 2 was shipped with a powerful, yet easy to use data control: the DataGrid.

The DataGrid can be customized in so many ways that there could (almost) be a book named *Silverlight DataGrid Unleashed*. This section gives you a good overview of this powerful control. For more details, check the "DataGrid" section in the SDK documentation. For now, follow the steps:

1. Open the ColorChooser application in Visual Studio and open Page.xaml.

2. Remove the ListBox we added earlier.

3. In the Visual Studio Toolbox, locate the DataGrid control, and drag and drop it on the XAML markup, in place of the ListBox we just removed.

   This operation takes care of adding a reference to the assembly System.Windows.Controls.Data in which the DataGrid is included. It also adds a new namespace to the XAML document, in the UserControl tag, and uses this prefix to reference the DataGrid control. Alternatively, you could perform these steps manually, like we did for the GridSplitter control in Chapter 16, in the section titled "Adding the System.Windows.Controls Assembly."

4. Edit the DataGrid markup to look like Listing 18.18:

LISTING 18.18   Simple DataGrid

```
<my:DataGrid x:Name="ColorsList" AutoGenerateColumns="True"
  ItemsSource="{Binding Mode=OneWay, Source={StaticResource MyColorBrushes}}"
  Margin="10,10,10,10" />
```

5. Click on the Preview tab in Visual Studio (bottom left) to see the result of our implementation (Figure 18.3). This is a very powerful feature of Visual Studio: Even the initialization code we added in the `ColorBrushes` class is run and you can see 10 rows in the `DataGrid`! Note however that the Preview tab is a bit slow....

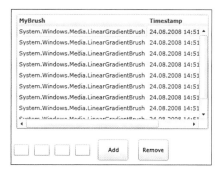

FIGURE 18.3   Simple `DataGrid`

By setting the `AutoGenerateColumns` property to `True`, the `DataGrid` automatically displays one column for each public property in the data item. In our case, the first column doesn't make much sense (it's just the `ToString` method of the `Brush` class being called). We change this a little later.

Because we named the new `DataGrid` ColorsList just like the `ListBox` before, and because the `DataGrid` control exposes the same interface as the `ListBox` control, you can run the application, then use the Add and Remove buttons without changing anything in the code.

Editing Values and Checking Them

When we defined the `MyColor` class, we made the `Name` and `Timestamp` properties writeable. As a consequence, the user can click in the corresponding columns and change these properties. You can prevent this by setting the whole `DataGrid` to read-only by using the `IsReadOnly` property. When we customize the columns later in this chapter, you can also set each column to read-only or read-write separately.

Since the value displayed in the `DataGrid`'s column is data bound to a property in the data object, you can add validation logic in the property setter to make sure that the value entered by the user complies with the rules of the application.

When Does a Value Get Updated, Exactly?

When you bind a property to a `TextBox` with a Two Way binding (which is exactly what happens in the `DataGrid`), the value gets updated only after the user sets the focus on a different element than the `TextBox`. This can be done by pressing the Tab key, or by clicking the mouse somewhere else.

In the `DataGrid`, you get an additional way to commit the change: Press the Enter key.

Customizing the Look and Feel

Because the properties are all set to default, the `DataGrid` displays a simple look and feel. To change this, you can set all kinds of brushes:

- ▶ `Foreground` changes the color of the texts in the rows and in the title.

- ▶ `RowBackground` and `AlternatingRowBackground` set the background color of the row and (if set) of every second row in the grid. This makes it easier to browse large grids.

18

▶ HorizontalGridlinesBrush and VerticalGridlinesBrush set the color of the grid lines.

The DataGrid control can also be edited comfortably in Expression Blend. Especially all the different brushes used by this control can be visualized and edited.

In addition to these brushes, you can set a large number of properties on the DataGrid to modify its appearance and behavior. For instance:

> **WARNING**
>
> Pressing Enter to commit the value works only in the DataGrid. When you data bind a standard TextBox to a property, pressing Enter will not commit the data.
>
> If you have one TextBox only, clicking on another location in the Silverlight application will not remove the focus from the control, and the value won't get committed. You can remove the focus by clicking on a control in the web browser, such as as the location bar, or by pressing the Tab key.

▶ CanUserReorderColumns and CanUserResizeColumns are set to True by default. If the user grabs a column and moves it, the column order is changed. By moving the "splitter" at the right of the column title, the user can resize the column. Changing these two properties to False prevents this from happening. The user changes to the columns are not preserved. If the user refreshes the web page by pressing F5 in the web browser, the order of the columns is lost. To prevent this, you can use the DisplayIndex property of each column in the Columns collection of the DataGrid, and save these values to the isolated storage. You can save any changes by handling the ColumnReordered event.

▶ CanUserSortColumns is also set to True by default. The columns can be sorted by clicking on their header. Note that the sorting algorithm might need to be customized to meet your needs.

▶ ColumnWidth, MinColumnWidth, and MaxColumnWidth govern the columns' size. Note that this affects each column in the grid in the same way. To set the columns' width individually, you must rather use the Width property in the DataGrid's Columns collection. For example, handle the AutoGeneratingColumn event in the DataGrid tag.

```
AutoGeneratingColumn="DataGrid_AutoGeneratingColumn"
```

The code in Listing 18.19 sets the first column's Width to 100 pixels.

LISTING 18.19   Setting the First Column's Width

```
private int _columnIndex = 0;
private void DataGrid_AutoGeneratingColumn(object sender,
  DataGridAutoGeneratingColumnEventArgs e)
{
  if (_columnIndex == 0)
  {
    e.Column.Width = new DataGridLength(100.0);
```

LISTING 18.19   Continued

```
  }
  _columnIndex++;
}
```

- ▶ The ScrollBars visibility is (as usual) set with the HorizontalScrollBarVisibility and VerticalScrollBarVisibility properties. If the user is allowed to scroll horizontally, the FrozenColumnCount property sets how many columns on the left of the DataGrid are always visible. This is similar to the Freeze Panes option in Microsoft Excel.

- ▶ ColumnHeaderHeight is pretty much self-explanatory. Note that you can also change the header's appearance by customizing its style, with the property ColumnHeaderStyle. The TargetType for this Style should be set to DataGridColumnHeader, and you can customize each of this class's properties (check the SDK documentation for more details).

Setting the RowDetails
A nice feature of the DataGrid is the ability to easily create a RowDetails, which expands when the corresponding row is selected. Simply set the RowDetailsTemplate property. Since we have a DataTemplate already (the one we used in the ListBox before), we can just reuse this:

```
<dg:DataGrid x:Name="ColorsList" AutoGenerateColumns="True"
  ItemsSource="{Binding Mode=OneWay, Source={StaticResource MyColorBrushes}}"
  Margin="10,10,10,10" RowDetailsTemplate="{StaticResource BrushTemplate}" />
```

Note that you can control the way the RowDetails is displayed by using the RowDetailsVisibilityMode property (see Figure 18.4). It can be set to Collapsed, Visible, or VisibleWhenSelected (this is the default value).

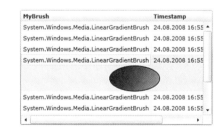

FIGURE 18.4   RowDetails

Refining the Columns
One column is still annoying: MyBrush really shouldn't be displayed this way, because it doesn't bring any information to the user. Generating the columns automatically is not enough, and we need to specify the columns individually.

Change the DataGrid as in Listing 18.20:

LISTING 18.20   DataGrid with Manually Defined Columns

```
<my:DataGrid x:Name="ColorsList" AutoGenerateColumns="False"
  ItemsSource="{Binding Mode=OneWay, Source={StaticResource MyColorBrushes}}"
  Margin="10,10,10,10">

  <my:DataGrid.Columns>
    <my:DataGridTextColumn Header="Name" DisplayMemberBinding="{Binding Name}" />

    <my:DataGridTemplateColumn Width="100" Header="Brush">
      <my:DataGridTemplateColumn.CellTemplate>
        <DataTemplate>
          <Grid>
            <Rectangle Fill="{Binding MyBrush}" />
          </Grid>
        </DataTemplate>
      </my:DataGridTemplateColumn.CellTemplate>
    </my:DataGridTemplateColumn>

    <my:DataGridTextColumn Header="Timestamp"
                           DisplayMemberBinding="{Binding Timestamp}" />
  </my:DataGrid.Columns>
</my:DataGrid>
```

▶ We set the `AutoGenerateColumns` property to false. It means that we need to specify the columns' look and feel ourselves.

▶ The first and last columns in the `Columns` collection are `DataGridTextColumn`. We tell the grid what to display by using the `DisplayMemberBinding` property. In this case, we want to display the `Name` and the `Timestamp` of the current item.

▶ The second column is specified with even more details. We create a `DataTemplate` to show exactly what we want. In that case, the template is simple: a `Rectangle` in a `Grid`, with its `Fill` property set to the current item's `MyBrush` property thanks to a binding. Of course, this template can be customized even more and can display anything you want.

In addition to the `DataGridTextColumn` and the `DataGridTemplateColumn`, the `DataGrid` also allows for a `boolean` property to be displayed by a `DataGridCheckBoxColumn`.

Each column can be customized by a set of properties, similar to the ones we studied earlier for the `DataGrid` itself (such as `MinWidth`, `CanUserReorder`, `CanUserResize`, and so on). Check the SDK documentation.

Editing Elements in the DataGrid

The last feature we present here is the ability to change a column's appearance when it is being edited. We saw earlier that a column can be edited when the corresponding property is writeable (and the `IsReadOnly` property is set to `false`, which is the default). Follow the steps:

1. Replace the first column `"Name"` with the template in Listing 18.21:

LISTING 18.21   TemplateColumn for the `Name` Column

```
<my:DataGridTemplateColumn Header="Name" Width="120">
  <my:DataGridTemplateColumn.CellTemplate>
    <DataTemplate>
      <TextBlock Text="{Binding Name}" />
    </DataTemplate>
  </my:DataGridTemplateColumn.CellTemplate>
  <my:DataGridTemplateColumn.CellEditingTemplate>
    <DataTemplate>
      <TextBox Text="{Binding Name, Mode=TwoWay}"
               Background="LightCoral" Foreground="Red" />
    </DataTemplate>
  </my:DataGridTemplateColumn.CellEditingTemplate>
</my:DataGridTemplateColumn>
```

2. Replace the last column `"Timestamp"` with Listing 18.22:

LISTING 18.22   TemplateColumn for the `Timestamp` Column

```
<my:DataGridTemplateColumn Header="Timestamp" Width="120">
  <my:DataGridTemplateColumn.CellTemplate>
    <DataTemplate>
      <TextBlock Text="{Binding Timestamp}" />
    </DataTemplate>
  </my:DataGridTemplateColumn.CellTemplate>
  <my:DataGridTemplateColumn.CellEditingTemplate>
    <DataTemplate>
      <my1:DatePicker DisplayDate="{Binding Timestamp, Mode=TwoWay}"
                      SelectedDate="{Binding Timestamp, Mode=TwoWay}"/>
    </DataTemplate>
  </my:DataGridTemplateColumn.CellEditingTemplate>
</my:DataGridTemplateColumn>
```

18

3. Run the application and notice how the `CellEditingTemplate` is used when you edit the `Name` column or the `Timestamp` column (see Figure 18.5).

NOTE

To add the `DatePicker` to the `Timestamp` column, drag and drop this control from the Toolbox in Visual Studio. Refer to Chapter 16, to the section called "Using the DatePicker."

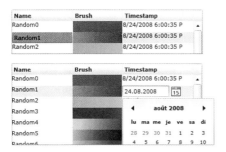

FIGURE 18.5   Editing the `Name` and `Timestamp` property

Using XML Data Sources

We saw how to bind a collection (in fact, any `IEnumerable`) of items to a data control. Often, however, we need to work with other kinds of data sources, and especially XML content. Binding to XML data in Silverlight involves a conversion from XML to a collection of objects. This can be done using a technology named *LINQ*.

Often, XML data is obtained as the result of a web service call. Silverlight is well equipped to communicate with web services, especially those returning an XML- or JSON-formatted response. We talk about Silverlight web communication and the various web-based data sources in Chapter 22, where we also build such an example for our Thumbnails application.

Summary

Data binding might be one of the most revolutionary additions to the .NET framework brought by WPF and Silverlight. Binding various properties to data objects brings a new dynamic to the applications, and a clean separation of presentation layer (mostly implemented in XAML) and data model.

The new data controls, and especially the `DataGrid` make it comfortable to work with collections of items. This last control is so powerful that it is impossible to study all the scenarios in just one chapter.

While many data operations can be done in code-behind, you are encouraged to use data binding as often as you can. It might seem difficult at first (especially for developers used to more traditional technologies), but it will quickly become second nature. The learning curve is worth it!

CHAPTER 19

Creating User Controls and Custom Controls

Controls are a convenient way to "pack" functionality and to provide encapsulation, reusability, and testability. When Silverlight was first released, the only control delivered was a TextBlock. Needless to say, it was not easy to create rich applications! Of course, you also had a set of "primitives" such as Rectangles, Ellipses, and even Paths, not to mention the powerful MediaElement. But the point remains, building an application without even a Button or a Slider is tough. Some (such as the team building the video player templates for Expression Encoder) created buttons and other controls from scratch (you can still see this if you open one of the player templates in Blend, as we did in Chapter 13, "Progressing with Videos").

Fortunately, we now have a rich set of controls. Even better, we have a framework that allows us to create new controls and also to customize existing controls' look and feel. This is liberating. However, creating controls is not easy—it's advanced Silverlight! This chapter and the next help you understand how such a complex task is done, and encourage you to continue the exploration.

Creating a Thumbnails Viewer User Control

A UserControl (as opposed to a custom control, which we create later) has a XAML front end in addition to the code-behind. In this section we customize the control in which our thumbnails are displayed and scrolled. To do this, we create a new UserControl composed of a ScrollViewer (without any scrollbars visible), an `ItemsControl`, and two `RepeatButtons`. We talked about `ItemsControls` in Chapter 18, "Data Binding and Using Data Controls," and saw how they can be used to display a collection of items. This enables us to move toward a model where the media items are totally external to the Thumbnails application (for example, placed on the web server).

The next step is use an XML file to describe the items, and to finally be free from any hard-coded value. Instead, we "feed" an XML file to our application, and the media files are loaded dynamically from the web server.

Creating the Data Objects

Our application and its extended functionality require some code-behind. Since we are experienced object-oriented programmers now, let's "break" our functionality in objects.

Making the Parent Class Media

We want a new class to hold our thumbnails information. This is the class that we will "fill" with data, add to a collection, and then *data bind* to our thumbnails viewer (that's the control we do next). Follow the steps:

1. In Visual Studio, open the Thumbnails application that we edited last in Chapter 17, "Using Resources, Styling, and Templating." Then right-click on the Thumbnails Solution (the first file on top of the Solution Explorer) and add a new project to the Thumbnails Solution. This should be a Silverlight class library named MediaInfo.

2. Rename the class file in Solution Explorer from Class1.cs to Media.cs.

3. Replace the Media class with the code in Listing 19.1:

> **NOTE**
>
> We will try to make this library and the classes it will contain as independent from the Thumbnails application as possible. Our intent is to make it so it can be reused in other applications. Actually, it would even make sense to develop it independently from the Thumbnails application (for example, in its own Solution), and to reference the MediaInfo.dll instead of the MediaInfo project. For more information, see the "Using an External Class Library" section in Chapter 20, "Taking Silverlight 2 One Step Further."

LISTING 19.1   `MediaType` Enumeration and `Media` Class

```
public enum MediaType
{
  Image = 0,
  Movie = 1,
}


public class Media : INotifyPropertyChanged
{
```

LISTING 19.1   Continued

```
#region INotifyPropertyChanged Members
public event PropertyChangedEventHandler PropertyChanged;
#endregion

public MediaType Type
{
  get; set;
}
public string MediaName
{
  get; set;
}
private string _description;
public string Description
{
  get { return _description; }
  set
  {
    _description = value;
    if (PropertyChanged != null)
    {
      PropertyChanged(this,
        new PropertyChangedEventArgs("Description"));
    }
  }
}
private string _mediaPath = "";
public string MediaPath
{
  get { return _mediaPath; }
  set { _mediaPath = (value == null) ? "" : value; }
}
public DateTime TimeStamp
{
  get; set;
}
}
```

► First we add an enumeration named MediaType that we will use to define the type of the current media.

► The Media class has five properties. Of these five, only the Description might be updated at runtime, so it's the only one that raises the PropertyChanged event.

▶ The property `MediaPath` may never be `null`, because it might be combined to the `MediaName` to form the full path of the media item. We check whether it's set to `null`, and we set it to an empty string instead.

Build the application now to make sure that everything is OK. You will have to add a using directive for the `INotifyPropertyChanged` interface.

Extending the `Media` Class

The `Media` class is an independent data object. When we build our Thumbnail template later, we will need a couple more properties, directly related to how we display our media elements. The best way to do this is to *extend* the `Media` class. Because this new class is extended, we name it `MediaEx`. Also, because it's really only used in our Thumbnails application, we create it in that project with the following steps:

1. Right-click on the Data folder in the Thumbnails project in Studio and select Add, Class. Name the new class MediaEx.cs.

2. We need a reference to the external DLL MediaInfo. We add it through a project reference. Right-click on the Thumbnails project again and select Add Reference. In the Add Reference dialog, choose the Projects tab and select the MediaInfo project.

3. The class looks like Listing 19.2:

LISTING 19.2   MediaEx Class

```
public class MediaEx : Media
{
  public Uri FileUri
  {
    get
    {
      return new Uri(
        System.IO.Path.Combine(MediaPath, MediaName).Replace('\\', '/'),
          UriKind.Relative);
    }
  }
  public BitmapImage ImageSource
  {
    get
    {
      return (Type == MediaType.Image)
        ? new BitmapImage(FileUri) : null;
    }
  }
  public Uri MovieUri
  {
    get { return (Type == MediaType.Movie)
```

LISTING 19.2   Continued

```
    ? FileUri : null; }
  }
}
```

▶ None of these properties change during runtime, so they don't raise the PropertyChanged event.

▶ The FileUri property is just a convenience property, but since it's read-only, it does no harm to make it public. Note the use of the helper method System.IO.Path.Combine. Unfortunately, this method uses the backslash separator ('\') and not the slash ('/'), which is needed for URIs. This is why we need to replace the '\' character with '/'.

▶ The ImageSource (of type BitmapImage) and MovieUri (of type Uri) are what we need to bind to an Image control, and respectively, a MediaElement control. If the Type doesn't correspond, they return null and nothing appears on the UI.

> **WARNING**
>
> In C#, the backslash has a special meaning: It helps define special characters (such as Tab '\t' and new line '\n'). If you want to use it alone, you must write '\\'.

4. We want the MediaEx items stored in an ObservableCollection. Since the data source class is very simple, you can write the code in Listing 19.3 in the same file MediaEx.cs. If you prefer, however, you can also create a new class file called MediaExCollection.cs in the Data folder. At this point, you can try and build the application. It should build fine, after you add a couple of using directives.

LISTING 19.3   MediaExCollection Class

```
public class MediaExCollection : ObservableCollection<MediaEx>
{
}
```

Packing the ThumbnailsViewerControl

With the data objects ready, let's work on the user interface now with the following steps:

1. Build the application in Visual Studio, and then open it in Expression Blend. If you see an error message, just recompile the application in Blend.

2. In Page.xaml, in the Objects and Timeline category, delete the ScrollViewer containing the Thumbnails.

3. Add a new `Grid` to the LayoutRoot, and name it ThumbnailsViewer. Move the new `Grid` in the Objects and Timeline category until it appears before the `StackPanel`, just under the LayoutRoot.

4. Set the ThumbnailsViewer `Grid`'s `Width` to 170 pixels and reset its `Height` to Auto. Reset the `HorizontalAlignment` and `VerticalAlignment` to Stretch and reset the `Margin` to 0. Set the `Column` to 1 and the `RowSpan` to 2 so that it appears in the same cells as the previous `ScrollViewer`.

5. Select the new `Grid` until it appears surrounded with a yellow border. Then, with the Selection tool selected in the toolbar, create three rows. The first and the last are going to "host" buttons to scroll the content. Make them 75 pixels high. The middle row will "host" the Thumbnails, and its `Height` should be set to 1 Star.

> **TIP**
>
> To set a `Grid`'s row's `Height`, click with the mouse on top of it, next to the "lock" icon. Then set the `Height` in the Properties panel. Note that this works only when the `Grid` is in Grid Layout mode, not in Canvas mode, so you may have to switch. Refer to Figure 5.7 for details.

6. Open the Asset Library by clicking on the last button on the toolbar.

7. Check the Show All box and select a `RepeatButton`. This control gets added as a tool to the toolbar, right above the Asset Library button.

8. Using the `RepeatButton` tool, add a button to the first cell of the ThumbnailsViewer `Grid` and make it fill the whole cell. Name this button ScrollButtonUp.

9. Repeat the operation in the last cell on the right, and name this new button ScrollButtonDown.

10. In the middle cell, add a `ScrollViewer` and make it fill the whole cell. Name it ThumbScrollViewer. Set its `HorizontalScrollbarVisibility` to Disabled and `VerticalScrollBarVisibility` to Hidden.

11. Select the `ScrollViewer` with a yellow border and add an `ItemsControl` to it. Here too, this control must be selected from the Asset library (like the `RepeatButton` before). And here, too, this control should fill the whole `ScrollViewer`. Name it ThumbItemsControl. The result should look like Figure 19.1.

FIGURE 19.1   ThumbnailsViewer control draft

12. Finally, we "pack" our `UserControl`. This gives us more flexibility to work with it and provides neater code. Right-click on the ThumbnailsViewer `Grid` in the Objects and Timeline category. Select Make Control (or press the F8 key).

13. Enter a name for the new control: ThumbnailsViewerControl (the name proposed by Blend) sounds all right. Do not check the Leave Original Content As Is And Create Duplicates As Necessary box. Click OK.

Blend creates a new `UserControl` and places the ThumbnailsViewer `Grid` within the new control's LayoutRoot `Grid`. That's not really necessary, since ThumbnailsViewer is a grid already. We will simply replace LayoutRoot with ThumbnailsViewer as shown in the following steps:

1. Select ThumbnailsViewer in the Objects and Timeline category, and drag it on the `UserControl` on top. Since the `UserControl` can have only one child, the LayoutRoot disappears.

2. Rename ThumbnailsViewer to LayoutRoot. Although not required, it's good practice to name the top container like this.

3. In the Properties panel, set the `Width` and `Height` of LayoutRoot to Auto. When you do this, even though all the elements' `Width` and `Height` are set to Auto, Blend sets a "design width and height" to help you work. If it didn't, our control would appear very small.

4. Save everything and go back to the Page.xaml.

5. In Page.xaml, set the `ThumbnailsViewerControl`'s `Width` to 170 pixels if needed. Reset the `Margin` to 0. Also make sure that the `Column` in which the ThumbnailsViewer is located is 1 and the `RowSpan` is 2!

6. Notice that the Design panel asks you to rebuild the project, which you should do now.

7. Finally, set the `ThumbnailsViewerControl` Name to ThumbnailsViewer. You can now run the application to see the result.

Communicating with the Outside World

Our `UserControl` should get some information from the `Page`, and also expose information when an item is selected.

Adding an `ItemsSource` Property

We need to provide the `Page` with a way to set the items that must be displayed. To do this, let's add a `DependencyProperty` that we will use as a gateway to set our `ItemsControl`'s `ItemsSource` property. We reuse the same name to make our intent clear.

We mentioned `DependencyProperties` in Chapter 15, "Digging into Silverlight Elements," and said that they are the mortar of Silverlight, holding pieces together.

DPs can be added to a `DependencyObject` (and remember that `FrameworkElement` derives from `DependencyObject`). A DP can be animated, it can be styled, and two DPs can be data bound together (as we saw in previous chapters). Generally, any property that could change during the life of the control, and any property that you want to data bind to should probably be a DP.

> **TIP**
>
> If you really want to sound cool when you talk about Silverlight, you should name `DependencyProperties` "DPs."
>
> By convention, all DPs are named with the suffix Property.

Actually, Windows Presentation Foundation uses DPs even more than Silverlight (and WPF DPs are also more powerful than Silverlight's one because WPF is a superset of Silverlight). In Silverlight, you cannot derive a class from `DependencyObject`, so you cannot use DPs with data items, but only with controls.

`DependencyProperties` are *registered* with the Silverlight framework. The registration process occurs once only for every class (it's a *static* registration), but every instance of the class gets a separate set of DPs anyway. Let's add a DP to our control with the following steps:

1. Open the file ThumbnailsViewerControl.xaml.cs in Visual Studio. You will have to reload the project there, as we changed it in Blend.

2. Add an event handler inside the `ThumbnailsViewerControl` class as in Listing 19.4. It will be called when the `ItemsSource` DP is set. Whenever this happens, we want to use the value to set the `ItemsControl` `ItemsSource`.

LISTING 19.4   `OnItemsSourceChanged` Event Handler

```
private static void OnItemsSourceChanged(DependencyObject d,
  DependencyPropertyChangedEventArgs args)
{
  ThumbnailsViewerControl sender = d as ThumbnailsViewerControl;
  sender.ThumbItemsControl.ItemsSource
    = (args.NewValue as MediaExCollection);
}
```

▶ Because this is a static event handler (remember that DPs are registered in a static way with the framework, so the event handler must be static too), we need to get a reference on the instance that sent the event. This is what the first parameter does. On the first line, we cast this object d to a `ThumbnailsViewerControl`.

▶ Note how we get the `NewValue` of the `MediaExCollection` instance in the args parameter of `OnMediaChanged`. You also get the `OldValue` if you need it.

3. Add the DP as shown in Listing 19.5:

LISTING 19.5   `ItemsSourceProperty DP`

```
1  public static readonly DependencyProperty ItemsSourceProperty
2    = DependencyProperty.Register("ItemsSource",
3    typeof(MediaExCollection), typeof(ThumbnailsViewerControl),
4    new PropertyMetadata(new PropertyChangedCallback(OnItemsSourceChanged)));
```

- ▶ On line 1, we declare the name of the DP.

- ▶ Line 2 is the call to the static method `Register` on the `DependencyProperty` class. The first parameter is the name of the property.

- ▶ Line 3 states the type of the DP, and then the type of the owner.

- ▶ Line 4 creates a new `PropertyMetadata` instance. This type contains additional information about the DP. In our case, we "wire" the event handler we implemented before, through a `PropertyChangedCallback` handler. This guarantees that our event handler is called every time the DP's value changes.

4. For convenience, add "normal" get and set accessors for the DP as in Listing 19.6. This makes it much easier to work with it, for example, to set the DP in code.

LISTING 19.6   Convenience Setter and Getter

```
public MediaExCollection ItemsSource
{
  get { return (MediaExCollection) GetValue(ItemsSourceProperty); }
  set { SetValue(ItemsSourceProperty, value); }
}
```

The DP's value for each instance can be read by a call to the method `GetValue`. To write, use the method `SetValue`. Build the code to make sure that everything is in order. You can build the application now.

Adding a `SelectedItem DependencyProperty`

Add the code as shown in Listing 19.7:

LISTING 19.7   `SelectedItem DP`

```
public MediaEx SelectedItem
{
  get { return (MediaEx) GetValue(SelectedItemProperty); }
  set { SetValue(SelectedItemProperty, value); }
}

public static readonly DependencyProperty SelectedItemProperty
```

19

LISTING 19.7   Continued

```
= DependencyProperty.Register("SelectedItem",
typeof(MediaEx), typeof(ThumbnailsViewerControl),
new PropertyMetadata(null));
```

We set this DP later in this chapter, when we handle the MouseLeftButtonDown event on each Thumbnail.

Adding an Event

To trigger the "expanding" and "collapsing" animations in the Page, we expose an event that will be raised when a Thumbnail is clicked. Here, too, we can inspire ourselves from the ListBox and its SelectionChanged event. We will in fact reuse the same delegate and the SelectionChangedEventArgs class for our purpose.

1. In the ThumbnailsViewerControl class, declare an event:

   ```
   public event SelectionChangedEventHandler SelectionChanged;
   ```

2. Create a helper method to raise this event (Listing 19.8):

LISTING 19.8   OnSelectionChanged Helper Method

```
private void OnSelectionChanged(FrameworkElement sender, MediaEx item)
{
  if (SelectionChanged != null)
  {
    object[] addedItems = new object[1];
    addedItems[0] = sender;
    object[] removedItems = new object[0];
    SelectionChangedEventArgs args
        = new SelectionChangedEventArgs(removedItems, addedItems);
    SelectionChanged(this, args);
  }
  SelectedItem = item;
}
```

▶ For more information, check the class SelectionChangedEventArgs in the SDK documentation.

▶ In the last line of the method set the SelectedItem property to the MediaEx instance currently selected. If any other property of another control is bound to that DP, it is notified of the change. We see how this works in Chapter 20.

At this point, you can build the application again to make sure that everything is OK. You can even run it, though you won't notice any changes, we still need to update the UI!

Creating the Items and Designing a DataTemplate

Our UserControl's functionality is ready. Now we need to create items to fill it, and a DataTemplate for these items. We also need to trigger the SelectionChangedEvent and set the SelectedItem correctly.

Creating the Media Instances in XAML

Since we don't know how to read an XML file yet (we learn this in Chapter 22, "Connecting to the Web"), we now create the Media instances in XAML markup. This is temporary. Follow the steps:

1. Open the file Page.xaml in Visual Studio.

2. Add a namespace in the UserControl tag pointing to the namespace Thumbnails.Data:

   ```
   xmlns:data="clr-namespace:Thumbnails.Data"
   ```

3. Because we use the items in Blend, we want to notify Blend that this is a data source. To do this, we need the namespaces in Listing 19.9 added to the UserControl tag (we talked about this in Chapter 18). Note however that it is very possible that Blend already added these namespaces. Make sure that they are not already available before you add them, or else you'll get an error.

LISTING 19.9   Adding Namespaces

```
xmlns:d="http://schemas.microsoft.com/expression/blend/2008"
xmlns:mc="http://schemas.openxmlformats.org/markup-compatibility/2006"
mc:Ignorable="d"
```

4. In the UserControl.Resources section, add the markup in Listing 19.10:

LISTING 19.10   MediaDataSource Collection

```
<data:MediaExCollection x:Key="MediaDataSource" d:IsDataSource="True">
  <data:MediaEx MediaName="mov1.wmv" MediaPath="MediaFiles" Type="Movie"
              Description="Nightly show at Singapore Zoo" />
  <data:MediaEx MediaName="pic1.png" MediaPath="MediaFiles" Type="Image"
              Description="The Matterhorn seen from Zermatt" />
  <data:MediaEx MediaName="pic2.jpg" MediaPath="MediaFiles" Type="Image"
              Description="The Matterhorn" />
  <data:MediaEx MediaName="pic3.jpg" MediaPath="MediaFiles" Type="Image"
              Description="Mountains seen from Klosters" />
</data:MediaExCollection>
```

19

▸ This markup creates four instances of the MediaEx class and initializes them with information about the files. The path MediaFiles is the name of a (yet to be created) folder in which we will copy the media files. If you want, you can create a more complex file structure.

▸ The four instances are added to an instance of the MediaExCollection class we created before. Remember that this class inherits ObservableCollection.

▸ We set the d:IsDataSource attribute to True. We talked about this Expression Blend attribute in Chapter 18.

To help us design the DataTemplate, we also add such a collection with test data in the ThumbnailsViewerControl.xaml file. We want test data there because it helps us visualize the items when we design them in Blend.

1. Open ThumbnailsViewerControl.xaml and set the data namespace in the UserControl tag.

   ```
   xmlns:data="clr-namespace:Thumbnails.Data"
   ```

2. Create a new UserControl.Resources section as in Listing 19.11:

LISTING 19.11   TEMPMediaDataSource Collection

```
<UserControl.Resources>
  <data:MediaExCollection x:Key="TEMPMediaDataSource"
                          d:IsDataSource="True">
    <data:MediaEx MediaName="pic1.png"
                  Type="Image" Description="Test1" />
    <data:MediaEx MediaName="pic2.jpg"
                  Type="Image" Description="Test2" />
  </data:MediaExCollection>
</UserControl.Resources>
```

3. Replace the existing ItemsControl in the XAML markup with Listing 19.12, including a data binding to our test data source:

LISTING 19.12   Data Bound ThumbItemsControl

```
<ItemsControl x:Name="ThumbItemsControl"
ItemsSource="{Binding Source={StaticResource TEMPMediaDataSource}}" />
```

If you click on the Preview tab in Visual Studio (or if you run the application), you should now see two lines in our ThumbnailsViewerControl, each with the text "Thumbnails.Data.MediaEx" (see Figure 19.2). Since we worked with data controls, we know that this occurs when the ItemsControl has items, but no template to represent them. So we can be happy, our "wiring" to the test data is working fine.

FIGURE 19.2   ThumbnailsViewerControl in Preview tab

By default, the ItemsControl uses a vertical StackPanel to display the items. This is exactly what we need, so no need to touch anything. Should you want to use another panel (for example a horizontal StackPanel) someday, you can do so in Blend with the following steps. Note that this is not needed here, it's just so that you see this functionality once:

1. In Blend, in Page.xaml, right-click on the ThumbnailsViewer control and choose Edit Control. This opens ThumbnailsViewerControl.xaml.

2. Right-click on the ItemsControl and select Edit Other Templates, Edit Items Panel, Create Empty.

3. Name the new template ThumbnailsPanelTemplate and click OK.

4. In the template, right-click on the Grid and select Change Layout Type, StackPanel.

5. Select the StackPanel, and set its Orientation to Horizontal in the Properties panel. Then set the scope back to the UserControl.

Now we "just" need to create a visual representation of the items.

Designing a DataTemplate

In fact, we want to use a similar representation to what we had until now. To make it a little simpler, we will, however, remove the reflection next to the Thumbnails. Also, one single template must be able to handle a video as well as an image!

Handling Images

The first action is to create a DataTemplate and to implement it so that it handles images, with the following steps:

1. In Blend, in ThumbnailsViewerControl.xaml, right-click on ThumbItemsControl and choose Edit Other Templates, Edit ItemTemplate, Create Empty.

2. Name this new DataTemplate ThumbnailTemplate and place it in the UserControl.

3. Select the main Grid in the template. Then, using the Search box on top of the Properties panel, find the Style property and set it to ThumbnailGridStyle. Use the

19

small square next to the `Style` property, then select Local Resource from the context menu. This `Style` is the one we created in Chapter 17. Don't worry if the `Grid` appears smaller than it should, this is a Blend issue and we will take care of that in a minute.

4. Inside the `Grid`, add a `Border` and reset its `Width`, `Height`, `HorizontalAlignment`, `VerticalAlignment` and `Margin` to their default value. Remember to use the small square next to the property and choose Reset.

5. Set the `Border`'s `Style` to ThumbnailBorderStyle using the same process as in step 3. This `Style` was also created in Chapter 17 and placed in App.xaml.

6. Inside the `Border`, add an `Image` control (you must select it from the Asset library with the Show All check box checked). If needed, reset the `Image`'s `Width` and `Height`, `Margin` and alignment.

7. Define an empty `Style` for the `Image`, name it ThumbnailImageStyle and place it in the Application. In the `Style`, set the `Image`'s `Stretch` property to Fill.

8. Save and set the scope back to the `DataTemplate`. Then, using the small square next to the `Source` property of the `Image`, set a `DataBinding` to the Explicit Data Context, with the custom path expression set to `ImageSource`.

9. Build the application in Blend. You should now see two images in the `ItemsControl`. See how handy it is to design the `DataTemplate` when you can actually see it? If you want, edit the `Styles` to make the thumbnails look just like you want them.

10. With the `Image` selected, add an event handler (use the small "lightning bolt" button located on top of the Properties panel). Enter the name `media_MouseLeftButtonDown` for the `MouseLeftButtonDown` event. Then click out of the text box to create the event in Visual Studio. We implement this event handler later.

Handling Videos

Our `DataTemplate` can handle pictures now, but we also have videos in the collection. Implement the following steps:

1. Go back to Blend and in the ThumbnailTemplate, add another `Border` in the main `Grid`. Make it fill the whole space like before.

2. Using the Properties panel, set the new `Border`'s `Style` to the local resource we created earlier, named ThumbnailBorderStyle (the small square next to the `Style` property helps you there).

3. In the `Border`, add a `MediaElement` from the Asset library. Set its `Width` and `Height` to Auto, set `Stretch` to Fill, and set `AutoPlay` to False. Remember that due to a bug in Blend, you might have to click on the check box a couple of times until the value gets set correctly. See in the XAML file whether the value `AutoPlay="False"` is written.

4. Using the small square next to the `Source` property, set a data binding to Explicit Data Context, with the "custom path expression" set to `MovieUri`.

5. Here, too, set the `MouseLeftButtonDown` event to the same event as before: `media_MouseLeftButtonDown`.

6. In addition, set the `MediaEnded` event to an event handler named `MediaElement_MediaEnded`. Remember we implemented this event handler before (in Chapter 5, "Using Media").

7. Open Page.xaml.cs in Studio and locate the old event handler `MediaElement_MediaEnded`. Then copy the content into the new event handler with the same name in ThumbnailsViewerControl.xaml.cs. You can delete the old event handler in Page.xaml.cs.

Again, you should build the application as a check that everything is fine.

Removing the Test Data Source

We can now remove the test markup we added before with the following steps:

1. In Visual Studio, remove the `TEMPMediaDataSource` collection from ThumbnailsViewerControl.xaml.

2. Remove the `ItemsSource` property from the `ItemsControl`. We don't need this anymore. The application should build just fine. You can run it, but nothing will appear yet.

Moving the Media Files

For the moment, our media files are *embedded* inside the assembly Thumbnails.dll. This is obviously far from ideal. The first task is to remove the files and place them on the web server instead, with the following steps:

1. In Visual Studio, find the folder ClientBin and create a new folder inside it. Name this new folder MediaFiles.

> **WARNING**
>
> Why do we create the MediaFiles folder inside ClientBin? Because we want to use relative paths for the media. However, in the current version of Silverlight, relative paths are all resolved relatively to the ClientBin folder (and not relative to the website root). And even more unfortunately, you cannot "exit" the ClientBin folder with the ".." syntax. Since the ClientBin folder is accessible from the web client, this is not a huge issue, and the media files you have there are also accessible from a standard HTML page.

2. Drag the files mov1.wmv, pic1.png, pic2.jpg, and pic3.jpg from Thumbnails to Thumbnails.Web/ClientBin/MediaFiles. This creates a copy of the files, so you can now delete them from the Thumbnails project.

3. Before you build the application, right-click on the Thumbnails project in the Solution Explorer and select Open Folder in Windows Explorer. Navigate to Thumbnails\bin\Debug and write down the size of Thumbnails.dll. Then, build the application in Studio and check the size again. Because all the media files are now removed from the DLL, the size should be much smaller.

4. Since we don't have the local media files anymore, open Page.xaml and remove the `TextBlock.Foreground` for both title `TextBlocks` (the ones saying "Welcome to my gallery" and "Have some fun"). We will set these in code instead.

5. While we are at it, and because we want to access these `TextBlocks` in code, let's name them `TitleTextBlock1` and `TitleTextBlock2`.

6. Then, add an `ImageBrush` in code. Add the code in Listing 19.13 in Page.xaml.cs, at the end of the `Page` constructor. Then save all the files and build the application.

LISTING 19.13   Setting the TextBlocks' Brushes in Code

```
MediaExCollection mediaCollection
  = Resources["MediaDataSource"] as MediaExCollection;
MediaEx mediaInfo1 = mediaCollection[1];
MediaEx mediaInfo2 = mediaCollection[2];

ImageBrush brush = new ImageBrush();
brush.ImageSource = mediaInfo1.ImageSource;
TitleTextBlock1.Foreground = brush;
brush = new ImageBrush();
brush.ImageSource = mediaInfo2.ImageSource;
TitleTextBlock2.Foreground = brush;
```

We create two different `ImageBrushes` according to the images we have in the `MediaEx` instances that we read from the resources. This is temporary and will change in Chapter 22.

WARNING

If you run the application with the Thumbnails project selected as startup, you will get errors. The media files are hard-coded in the Page.xaml file, but they are not available in the Thumbnails project anymore. This state is temporary until Chapter 22. To solve the issue, make sure that the test project Thumbnails.Web is selected as the startup project and its index.html as the startup page. Do this in Blend and in Studio!!

Connecting the ThumbnailsViewer to the Real Data

Remember the `ItemsSource` DP that we added into our ThumbnailsViewerControl before? We will use this DP to connect the control to the real data files. Since we internally "wire" the `ItemsControl` to this DP, this should work just fine. Follow the steps:

1. Open Page.xaml in Blend and click on ThumbnailsViewer.

2. In the Properties panel, look for the `ItemsSource`.

3. Use the small square next to this property to set the value to a data binding. Select the `MediaDataSource` in the Data Sources panel. Then click Finish. We see the `MediaDataSource` in the Create Data Binding dialog because we set the `d:IsDataSource` attribute to `True` earlier.

At this point, you should see four empty borders in the `ItemsControl` in Blend. They are empty because the actual media files are not in the Silverlight project anymore (we moved them in the section titled "Moving the Media Files" earlier). If you run the application (and make sure that you set the website project Thumbnails.Web and index.html as Startup), you will see the four media thumbnails.

Raising and Handling the SelectionChanged Event

We don't do anything yet when a media gets clicked, but we have an event handler already. What we want is simple: We just need to raise the `SelectionChanged` event.

Raising the Event in the `UserControl`

In Visual Studio, in ThumbnailsViewerControl.xaml.cs, get the clicked element and the corresponding `MediaEx` instance. Thankfully we know that the data item is automatically set as the `DataContext` of the `FrameworkElement`, and that it is passed to all its children. We already have an empty method for the media_MouseLeftButtonDown event. You can now replace it with Listing 19.14.

LISTING 19.14   media_MouseLeftButtonDown Event Handler

```
private void media_MouseLeftButtonDown(object sender,
  MouseButtonEventArgs e)
{
  FrameworkElement clickedElement = sender as FrameworkElement;
  MediaEx media = clickedElement.DataContext as MediaEx;
  OnSelectionChanged(clickedElement, media);
}
```

Handling the Event in the Page

When an item gets clicked, we want the animation to start, the Thumbnail to expand and be displayed in the frame, the movie to start running, and so on. In short, we want the method named `media_MouseLeftButtonDown` in Page.xaml.cs to be executed. We can do this with the following steps:

1. This method was initially an event handler, but it's not anymore. Let's modify its name to make this more obvious. We can also change its signature:

```
void ExpandCollapseMedia(FrameworkElement castedSender)
```

2. Because we now pass the `castedSender` directly to the method, we don't need the first line of the method, the line where the `sender` was casted. Remove that line.

3. The name `castedSender` doesn't make much sense anymore, so here is a trick to change it everywhere in the code in two easy steps:

   ▶ In the method signature, rename `castedSender` to `media`.

   ▶ Press Shift+Alt+F10 and select Rename 'castedSender' to 'media'. This replaces the name everywhere in the method. You can also use this trick for attributes, properties, methods, and have Studio replace the name everywhere in the application. If you get a message from Studio, just click on "Continue".

4. Try to build now: You should get a compilation error. Remember that we did the "wiring" to the `MouseLeftButtonDown` event handler in code before. You need to remove this part. In the `Page` constructor, delete the lines from

```
UIElement media = null;
```

to

```
while (media != null);
```

Finally, let's hook the `SelectionChanged` event of the ThumbnailsViewer control to the ExpandCollapseMedia method.

1. At the end of the `Page` constructor, add the event handler as in Listing 19.15:

LISTING 19.15   Adding the `SelectionChanged` Event Handler

```
ThumbnailsViewer.SelectionChanged
  += new SelectionChangedEventHandler(ThumbnailsViewer_SelectionChanged);
```

2. And then implement it as in Listing 19.16:

LISTING 19.16   ThumbnailsViewer_SelectionChanged Event Handler

```
void ThumbnailsViewer_SelectionChanged(object sender,
  SelectionChangedEventArgs e)
{
  if (e.AddedItems.Count > 0)
```

LISTING 19.16   Continued

```
  {
    ExpandCollapseMedia(e.AddedItems[0] as FrameworkElement);
  }
}
```

You can now build and run the application, and click on the Thumbnails. We restored the functionality we had before, but this time in a much more flexible and extendable way. Note that the ScrollViewer doesn't scroll yet. We will take care of that in Chapter 20.

Creating a MediaInfoDisplay Custom Control

Custom controls have a different purpose than user controls.

▶ User controls are a *group of controls* fulfilling a certain purpose. It is more of a logical encapsulation of functionality within an application. A user control is not lookless; it has a XAML front-end.

▶ Custom controls are *reusable UI elements* designed as *lookless* objects. They do not have a XAML front end (but a template can be attached to them to define their look and feel). They are usually distributed in a separate assembly and referenced from the application.

In practice, you can also store user controls in a separate assembly and reuse them in multiple applications. This separation in custom controls versus user controls is also a matter of personal preference, technical expertise, what you really want to do with the control, and so on. Generally, user controls are easier and faster to develop than custom controls, but they do not offer the same level of separation between behavior and appearance as custom controls.

Creating a new custom control from scratch is a big job and requires a good understanding of Silverlight. This section gives you an overview of how to build a simple custom control, but you might want to explore more on your own. In that case, check out the "Digging Deeper" section in Chapter 20.

Making a Blueprint

The control we create now displays information about media. In this simple implementation, we only provide a short description and a long description. Of course the control can be extended later to display a name, date, and other information for the current media. For the moment, we will not worry about the way the information will be displayed. This will be for later, when we wear our "designer's hat" and create a template for the control. For now, we only worry about the implementation. The control must do the following:

1. Accept an instance of the class `Media` that we created earlier.

2. Provide the `Media.Description` as a `LongDescription` property.

3. Create a `ShortDescription` property, calculated according to a maximum number of characters.

4. Should these properties change, the controls bound to them must update their view automatically (you see where I am going with that, don't you?).

5. Be encapsulated and easily reusable in other applications if needed.

6. Provide a simple default look and feel as a designer will create a new template anyway.

Now that we have a better idea of what our control must fulfill, let's implement!

Creating the "Shell"

To fulfill requirement number 5, we want to place the `MediaInfoDisplay` control in a class assembly. Also, due to the relationship between the control and the `Media` data object, let's put `MediaInfoDisplay` in the MediaInfo assembly. Follow the steps:

1. In Visual Studio, add a new class to the project MediaInfo. Name it MediaInfoDisplay.cs.

2. Let the new control derive from the `Control` class:

```
public class MediaInfoDisplay : Control
```

3. In the class, declare a constant. This is the number of characters that the `ShortDescription` will display. Note that, in this simple implementation, we do not provide a way for the user to change this value. Constants are static, even though they are not declared explicitly so. A constant always has the same value for every instance of this type.

```
private const int SHORT_LENGTH = 30;
```

4. Add a default constructor to the class as in Listing 19.17. The only operation is to specify the `DefaultStyleKey` property.

LISTING 19.17   `MediaInfoDisplay` Constructor

```
public MediaInfoDisplay()
{
  DefaultStyleKey = typeof(MediaInfoDisplay);
}
```

▶ This property is inherited from the `FrameworkElement` class.

▶ It notifies the framework that if nothing else is specified, it must look for a `Style` corresponding to this control's type, and apply it.

▶ We use this later to create a default look and feel for the `MediaInfoDisplay` control and include it in our class library.

Specifying the Parts and States

We now specify what parts and states the control will contain. This is not strictly needed by the Silverlight framework itself, but will enable a good workflow in Blend. This also helps us visualize what we need to do. Parts are components of the control. Typically, a *part* is an element to which event handlers will be attached. A complex control can have many parts. A more simple control might have no parts at all. Our control will have one part—one element that can be clicked—and we will call it the `DescriptionPanel`.

Parts and states are specified using attributes. Remember them? We talked about them in Chapter 14, "Letting .NET and JavaScript Talk," and mentioned they are used to *decorate* classes or other elements with information. That's what we do here. Expression Blend reads this *metainformation* and reacts accordingly. On top of the class declaration, add an attribute for the `DescriptionPanel` part:

```
[TemplatePart(Name="DescriptionPanel", Type=typeof(FrameworkElement))]
```

We mention that `DescriptionPanel` will be a `FrameworkElement`. For example, it could be a `Border`, `Grid`, or anything the designer wants to use. We don't want to restrain the designer's creativity by restricting the type of the `DescriptionPanel` part.

Now we use another attribute to specify the control's states. We use two *states groups*: `CommonStates` gathers states that have to do with the general appearance of the control. `DescriptionStates` gathers states that have to do with the way the description is displayed.

For this last group, we specify two states: The control displays either a `ShortDescription` or a `LongDescription` (that's requirement numbers 2 and 3 in the previous list). So we specify `DescriptionNormal` for when the `ShortDescription` is displayed, and `DescriptionExpanded` for when the `LongDescription` is shown.

In addition we define a `Normal` state and a `MouseOver` state, which are pretty much self-explanatory.

Add the following attributes right below the `TemplatePart` one and before the class declaration, so that we have Listing 19.18:

LISTING 19.18   Parts and States

```
[TemplatePart(Name="DescriptionPanel", Type=typeof(FrameworkElement))]
[TemplateVisualState(Name = "Normal", GroupName = "CommonStates")]
[TemplateVisualState(Name = "MouseOver", GroupName = "CommonStates")]
```

19

LISTING 19.18   Continued

```
[TemplateVisualState(Name = "DescriptionNormal",
  GroupName = "DescriptionStates")]
[TemplateVisualState(Name = "DescriptionExpanded",
  GroupName = "DescriptionStates")]
public class MediaInfoDisplay : Control
```

Adding DependencyProperties

To fulfill the functionality, our control needs to expose three DPs. We define them now.

1. Add a DP for the ShortDescription property as in Listing 19.19:

LISTING 19.19   ShortDescription DP

```
// Short description DP
public string ShortDescription
{
  get { return (string) GetValue(ShortDescriptionProperty); }
  set { SetValue(ShortDescriptionProperty, value); }
}

public static readonly DependencyProperty ShortDescriptionProperty
  = DependencyProperty.Register("ShortDescription",
  typeof(string), typeof(MediaInfoDisplay),
  new PropertyMetadata(null));
```

2. When the LongDescription is changed, the ShortDescription should be updated too. Let's do this by creating an event handler for the PropertyChangedCallback event as in Listing 19.20. We see in step 3 how to "wire" this event handler to the event.

LISTING 19.20   OnLongChanged Event Handler

```
// Long description DP
private static void OnLongChanged(DependencyObject d,
  DependencyPropertyChangedEventArgs args)
{
  MediaInfoDisplay sender = d as MediaInfoDisplay;

  sender.ShortDescription
    = (sender.LongDescription.Length > SHORT_LENGTH)
    ? sender.LongDescription.Substring(0, SHORT_LENGTH - 3) + "..."
    : sender.LongDescription;
}
```

We calculate the value of the `ShortDescription` for the sender based on the `LongDescription` and on the constant value `SHORT_LENGTH`.

3. Now register the DP for the long description (Listing 19.21):

LISTING 19.21   LongDescription DP

```
public string LongDescription
{
  get { return (string) GetValue(LongDescriptionProperty); }
  set { SetValue(LongDescriptionProperty, value); }
}

public static readonly DependencyProperty LongDescriptionProperty
  = DependencyProperty.Register("LongDescription",
  typeof(string), typeof(MediaInfoDisplay),
  new PropertyMetadata(new PropertyChangedCallback(OnLongChanged)));
```

Notice how the first parameter of the `PropertyMetadata` is a `PropertyChangedCallback`, and how it is "wired" to our event handler. This way, every time that `LongDescription` changes, the `ShortDescription` will also be updated.

The last DP we need is an instance of the class `Media` that our control will represent. We must handle changes to this property. We set the `LongDescription` DP according to the instance, and in turn this automatically updates the `ShortDescription`.

Add the following event handler and register the DP as in Listing 19.22:

LISTING 19.22   MediaInfo DP

```
// Media info DP
private static void OnMediaChanged(DependencyObject d,
  DependencyPropertyChangedEventArgs args)
{
  MediaInfoDisplay sender = d as MediaInfoDisplay;

  Binding binding = new Binding();
  binding.Source = args.NewValue as Media;
  binding.Path = new PropertyPath("Description");
  sender.SetBinding(LongDescriptionProperty, binding);
}

public Media MediaInfo
{
  get { return (Media) GetValue(MediaInfoProperty); }
  set { SetValue(MediaInfoProperty, value); }
```

LISTING 19.22   Continued

```
}

public static readonly DependencyProperty MediaInfoProperty
  = DependencyProperty.Register("MediaInfo",
  typeof(Media),
  typeof(MediaInfoDisplay),
  new PropertyMetadata(new PropertyChangedCallback(OnMediaChanged)));
```

We data bind the LongDescription to the property Media.Description, which raises the PropertyChanged event when it is set. So we will be automatically notified if it changes. For example, if later you decide to implement a user interface to let the user edit the media description, the rest of the UI will be updated according to the user's changes! At this point, build the application to check if the code has errors.

Handling the States

The states of the control are managed by a neat class called VisualStateManager or VSM. This class provided by the Silverlight framework handles all the transitions between the control's states. Of course it needs input from us:

▶ We need to trigger the transition when the event handlers are raised.

▶ We also need to tell the VSM what the transitions are. We will customize these transitions later when we put our designer's hat on and create a template for our MediaInfoDisplay control.

To make things easier, we create a couple of private attributes and a helper method in the class MediaInfoDisplay. Add two private attributes holding the control's desired state and create a helper method named GoToState as in Listing 19.23:

LISTING 19.23   GoToState Method

```
// Handling the states
private bool _isMouseOver = false;
private bool _isDescriptionExpanded = false;
private void GoToState(bool useTransitions)
{
  if (_isMouseOver)
  {
    VisualStateManager.GoToState(this,
      "MouseOver", useTransitions);
  }
  else
  {
```

LISTING 19.23   Continued

```
  VisualStateManager.GoToState(this,
    "Normal", useTransitions);
}

if (_isDescriptionExpanded)
{
  VisualStateManager.GoToState(this,
    "DescriptionExpanded", useTransitions);
}
else
{
  VisualStateManager.GoToState(this,
    "DescriptionNormal", useTransitions);
}
}
```

- ▶ Depending on the desired states, the VSM changes the control to the corresponding state.

- ▶ Note the parameter useTransitions: If it is true, the Silverlight framework will set the state of the control using an animation. If it's false, the transition will be immediate. This can be useful to place the control in its initial state, for example. We see a little later how to set the transitions.

Be careful here: the names of the states you use here must match the names of the states you declared for the class in the attributes before. This is annoying, but it's the way it is. Build the application to check is everything if OK.

Handling the Part

Our control declared one part, which is the element (of type FrameworkElement) containing the description strings. It can be a Border or a panel of any kind, depending on the graphics designer's fantasy. We declare it as a part, because we want to change the state of the description when this panel is clicked. The control's state can go from DescriptionNormal to DescriptionExpanded.

Let's handle the case where the part is found. In that case, we must add event handlers to it (Listing 19.24):

LISTING 19.24   DescriptionPanelPart Property

```
  // Handling the part
1 private FrameworkElement _panelPart = null;
2 private FrameworkElement DescriptionPanelPart
3 {
```

19

LISTING 19.24   Continued

```
 4    get { return _panelPart; }
 5    set
 6    {
 7      FrameworkElement _oldPart = _panelPart;
 8      if (_oldPart != null)
 9      {
10        _oldPart.MouseEnter
11          -= new MouseEventHandler(_panelPart_MouseEnter);
12        _oldPart.MouseLeave
13          -= new MouseEventHandler(_panelPart_MouseLeave);
14        _oldPart.MouseLeftButtonDown
15          -= new MouseButtonEventHandler(
16            _panelPart_MouseLeftButtonDown);
17      }
18
19      _panelPart = value;
20      if (_panelPart != null)
21      {
22        _panelPart.MouseEnter
23          += new MouseEventHandler(_panelPart_MouseEnter);
24        _panelPart.MouseLeave
25          += new MouseEventHandler(_panelPart_MouseLeave);
26        _panelPart.MouseLeftButtonDown
27          += new MouseButtonEventHandler(
28            _panelPart_MouseLeftButtonDown);
29      }
30    }
31  }
```

▶ Line 7 gets the part that we saved before (in case it's not the first call). If it's not null, we remove the event handlers that we had attached to it (lines 10 to 16). That's a bit confusing, but check lines 22 to 28; this is where we attach the event handlers.

▶ On line 19, we assign the value to the private attribute, saving it for later.

WARNING

Not removing the event handlers does not create errors but does affect the way your application works. If you leave the event handlers when the DescriptionPanelPart changes, you prevent the memory from being freed. Granted, the risk of this becoming a problem in this simple application is small, but preventing *memory leaks* is always a good policy!

▶ In case the panelPart is not null, we assign new event handlers to it. We handle the case where the mouse passes over the panel, where it exits the panel, and finally where the element is clicked.

▶ Your control should always handle the case where the part is null. After all, nothing forces the designer to use the named part in a template. Your control must be robust enough and avoid crashing if that's the case.

Finally, let's implement the event handlers (see Listing 19.25). Fortunately, it's easy thanks to our helper method GoToState.

LISTING 19.25   Event Handlers

```
// Event handlers
void _panelPart_MouseEnter(object sender,
  MouseEventArgs e)
{
  _isMouseOver = true;
  GoToState(true);
}
void _panelPart_MouseLeave(object sender,
  MouseEventArgs e)
{
  _isMouseOver = false;
  GoToState(true);
}
void _panelPart_MouseLeftButtonDown(object sender,
  MouseButtonEventArgs e)
{
  _isDescriptionExpanded = !_isDescriptionExpanded;
  GoToState(true);
}
```

▶ We ask the method GoToState to use transitions when the events are raised: The user interaction should cause smooth transitions!

▶ The "expanding" of the description is a toggle between two states. So every time the panel is clicked, we toggle the boolean value _isDescriptionExpanded.

At this point, build the application again.

Applying the Template

Finally (and yes, that's the last operation in this class), we need to trigger all these actions! The right moment to do so is when the ControlTemplate is applied to the control. When this occurs, the Silverlight framework calls the method OnApplyTemplate on the Control class that we derive from.

However, if we don't do anything, the Control parent class doesn't notify us when this happens. We need to *override* this method and redefine its behavior as in Listing 19.26.

LISTING 19.26   Applying the Template

```
  // Applying the template
1 public override void OnApplyTemplate()
2 {
3   base.OnApplyTemplate();
4   DescriptionPanelPart
5     = (FrameworkElement) GetTemplateChild("DescriptionPanel");
6   GoToState(false);
7 }
```

▶ On line 3, we call the base class's method. This is needed, because in addition to performing our own operations, the base class needs to do the default tasks such as applying the template and wiring up everything.

▶ On lines 4 and 5, we get the named part, using the Control's method GetTemplateChild. Here, too, the name of the part must match the name you declared in the beginning with the TemplatePart attribute. We assign this value to our DescriptionPanelPart property, which wires up the event handlers to the part (except if it is null!).

▶ GetTemplateChild is a protected method of the Control class. It means that you can use it only in a derived class (this is the case here). You cannot use this method outside the MediaInfoDisplay class.

▶ Then on line 6 we instruct the VSM to set the control in its default state. This stage is needed, because we want the control to be in a defined state, so that all the transitions run correctly when the user passes the mouse over it or clicks it.

If anyone wants to use our control now, well they can't yet: It is totally lookless. Creating a look and feel for this control will be done in Chapter 20. First we create a *generic style and template* for the control and embed it in the same assembly. Then we use our control in the Thumbnails application and wear our designer's hat to create a slightly more complex template for the control. You can, however, build and run the application.

Summary

You were warned: creating controls is not easy. In this chapter we performed a lot of ground work, but our controls are neither finished nor functional yet. We continue working on them in the next chapter!

CHAPTER 20

Taking Silverlight 2 One Step Further

W e worked a lot on our Thumbnails application in Chapter 19, "Creating User Controls and Custom Controls," and started creating controls to "pack" the functionality, make it easier to manage and maintain, modify the look and feel, and so on. In this chapter, we continue this task. This will not take the whole chapter, however, because Silverlight, Blend, and Visual Studio enable us to work in an efficient and comfortable way. In the remaining time, we begin a discussion of advanced Silverlight and .NET topics.

Creating a Default Template for the MediaInfoDisplay Control

When a developer wants to use our control in an application, he should see something—even if it's not the look and feel that he will use later, even if a designer will re-template the control. This is also what happens when you add a Silverlight button to your application: Even though the Button (like all Silverlight controls) is lookless, you can actually see something because a default look and feel is included.

We will do now what the Silverlight framework's developers and designers also did with the standard controls set, and define the generic look and feel for our MediaInfoDisplay control with the following steps:

1. In Visual Studio, open the Thumbnails application that we last edited in Chapter 19. Right-click on the MediaInfo project and select Add, New Folder. Name this new folder Themes.

2. Right click on the Themes folder, and choose Add, New Item. Select a Text file and enter the name generic.xaml.

The generic file must be a `ResourceDictionary`. We talked about this specialized collection in Chapter 17, "Using Resources, Styling, and Templating." Back then, you were told that Silverlight doesn't handle "loose" `ResourceDictionary` files yet, and that you always have to add resources in the main XAML file or in App.xaml. Well guess what: It was a lie, or almost. The file generic.xaml is an exception. It can (and should) be a loose file included in the assembly with the controls you want to create default styles for. Because its name and location (the Themes folder) are reserved, the Silverlight framework knows how to handle it. You can implement the default look and feel with the following steps:

1. Enter a `ResourceDictionary` tag to generic.xaml as in Listing 20.1:

LISTING 20.1   Empty `ResourceDictionary`

```
<ResourceDictionary
  xmlns="http://schemas.microsoft.com/winfx/2006/xaml/presentation"
  xmlns:x="http://schemas.microsoft.com/winfx/2006/xaml">
</ResourceDictionary>
```

2. Add a namespace in the `ResourceDictionary` tag pointing to the `MediaInfo` namespace in the local assembly:

```
xmlns:controls="clr-namespace:MediaInfo"
```

3. Then add the default style for the `MediaInfoDisplay` control inside the `ResourceDictionary` as shown in Listing 20.2:

LISTING 20.2   Default `Style` for `MediaInfoDisplay`

```
1   <Style TargetType="controls:MediaInfoDisplay">
2     <Setter Property="Template">
3       <Setter.Value>
4         <ControlTemplate TargetType="controls:MediaInfoDisplay">
5           <Border BorderBrush="{TemplateBinding BorderBrush}"
6                   BorderThickness="{TemplateBinding BorderThickness}"
7                   Background="#FFDDDDDD"
8                   Padding="10" x:Name="DescriptionPanel">
9             <StackPanel Cursor="Hand">
10              <TextBlock Text="{TemplateBinding ShortDescription}" />
11              <TextBlock Text="{TemplateBinding LongDescription}"
12                         TextWrapping="Wrap"/>
13            </StackPanel>
14          </Border>
15        </ControlTemplate>
```

LISTING 20.2   Continued

```
16        </Setter.Value>
17      </Setter>
18    </Style>
```

- ▶ On line 1, we create the new `Style`, and we set its `TargetType`. This `Style`, even though it is included in a `ResourceDictionary`, does not have a key! Remember before, when we set the property `DefaultStyleKey = typeof(MediaInfoDisplay);`. This line enables us to specify a generic style by setting the `TargetType` only. This `Style` is automatically applied to all `MediaInfoDisplay` instances (unless of course the designer specifies something different).

- ▶ Lines 4 to 15 specify the template for our control.

- ▶ Note the use of `TemplateBinding` for the properties `BorderBrush` and `BorderThickness` and in the `TextBlocks` for `ShortDescription` and `LongDescription`. This default template is rather simple, and doesn't specify any transitions. But it allows the developer to position, size, and test the control in an application before a designer creates a new template.

- ▶ We test this default look and feel later in this chapter, when we add the control to our Thumbnails application!

- ▶ To make sure that all changes are visible, build your application in Visual Studio before going further.

Using the `MediaInfoDisplay` Control

Because we created a default template, we can manipulate the control in its generic look and feel. Later, we wear our designer's hat and create a template that looks better than the default one. We add smooth transitions between the states. When we do this, we see how we can add test data again, as we did in Chapter 19, to make the work in Blend even easier. Then, we connect the `ThumbnailsViewerControl` and the `MediaInfoDisplay` to have a functional application.

Adding Test Data

Adding test data is useful to make the workflow easier in Blend. This is easy with the following steps:

1. Open Page.xaml in Visual Studio.

2. In the `UserControl.Resources` section, add the instance of the `MediaEx` class shown in Listing 20.3. This is what we will use as test data for the styling and templating exercise.

20

LISTING 20.3   Default Style for MediaInfoDisplay

```
<data:MediaEx x:Key="TEMPMediaInfo"
            Description="[Your description here]"
            d:IsDataSource="True" />
```

3. Enter your own description instead of the [Your description here]. You should make it longer than 30 characters to see whether the "trimming" works.

4. Choose File, Save all from the menu.

Adding the Control to the Scene

The next step is to include and position the control in our application's page. We will position it so that it takes as little space as possible, but that it can be expanded above the two title TextBlocks if needed, with the following steps:

1. Open Page.xaml in Blend.

2. Select the Grid LayoutRoot's first row by clicking next to the small lock (reminder: The Grid must be in Grid Layout Mode; to do that, see Figure 5.7). Then set the row's Height to 380 pixels.

3. Select the MediaInfoDisplay control from the Asset library (use the Custom Controls tab). If you cannot see the control in the library, try rebuilding your solution in Blend first.

4. Add an instance of the MediaInfoDisplay in the same cell as the two title TextBlocks. You should see the default template that we defined before in generic.xaml.

5. To see some text, wire the new control to the test data: Using the Search text box in the Properties panel, find the MediaInfo property. Note that even though this property is a custom DependencyProperty (DP) that we added, it appears in Blend's Properties panel anyway.

6. Click on the small square next to the property and select Data Binding.

7. From the Create Data Binding dialog, select the TEMPMediaInfo data source and click on Finish. You should now see the text that you just entered.

8. Remember that we data bound the BorderBrush and BorderThickness in generic.xaml, so let's try and set them to see whether that works. Set the BorderBrush to #FF000B70 and the BorderThickness to 2,2,2,2.

9. Then do a little layout: Set the
Width to 340, the Height to 200,
the HorizontalAlignment to Left,
VerticalAlignment to Top, and the
Margin to Left = 30, Top = -65,
Right = Bottom = 0. Also make sure
that the Row is set to 1 and the
Column to 0. The result should look
like Figure 20.1.

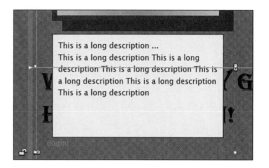

> This is a long description ...
> This is a long description This is a long
> description This is a long description This is
> a long description This is a long description
> This is a long description

FIGURE 20.1   Default look and feel

Creating a Template

Now we create a better template and add some transitions with the following steps:

1. Right-click on the MediaInfoDisplay control and select Edit Control Parts (Template),
   Create Empty.

2. Name the new template MediaInfoDisplayControlTemplate and place it in This
   Document.

3. Make sure that the Grid fills the whole space.

4. Inside the Grid, place a Border. Set its Width to Auto and its Height to 50. Set the
   Margin to 0, reset the HorizontalAlignment. Set the VerticalAlignment to Top. Set the
   Cursor to Hand and the Background to #FFDDDDDD. Set the Padding to Left = Right
   = 10 pixels. Leave the Top and Bottom Padding set to 0.

5. Make a TemplateBinding between the Border's BorderBrush and BorderThickness and
   the equivalent properties in the control. Note how the display is updated according
   to the properties that you set just before on the MediaInfoDisplay control in the
   Page.

6. Continue designing the ControlTemplate according to your fantasy, for example, set
   the CornerRadius to 16.

7. In the Border, add a TextBlock and set its HorizontalAlignment to Center and the
   VerticalAlignment to Top. Set the Top Margin to 10 pixels. Leave the other Margins
   set to 0. Reset the TextWrapping property to NoWrap.

8. Make a TemplateBinding between the TextBlock's Text property and the
   ShortDescription.

9. In the Grid, add another Border. It will be positioned on top of the
   ShortDescription one. However, we don't want it to interfere with the rest of the
   UI, so set its IsHitTestVisible property to False.

10. Create a TemplateBinding for the BorderBrush and BorderThickness. Set the Width
    and Height of this Border to Auto; reset the HorizontalAlignment and the

VerticalAlignment. Also set its Background to #FFDDDDDD and the CornerRadius to 16 pixels, Padding to Left = Right = Bottom = 10 pixels and leave the Top Padding to 0 pixels.

11. Add a TextBlock to the second Border. Set the HorizontalAlignment to Center, and VerticalAlignment to Stretch. Set the Top Margin to 10 pixels. Create a TemplateBinding between the Text property and the LongDescription.

Making Transitions

Now we add transitions to our control. Remember that we have two states groups (one with Normal and MouseOver, the other with DescriptionExpanded and DescriptionNormal). These states should be visible in the Interaction panel, in the States category.

Also, remember that the event handlers triggering the transitions are set when the DescriptionPanel part is found. So let's name one of the elements in the template accordingly! Follow the steps:

1. Rename the template's main Grid to DescriptionPanel.

2. With the Base state selected in the States category, set the second Border's Opacity to 0%.

3. Select the MouseOver state. Blend changes in State recording mode. Select the first Border and set its Background to #FFF3FF2C. Do the same for the second Border too.

4. Set the transition time for the CommonStates group to 0.2 seconds.

5. Then click on the DescriptionExpanded state.

6. Select the second Border (the invisible one) and set its Opacity to 100%.

7. Add a transition from DescriptionExpanded to DescriptionNormal and set the time to 0.2 seconds.

8. Then add a transition from DescriptionNormal to DescriptionExpanded and set this time to 0.5 seconds (see Figure 20.2).

9. Stop the State recording mode and set the scope back to the Page.

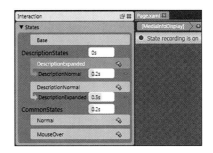

FIGURE 20.2   States and Transitions

At this stage, you can test your application to see whether the states and transitions are working. The MediaInfoDisplay should turn to yellow when the mouse is over the ShortDescription border. Because we set the IsHitTestVisible to False for the bigger Border, it shouldn't react to the mouse.

If you click on the panel when it's yellow, you should see the `LongDescription` appear. Click again to make it fade. Notice that the "expanding" time is slightly longer than the "fading" time, which is what we wanted.

Removing the Test Data

Now we can remove the test data; we don't need it anymore. Simply delete `TEMPMediaInfo` from the resources in Page.xaml in Studio.

Wiring Up

And now for the last step: We connect the item currently displayed with the `MediaInfoDisplay` control. Remember that the `ThumbnailsViewerControl` has a `SelectedItem` property, and this is a DP. So we can create a data binding between that DP and the `MediaInfo` DP on the `MediaInfoDisplay` control.

However, in Silverlight 2 (unlike in Windows Presentation Foundation), you cannot bind two UI elements together directly. You must do this through a data object (this is cleaner anyway, but that's another story).

1. In Visual Studio, add a class to the Data folder in the Thumbnails project. Name this class Settings.cs.

2. Implement the class shown in Listing 20.4:

LISTING 20.4   Settings Class

```
public class Settings : INotifyPropertyChanged
{
  #region INotifyPropertyChanged Members
  public event PropertyChangedEventHandler PropertyChanged;
  #endregion

  private MediaEx _currentMediaInfo = null;
  public MediaEx CurrentMediaInfo
  {
    get { return _currentMediaInfo; }
    set
    {
      _currentMediaInfo = value;
      if (PropertyChanged != null)
      {
        PropertyChanged(this,
          new PropertyChangedEventArgs("CurrentMediaInfo"));
      }
    }
  }
}
```

20

One property only! When it changes, the `PropertyChanged` event is raised.

3. Click on File, Save All and build the application. You will have to add one `using` statement.

4. In Blend, build the application. Then, in the Data panel, click on +CLR Object and select the `Settings` class. Set the Data Source Name to `Settings` and click OK.

5. Select the ThumbnailsViewer and create a binding between its `SelectedItem` property and the `Settings` data source. In the Fields panel of the Create Data Binding dialog, choose the `CurrentMediaInfo` property.

6. Expand the Advanced Properties section and set the Binding direction to TwoWay. Then click Finish.

7. Select the `MediaInfoDisplay` control and set a binding between its `MediaInfo` property and the same `CurrentMediaInfo` property on the `Settings` data source. You can leave this binding set to OneWay.

> **NOTE**
>
> TwoWay is not ideal, because the `SelectedItem` property should not be written to. Only the ThumbnailsViewer should be able to change this property. The OneWayToSource mode available in Windows Presentation Foundation would be better. Unfortunately, Silverlight doesn't allow this mode for the moment.

Our application is functional now. Try it: Run the application and select a thumbnail. The description should appear. For some of them, the `ShortDescription` might be truncated, but it's okay; you can click on the panel and expand the `LongDescription`.

In Chapter 22, "Connecting to the Web," we remove all hard-coded information about the media files, and import them from an XML file instead. This makes your application fully functional to work on the Web. We also see how we can get some pictures to be loaded from Flickr directly, through a web service.

Digging Deeper

As we said before, creating custom controls is a big job. The previous section gave you an overview, but if you intend to create relatively complex custom controls, you may want to "dig deeper." Karen Corby, program manager for Silverlight 2, created a good series of four blog posts about custom controls. This is where you want to start! The first of her posts and the starting point to the series is located at http://scorbs.com/2008/06/11/parts-states-model-with-visualstatemanager-part-1-of.

Scrolling the Items

What else is missing? Oh yes, we have a `ScrollViewer`, but it doesn't scroll yet! Since we set the vertical scrollbar's visibility to Hidden, we can scroll programmatically. Let's try this with the following steps.

1. Open the file ThumbnailsViewerControl.xaml in Visual Studio and add a `Click`
   event handler to `ScrollButtonUp`. It should be named `ScrollButtonUp_Click`.

2. Do the same with `ScrollButtonDown` and `ScrollButtonDown_Click`.

3. In ThumbnailsViewerControl.xaml.cs, disable both buttons in the constructor. Add
   the code shown in Listing 20.5 under the call to `InitializeComponent`.

LISTING 20.5   Disabling Both `RepeatButtons`

```
ScrollButtonUp.IsEnabled = false;
ScrollButtonDown.IsEnabled = false;
```

4. Then, implement the handlers as shown in Listing 20.6:

LISTING 20.6   Event Handlers for `RepeatButtons`

```
1   private double _scrollOffset = 0.0;
2   private void ScrollButtonUp_Click(object sender, RoutedEventArgs e)
3   {
4     ScrollButtonDown.IsEnabled = true;
5     _scrollOffset -= ThumbScrollViewer.ActualWidth / 10;
6     if (_scrollOffset <= 0)
7     {
8       _scrollOffset = 0;
9       ScrollButtonUp.IsEnabled = false;
10    }
11    ThumbScrollViewer.ScrollToVerticalOffset(_scrollOffset);
12  }
13
14  private void ScrollButtonDown_Click(object sender, RoutedEventArgs e)
15  {
16    ScrollButtonUp.IsEnabled = true;
17    _scrollOffset += ThumbScrollViewer.ActualHeight / 10;
18    if (_scrollOffset >= ThumbScrollViewer.ScrollableHeight)
19    {
20      _scrollOffset = ThumbScrollViewer.ScrollableHeight;
21      ScrollButtonDown.IsEnabled = false;
22    }
23    ThumbScrollViewer.ScrollToVerticalOffset(_scrollOffset);
24  }
```

▶ Line 1 declares a private attribute to store the value of the offset. Like most values
   having to do with layout in Silverlight, this is a `double`.

▶ Whenever the user clicks on the up button, we make sure that the down button is enabled. Even if it was disabled before, clicking on the up button restores the down button's capability to scroll.

▶ When you click on the up button (lines 2 to 12), you want to scroll up. We must calculate a smaller offset than the current one. However, we cannot scroll lower than 0 (line 6 to 10). Also, if the calculated value is equal to 0, we disable the button to notify the user.

▶ Line 11 does the magic, and calls the ScrollViewer's ScrollToVerticalOffset method. Remember that this method only works when the corresponding ScrollBar's visibility has been set to Hidden, not Disabled!

NOTE

Disabling a control when it cannot be used is usually a good idea. It informs the user about the status of the application, and it also prevents the event handler to be called again, which can improve the performance of your application.

▶ Finally, lines 14 to 24 do the corresponding operation for the other direction. Notice the usage of ThumbScrollViewer.ScrollableHeight to make sure that we don't exceed the scrollable area.

To make the state of the buttons consistent with the control's size, we now handle the LayoutUpdated event. This event gets called when the application starts and also every time that something causes the layout to change, so the buttons get enabled or disabled depending on the size of the control, the number of items it contains, and so on.

1. In ThumbnailsViewerControl.xaml, add this event to the ThumbItemsControl.

   LayoutUpdated="ThumbnailsViewerControl_LayoutUpdated"

2. Create the corresponding event handler in ThumbnailsViewerControl.xaml.cs (Listing 20.7):

LISTING 20.7   ThumbnailsViewerControl_LayoutUpdated Event Handler

```
1  private void ThumbnailsViewerControl_LayoutUpdated(object sender,
2    EventArgs e)
3  {
4    if (ThumbScrollViewer.ScrollableHeight == 0)
5    {
6      ScrollButtonUp.IsEnabled = false;
7      ScrollButtonDown.IsEnabled = false;
8    }
9    else
10   {
11     if (ThumbScrollViewer.VerticalOffset > 0)
12     {
13       ScrollButtonUp.IsEnabled = true;
```

LISTING 20.7   Continued

```
14        }
15        if (ThumbScrollViewer.VerticalOffset
16              < ThumbScrollViewer.ScrollableHeight)
17        {
18          ScrollButtonDown.IsEnabled = true;
19        }
20      }
21      _scrollOffset = ThumbScrollViewer.VerticalOffset;
22  }
```

▶ Here too, we use the convenient property `ScrollableHeight` to check whether we are in a state where scrolling is even possible. If not, we disable both buttons.

▶ If we can scroll, we check in which direction(s) we can do this and enable or disable the buttons accordingly.

▶ Finally, maybe the offset changed during this operation, so we save the new value on line 21.

3. Test the application. Observe what happens when you resize the window to a small size or a big size. The buttons should get enabled or disabled accordingly. Then try scrolling the thumbnails. Since we used `RepeatButtons`, you can press and hold a button to scroll in successful steps.

The scrolling algorithm we use now is simple and could probably be improved. For example, using a smaller "step" when the button is clicked, making the `Interval` property shorter, and so on.

Creating a New `RepeatButton` Template

Let's make our buttons look nicer! Keep in mind, however, that this author is a developer and no designer—and that he does his best. So please don't laugh too hard!

Creating the Template

First we will change the appearance of the buttons, by creating a new template for them. Follow the steps:

1. In Expression Blend, open ThumbnailsViewerControl.xaml. Right-click on the top `RepeatButton` in Blend and select Edit Control Parts (Template), Create Empty.

2. Enter the name ScrollButtonTemplate and create the template in the `UserControl`.

3. In the template editor, rename the `Grid` to "Root". This is needed to work around a bug in Silverlight with `RepeatButtons`. Then add an `Ellipse` to the `Grid` and make it fill the whole cell. Set its `Fill` property to blue temporarily and reset the `Stroke` to No brush. Name the `Ellipse` BackgroundPath.

4. Convert the `Ellipse` to a `Path` (select Object, Path, Convert to Path).

5. Using the Pen and the Direct Selection tool, modify the `Path` to make it look roughly like Figure 20.3.

6. In the template editor, make sure that the `Grid` is selected with a yellow border. Then copy and paste the same `Path` again. Name the second path Highlight so that it's easier to recognize it.

7. Set the Highlight's `Fill` property to a `RadialGradientBrush`. Set the first `GradientStop` to #CCFFFFFF and the second stop to #00FFFFFF.

8. Use the Brush Transform tool to move the brush until you get the effect shown in Figure 20.4.

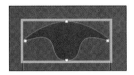

FIGURE 20.3   `RepeatButton` template path

TIP

With the Pen tool selected, press and hold down the Alt key; then move the point on the left of the ellipse. This changes the `Path` using a spline. Doing this might take a little practice, but don't worry if it doesn't look too good first. You can always modify it later. Use the Zoom tool to make the editing easier! Then repeat the operation for the point on the right of the ellipse. Try to make the new `Path` symmetrical.

You might have to reset the `Margin` to 0 after editing a spline.

Changing the Transitions

1. Select the Base state. Then select the Highlight and set its `Opacity` to 0%. Set the BackgroundPath's `Opacity` to 80%.

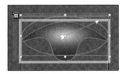

FIGURE 20.4   `RepeatButton` with highlight

2. Select the `MouseOver` state. This puts Blend in State recording mode. Select the Highlight and make sure that its `Opacity` is 100%. Also set the BackgroundPath's `Opacity` to 100%.

3. Select the `Disabled` state, and set the BackgroundPath's `Opacity` to 20%.

4. Select the `Pressed` state. Select the Highlight element and set its Opacity to 50%.

5. Exit the State recording mode.

6. Add the following transitions and set their transition time to 0.1 seconds: from `Normal` to `MouseOver`; from `Normal` to `Pressed`; from `MouseOver` to `Normal`; from `MouseOver` to `Pressed`; from `Pressed` to `MouseOver`; from `Pressed` to `Normal`.

We set the transitions from Normal to Pressed to Normal, because the RepeatButton has a ClickMode property (we saw that in Chapter 16, "Digging Deeper into Silverlight Elements," remember?). When ClickMode is set to Hover, the button goes directly from Normal to Pressed without going over the MouseOver state.

Binding the Template

We want to be able to use the same template on multiple buttons and change the colors.

1. Select the BackgroundPath's Fill property and click the small square next to it. Choose TemplateBinding, Background.

2. Do the same for the Path's Stroke and bind it to the BorderBrush.

Testing the New Button

We have all we need to set up the new button and test it with the following steps:

1. Give the scope back to the UserControl.

2. Change the button's Background to red and check whether the BackgroundPath also changes its color. Do the same for the button's BorderBrush.

3. Run the application and pass the mouse over the button. The Highlight should appear in 0.1 seconds. Then press the button and check whether the Highlight changes as specified. You must click on the down button first, so that the up button is enabled.

4. Then reset the Background and BorderBrush to the default. We create a Style in the next section to handle this.

At this stage, feel free to change the design as you want. Remember that the Visual State editor allows you to change any property of the button template. Keep it tasteful though!

Styling the RepeatButton

In this section, we set all the RepeatButton's properties through a Style. Remember that this is a better practice, especially because we use two RepeatButtons with the same look and feel.

Also, it is better to set the template within the Style instead of directly in the RepeatButton. Without going into too much detail, let's just say that this makes the workflow designer/developer easier, especially when the Style is placed in the App.xaml file. Follow the steps:

1. With the top RepeatButton selected, choose Object, Edit Style, Create Empty from the menu. Name the new style ScrollButtonStyle and place it in the UserControl.

2. In the Style, set the Margin to 10. Set the Background and the Stroke brush to a SolidColorBrush of #FF4D009E.

3. Set the `Template` property in the `Style` to Local Resource, ScrollButtonTemplate.

4. Set the scope back to the `UserControl`. Find the `RepeatButton`'s `Template` property and reset it to default if needed.

You can now set the scope back to the `UserControl`.

Styling the Other Button

Let's take care of the other `RepeatButton`. Thankfully, it is easy to do so, even though the button "looks in the other direction." We simply flip it! Follow the steps:

1. Select the `RepeatButton` on the bottom.

2. Select Object, Edit Style, Apply Resource and apply the ScrollButtonStyle.

3. Use the Transform section in the Properties panel to "flip" the button along the Y axis.

That's it; we now have two cool-looking (well, at least I think so) buttons to scroll our Thumbnails collection (see Figure 20.5). You can now build and test the application.

FIGURE 20.5   Thumbnails application during an animation

Exporting Classes to an External Assembly and Refactoring

A .NET application is always composed of multiple assemblies (EXEs or DLLs). A *DLL (Dynamic-Link Library)* contains *intermediate language (IL)* code as we discussed in previous chapters. The classes stored in the DLL can be reused in multiple applications. This is exactly what is done when we create a new project:

▸ Expand the References folder.

▸ This folder contains references to multiple external assemblies, which contain the code needed to run even the simplest Silverlight application (see Figure 20.6).

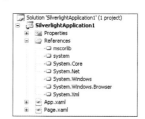

FIGURE 20.6   References folder

You can also create a Silverlight class library and use it to store utility code, custom controls, or any code that you want to separate from the main assembly for any reason.

Creating a Silverlight Class Library

We already saw that object-oriented code allows creating modular code. A specific class can be instantiated in multiple

NOTE

Usually a referenced assembly is copied to the XAP file and must be deployed to the client computer so that the code is available for the application. The default assemblies shown in Figure 20.6 don't need to be deployed, however, because they are part of the standard Silverlight installation.

places and used in multiple configurations. Sometimes you want to be even more modular than this and reuse a particular object in a new application that you are developing. This is where a class library can be useful.

For example, let's imagine that we want to reuse the classes `DataFile` and `User` that we created for our Thumbnails application. After all, there are multiple scenarios where you may want to log a user's name, password, and last visit. We don't want to have to rewrite that code over and over again.

Of course you could imagine copying and pasting the code you want to reuse in every application where it's needed. This is not a good idea; however, if you find a bug in your code, or simply want to make a modification, you will need to make that change in every single copy of the code. Not very efficient!

Creating the Project and Moving the Classes

Visual Studio is a great help for refactoring an application and moving classes around if needed. Follow the steps:

1. Open the application Thumbnails in Visual Studio.

2. In the Solution Explorer, right-click on the Thumbnails Solution (*not* on the project!) and select Add, New Project, as shown in Figure 20.7.

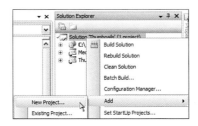

FIGURE 20.7   Selecting Add, New Project from the Solution Explorer

3. In the Add New Project dialog under Silverlight, select Silverlight Class Library.

4. Enter a name for the new class library, for example, UserManagement.

5. Because we want to reuse this class library in various projects, it makes sense to save it in a location independent from the Thumbnails project. You can choose any location to save the new UserManagement project.

6. The newly created project contains a class created by default and named `Class1`. We don't need this class, so you can safely delete this file in the Solution Explorer.

7. In the Solution Explorer, drag the file DataFile.cs from the Data folder in the Thumbnails project. Drop this file on the new UserManagement project. Then repeat the operation for the file User.cs.

8. Dragging and dropping creates a copy of the files. Since we only use the ones from the UserManagement project, you can delete these files from the Data folder in the Thumbnails project.

Changing the Namespace

It is good practice to modify the namespace containing the objects according to the project containing them. This makes looking for bugs easier and provides a neater organization. This is not required, because nothing requires a namespace to be named according to its containing project, but it is good to do so.

1. Open the files DataFile.cs and User.cs and modify the namespace to read:

```
namespace UserManagement
```

After compilation, the classes `DataFile` and `User` will be placed into a new assembly named UserManagement.dll, just like the project. For each project, Visual Studio creates a separate assembly when you build. If you compile the application now, you will get errors: DataFile is not found. To use the objects, you need to add a reference to the newly created project.

2. In the Solution Explorer, right-click on the Thumbnails project and select Add Reference.

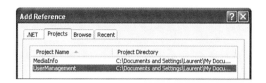

3. Select the Projects tab. You should see the UserManagement project that we just created (see Figure 20.8). Select this project and click OK.

FIGURE 20.8   The Add Reference dialog

4. Expand the References folder in the project Thumbnails (in the Solution Explorer). Notice that, in addition to the assemblies we mentioned earlier, you now have a reference to the UserManagement assembly.

5. Double-click on the error in the Error List panel in Visual Studio. This should lead you to the `Page` class. Add the `UserManagement` namespace to the `using` section of the `Page` class. You must *not* delete the namespace `Thumbnails.Data`, because other classes are included in that, such as `MediaEx`.

6. After replacing the namespace, build the application.

Updating the Visibility

This last step causes a lot of errors in Visual Studio, like `'UserManagement.DataFile'` does not contain a definition for `'LoadUsers'` and no extension method `'LoadUsers'` accepting a first argument of type `'UserManagement.DataFile'` could be found (are you missing a using directive or an assembly reference?)"

So what happened? The method `LoadUsers` exists, it is defined, and we didn't change anything in the code! The reason for the error is the method's visibility: We defined it as `internal`, which makes it visible only within its own assembly. If you want to use this method outside the assembly, you need to make it `public`.

It is good practice to use the lowest possible visibility for a class or its members. However, it causes this kind of errors when you *refactor* your application and move classes in other assemblies. This is what software design is about, carefully planning components (assemblies), classes, their members, and their features.

Let's correct these errors now:

1. Open the Error List panel in Visual Studio, and double-click on the first error. This takes you in the source code, at the location where the `LoadUsers` method is called.

2. Right-click on the method's name, and select Go to Definition from the context menu.

3. In the method's definition, replace the `internal` keyword with `public`.

> **TIP**
>
> Another type of error to be solved this way is Property or indexer `'UserManagement.User.Password'` cannot be assigned to -- it is read only.
>
> The cause for this error is also the visibility: The setter is set to `internal`, so it cannot be used outside the local assembly. Simply remove the `internal` keyword to make the setter and getter accessors both `public`.

20

4. Build the application. You still have errors, but there are less of them.

5. Repeat steps 1 to 4 as many times as needed, until all the errors are gone.

Testing the New Component

After all the errors have been corrected, run the application and try to log in using a previously defined user name and password combination. You see that the user name is still available! The reason is that isolated storage files are available to the application that created them. Even though we moved the code to a different assembly, the application is still the same and it may reuse the same file.

Note that even though refactoring is relatively easy with Visual Studio, creating class libraries comes with a responsibility: If you make changes to code that is already integrated in another application, there is a risk of breaking it. Such changes must be considered carefully to avoid any side effects.

Checking the DLL

As a final step, right-click on the Thumbnails project in the Solution Explorer. Select Open Folder in Windows Explorer. Then navigate to the folder bin/Debug.

If you scroll down, you see a new DLL named UserManagement.dll. This component was created when we built the new project. Because the Thumbnails project has a reference on the UserManagement project, this DLL is copied to the Silverlight application.

Using an External Class Library

To reuse a class library, you don't always need a reference to the *project* that created it. It is enough to have a copy of the DLL and to add a reference to it. We can demonstrate this with the following steps:

1. Navigate to the folder UserManagement\bin\Debug in Windows Explorer.

2. Copy the assembly UserManagement.dll.

3. Create a new folder in the project root, at the same level as the file UserManagement.csproj. Name this folder Reference.

4. Paste the UserManagement.dll into the References folder.

5. Create a new Silverlight application in Visual Studio. Name it SimpleUserLogin.

6. Right-click on the project and choose Add Reference. In the Browse tab, navigate to the Reference folder we created just before, and select the UserManagement.dll.

7. In Page.xaml, change LayoutRoot as in Listing 20.8. Note how we use a new control named `PasswordBox`, useful to mask a user's input from prying eyes.

LISTING 20.8   SimpleUserLogin UI

```
<StackPanel x:Name="LayoutRoot" Background="White">
  <TextBlock Text="User name" Margin="10,10,10,0" />
  <TextBox x:Name="UserNameTextBox" Margin="10" />
  <TextBlock Text="Password" Margin="10,10,10,0" />
  <PasswordBox x:Name="PasswordTextBox"
               Margin="10"/>
  <Button Content="Login" Margin="10"
          x:Name="LoginButton"
          Click="LoginButton_Click" />
  <Button Content="New User" Margin="10"
          x:Name="NewUserButton"
          Click="NewUserButton_Click" />
  <TextBlock x:Name="StatusTextBlock" Margin="10" />
</StackPanel>
```

8. Modify the Page class like Listing 20.9:

LISTING 20.9   SimpleUserLogin Logic

```
private DataFile _dataFile;

public Page()
{
  InitializeComponent();
  _dataFile = new DataFile();
  _dataFile.LoadUsers();
}

private void LoginButton_Click(object sender, RoutedEventArgs e)
{
  User inputUser = new User();
  inputUser.Name = UserNameTextBox.Text;
  inputUser.Password = PasswordTextBox.Password;
  if (_dataFile.ValidateUser(inputUser))
  {
    User savedUser = _dataFile.GetUser(inputUser.Name);
    StatusTextBlock.Text = "(Your last visit was: "
      + savedUser.LastVisit.Value.ToShortDateString()
      + " " + savedUser.LastVisit.Value.ToLongTimeString() + ")";
    savedUser.SetLastVisit();
    _dataFile.SaveUsers();
  }
  else
```

20

LISTING 20.9   Continued

```
    {
      StatusTextBlock.Text = "Invalid user/password combination";
    }
  }

private void NewUserButton_Click(object sender, RoutedEventArgs e)
{
  try
  {
    User newUser = new User();
    newUser.Name = UserNameTextBox.Text;
    newUser.Password = PasswordTextBox.Password;
    newUser.SetLastVisit();
    _dataFile.AddUser(newUser);
    StatusTextBlock.Text = "(This is your first visit)";
  }
  catch (Exception ex)
  {
    StatusTextBlock.Text = ex.Message;
  }
}
```

You will need to add the UserManagement namespace to the using section to build the application. Then you can run and test it. This code is similar to what we have in the Thumbnails application. In fact, we delegate the whole user management scenarios to the UserManagement component, with its classes DataFile and User. This way, the whole isolated storage management is *encapsulated*, and we don't need to worry about it.

If you think that your component's functionality is interesting enough, you can even *distribute* your assembly, for example, on the Web. Creating external class assemblies allows you to easily manage and reuse functionality.

> **NOTE**
>
> Standalone components and application assemblies are usually *versioned*. The versioning of a .NET component is done in the file AssemblyInfo.cs available in the Properties folder. .NET versioning is a topic more complex than it seems, and we won't go into the details of it here. For more information, check http://msdn.microsoft.com/en-us/library/51ket42z.aspx

Talking About the Application Object

In the next chapter, we work with the Application object. While we already mentioned this object a few times, we never discussed it in details. Let's take a closer look at this fundamental object in Silverlight applications, with the following steps.

1. In any Silverlight application, open the file App.xaml.cs.

2. The class named `App` (deriving from the `Application` class) contains all kinds of global information, valid for the whole Silverlight application. For example:

   ▶ The `Startup` event is called when the application is starting up. Note that this object is responsible for creating the `Page` instance where our code is running. If you decide to create additional pages, this is where you can decide which one should be the initial one.

   ▶ The `Exit` event is called when the application is, you guessed it, exiting. This can be because the user navigates to a different HTML page or refreshes the page using the F5 key, for example.

   ▶ The `UnhandledException` event is called when an exception occurs in the code, but is not handled anywhere. We talk more about exceptions in Chapter 23, "Placing Cross-domain Requests and Handling Exceptions."

You can modify these events to handle special scenarios in your code. If needed, you can also add your own properties to the `App` object. For example, Listing 20.10:

LISTING 20.10   Property in `Application` Object

```
public partial class App : Application
{
  private DateTime _initializationDate = DateTime.Now;
  public DateTime InitializationDate
  {
    get { return _initializationDate; }
  }

  // ...
}
```

Then you can get this value anywhere in the Silverlight application with:

```
DateTime _initTime = (App.Current as App).InitializationDate;
```

Note that the type of `App.Current` is `Application`, so to access the properties you add you need to cast it to `App`.

`App.Current` is a global object that can be retrieved from anywhere in the rest of the code, even in data objects. That makes it handy to store values that are shared everywhere.

Using Generics

When you need a method (or a class) to deal with multiple types, but you are not sure in advance what these types will be, you want to use generics. It's a little like saying "I create a method now, and it will accept multiple parameters types." In Silverlight (and generally in .NET), one of the most common uses of generics is for strongly typed collections. Before generics, filling a collection and then accessing the content was something like Listing 20.11:

LISTING 20.11   ArrayList (Old Implementation)

```
ArrayList myArrayList = new ArrayList();
myArrayList.Add("hello");
myArrayList.Add("world");
// ...
string element1 = (string) myArrayList[0];
string element2 = (string) myArrayList[1];
```

Notice how, even though each element is a string, it is necessary to cast them back to `string` when accessing them. This is because an `ArrayList` stores elements of type `object` only. Remember, each and every class in .NET always derives from `object`, even if nothing explicit is specified.

With generics, you can write (Listing 20.12):

LISTING 20.12   Generic List (New Implementation)

```
List<string> myList = new List<string>();
myList.Add("hello");
myList.Add("world");
// ...
string element1 = myList[0];
string element2 = myList[1];
```

No more casting, because the .NET compiler knows that the List contains only elements of type `string`.

To define your own generics method, use the syntax shown in Listing 20.13:

LISTING 20.13   Generic Method Implementation

```
public void DoSomethingGenerics<T>(T myParameter)
{
  // ...
}
public void UseMyMethod()
{
```

LISTING 20.13   Continued

```
DoSomethingGenerics<string>("hello"); // OK
DoSomethingGenerics<int>(2);          // OK
}
```

You can also create generics classes as in Listing 20.14:

LISTING 20.14   Generic Class Implementation

```
public class MyClass<T>
{
  private T myAttribute;
  public MyClass(T myParameter)
  {
    myAttribute = myParameter;
  }
}
```

And then Listing 20.15:

LISTING 20.15   Using a Generic Class

```
Uri uri = new Uri("http://www.galasoft.ch");
MyClass<Uri> myObject = new MyClass<Uri>(uri);
Rectangle shape = new Rectangle();
MyClass<Rectangle> myObject2 = new MyClass<Rectangle>(shape);
```

Notice how we use the same object with two totally different parameters, just like when we use a generics collection such as List<>. The notation <T> tells the compiler that the type can vary.

Summary

In this chapter, we finished what we started in Chapter 19 and gave our Thumbnails application a different look. Also, and maybe more importantly, the media files we display are not located in the Thumbnails assembly anymore, but on the web server. We still have information about them hard-coded, but that will change soon. We now understand how to create user controls and custom controls, how to modify an existing control's look and feel, and why controls in Silverlight are lookless.

We also talked about advanced Silverlight topics: Exporting classes to a class library, reusing these components in another application; then we talked about the Application object and finally about generics.

We continue our discussion of advanced topics in Chapter 21, "Taking Silverlight 2 Even Further."

20

CHAPTER 21

Taking Silverlight 2 Even Further

Since we started learning Silverlight 2 and .NET topics, we have moved forward quickly and without looking back. Now it's time to take a deep breath and study a few advanced subjects.

The first sections of this chapter use the JavaScriptDotNet application that we created in Chapter 14, "Letting .NET and JavaScript Talk." If you didn't keep this application, you can download the file from www.galasoft.ch/SL2U/Chapter14/JavaScriptDotNet.zip.

TIP

Because Silverlight applications are cached by the web browser, sometimes changes you make will not appear immediately when you refresh the web browser. To solve this, try the following:

▶ Press Shift+F5 to refresh the web browser instead of just F5.

▶ In Visual Studio, right-click on the Solution and select Clean Solution from the context menu. Then restart the Silverlight application.

▶ Clear the cache of your web browser before running the application again.

Registering Multiple JavaScript Event Handlers

We learned a lot about .NET to JavaScript to .NET communication in Chapter 8, "Programming Silverlight with JavaScript," and Chapter 14. We also learned how to register a JavaScript handler for a .NET event. Consider the following steps:

1. In Visual Studio, open the application JavaScriptDotNet that we created in Chapter 14. Make sure that JavaScriptDotNetWeb is set as start project and the page JavaScriptDotNetTestPage.html as start page.

2. In JavaScriptDotNetTestPage.html, in the constructor, see how we registered the event handler for the `CounterTicked` event (see Listing 21.1):

LISTING 21.1   Registering One Event Handler

```
page.CounterTicked = JavaScriptDotNet.createDelegate(this,
  this.handleCounterTicked);
```

3. With this method of registering, you can have only one JavaScript method handling the .NET event. For example, modify the application as shown in Listing 21.2. Then, run the code and click 5 times on the Count button. Only one "alert" will be displayed. The first attached handler is overwritten by the second.

LISTING 21.2   Trying to Register Two Event Handlers

```
JavaScriptDotNet = function(page)
{
  page.CounterTicked = JavaScriptDotNet.createDelegate(this,
    this.handleCounterTicked);
  page.CounterTicked = JavaScriptDotNet.createDelegate(this,
    this.doSomethingElse);
}

// ...

JavaScriptDotNet.prototype =
{
  handleCounterTicked : function(sender, e)
  {
    alert("Counter ticked: " + e.CounterValue);
  },
  doSomethingElse : function(sender, e)
  {
    alert("This is another event handler");
  },
  saySomething : function(message1, message2, message3)
  {
```

LISTING 21.2   Continued

```
    alert(message1 + "/" + message2 + "/" + message3);
  }
}
```

4. To register multiple handlers for one event, you must use the method
   addEventListener. This method allows adding as many handlers as you need for a
   given event. To demonstrate this, modify the JavaScriptDotNet constructor as
   shown in Listing 21.3:

LISTING 21.3   Registering Two Event Handlers

```
JavaScriptDotNet = function(page)
{
  page.addEventListener("CounterTicked",
    JavaScriptDotNet.createDelegate(this, this.handleCounterTicked));
  page.addEventListener("CounterTicked",
    JavaScriptDotNet.createDelegate(this, this.doSomethingElse));
}
```

If you execute this code now, both alerts will be displayed.

Finding Silverlight Elements in JavaScript

Events can also be added to other elements in the Silverlight page, for example with the
following steps:

1. In JavaScriptDotNetTestPage.html, replace the function onSilverlightLoaded with
   the code shown in Listing 21.4. We use the sender we get as parameter of the
   onload event handler and find a Silverlight element (the CounterButton) by its name.
   Then we add event handlers for the MouseEnter and the MouseLeave events.

LISTING 21.4   Registering and Unregistering Event Handler to a Silverlight Element

```
var jsDotNetInstance;
var token1 = null;
var button = null;
function onSilverlightLoaded(sender, args)
{
  jsDotNetInstance
    = new JavaScriptDotNet(sender.getHost().Content.Page);

  button = sender.findName("CounterButton");
  token1 = button.addEventListener("MouseEnter",
    JavaScriptDotNet.createDelegate(jsDotNetInstance,
```

LISTING 21.4   Continued

```
      jsDotNetInstance.handleMouseEnter));

  button.addEventListener("MouseLeave",
    JavaScriptDotNet.createDelegate(jsDotNetInstance,
      jsDotNetInstance.handleMouseLeave));
}
```

2. Implement the event handlers in the JavaScriptDotNet prototype (see Listing 21.5). Note that the last , (comma) should be added only if another event handler comes after handleMouseLeave.

LISTING 21.5   Two Event Handlers

```
handleMouseEnter : function()
{
  document.title = "Mouse over";
},
handleMouseLeave : function()
{
  document.title = "Mouse leave";
},
```

3. Run this code now. You will see the HTML page's title change when you pass the mouse over and out of the Count button. The Silverlight event is handled directly in JavaScript.

4. Using the saved token, you can also remove an event handler. This can be done with the following code. Replace the method saySomething with the code in Listing 21.6. After you do this, run the code. The title will get updated when you pass the mouse over the Count button, but if you click on the Say button once, the title will not get updated anymore afterwards (the event handler has been removed).

LISTING 21.6   Method saySomething

```
saySomething: function(message1, message2, message3)
{
  alert("Removing event handler");
  if (button != null
    && token1 != null)
  {
    button.removeEventListener("MouseEnter", token1);
    token1 = null;
  }
}
```

Removing the event handler is possible because we saved the `button` and the `token1` as global variables. Note also that you must always test whether the `token1` is null, because on some elements, the method `addEventListener` doesn't return a valid token. In that case, the event handler cannot be removed.

Accessing the HTML Page From .NET

In Chapter 14, we talked about the Silverlight `HtmlPage` class as a gateway to the HTML page (hence the name) containing the application. We talked about the `HtmlPage.Window` property and used it to get JavaScript object instances, and to call the `Alert`, `Confirm`, and `Prompt` methods.

Another handy property of the `HtmlPage` class is the `Document`. This is the exact equivalent of calling `document` in JavaScript. Using the well-known methods `GetElementById` and `GetElementsByTagName`, you can access any HTML element and modify it.

Silverlight can modify the HTML page directly. This is yet another framework that our Silverlight application can talk to, called the *DOM (Document Object Model)*. In this model, the HTML document is made available as a collection of *nodes* and *elements*. Some have children that in turn are nodes and elements (this is similar to what we know of XML, and in fact HTML is close to the XML format).

> **WARNING**
>
> When accessing the HTML document, the .NET code must have a deep knowledge of the structure of the HTML page hosting it. From an architectural point of view, it's not the best way to solve things. On the other hand, raising .NET events and catching them in JavaScript is a much cleaner way to communicate: If the HTML page changes, the Silverlight application doesn't need any modification. The event introduces a better level of *abstraction* between .NET and JavaScript.

If an application modifies attributes of a node (such as its background color, for example), or if it adds or removes nodes from the document, the changes are immediately reflected visually. Generally, the DOM is programmed by JavaScript applications (this is known as *DHTML, Dynamic HTML*). But Silverlight also gets a direct access to the DOM.

Here is an example. Implement the following steps:

1. In the JavaScriptDotNet application, open the file JavaScriptDotNetTestPage.html in Studio.

2. In the HTML header, set the `silverlightControlHost` CSS selector as shown in Listing 21.7:

LISTING 21.7   CSS Class `silverlightControlHost`

```
#silverlightControlHost {
  height: 300px;
  width: 400px;
}
```

3. Add a `div` to the HTML document, below the `div` containing the Silverlight `object` tag, as in Listing 21.8.

LISTING 21.8   Test `div` Element

```
<div style="position: absolute;
          left: 450px; top: 0px;
          width: 300px; height: 100px;
          background-color: Red;
          color: White;"
     id="TestDiv">
  <span id="TestSpan"> </span>
</div>
```

4. In Page.xaml, add the following controls in LayoutRoot (Listing 21.9):

LISTING 21.9   XAML Test Markup

```
<TextBox x:Name="ValueTextBox"
  HorizontalAlignment="Left" VerticalAlignment="Top"
  Margin="49,21,0,0" Width="300" />
<Button x:Name="SetTitleButton"
  HorizontalAlignment="Right" Height="40" Width="80"
  Content="Set title" Margin="0,-120,100,0"
  Click="SetTitleButton_Click" />
<Button x:Name="SetTopButton"
  HorizontalAlignment="Left" Height="40" Width="80"
  Content="Set top" Margin="100,-120,0,0"
  Click="SetTopButton_Click" />
```

5. Then in Page.xaml.cs, implement the event handlers inside the `Page` class, like in Listing 21.10:

LISTING 21.10   Event Handler `SetTitleButton_Click`

```
1    private void SetTitleButton_Click(object sender, RoutedEventArgs e)
2    {
3      HtmlPage.Document.SetProperty("title", ValueTextBox.Text);
4    }
5    private void SetTopButton_Click(object sender, RoutedEventArgs e)
6    {
7      HtmlElement div = HtmlPage.Document.GetElementById("TestDiv");
8      div.SetStyleAttribute("top", ValueTextBox.Text);
9
10     HtmlElement span = HtmlPage.Document.GetElementById("TestSpan");
```

LISTING 21.10   Continued

```
11    span.SetAttribute("innerHTML",
12       "<span style='font-style: bold'>"
13       + ValueTextBox.Text + "</span>");
14  }
```

▶ On line 3 (called when the Set title button is pressed), we set the `title` property of the `document` object. This changes what is displayed in your web browser's title bar. You can enter any text in the `TextBox` and press the Set title `Button`.

▶ Line 7 gets a reference to the `div` element we just added to the HTML page.

▶ Line 8 changes an attribute in the CSS style of this `div` element. The effect is to move the element vertically according to the value in the `TextBox`.

▶ Line 10 gets a reference to the `span` element located within the `TestDiv`.

▶ Lines 10 to 13 set the `innerHTML` attribute of the `div`. You can use any HTML code, and it will be displayed. The `SetAttribute` method applies a value to any HTML attribute of the `HtmlElement`.

Run the application and enter text in the text box, then press the Set title button. The page's title changes, directly set in HTML from the Silverlight application. Then, enter a CSS length in the text box, and press the Set top button. The red `div` will move accordingly. Here too, the CSS style has been set in HTML directly from Silverlight. Note that you must use a CSS formatted length value, such as 2em, or 45px, and so on.

TIP

You can prevent a Silverlight application from accessing the HTML document by setting the `enableHtmlAccess` parameter to `false` in the `object` tag (in the HTML page). This can be useful for security reasons, if you use a third-party application in your own page, and you are not sure what it does exactly. The default is `true`.

```
<param name="enableHtmlAccess" value="false" />
```

Exchanging Data Between .NET and JavaScript

We talked a little about converting data from JavaScript to .NET and back, and of the problems it may cause. This deserves more attention.

Converting data from one technology to another is not straightforward. In Silverlight, a conversion is only easy if the given type exists in both the .NET world and the JavaScript world. A .NET `int` can be converted into a JavaScript `Number` without troubles. However, other types cause problems, for example, converting a JavaScript `Number` into a .NET `byte` because `byte` only goes from 0 to 255.

Attempting Conversion

Other conversions simply cannot be done. This is easy to verify with the following steps:

1. In the JavaScriptDotNet project, in Page.xaml.cs, add a new class under the existing class CounterTickedEventArgs (see Listing 21.11):

LISTING 21.11   Class MyDate

```
public class MyDate
{
  [ScriptableMember]
  public DateTime When
  {
    get;
    internal set;
  }
}
```

2. Add a property to the CounterTickedEventArgs class, right under the property CounterValue (Listing 21.12):

LISTING 21.12   Property CustomTimestamp

```
[ScriptableMember]
public MyDate CustomTimestamp
{
  get;
  internal set;
}
```

3. When the event in CounterButton_Click is raised, set CustomTimestamp to the current date and time. Replace this event handler with the code in Listing 21.13:

LISTING 21.13   Event Handler CounterButton_Click

```
private int _counter = 0;
private void CounterButton_Click(object sender, RoutedEventArgs e)
{
  _counter++;
  if ((_counter % 5) == 0)
  {
    // true every time the counter is a multiple of 5
    CounterTickedEventArgs args = new CounterTickedEventArgs();
    args.CounterValue = _counter;
    MyDate customTimeStamp = new MyDate();
    customTimeStamp.When = DateTime.Now;
```

LISTING 21.13   Continued

```
   args.CustomTimestamp= customTimeStamp;
   OnCounterTicked(args);
 }
}
```

4. In JavaScript, in JavaScriptDotNetTestPage.html, modify the method handleCounterTicked to try and read the CustomTimestamp property as in Listing 21.14:

LISTING 21.14   Event Handler handleCounterTicked

```
handleCounterTicked : function(sender, e)
{
  alert("Counter ticked: " + e.CounterValue + " - " + e.CustomTimestamp);
},
```

Run the application now and press the Count button five times (see Figure 21.1).

FIGURE 21.1   Unknown custom type

The framework doesn't know how to convert the MyDate class and simply displays its type name. This error message makes us realize that the framework calls the method ToString on unknown types. Remember that every .NET object automatically inherits this method. However, we need to tell the framework what to do with our custom type, with the following steps.

1. In Page.xaml.cs, in the MyDate class, *override* the inherited method ToString. Simply add the code in Listing 21.15 in the class:

LISTING 21.15   Method ToString

```
public override string ToString()
{
  return When.ToString();
}
```

TIP

Visual Studio assists you there: Simply type "override" and then choose from the Intellisense box which method you want to override. Visual Studio automatically adds the correct method signature. The default implementation of the overridden method is calling the *parent class*, the class of which the current type is derived. You'll need to replace the default implementation with your own.

2. Execute the code again. This time you see the message shown in Figure 21.2. Note that depending on your system's settings, the message displayed may be formatted differently.

FIGURE 21.2   Unknown custom type with ToString override

Passing Standard Formats

The preceding solution is not quite satisfying. JavaScript also has a Date object. It would be better if we could use the string returned by CustomTimestamp to build that JavaScript Date object. Because the formatting of the DateTime class varies depending on your system's settings, JavaScript doesn't know how to create a JavaScript Date object out of this string. We need a convention, a "contract" between both worlds.

At this stage, it is useful to check the documentation to see what string format JavaScript understands, and how Silverlight can create such formatted strings. A good complete reference of the JavaScript language can be found at http://developer.mozilla.org/en/docs/Core_JavaScript_1.5_Reference.

> **NOTE**
>
> Agreeing on formats between JavaScript and .NET creates an issue if you decide to change this format. If you change the contract, both parties must agree on the changes. This can cost time and money. This is why it is important to design the interfaces (and to consider changes to existing interfaces) carefully.

Even though this is a Mozilla help page, JavaScript is standardized enough that it can be used (for the most part) in Internet Explorer and in other web browsers too. The JavaScript Date object reference can be found here: http://developer.mozilla.org/en/docs/Core_JavaScript_1.5_Reference:Global_Objects:Date. According to this specification, a new Date object can be created out of a string with the parse method of the Date class. A peek into the parse method reference teaches us that JavaScript (among other formats) understands the standardized notation RFC 1123. Because this notation is a standard, .NET also can output such a formatted string. Implement the following steps:

1. Check the .NET DateTime's ToString method documentation at http://msdn2.microsoft.com/en-us/library/zdtaw1bw.aspx.

2. The ToString method accepts a format parameter. We need to find out what to do to get the RFC 1123 format.

3. The Standard Date and Time Format Strings page at http://msdn2.microsoft.com/en-us/library/az4se3k1.aspx teaches us that the RFC 1123 format is obtained using the "R" parameter. We can modify our code as Listing 21.16 shows (in the MyDate class):

LISTING 21.16   New Method ToString

```
public override string ToString()
{
  return When.ToString("R");
}
```

4. And in JavaScript (Listing 21.17):

LISTING 21.17   New Event Handler handleCounterTicked

```
handleCounterTicked : function(sender, e)
{
  var when = new Date(e.CustomTimestamp);
  alert("Counter ticked: " + e.CounterValue
    + " - "+ when.getDate()
    + "." + when.getMonth()
    + "." + when.getFullYear());
},
```

Unlike what we did before, the when variable is now a genuine JavaScript Date object that we can manipulate (see Figure 21.3).

FIGURE 21.3   Custom Silverlight type converted in a JavaScript Date

All these standards and the documentation can seem complex, and in fact they are. A big part of the software developer's job nowadays consists of reading (and understanding) documentation, finding how systems and frameworks work, and most importantly, figuring out how they *communicate* together.

Converting the ScriptObject Class

When .NET calls a JavaScript method, the result can be converted to a simple type (such as int, bool, string, and so on) or to a ScriptObject. This last type is used every time .NET doesn't know how to convert the returned object, either because it is a complex type, or because it is an array. To demonstrate this, implement the following steps:

1. In JavaScriptDotNetTestPage.html, add the methods shown in Listing 21.18 to the JavaScriptDotNet prototype, before the other event handlers.

LISTING 21.18   Test Methods

```
getMeANumber : function()
{
  return 1234;
},
getMeAString : function()
{
  return "Hello";
},
getMeABoolean : function()
{
  return true;
},
getMeAnObject : function()
{
  var myObject = {
    Property1 : "Hello",
    Property2 : 1234 };
  return myObject;
},
getMeAnArray : function()
{
  var myArray = [ 123, 456, 789 ];
  return myArray;
},
```

2. In Page.xaml, add the three TextBlocks shown in Listing 21.19:

LISTING 21.19   Three TextBlocks

```
<TextBlock x:Name="SimpleTextBlock"
           Cursor="Hand" Margin="10,0,0,100"
           Text="Click to get simple values"
           MouseLeftButtonDown="SimpleTextBlock_MouseLeftButtonDown"
           VerticalAlignment="Bottom" />
<TextBlock x:Name="ObjectTextBlock"
           Cursor="Hand" Margin="10,0,0,75"
           Text="Click to get a JavaScript object"
           MouseLeftButtonDown="ObjectTextBlock_MouseLeftButtonDown"
           VerticalAlignment="Bottom" />
<TextBlock x:Name="ArrayTextBlock"
           Cursor="Hand" Margin="10,0,0,50"
           Text="Click to get a JavaScript array"
           MouseLeftButtonDown="ArrayTextBlock_MouseLeftButtonDown"
           VerticalAlignment="Bottom" />
```

3. In Page.xaml.cs, add the event handlers as in Listing 21.20. Make sure that you add them inside the `Page` class, or else you'll have a compilation error.

LISTING 21.20   Three Event Handlers

```csharp
private void SimpleTextBlock_MouseLeftButtonDown(object sender,
  MouseButtonEventArgs e)
{
  ScriptObject instance = HtmlPage.Window.GetProperty("jsDotNetInstance")
    as ScriptObject;

  int valueInt = (int) (double) instance.Invoke("getMeANumber", null);
  string valueString = (string) instance.Invoke("getMeAString", null);
  bool valueBool = (bool) instance.Invoke("getMeABoolean", null);
  SimpleTextBlock.Text = valueInt.ToString()
    + " - " + valueString + " - " + valueBool.ToString();
}
private void ObjectTextBlock_MouseLeftButtonDown(object sender,
  MouseButtonEventArgs e)
{
  ScriptObject instance = HtmlPage.Window.GetProperty("jsDotNetInstance")
    as ScriptObject;

  ScriptObject value = instance.Invoke("getMeAnObject", null) as ScriptObject;
  ObjectTextBlock.Text = (string) value.GetProperty("Property1")
    + " - " + (int) (double) value.GetProperty("Property2");
}
private void ArrayTextBlock_MouseLeftButtonDown(object sender,
  MouseButtonEventArgs e)
{
  ScriptObject instance = HtmlPage.Window.GetProperty("jsDotNetInstance")
    as ScriptObject;

  ScriptObject value = instance.Invoke("getMeAnArray", null) as ScriptObject;
  int length = (int) (double) value.GetProperty("length");
  ArrayTextBlock.Text = "";
  for (int index = 0; index < length; index++)
  {
    ArrayTextBlock.Text += value.GetProperty(index);
  }
}
```

Run the application and try to click on the `TextBlocks`. Refer to the next sections for explanations.

Simple Values

If the JavaScript method returns a simple value (as when the `SimpleTextBlock` is pressed), the following conversions take place:

- ▶ JavaScript `Number`—Because JavaScript doesn't distinguish between integer and floating point, every `Number` can be casted to a .NET `double`. From there, it can be casted again, for example, to an `int`.

- ▶ JavaScript `string`—They can be casted directly to a .NET `string`.

- ▶ JavaScript `Boolean`—The result of `Invoke` can be casted to a .NET `bool`.

Pressing the first `TextBlock` displays the value 1234 – Hello – True (according to what we implemented in Listing 21.20).

JavaScript Objects

The JavaScript method `getMeAnObject` returns a JavaScript `Object` built using the JSON notation. This object has two properties. The first one is a `string`, and the second one is a `Number`.

The result of the .NET `Invoke` method (when the `ObjectTextBlock` is pressed) can be casted to a `ScriptObject`. This .NET object uses the method `GetProperty` to access the JavaScript object's properties. Since these are simple values, the same rules as above apply.

Note that a JavaScript object's property can be, in turn, another JavaScript object. In that case, the result of `GetProperty` is also a `ScriptObject` on which `GetProperty` can also be called, and so forth.

The second `TextBlock` displays the value Hello – 1234 when pressed.

Arrays

JavaScript arrays are a special type of object. They have a `length` property (the number of cells in the array). In addition, all the cells can be accessed through an index.

To handle this case, the `GetProperty` method can be called with an index as parameter. Note that since the `length` property is a JavaScript `Number`, it must also be casted to a `double` first, and then to an `int`.

After we get the `length` property, we can use a `for` loop to get all the cells. This is what we do when the `ArrayTextBlock` is pressed and displays 123456789.

This works in our case because we are sure that all the JavaScript array cells are of the same type (`Number`). However, JavaScript is flexible, and nothing prevents the developer from saving mixed types in the cells (this is not a good practice, but it's possible). If that's the case, you must access and convert each cell separately.

Passing Initialization Parameters

Apart from passing values to a Silverlight application using JavaScript, you can also initialize it using the `initparams` parameter in the `object` tag (in the HTML page). The initialization parameters can be retrieved in .NET when the application starts.

Note however that this method of initializing a Silverlight application is more "static." Once the application starts, the parameters cannot be modified anymore.

Setting Initialization Parameters

Passing initialization parameters from the HTML page is very straightforward. Simply add the `initparams` parameter within the `object` tag, as a comma-separated list of key=value pairs. For example, add the following parameter to the object tag in JavaScriptDotNetTestPage.html.

```
<param name="initparams" value="param1=1234,param2=Hello" />
```

If you instantiate the Silverlight application using JavaScript as we did in Chapter 8, you can also pass initialization parameters, as shown in Listing 21.21:

LISTING 21.21   Passing Initialization Parameters in JavaScript

```
Silverlight.createObjectEx({
  source: xapUrl,
  parentElement: document.getElementById(hostId),
  id: controlId,
  properties: {
    width: "100%",
    height: "100%",
    version: "2.0",
    isWindowless : "True",
    background : "#00000000"
  },
  events: {
    onLoad: GalaSoftLogo.createDelegate(page, page.handleLoad),
    onError: GalaSoftLogo.createDelegate(page, page.handleError)
  },
  initParams : "param1=1234,param2=Hello"
});
```

Retrieving Initialization Parameters

The initialization parameters are *parsed* by the Silverlight framework when the application starts, and passed in a property of the `StartupEventArgs`, in the `Application_Startup` event handler (in App.xaml.cs). Since this event is handled in the `App` class, you can get the parameters there, for example, before instantiating the Page class. Let's see how with the following steps:

1. In JavaScriptDotNet, modify the Page constructor in the Page.xaml.cs file:

```
public Page(int initParam1, string initParam2)
```

2. To prove that we actually retrieved the parameters in Silverlight, add the code in Listing 21.22 at the end of the Page constructor, after the call to HtmlPage.RegisterScriptableObject.

LISTING 21.22   Displaying the Parameters

```
HtmlPage.Window.Alert("Retrieved init params:"
  + Environment.NewLine + "initParam1 = " + initParam1
  + Environment.NewLine + "initParam2 = " + initParam2);
```

3. In App.xaml.cs, change the Application_Startup event handler as shown in Listing 21.23:

LISTING 21.23   Getting the Parameters at Start Up

```
private void Application_Startup(object sender, StartupEventArgs e)
{
  int param1 = -1;
  if (e.InitParams.ContainsKey("param1"))
  {
    param1 = Int32.Parse(e.InitParams["param1"]);
  }
  string param2 = "- not set -";
  if (e.InitParams.ContainsKey("param2"))
  {
    param2 = e.InitParams["param2"];
  }
  this.RootVisual = new Page(param1, param2);
}
```

Note that since the initialization parameters might not be set, it is important to check for their existence before you try retrieving them! Try running the application now. The two initialization parameters should be displayed in an alert box.

Attaching .NET Events to HTML Elements

In Chapter 14, we saw how a JavaScript method can call a Silverlight method. For this, the Silverlight application needs to expose the method using the Scriptable attribute and to register itself using the method HtmlPage.RegisterScriptableObject.

Another way to initiate a web page-to-.NET communication is to attach a Silverlight event handler to an HTML event, for example with the following steps:

1. In the JavaScriptDotNetTestPage.html, replace the `div` named `TestDiv` with the content of Listing 21.24. This adds an HTML button under the `TestSpan`:

LISTING 21.24   Modified Test `div` Element

```
<div style="position: absolute;
  left: 450px; top: 0px; width: 300px; height: 100px;
  background-color: Red; color: White;"
  id="TestDiv">
  <span id="TestSpan"> </span>
  <form action="TestPage.html">
    <input type="button" id="htmlButton"
           value="Click me from HTML" />
  </form>
</div>
```

2. The HTML button executes the same code as the Silverlight Count button. To make things neater, we move this code into a method. Open the file Page.xaml.cs.

3. Select all the code inside the method `CounterButton_Click`.

4. With the content of this method selected, right-click and choose Refactor, Extract Method from the context menu (see Figure 21.4).

FIGURE 21.4   Choosing Refactor, Extract Method from the context menu

5. In the Extract Method dialog, enter a name for this new method: TickAndCheckCounter. Visual Studio is helpful in refactoring code. Notice how it creates the new method and even adds a call to this method in the `CounterButton_Click` event handler! Refactoring code is a good practice. Going through the code you wrote and using Visual Studio's refactoring capabilities creates clearer and cleaner code.

6. Add the code in Listing 21.25 at the end of the `Page` constructor:

LISTING 21.25   Attaching an Event

```
HtmlDocument document = HtmlPage.Document;
HtmlElement button = document.GetElementById("htmlButton");
button.AttachEvent("onclick", HtmlButton_Click);
```

7. Implement the `HtmlButton_Click` event handler as in Listing 21.26:

LISTING 21.26   Event Handler HtmlButton_Click

```
void HtmlButton_Click(object sender, HtmlEventArgs e)
{
  TickAndCheckCounter();
}
```

With the XAML event handler and the HTML event handler calling the same method, you can run the application and click on either the XAML or HTML button. After five clicks on either button, the alert is displayed.

This gives you a great deal of flexibility: You can choose to keep an existing HTML user interface and move the functionality in an invisible Silverlight application, or you can design a brand-new user interface in XAML. The choice is yours!

Note however that the HTML button needs a little more time to react than the XAML button, because of the communication between the HTML world and the Silverlight framework. If you need a responsive and fast user interface, you may want to develop it in XAML directly.

Using the HtmlEventArgs Class

When an HTML event is handled by a .NET event handler, an instance of HtmlEventArgs is passed to the method. This is useful, because this class contains a wealth of information about the HTML element having caused the event.

For example, why not modify the button's caption from Silverlight to display the number of clicks? In Page.xaml.cs, replace the HtmlButton_Click event handler we added in the previous section as shown in Listing 21.27:

LISTING 21.27   New Event Handler HtmlButton_Click

```
1   string _originalButtonValue = null;
2   void HtmlButton_Click(object sender, HtmlEventArgs e)
3   {
4     TickAndCheckCounter();
5
6     HtmlElement element = e.Source as HtmlElement;
7     if (element != null)
8     {
9       if (_originalButtonValue == null)
10      {
11        _originalButtonValue = element.GetAttribute("value");
12      }
13      element.SetAttribute("value", _originalButtonValue
14        + " (" + _counter.ToString() + ")");
15    }
16  }
```

▶ On line 1, we declare a private attribute to store the original text displayed by the HTML button. We want to reuse whatever text the HTML designer used.

▶ On line 4, we keep the call to the method `TickAndCheckCounter`.

▶ On line 6, we cast the attribute `e.Source` to an `HtmlElement`. Depending on the source of the event, the `e.Source` can be either an `HtmlDocument` or an `HtmlElement`. In our case, the source is the button, so it's an `HtmlElement`.

▶ On lines 9 to 12, we store the original text of the HTML button. Note that this is done only if it was never saved before. We use the method `GetAttribute` to access the attributes of the HTML element.

▶ Finally, on lines 13 and 14, we write a new `value` to the HTML button. The method `SetAttribute` takes care of setting this HTML attribute. As a result, the text displayed by the HTML button will change.

Run the application and click on the HTML button. Its text should be modified on each click. `HtmlEventArgs` has many more properties, such as the state of the Alt or Ctrl key when the event is caused by the user, the position of the mouse when it is clicked, and so on. For more information, check the SDK documentation.

Publishing Directly from Visual Studio

Visual Studio is a powerful Integrated Development Environment (IDE) and allows you to copy your website project code directly to your web server. This is a handy feature! We can test this with the following steps:

1. Open the Thumbnails application in Visual Studio. We edited this application the last time in Chapter 20, "Taking Silverlight 2 One Step Further."

2. Right-click on the Thumbnails.Web website project and select Publish Web Site from the context menu.

3. In the Publish Web Site dialog, click on the ... button next to the location text box (see Figure 21.5).

FIGURE 21.5   The Publish Web Site dialog

4. In the new dialog, select FTP Site. Enter the information about your website (as we did in Chapter 7, "Deploying to a Web Page").

5. Click on Open and then OK.

The website will be built if needed, and then published. This can take a long time, especially if you have media files. During this time, you can check the progress in the Output window in Studio.

Debugging Your Silverlight Application

An important truth in software engineering is that if you write code, you also write bugs. Software code is so complex that it is simply impossible to think of all the possible cases that the code must cover. Nowadays, modern development techniques (such as *Test Driven Development—TDD*) are focused on improving the testability of software and minimizing the risk of adding bugs to the code (we talk about unit tests and TDD in Chapter 24, "Silverlight: Continuing the Journey"). Nonetheless, finding and correcting bugs is an important part of a software programmer's life, and thankfully we have tools to help us.

In this section, we concentrate on the Visual Studio debugger. Many other tools can help you improve your application's performance, detect *memory leaks* (we mentioned that earlier; this is when memory is not freed by the application even though it is not used anymore), and make other program enhancements. These are advanced programming topics, and other authors can help you there. For now, let's debug with the tools we have already.

Comparing Debug Version and Release Version

Do you remember when we were looking at the DLLs earlier? They are placed in a bin\Debug folder. That's because so far, we always compiled the application in the Debug configuration. This mode (which is the default in Visual Studio) adds information to the assemblies, allowing you to attach a debugger to the application (as we will do in a moment).

During development, you usually deploy the Debug version of the application, because it makes debugging much easier. In production mode, however, you should deploy the Release version. Your application will be slightly smaller (because the debug information is taken out), and it will run faster.

Creating the Release Version

If you want to create a Release version of your application, you need to change the configuration in Visual Studio with the following steps.

1. Open the Thumbnails application in Visual Studio. Make sure that the Thumbnails project is selected in the Solution Explorer.

2. In the Standard toolbar, open the Debug combo box (or open the Release combo box, if you had already changed this), as shown in Figure 21.6.

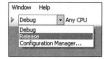

FIGURE 21.6   Select configuration

3. Select Release and build the application.

4. Next to the directory bin\Debug, you should now see a folder named bin\Release.

This directory's content is similar to the Debug folder. All the referenced assemblies (such as our UserManagement.dll and the MediaInfo.dll) should be there too (or the application will crash!).

You can even run your application in Release mode (by pressing Ctrl+F5). In fact, you should *always* test your application in Release mode before deploying it. Even though most of the code will run the same in Debug or Release configuration, there might be some differences.

Stepping Through the Code

The best way to look for errors, or even simply make sure that your application works as you expect, is to use the debugger and to step through your code, for example with the following steps:

1. Set the Thumbnails project in Debug mode again. Then right click on the Thumbnails project (the Silverlight project, not the web site project!) and select Set as StartUp Project.

2. Open the file App.xaml.cs. As we saw previously, this is the entry point of the application.

3. In the OnStartup event handler, place the cursor on the line starting with this.RootVisual.

4. Choose Debug, Toggle Breakpoint from the menu or press F9 (see Figure 21.7).

FIGURE 21.7   Breakpoint

5. Press the F5 key to start the application in the debugger.

When the running code reaches this location, the debugger stops the execution (in that particular case, it's just once when the application starts), as shown in Figure 21.8.

```
17   private void OnStartup(object sender, StartupEventArgs e)
18   {
19       // Load the main control here
20       this.RootVisual = new Page();
21   }
```

FIGURE 21.8   Active breakpoint

Stepping In

If you want to inspect what the Page method does, press the F11 key. This opens the Page.xaml.cs file in which the code is located and advances the debugger one step at a time.

1. You can now press F10 to execute the code step by step.

2. If the cursor is positioned over a method call (for example, the call to dataFile.LoadUsers();), press F11 to *step inside* the method, or press F10 to *step over* the method.

3. If your cursor reaches a loop (for example the do...while loop inside the method dataFile.LoadUsers), you can avoid having to step through every cycle of the loop. Simply position the cursor under the loop (it can even be on a curly bracket }), right-click, and select Run to Cursor from the context menu.

4. If you want to get out of a method without stepping through the rest of its code, press Shift+F11 to *step out*. The code is still executed, but not step by step.

5. If you just want to run the code without stepping, press F5 to run until the next breakpoint is met.

6. You can also *stop* the execution altogether. This closes the application and stops the debugger.

Note that all the debugger's commands are also available through the Debug menu or the Debug toolbar (see Figure 21.9).

FIGURE 21.9   Debug toolbar in Studio

NOTE

In the bin\Debug folder, you should also see files named *.pdb (for example, Thumbnails.pdb). PDB (Program DataBase) files contain additional debug information about your assembly. If you want to use the debugger and step through the code, you must have these files.

Usually, they are created by Visual Studio (that's the default configuration). However, it is not required to deploy them with the rest of the application. Also, you can actually change the configuration to avoid creating PDB files. This is advanced, so we won't go into more detail, but if you cannot step through the code you're debugging, make sure the PDB files are available.

Why Can't We Step Through InitializeComponent**?**
You might have noticed that the method InitializeComponent in the Page constructor cannot be stepped in, not even if you press F11. The reason is that this generated method has an attribute that explicitly prevents this from happening. You can see that with the following steps:

1. Position the mouse on the call to InitializeComponent and right-click.

2. From the context menu, select Go to Definition. This opens the Page.g.cs file.

3. On top of the InitializeComponent method, you should see the attribute DebuggerNonUserCodeAttribute. Because of this attribute, the debugger will not step in this method.

The generated file Page.g.cs contains all the code needed to wire the XAML markup to the code-behind. It is created by the compiler when the application is built. There is one such generated file for each XAML file (except in some special cases). Do not under any circumstances modify the content of Page.g.cs. This

> **NOTE**
>
> The generated code runs in the same Page class as our own code. This is possible thanks to the partial keyword available in .NET, which allows us to split our class declaration into multiple files.

class is *generated*, and your changes will be lost every time that you build the application.

Conditional Breakpoints
If you want your code to stop only if a certain condition is met, you can use *conditional breakpoints*, for example with the following steps:

1. In the Thumbnails application, open DataFile.cs file and place a breakpoint on the line reading while (line != null);.

2. Right-click on the breakpoint and select Condition from the context menu.

3. In the Condition text box, enter the condition line == null, as shown in Figure 21.10.

4. Click OK to close the dialog. The breakpoint now appears with a small white cross in the middle.

5. Run the application. The whole loop (reading the file) is executed,

FIGURE 21.10   Breakpoint condition

and the execution only breaks when the end-of-file is reached, and the breakpoint condition is reached.

Inspecting and Modifying Variables

Stepping through the code is a good start to understanding what is happening with your code, for example, when you have an `if` or a `switch` statement. However, you need more: How about being able to check what the value of a variable is, and to modify it while the code is being debugged? You can do it with the following steps:

1. In DataFile.cs, in the method `LoadUsers`, place a breakpoint on the line with `line = reader.ReadLine();`.

2. Press F5 to execute the application in debug mode.

3. When the debugger reaches the breakpoint, press F10 to step once.

4. Place the mouse over the `line` variable, as shown in Figure 21.11.

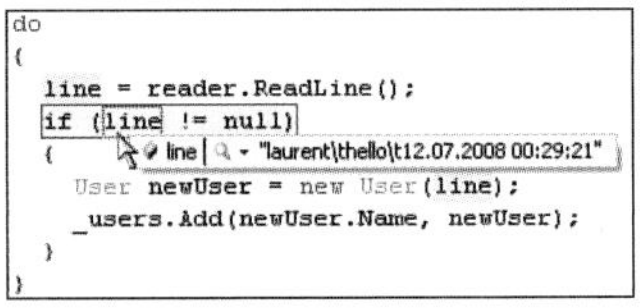

FIGURE 21.11   Inspecting a variable

▶ The value of the `line` variable is displayed. In our case, it is a string, with the user name, password, and date of last visit.

▶ Clicking on the string value allows you to modify it before you resume execution. This can help you to test what happens when some special values are found. For example, is the code robust enough to handle invalid values—for example, if you remove the `'\t'` characters (these are "tabs")? (*Answer: No it's not. If you remove the tabs from the string, you will get a System.IndexOutOfRangeException.*)

▶ For some types, you will notice a small magnifier icon. This is displayed only if a visualizer is available for this type. For strings, for example, you can use Text, XML, or HTML visualizers. You can also get additional visualizers on the Internet.

Objects can also be inspected:

1. Place the mouse cursor on the `reader` variable.

2. Click on the small "+" sign on the left.

3. This expands an additional popup with all the reader's properties and attributes. If a property is also an object, you can also expand it, and so on.

4. If the application is already running in the web browser, you can restart it simply by refreshing the web page. This reexecutes the whole code, allowing you to check your startup code again.

The variables can also be inspected in other locations:

- ▶ You can drag a variable name into one of the Watch windows. There are four of them, which you can open by choosing Debug, Windows, Watch, Watch 1-4 from the menu.

- ▶ The Locals window (select Debug, Windows, Locals) shows the values of all the local variables.

- ▶ The Auto window (select Debug, Windows, Auto) shows you the variables that the debugger thinks you want to see depending on the cursor location.

Debugging in a Web Site Project

When you have a web site project with a link to a Silverlight application (as we have here for the Thumbnails application and its Thumbnails.Web web site project), you can also debug Silverlight. Note, however, that you can either debug JavaScript (see the next section, "Debugging JavaScript") or Silverlight, but not both at the same time.

1. Right click on the Thumbnails.Web web site project now and select it as StartUp Project. Set the page index.html as StartUp Page.

2. To select which platform you will debug, right-click on the project Thumbnails.Web.

3. Select Property Pages.

4. Under Start Options, in the Debuggers section, switch the Silverlight check box on or off depending on what you want to do (on for Silverlight, off for JavaScript).

Debugging JavaScript

Debugging JavaScript, stepping in the code, and inspecting/modifying variables are also possible in Visual Studio with the following steps:

1. First make sure that JavaScript debugging is enabled (see the preceding section "Debugging in a Web Site Project").

2. Open the JavaScript file Thumbnails.js.

3. Inside the handler `handleSubmitClicked`, place a breakpoint on the line reading `var name = this._nameTextBox.value`.

4. Run the application in debug mode by pressing F5.

5. Click on the login link, enter a user name and password, and click Submit.

6. The debugger breaks at the location of the breakpoint we placed right before.

Here too, you can step inside functions and inspect or modify variables' values, with the two following remarks:

▶ If you want to watch the value of a complex expression, for example `this._passwordTextBox.value`, you must select the whole expression with the mouse before passing the cursor over the expression.

▶ Sometimes, when you try to place a breakpoint on the first line of a function, the whole function gets selected instead. To avoid this, you must place the breakpoint on the second line only. If needed, add a dummy line before the first line (for example, `alert("Dummy");`). Don't forget to remove it later.

Debugging Running Applications

The last exciting feature we cover in this chapter is the ability to load a Silverlight application from the Internet and to attach the debugger to it even after it has been started. This is convenient if your application connects to the web server of origin to get values, for example, and you notice a different behavior between the local and remote execution. Let's see how with the following steps:

1. Follow the directions in the "Publishing Directly from Visual Studio" section earlier in this chapter to copy the project Thumbnails.Web to the web server. In theory you can also copy the files to the web server using an FTP server as we did in Chapter 7. However, debugging a Silverlight application served from a web

> **NOTE**
>
> Even if your Silverlight application connects to an ASP.NET application, you will only be able to debug the code running locally on your PC—that is, the Silverlight code and the JavaScript code. If you want to debug the server-side code, you must attach your debugger to the web server.

server works much better if you publish from Visual Studio directly. This ensures that all the components on the web server are totally up-to-date with the code.

2. Point your web browser to the address of the index.html file, for example www. galasoft.ch/SL2U/Thumbnails/index.html.

3. In Visual Studio, place a breakpoint in Page.xaml.cs, in the handler `ThumbnailsViewer_SelectionChanged`.

Now we must *attach* the debugger to the application:

1. Choose Debug, Attach to Process from the menu.

2. In the process list, select iexplore.exe (or firefox.exe if you run the Silverlight application in Firefox).

3. Above the available processes list, make sure that Silverlight Code appears next to the Attach To label. If that's not the case, click on Select and check the box next to the Silverlight code type.

4. Click Attach.

5. Click on a Thumbnail. The debugger breaks at the location of your breakpoint.

You can now debug the application as we did before. Just remember, you are debugging the code *running locally* on your PC, even though it is *served from a remote web server*. After you are done, *detach* the debugger by choosing Debug, Stop Debugging from the menu (or press Shift+F5).

Debugging Silverlight Running on a Macintosh

Silverlight running on Apple Macintosh computers should behave exactly the same as on Windows computers. But sometimes you might need to debug this configuration anyway. Since Visual Studio doesn't run on Macintosh computers, however, you cannot install it and debug directly.

Thankfully, it is possible to attach Visual Studio on one PC to a Silverlight application running on a Macintosh computer. For more information, check the following links:

http://blogs.msdn.com/ddietric/archive/2008/03/05/setting-up-silverlight-2-remote-debugging-on-mac-os-x.aspx

www.microsoft.com/silverlight/resources/readme.aspx?v=2.0

Summary

In this chapter, we sharpened our knowledge of Silverlight and studied a few topics in more detail, especially involving JavaScript, HTML, and Silverlight communication. Data conversion, `ScriptObject`, initialization parameters, events and event handlers—this infrastructure allows building rich *integrated* applications.

Later, we learned how to use advanced functionalities of Visual Studio, such as publishing to your web server directly from the development environment, debugging Silverlight and JavaScript code, attaching the debugger to a running application (even if it is served from your web server), and so on.

Chapter 22, "Connecting to the Web," is all about communication and web services of all kinds. After opening Silverlight's interfaces to the hosting web page, we now open the gates of communication to the World Wide Web.

Connecting to the Web

So far, our Silverlight applications have run isolated from the server they originated from. We loaded images and videos, but after that the application didn't communicate with the server anymore. In this chapter, we change this and demonstrate three different ways to place calls to the web server.

Creating and Loading an XML File

We talked about XML as early as Chapter 2, "Understanding XAML," as a good and modern way to store information. In this chapter, we will apply this to our Thumbnails application. After taking the media files themselves out of the application, we finally do the same with the media information.

Removing the Media Information from the Application

The first step in creating and loading an XML file is to export the media information from the Page.xaml resources into an external file. It will be easier to modify this file, to add or remove media, without having to recompile the application. Follow the steps:

1. Open the Thumbnails application in Visual Studio. In Thumbnails.Web, right click on the ClientBin folder in the Solution Explorer and select Add New Item.

2. Select an XML file and name it media.xml.

3. Set the content shown in Listing 22.1.

LISTING 22.1   XML Media Information File

```xml
<?xml version="1.0" encoding="utf-8" ?>
<medias>
  <media type="Movie" name="mov1.wmv"
         description="Nightly show at Singapore Zoo"/>
  <media type="Image" name="pic1.png"
         description="The Matterhorn seen from Zermatt"/>
  <media type="Image" name="pic2.jpg"
         description="The Matterhorn"/>
  <media type="Image" name="pic3.jpg"
         description="Mountains seen from Klosters"/>
</medias>
```

4. In the Thumbnails project, open Page.xaml and *empty* the MediaDataSource:

```xml
<data:MediaExCollection x:Key="MediaDataSource"
                        d:IsDataSource="True" />
```

5. In Page.xaml.cs, to avoid errors, in the Page constructor, *delete* the code used to initialize the TextBlocks Foreground brush. Delete the lines starting at MediaExCollection mediaCollection and ending at TitleTextBlock2.Foreground = brush;.

You can build the application to make sure that everything is OK. You can even run it, but of course the viewer will be empty, since we removed the content of the data source.

Showing and Hiding a Startup Screen

We will now add a startup screen to the application. It will simply cover the whole screen and be half transparent. We will also use it to display information to the user. If you want, you can of course place additional features on this screen, such as an animation, a logo, and so on. We will make sure that the startup screen is displayed before we load the XML file and the thumbnails. This way, if the network is slow, the user gets information, instead of staring at an empty screen.

In Page.xaml, add a "cache" at the end of the main Grid LayoutRoot (but still inside it). Since the "cache" appears after every other element, it will be on top of them and intercept every mouse click. By making it half transparent (well, 70% opaque, actually), we let the user get a preview of what to expect. Of course, the cache must cover everything, so we use the Grid.RowSpan and

> **NOTE**
>
> We use a StackPanel because the user might resize the web browser's width, and the first TextBlock can wrap on multiple lines. By using a StackPanel, we make sure that the second TextBlock (used to display error information) is "pushed" down if that happens. Of course, there is the risk that it is "pushed" outside the screen. To handle this, you could wrap a ScrollViewer around the StackPanel.

`Grid.ColumnSpan` attributes as shown in Listing 22.2. Add this markup at the end of the file, but still in the LayoutRoot:

LISTING 22.2   Cache Panel

```
<StackPanel x:Name="Cache" Background="#CCFFFFFF"
            Grid.RowSpan="2" Grid.ColumnSpan="2">
  <TextBlock Text="Please wait..." TextWrapping="Wrap"
   x:Name="StatusTextBlock" FontSize="36"
   RenderTransformOrigin="0.5,0.5"
   Margin="25,80,25,0" HorizontalAlignment="Left">
    <TextBlock.RenderTransform>
      <RotateTransform Angle="-10" />
    </TextBlock.RenderTransform>
  </TextBlock>
  <TextBlock TextWrapping="Wrap" x:Name="ErrorTextBlock"
   Margin="25,70,25,0" HorizontalAlignment="Stretch" />
</StackPanel>
```

We don't want to simply hide the "cache," so we draft a simple fade out animation. You can do this in Blend, or simply type the XAML markup in Listing 22.3 at the end of the `UserControl.Resources`:

LISTING 22.3   Storyboard to Hide the Cache

```
<Storyboard x:Name="CacheFadeOutStoryboard">
  <DoubleAnimationUsingKeyFrames BeginTime="00:00:00"
   Storyboard.TargetName="Cache"
   Storyboard.TargetProperty="(UIElement.Opacity)">
    <SplineDoubleKeyFrame KeyTime="00:00:00.5000000" Value="0" />
  </DoubleAnimationUsingKeyFrames>
</Storyboard>
```

Loading the XML Media Information File

We encapsulate the loading and parsing of the XML media file in a separate object. This way, it is easier to modify it if the structure of the XML file changes, if we decide to create a web service to deliver this information, for example.

1. Inside the Data folder in the Thumbnails project, add a new class and name it MediaInformationFile.cs.

2. Before the `MediaInformationFile` class itself, add a new class deriving from `EventArgs` (Listing 22.4). We use this class to communicate the results to the outside world.

LISTING 22.4   MediaFileLoadedEventArgs Class

```
public class MediaFileLoadedEventArgs : EventArgs
{
  public IEnumerable<MediaEx> Collection
  {
    get; set;
  }
  public Exception Error
  {
    get; set;
  }
}
```

3. In the beginning of the `MediaInformationFile` class, add two constants to store the name of the XML media file and the path to the media files:

```
public const string MEDIA_FILE_NAME = "media.xml";
public const string MEDIA_PATH = "MediaFiles";
```

4. Declare a new event inside the class. We use that event to inform any subscriber that the information contained in the XML file is loaded and ready for use. Together with this event, let's declare a companion method like we did a couple of times before, as shown in Listing 22.5:

> **NOTE**
>
> It would be better to pass these two parameters to the Silverlight application using the `initParams` we saw in Chapter 21, "Taking Silverlight 2 Even Further." This would add modularity to the application.

LISTING 22.5   Loaded Event and Companion Method

```
public event EventHandler Loaded;

private void OnMediaFileLoaded(IEnumerable<MediaEx> xmlMedias,
  Exception lastError)
{
  if (Loaded != null)
  {
    MediaFileLoadedEventArgs args = new MediaFileLoadedEventArgs();
    args.Collection = xmlMedias;
    args.Error = lastError;
    Loaded(this, args);
  }
}
```

▶ If someone subscribed to the event, the method creates a new `MediaFileLoadedEventArgs` and stores the collection of loaded `MediaEx` instances (as read from the XML file).

▶ In case something bad happened, we also pass the last error to the event subscriber. This error is of type `Exception`. We talk more about them in Chapter 23, "Placing Cross-Domain Requests and Handling Exceptions."

Instead of passing an `ObservableCollection` (such as an instance of the `MediaExCollection` that we created before), we use an `IEnumerable<MediaEx>`. This gives us a great freedom: The only thing that the subscriber knows for sure is that they can enumerate (for example, with a `foreach` loop) through the content of the collection. The reason we prefer to use an `IEnumerable<MediaEx>` is that it avoids an additional conversion as we see in a moment. Besides, since `ObservableCollection` (and thus `MediaExCollection`) *implements* `IEnumerable`, too, we can change this later without having to modify the `MediaFileLoadedEventArgs` at all.

Sending the Request

Let's add some flesh to the `MediaInformationFile` class.

1. Add the DLL System.Net to the application. This DLL contains the `WebClient` class that we want to use. Because it is not part of the standard distribution of Silverlight, we must add it explicitly. Right click on the Thumbnails project and select Add Reference. Then, choose the System.Net DLL from the .NET tab.

2. Create a public method in the `MediaInformationFile` class as shown in Listing 22.6:

LISTING 22.6   LoadMediaFile Method

```
1  public void LoadMediaFile()
2  {
3    WebClient client = new WebClient();
4    client.DownloadStringCompleted
5      += new DownloadStringCompletedEventHandler(
6        client_DownloadStringCompleted);
7    client.DownloadStringAsync(new Uri(MEDIA_FILE_NAME, UriKind.Relative));
8  }
```

▶ The `WebClient` class is one of the two main classes you will use for web communication. This is the simplest way to send a request and get a response.

▶ This class has various methods. Since we need to download XML content, and we know that this is text, we use the method `DownloadStringAsync`, the easiest way to get text content from the web server.

▶ The suffix `Async` is short for *asynchronous*. In Silverlight, all the web communication occurs asynchronously. Once the request is sent, the Silverlight application continues to run without waiting for the response. When the response arrives, an event is raised by the framework.

▶ In the full version of .NET, there is a way to send synchronous requests to a web server, and to block the application as long as the response doesn't arrive, but synchronous communication is not included in Silverlight.

▶ As we said previously, we need to handle an event when the response from the web server reaches the Silverlight application. The event corresponding to the `DownloadStringAsync` method is the `DownloadStringCompleted` event. So we need to register a `DownloadStringCompletedEventHandler` event handler (lines 4 to 6).

▶ Finally, we call the method itself, providing a relative URI to the media files (line 7).

This method presupposes that the media will be placed into the MediaFiles folder and the XML information file in ClientBin. These types of constraints are exactly what user documentation is for: Don't forget to mention this fact to your users, to make sure that they comply.

Getting a Response

After the request is sent, the user can continue to work, but in this case it's not very interesting, since this is an initial download, and the user is just waiting. There is a way to provide information about the progress of the download, and we talk about this later in the chapter. For now, since the XML file is usually rather small, we just wait. Once the request arrives, the event is raised, and we handle it with Listing 22.7. Add this code in the `MediaInformationFile` class.

LISTING 22.7   client_DownloadStringCompleted Event Handler

```
1   void client_DownloadStringCompleted(object sender,
2     DownloadStringCompletedEventArgs e)
3   {
4     // Prepare data
5     IEnumerable<MediaEx> output = null;
6     Exception lastError = null;
7     try
8     {
9       // Get media collection here
10    }
11    catch (Exception ex)
12    {
13      // Failure, inform user
14      if (ex.InnerException != null
15        && ex.InnerException is WebException)
16      {
```

LISTING 22.7   Continued

```
17        lastError = ex.InnerException;
18      }
19      else
20      {
21        lastError = ex;
22      }
23      output = null;
24    }
25
26    OnMediaFileLoaded(output, lastError);
27  }
```

▶ On line 5, we declare an `IEnumerable<MediaEx>`. We know that an interface cannot be instantiated (because it is abstract), but the framework returns a class *implementing* this interface when we parse the XML file later. In fact we don't really care what exact class we get from the framework. The only thing that we are interested in is being able to enumerate all the items.

> **TIP**
>
> If the XML file cannot be found on the web server, the framework throws a `TargetInvocationException` as soon as you try to get the invocation's result. In that case, we catch this exception in this same method (lines 11 to 24) and handle it. For a "file not found" error, the exception's `InnerException` property is a `WebException` notifying us that the file we look for doesn't exist. This is the exception we want to pass to the user.

▶ On line 6 we create a variable for an error that could occur when loading the XML file.

▶ Because we don't know what other errors can occur, we catch just any `Exception` type (line 11). In fact, it is not very good practice. As we see in Chapter 23, it is better to differentiate according to the `Exception`'s type.

▶ Finally, we raise the `Loaded` event on line 26, to notify anyone interested that the collection is ready (or that an error occurred, in which case the `Error` property is set, and the `Collection` property is null).

At this point, you can build the application after adding a couple of `using` directives. Something big is missing though: Did you notice that we never actually read the media information from the response? This part deserves a section of its own.

Reading an XML File with LINQ

On line 9 in the Listing 22.7 example, we must `Get media collection here`. To perform this task, the easiest way is to use *LINQ*.

LINQ stands for *Language Integrated Query* and certainly deserves a book just for itself. Let's summarize aggressively, and say that LINQ is a *query framework* integrated in the .NET framework (and as a subset in Silverlight). The whole version of LINQ (available in .NET) can perform queries against a number of data sources, including databases, object collections (for example, arrays, lists, and so on). In this section, we use LINQ to perform queries against XML data stores. In Chapter 23, we will also see that you can use LINQ to perform queries from JSON-formatted data sources.

Before LINQ was created, the usual way to perform queries was by using another specialized and complex programming language called *SQL*. However, SQL has many disadvantages: It's text-based (so it's easy to make mistakes); it is only available to query against databases; it comes in different flavors, depending on the "brand" of database you work with; and it is not integrated but is external to .NET.

Although LINQ is comfortable to use (after you overcome the small learning curve), it is not the fastest method to parse XML data. For very big documents, to avoid waiting for the whole structure to be loaded in memory, you should instead use the XmlReader class. This is outside the scope of this book, however. Check the SDK documentation for details.

We lack the time to go into much detail about LINQ, even the reduced version available in Silverlight. In this section, we show how to load a collection of MediaEx items with the following steps:

1. LINQ is also not part of the standard Silverlight distribution, so we need to add the DLL to the application (just like the System.Net DLL before). Add a reference to the System.Xml.Linq DLL.

2. Add a private attribute on top of the class MediaInformationFile:

   ```
   private XDocument _document;
   ```

3. Additionally to the namespace System.Xml.Linq that you can add for the XDocument attribute we added in step 2, you need to add another using statement. This cannot be added automatically (pressing Shift+Alt+F10 doesn't work here), so simply type the following in the using section on top of MediaInformationFile.cs:

   ```
   using System.Linq;
   ```

4. Replace line 9 of Listing 22.7 (// Get media collection here) with the code shown in Listing 22.8. Then, you can build the application.

LISTING 22.8   Making a LINQ Query

```
1  StringReader reader = new StringReader(e.Result);
2  _document = XDocument.Load(reader);
3  output = from xmlMediaInfo
```

LISTING 22.8   Continued

```
4      in _document.Descendants("media")
5      select new MediaEx
6      {
7        MediaPath = MEDIA_PATH,
8        MediaName = (string) xmlMediaInfo.Attribute("name"),
9        Type = (MediaType) Enum.Parse(typeof(MediaType),
10         (string) xmlMediaInfo.Attribute("type"), true),
11       Description = (string) xmlMediaInfo.Attribute("description")
12     };
```

▶ For once, let's start with line 2: The flavor of LINQ that we use here (called *LINQ to XML*) uses a class named XDocument. Once an XML file is loaded into an instance of this class, we can query against it. Here, we use the Load method, which takes a *reader* as parameter.

▶ Depending on which kind of input you deal with, you can use various readers. We already know the StreamReader is suited to load *streams* (and we use it again soon). There are many other types of readers however.

▶ On line 1, we use the property e.Result to build the reader. For the DownloadStringAsync method, e.Result is of type string. This is really simple: We asked for a string, and we got one. The logical choice for a reader is a StringReader, created on line 1.

▶ Line 3 uses the from keyword to declare a variable named xmlMediaInfo. The next line specifies where we get this variable (this is the input taken from the XML file). Note that this is only the beginning of the query, which ends on line 12 with a semicolon.

▶ Line 4 specifies the collection in which we find the items to query. Here, this collection is returned by the XDocument: We get all the Descendants (children) of the main root that use the tag media. If you take a look back at Listing 22.1, you'll see that a media element describes one media item.

▶ Line 5 uses the select keyword. Like the name suggests, this keyword selects items inside the input collection. We do not set a condition, so all items will be loaded. Also on line 5 we inform the framework that we will create instances of the MediaEx class according to the XML data. Because of this statement, the LINQ query returns an IEnumerable<MediaEx> that we store in the output variable.

TIP

LINQ allows *filtering* an input collection with the `where` keyword. For example, you could get only the image files from the XML file by adding the following between lines 4 and 5 in Listing 22.8:

```
where (xmlMediaInfo.Attribute("type").Value
    == MediaType.Image.ToString())
```

LINQ even allows creating so-called *anonymous types*. These are similar to what we do in JavaScript when we declare new objects using the JSON notation. In this example, we use the explicit `MediaEx` type that is available anyway.

▶ We need to specify how to create the instances of `MediaEx` that will be stored in the collection. This is the purpose of lines 6 to 12. In these lines, the properties of the `MediaEx` instance are set one by one.

   ▶ Line 7 sets the `MediaPath` property to the constant we declared before.

   ▶ Line 8 gets the `name` attribute from the XML element and assigns it to the `MediaName` property.

   ▶ Lines 9 and 10 also get an attribute (`type`) from the XML element. XML attributes are `strings` and must be converted before we can use them in Silverlight (unless, of course, they really are `strings`, like the `MediaName` property). Here, the `Type` property is a `MediaType`. This *enumeration* is declared in the file Media.cs. To convert a `string` into an `enum`, we need to *parse* it using the static method `Enum.Parse` described in the next section, "Parsing Enums."

   ▶ Finally, the `Description` is also a `string`, so it is read directly from the XML element.

Parsing Enums

The method `Enum.Parse` is complex, so let's review it:

▶ The first parameter of this method is the *type* of enumeration we want to get, for example `typeof(MediaType)`.

▶ The second parameter is the string we want to parse. This could be the string `"Image"`, for example, or the value of an XML attribute.

▶ The third parameter is a `bool`. If it's `true`, the parser ignores the casing of the `string`. In that case the `strings` `"Image"`, `"image"`, and `"ImAgE"` are interpreted the same. If it's `false`, wrongly cased strings are not parsed, and an error is thrown.

▶ The `Parse` method returns an `object` that needs to be *casted* to the desired enumeration type.

Triggering the Request

Once again the entire infrastructure is in place now and needs to be triggered. This is the role of the Page class. We send the request after the whole page has been loaded. The right moment for this is when the Page.Loaded event is raised.

1. In Page.xaml.cs, add a private attribute to hold the instance of MediaInformationFile that loads the XML file.

   ```
   private MediaInformationFile _mediaFile;
   ```

2. Add an event handler for the Page.Loaded event. You should place this line at the end of the Page constructor.

   ```
   this.Loaded += new RoutedEventHandler(Page_Loaded);
   ```

3. Implement the event handler (Listing 22.9):

LISTING 22.9   Page_Loaded Event Handler

```
void Page_Loaded(object sender, RoutedEventArgs e)
{
  _mediaFile = new MediaInformationFile();
  _mediaFile.Loaded += new EventHandler(_mediaFile_Loaded);
  _mediaFile.LoadMediaFile();
}
```

Because the whole request/response/parsing business is encapsulated into the MediaInformationFile class, we simply need to create an instance of this class, subscribe to its Loaded event, and then call the LoadMediaFile method, using the path of the media files as a parameter.

Handling the Results

Like we mentioned, the file gets loaded asynchronously. Once it is fully loaded, and the collection of MediaEx instances has been parsed, we are notified by an event raised by the MediaInformationFile class, and we handle it with the following steps.

1. We registered for the MediaInformationFile.Loaded event earlier, so now we implement the _mediaFile_Loaded event handler in the Page class. The code in Listing 22.10 shows the empty event handler.

LISTING 22.10   _mediaFile_Loaded Event Handler

```
void _mediaFile_Loaded(object sender, EventArgs e)
{
}
```

2. Inside the event handler, cast the generic EventArgs instance to
   MediaFileLoadedEventArgs. Note that we could also have declared a specific delegate
   type for the MediaInformationFile.Loaded event like we did in Chapter 10,
   "Progressing with .NET," in the section titled "Raising Events and Using Delegates."

   ```
   MediaFileLoadedEventArgs args = e as MediaFileLoadedEventArgs;
   ```

3. In case there was an error, the args.Collection will be null. Additionally, the
   args.Error might contain additional information about the cause of the error. If
   that's the case, we display this to the user and we exit. Note that the cache will
   never be removed. At this point, the user should contact her support department.
   The code in Listing 22.11 comes after what we added in step 2.

LISTING 22.11   Error Handling

```
if (args.Collection == null)
{
  StatusTextBlock.Text = "There was an error";
  if (args.Error != null)
  {
    ErrorTextBlock.Text = args.Error.Message
      + Environment.NewLine + args.Error.StackTrace;
  }
  return;
}
```

4. Then get the data source collection out of the resources. Because this is an
   ObservableCollection, when we add new items to it (those taken from the XML
   file), the Silverlight framework automatically looks for the DataTemplate specified in
   the ItemsControl and creates a visual representation.

   ```
   MediaExCollection mediaCollection
     = Resources["MediaDataSource"] as MediaExCollection;
   ```

5. Since the result of the XML parsing is an IEnumerable<MediaEx>, we can enumerate
   it and add the items to our own collection. We also use the occasion to look for
   content appropriate to use as a brush for the title TextBlocks on the page. Add the
   code in Listing 22.12 in _mediaFile_Loaded.

LISTING 22.12   Enumerating the Items and Setting Brushes

```
bool foundBrush = false;
foreach (MediaEx mediaInfo in args.Collection)
{
  mediaCollection.Add(mediaInfo);

  if (!foundBrush
```

LISTING 22.12   Continued

```
   && mediaInfo.Type == MediaInfo.MediaType.Image)
  {
    ImageBrush brush = new ImageBrush();
    brush.ImageSource = mediaInfo.ImageSource;
    TitleTextBlock1.Foreground = brush;
    TitleTextBlock2.Foreground = brush;
    foundBrush = true;
  }
}
```

▶ Adding the items to the collection is straightforward since LINQ created them already of the right type. No need to cast.

▶ If the item represents an image, and if this is the first image that we find, we use it to create an `ImageBrush` for the `TextBlocks`.

6. If everything went well, the cache must disappear, so that the user can start clicking on the thumbnails. We created an animation for this, so let's retrieve it and use it with Listing 22.13, to be added in _mediaFile_Loaded.

LISTING 22.13   Getting and Starting the `Storyboard`

```
Storyboard cacheFadeOut
  = Resources["CacheFadeOutStoryboard"] as Storyboard;
cacheFadeOut.Completed
  += new EventHandler(cacheFadeOut_Completed);
cacheFadeOut.Begin();
```

7. Because the cache is in front of every other element, simply setting its `Opacity` to 0% still prevents us from using the application. This is why we set a handler for the storyboard's `Completed` event, as shown in Listing 22.14:

LISTING 22.14   cacheFadeOut_Completed Event Handler

```
void cacheFadeOut_Completed(object sender, EventArgs e)
{
  Cache.Visibility = Visibility.Collapsed;
}
```

As soon as the cache is completely transparent, we *collapse* it so that it doesn't get in the way anymore.

Testing the Application

Run the application now. The media files are loaded according to the information contained in the XML media file. To verify this, exit the web browser application and modify the XML file, for example, change a description, add or remove an item, or change the order of the thumbnails. Then load the page again. You should now see the thumbnails according to the new XML file, without having to recompile the application.

Remember what we said in the very beginning of Chapter 21: The Silverlight application is cached by the web browser (and that includes the XML file that it downloads). Simply refreshing the web page might not be enough. To load the file anew, you need to empty the cache first. Check Chapter 21 for details.

Loading a Zip File and Showing Progress

Our application sends separate requests for each of the media files. We simply set the URI of a `MediaElement`, an `Image`, or an `ImageBrush`, and the web browser sends the corresponding HTTP request. Depending on your configuration, this might not be the best way to do things.

We show another way to handle this: Pack all the media files into a Zip file and download this big file with the `WebClient` class.

It is difficult to say which method is the best.

▶ Handling multiple smaller responses might be more suited for slow connections, while one big download is better for a faster line.

▶ Loading the media files one by one displays them faster to the user, because as soon as one picture or video is down, it appears in the ThumbnailsViewer control.

▶ The big Zip file, once loaded, contains all the media needed to run the application. The application starts slower but is more responsive then, because the media is already available on the computer when the cache disappears.

▶ If you load all the media files in a Zip file, your application has full control over the content; it can modify the files before displaying them, for example, resizing them, filtering them, and so on.

Choosing one or the other requires a fine analysis of the conditions in which your application will run, of the requirements, and so on.

Creating the Zip File

Our first task is to create a Zip file instead of a folder. Use your preferred compression application to pack the whole MediaFiles folder into a Zip file. The Zip file should remain in the ClientBin folder.

You must make sure that the elements inside the Zip file are under the path MediaFiles and *not* in the root of the Zip file. With WinZip, for example, you can right-click on the ClientBin/MediaFiles folder and choose the Windows context menu WinZip, Add to MediaFiles.zip.

Extending the MediaEx Class to Store the Stream

The MediaEx class gets two new properties. Now that we have the whole media file in the Zip file, we extract it and save it in memory.

In MediaEx (in the Data folder of the Thumbnails project), delete the existing properties named ImageSource and MovieUri and instead add the properties shown in Listing 22.15:

LISTING 22.15   Two New Properties

```
public Stream MediaSource
{
  get; set;
}
public BitmapImage ImageSource
{
  get
  {
    if (MediaSource == null)
    {
      return null;
    }
    BitmapImage bitmap = new BitmapImage();
    bitmap.SetSource(MediaSource);
    return bitmap;
  }
}
```

▶ The first property is the actual media file, saved as a Stream. We worked with streams a couple of times before (for example to read and write files in the isolated storage). Later, we load this stream inside the MediaElement (if it's a movie) or inside the Image (if it's, well, an image).

▶ The second property is just a convenience property to make it easier to convert the stream into an image. Should the stream be null, the property simply returns null too, and nothing is displayed. If the stream is valid, however, a BitmapImage is created and loaded with the stream's content. We use the method SetSource. This method accepts a stream as input and converts it to an image file.

You can build the application, but running it at this point will create an error, because some properties referenced in the DataTemplates are now missing or have changed.

Loading the Zip File

Let's modify the class MediaInformationFile now. First, we add a new event to notify the Page (or any subscriber) when the download progress of the Zip file changes. Later we see how that works.

1. In MediaInformationFile, add the following line under the Loaded event:

   ```
   public event DownloadProgressChangedEventHandler DownloadProgressChanged;
   ```

2. Replace the last line of the client_DownloadStringCompleted event handler (the call to OnMediaFileLoaded) with the code in Listing 22.16:

LISTING 22.16   Loading the Zip File

```
if (output == null)
{
  OnMediaFileLoaded(output, lastError);
}
else
{
  LoadZipFile(output);
}
```

The method LoadZipFile is called only if the XML file is found and could be parsed. No need to load a big Zip file if there are errors anyway.

3. Implement LoadZipFile as shown in Listing 22.17:

LISTING 22.17   LoadZipFile Method

```
private void LoadZipFile(IEnumerable<MediaEx> mediaInfos)
{
  WebClient client = new WebClient();
  client.OpenReadCompleted
    += new OpenReadCompletedEventHandler(
      client_OpenReadCompleted);
  client.DownloadProgressChanged
    += new DownloadProgressChangedEventHandler(
      client_DownloadProgressChanged);
  client.OpenReadAsync(new Uri(MEDIA_PATH + ".zip", UriKind.Relative),
    mediaInfos);
}
```

▶ We assume the name of the Zip file to be MediaFiles.zip. Here, too, the user must be notified in the user documentation.

▶ The WebClient is the same class as before, but instead of the method
DownloadStringAsync, we use the more generic OpenReadAsync. While
DownloadStringAsync can only load text content, OpenReadAsync can load any
file type into a Stream.

▶ The Completed event for the OpenReadAsync method is called
OpenReadCompleted. The event handler signature is different too.

▶ Additionally to the Completed event, we handle the DownloadProgressChanged
event. This event is raised by the WebClient class every time a noticeable
change occurs in the download progress.

▶ The method OpenReadAsync is called with a relative URI just like before, but
instead of loading the XML file, we now load the Zip file.

▶ We preserved the result of the LINQ query and passed it to the LoadZipFile
method (as the mediaInfos parameter). Now we preserve it even further: By
passing it as the last parameter of the method OpenReadAsync, we save it as a
UserState. When the response arrives, we can get this object again and use it.
This is just a way to save information without having to allocate a private
attribute.

4. As we said previously, when the WebClient warns us about any change in the download progress, we want to notify the Page. Every time the client's
DownloadProgressChanged event is raised, we raise our own event. This is why it is
declared with the same handler type as the WebClient class, as shown in Listing
22.18:

LISTING 22.18   client_DownloadProgressChanged Event Handler

```
void client_DownloadProgressChanged(object sender,
  DownloadProgressChangedEventArgs e)
{
  if (DownloadProgressChanged != null)
  {
    DownloadProgressChanged(sender, e);
  }
}
```

Reading the Zipped Files

Let's now concentrate on the Completed event. The event handler's structure is similar to
the one we use for the XML file. Simply add Listing 22.19 to the MediaInformationFile
class:

LISTING 22.19   `client_OpenReadCompleted` Event Handler

```
void client_OpenReadCompleted(object sender,
  OpenReadCompletedEventArgs e)
{
  MediaExCollection output = new MediaExCollection();
  Exception lastError = null;
  try
  {
    // Get media stream here
  }
  catch (Exception ex)
  {
    // Failure, inform user
    if (ex.InnerException != null
      && ex.InnerException is WebException)
    {
      lastError = ex.InnerException;
    }
    else
    {
      lastError = ex;
    }
    output = null;
  }

  OnMediaFileLoaded(output, lastError);
}
```

▶ Instead of using an `IEnumerable`, we now return a `MediaExCollection`. This works because `MediaExCollection` derives from `ObservableCollection<MediaEx>`, and this last class implements `IEnumerable<MediaEx>`. So we can say that `MediaExCollection` is an `IEnumerable<MediaEx>`.

▶ If the Zip file is not found, accessing the property `e.Result` throws an exception like with the XML file before.

WARNING

The content of the `IEnumerable` returned by the LINQ query cannot be modified after the query has been executed. You cannot simply loop through the `MediaEx` instances contained in the `IEnumerable` and set their `MediaSource` property. Instead, you need to take the `MediaEx` instance, and save it in a different collection. We do that in just a moment.

Replace the line reading `// Get media stream here` with the code in Listing 22.20:

LISTING 22.20   `client_OpenReadCompleted` Event Handler

```
StreamResourceInfo zipInfo = new StreamResourceInfo(e.Result, null);
IEnumerable<MediaEx> mediaInfos = e.UserState as IEnumerable<MediaEx>;

foreach (MediaEx mediaInfo in mediaInfos)
{
  StreamResourceInfo streamInfo
    = Application.GetResourceStream(zipInfo, mediaInfo.FileUri);
  mediaInfo.MediaSource = streamInfo.Stream;
  output.Add(mediaInfo);
}
```

▶ Using the property `e.Result` (which is now a `Stream`, returned by the `WebClient` class) we create a new instance of `StreamResourceInfo`. This helper class assists us in reading the content of the Zip file.

▶ In `e.UserState`, we retrieve the result of the LINQ query that we had saved before by passing it to the `OpenReadAsync` method. Since it's an `object`, we need to cast it.

▶ We loop through each `MediaEx` instance, retrieve the corresponding `Stream`, and then save the instance in the `MediaExCollection`.

▶ The static method `Application`.`GetResourceStream` can read inside the Zip file. The first parameter is the `StreamResourceInfo` of the Zip file itself. The second parameter is a relative URI pointing to the file we want to extract. The result is another `StreamResourceInfo` instance, holding the XML file's stream as well as other information.

▶ Remember that a Zip file is organized like a tiny file system, with folders and files. Since we took care of preserving the path MediaFiles within the Zip file, the relative URI of the XML file doesn't change. Only, instead of being relative to the ClientBin folder, it is now relative to the root of the Zip file.

▶ We get a `StreamResourceInfo` corresponding to the URI of the current media file. This is yet another use for the handy helper property `FileUri`.

▶ The `Stream` is directly assigned to our `MediaSource` property.

That's it! The `MediaInformationFile` class is now ready to handle Zip files. You can build the application to make sure that everything is fine. The next step is to modify the UI to display the information about the download progress and load the thumbnails using the in-memory Stream.

Updating the UI

The user interface requires a few modifications to handle the new functionality.
Implement the following steps:

1. In Page.xaml.cs, "hook" the following event handler. Add the code in Listing 22.21
in the event handler `Page_Loaded`, just before the call to
`_mediaFile.LoadMediaFile`:

LISTING 22.21   Adding an Event Handler

```
_mediaFile.DownloadProgressChanged
  += new DownloadProgressChangedEventHandler(
    _mediaFile_DownloadProgressChanged);
```

2. Implement the event handler (Listing 22.22):

LISTING 22.22   mediaFile_DownloadProgressChanged Handler

```
void _mediaFile_DownloadProgressChanged(object sender,
  DownloadProgressChangedEventArgs e)
{
  StatusTextBlock.Text = string.Format("Loading {0}% ({1} / {2})",
    e.ProgressPercentage, e.BytesReceived, e.TotalBytesToReceive);
}
```

▶ The `DownloadProgressChangedEventArgs` parameter has all kinds of information
about the current progress of the download. In this example, we use the
`ProgressPercentage` property (this is an `int` from 0 to 100), the
`BytesReceived` property (indicating how many `bytes` are already available),
and the `TotalBytesToReceive` property (indicating the total size of the download).

▶ We use the method `string.Format` to create the status message. This method's
first parameter is a `string` in which you can add placeholders in the form {0},
{1}, and so on. When the method is executed, the placeholders are replaced
by the second and third parameters, for example.

▶ Using this information, you can also create a progress bar showing a visual
indication of the progress. You can see an example in the SDK documentation,
under Downloading Content on Demand.

3. In ExpandCollapseMedia, replace the `ImageBrush` assignment to `ThumbDisplay1.Fill`
as shown in Listing 22.23:

LISTING 22.23   Setting the `ThumbDisplay1`

```
if (media is Image)
{
  ImageBrush brush = new ImageBrush();
  MediaEx context = (media as Image).DataContext as MediaEx;
  brush.ImageSource = context.ImageSource;
  ThumbDisplay1.Fill = brush;
}
```

You should be able to build the application now.

We saw that a BitmapImage can be created from a Stream using the SetSource method. The same method is also available in the MediaElement class. However, this cannot be done in a binding. Instead, we need to create an event handler when each thumbnail is loaded in the UI and call the SetSource method in the code. Follow these steps:

1. In ThumbnailsViewerControl.xaml, find the DataTemplate named ThumbnailTemplate that we use for the ItemsControl. In the Image tag, remove the Source attribute. Instead, add the following event handler:

   ```
   Loaded="Media_Loaded"
   ```

2. Similarly, remove the Source attribute from the MediaElement tag, and replace it with the exact same event handler for Loaded.

3. Then, in ThumbnailsViewerControl.xaml.cs implement the event handler as shown in Listing 22.24:

LISTING 22.24   Media_Loaded Event Handler

```
private void Media_Loaded(object sender, RoutedEventArgs e)
{
  MediaEx context
    = (sender as FrameworkElement).DataContext as MediaEx;
  if (context.Type == MediaInfo.MediaType.Movie
    && sender is MediaElement)
  {
    MediaElement senderAsMedia = sender as MediaElement;
    senderAsMedia.SetSource(context.MediaSource);
  }
  if (context.Type == MediaInfo.MediaType.Image
    && sender is Image)
  {
    Image senderAsImage = sender as Image;
    senderAsImage.Source = context.ImageSource;
  }
}
```

▶ Getting the `DataContext` (the `MediaEx` instance) is something we know how to do.

▶ Depending on the type of media, we can use `SetSource` on the `MediaElement` (for Movies) or reuse our utility property `ImageSource` on the `Image`.

You can now run the application. The download progress is displayed, and when 100% is reached, the cache disappears and you can use the application.

Since the Zip file is local when you test, the download progress will move quickly. To make it more obvious and easier to test, you can add a very big file (for example, a big video) to the Zip file. The download will last longer and you can see the progress being updated. Don't forget to remove that big dummy file, though.

Making Requests to WCF Services

Silverlight is also equipped with more complex request mechanisms. In Chapter 23, we see how to place cross-domain calls to external services, such as Flickr. We can also place calls to web services (either so-called ASMX web services or Windows Communication Foundation [WCF] based). ASMX web services were used a lot before WCF became available. Although Silverlight supports both, and ASMX web services continue to have a bright life, we only demonstrate a WCF-based service here.

In this example, we move the password-checking functionality from the client to the web server and provide a WCF-based service to check it.

Moving the User and DataFile Classes to the Server

The functionality we use to check the user name and password is already defined, but it runs on the web client, in the Silverlight application. As we said already, this is not the cleanest way to handle password check. We will now move this functionality to the web server with the following steps:

1. In Visual Studio, right click on the Thumbnails Solution (not the project!!), which is the first file available on top of the Solution Explorer. Choose Add, New Project.

2. In the Add New Project dialog, select Windows and then Class Library. The library we create now will run on the web server, with the full version of .NET. This is different from a Silverlight class library, which runs with a subset of .NET. Name the new library UserManagementServer.

3. Drag the files User.cs and DataFile.cs from the existing project UserManagement to the new UserManagementServer project. You can also delete the existing file Class1.cs in this server-side project.

4. Once this is done, you can right-click on the UserManagement project and select Remove. We don't need this project anymore, since we delegate the whole user management to the web server now. Removing the project doesn't delete it. All the

files are still available on your hard drive, but the project is not compiled in this application anymore. If you think you'll never need this project anymore, you can also delete it from your hard disk (but maybe keeping a backup copy is a good idea!).

With the UserManagement project not available anymore, we need to make a few updates to the `Page` class:

1. In the file Page.xaml.cs, remove the namespace `UserManagement` from the `using` section.

2. Remove the whole content of the method `AddUser` except the line `return null; //` `success`.

3. Do the same for the method `ValidateUser` (here, too, leave only one line saying `return null; // success`).

4. Remove the private attribute `_dataFile` from the Page class and delete every statement that references this attribute.

   Try to compile the application. You get a series of errors warning you that `"The type or namespace name 'Windows' does not exist in the namespace 'System'"`. This is correct, because these references to Silverlight libraries are not available on the web server. We don't need them anyway (in fact, we could very well have removed them before).

5. In DataFile.cs, remove all the statements starting with `using System.Windows`. Then do the same operation in the User.cs files.

Our application still cannot be built. A couple of additional changes are needed.

Changing the DataFile to Run on the Server

The full version of .NET is outside the scope for this book, so we do not go into too much detail. If you need to write web server code, either in ASP.NET or in Windows Communication Foundation, we recommend other books such as *Sams Teach Yourself ASP.NET 2.0 in 24 Hours* and *WCF Unleashed*.

The class `DataFile` runs on the web server now, and with the full .NET. We modify it to save files on the hard disk instead of the isolated storage with the following steps.

WARNING

If the directory c:\temp is not available, saving the users will fail every time. Make sure that this folder exists. When your application runs on the web server, consult your Internet service provider to see where you can store such configuration files. It should be a location within the reach of your web service application, but not accessible from the Internet for security reasons.

1. In DataFile.cs, set the path to the user management file to the following. The @ syntax in @"c:\temp\ThumbnailsData.3.txt" tells .NET to use the \ character as a real backslash, instead of an escape sequence.

```
private const string DATA_FILE_NAME = @"c:\temp\ThumbnailsData.3.txt";
```

2. The method LoadUsers now becomes Listing 22.25:

LISTING 22.25   LoadUsers Method

```
1  public void LoadUsers()
2  {
3    _users = new Dictionary<string, User>();
4
5    if (File.Exists(DATA_FILE_NAME))
6    {
7      using (StreamReader reader = File.OpenText(DATA_FILE_NAME))
8      {
9        string line;
10       do
11       {
12         line = reader.ReadLine();
13         if (line != null)
14         {
15           User newUser = new User(line);
16           _users.Add(newUser.Name, newUser);
17         }
18       }
19       while (line != null);
20     }
21   }
22 }
```

▶ Instead of reading from the isolated storage, we use the web server's file system now. Lines 5 to 7 are different than before, but the result is the same: We check whether the user management file exists, and if it does, we open it for reading. The result is a StreamReader.

▶ The rest of the method is the same as before.

▶ Note that the full version of .NET also has access to an isolated storage located (in our case) on the web server. The syntax to access it is not totally compatible with Silverlight though.

3. The method SaveUsers also accesses the file system, and must be modified too (Listing 22.26):

LISTING 22.26 `SaveUsers` Method

```
1  public void SaveUsers()
2  {
3    using (StreamWriter writer = File.CreateText(DATA_FILE_NAME))
4    {
5      foreach (User user in _users.Values)
6      {
7        writer.WriteLine(user.ToString());
8      }
9    }
10 }
```

Here, too, the only difference is that we write to the file system instead of the isolated storage. Line 3 creates a `StreamWriter`, and the rest of the method is the same.

The rest of the methods remain exactly the same! The application should build now without errors.

Creating the WCF Service

As usual, Visual Studio provides great support for creating the new WCF service, as shown with the following steps:

1. In the Thumbnails application, right-click on the project Thumbnails.Web.

2. Select Add New Item from the context menu, and then choose Silverlight-enabled WCF Service. Name the new service UserManagementService.svc.

> **WARNING**
>
> A Silverlight-enabled WCF Service is very similar to a "normal" WCF Service. The only difference is that Silverlight only supports calls to WCF services configured with BasicHttpBinding. More advanced profiles are not supported at the moment. It is also possible to take a "normal" WCF Service, to reconfigure it to work with BasicHttpBinding, and to call it from Silverlight.

The service we write now runs on the web server and is written with the whole .NET framework and not "just" Silverlight. It is important that you understand the difference.

▶ Web site project, ASMX and WCF services → web server

▶ Silverlight application and class libraries → web browser

This operation creates a new file named UserManagementService.cs in the App_Code folder. This is a special ASP.NET folder: Each source code file placed into it is compiled on demand as needed. Note that this folder and the source code files it contains must be copied to the web server (this happens automatically when you *publish* from Visual Studio anyway). The file UserManagementService.cs is the entry point to our WCF service. Note that if you change the name of this WCF service class, you must update the file Web.config. This configuration file defines (among other things) what services are available on the web server.

Implementing the Service

The functionality to check the user name and password is now available on the server, but we still need to access it from the Silverlight application. This is what the WCF service is for, a gateway to the server-side code. Follow the steps:

1. We need a reference to the server-side library UserManagementServer that we created before. Right click on the Thumbnails.Web project and select Add Reference from the context menu. In the dialog, choose the UserManagementServer from the Projects tab and click OK.

2. In the file UserManagementService.cs, set the `Namespace` parameter in the `ServiceContract` attribute to something unique. Typically, the parameter is set to a URI, for example `http://www.galasoft.ch`.

3. In the same file, add a new class that we use to transfer information from the web server to the client (Listing 22.27). You must add this class below the `UserManagementService`. Alternatively, you can also create a new file in the App_Code folder to host this class.

LISTING 22.27   `UserInformation` Class

```
[DataContract]
public class UserInformation
{
  [DataMember]
  public bool PasswordOk
  {
    get; internal set;
  }

  [DataMember]
  public DateTime? LastVisit
  {
    get; internal set;
  }
}
```

▶ The `DataContract` attribute warns the framework that this class will be used on the server and on the client. A *proxy* (or representation) is created for this class in the Silverlight application.

▶ Similarly, the `DataMember` attribute specifies which members of this class are made available to the client application. Only public members marked with this attribute are created in the proxy.

4. In the `UserManagementService` class, remove the method `DoWork`:

5. Implement a new method `ValidateUser` as shown in Listing 22.28:

LISTING 22.28   ValidateUser Method

```
[OperationContract]
public UserInformation ValidateUser(string name, string password)
{
  DataFile dataFile = new DataFile();
  dataFile.LoadUsers();
  UserInformation userInfo = new UserInformation();

  User inputUser = new User();
  inputUser.Name = name;
  inputUser.Password = password;
  if (dataFile.ValidateUser(inputUser))
  {
    User savedUser = dataFile.GetUser(name);
    userInfo.LastVisit = savedUser.LastVisit;
    userInfo.PasswordOk = true;
    savedUser.SetLastVisit();
    dataFile.SaveUsers();
  }
  else
  {
    userInfo.PasswordOk = false;
  }
  return userInfo;
}
```

We pass data to the client in an instance of the `UserInformation` class. This data is encoded by the WCF framework and passed to the client. The `OperationContract` attribute notifies the framework that this method is available as a service.

6. As for `AddUser`, the code is similar to what we did previously in the `Page` class. Add the code in Listing 22.29 to the `UserManagementService` class.

LISTING 22.29   AddUser Method

```
[OperationContract]
public string AddUser(string name, string password)
{
```

LISTING 22.29   Continued

```
DataFile dataFile = new DataFile();
dataFile.LoadUsers();

try
{
  User newUser = new User();
  newUser.Name = name;
  newUser.Password = password;
  newUser.SetLastVisit();
  dataFile.AddUser(newUser);
}
catch (Exception ex)
{
  return ex.Message;
}
return null; // success
}
```

Building the application should work fine now, after adding a using directive referencing the UserManagement namespace where the classes DataFile and User are placed.

Updating the Client Application

With the web service ready to work, we need to connect the Silverlight application to the new service, with the following steps:

1. Add a *Service Reference* in our client application. To do this, right click on the Thumbnails project and select Add Service Reference from the context menu.

2. In the next dialog, click on Discover. In the Services panel, you should now see your WCF service.

3. Expand the service by clicking on the small + sign next to it. This operation can take a few moments. After the service expands, you should see the UserManagementService we created before. What happens here is that Visual Studio asks the WCF service what operations it offers.

4. Enter a name for the new namespace—for example, UserManagement (instead of ServiceReference1). Then click OK. This operation also takes time, as Visual Studio prepares a client-side representation (or proxy) of the web based WCF service.

5. Open Page.xaml.cs and add a private attribute in the Page class to hold the reference to the service.

   ```
   private UserManagementServiceClient _serviceClient
     = new UserManagementServiceClient();
   ```

> ### TIP
>
> Adding a service reference created a new namespace named (according to what you specified in step 4) `Thumbnails.UserManagement`. As usual, you need to add this reference to the `using` section. This new namespace contains all the *proxy* classes you need to connect to the WCF service. The classes marked with the `DataContract` attribute are used to pass data back and forth, while the classes marked with `ServiceContract` offer an access to the set of methods that you decorated with the `OperationContract` attribute. The proxies encode the call to the remote methods, send the request, get and decode the response, and call the callbacks.
>
> If you copy your application to the web server or make any other change to the server-side code, you need to update the Service Reference on the client. We see how to do this in Chapter 24, "Silverlight: Continuing the Journey."

22

6. At the end of the `Page` constructor, add event handlers for the `Completed` events for the two asynchronous methods as in Listing 22.30. As before, Silverlight only allows asynchronous calls to WCF services.

LISTING 22.30   Adding Event Handlers

```
_serviceClient.AddUserCompleted
  += new EventHandler<AddUserCompletedEventArgs>(
    _serviceClient_AddUserCompleted);
_serviceClient.ValidateUserCompleted
  += new EventHandler<ValidateUserCompletedEventArgs>(
    _serviceClient_ValidateUserCompleted);
```

For each method marked with the `OperationContract` attribute, the framework creates a `Completed` event and the corresponding `EventArgs` class.

7. The two existing methods `AddUser` and `ValidateUser` are now just calling the service methods (Listing 22.31):

LISTING 22.31   AddUser and ValidateUser Methods

```
[ScriptableMember]
public string AddUser(string name, string password)
{
  _serviceClient.AddUserAsync(name, password);
  return null; // success
}
[ScriptableMember]
public string ValidateUser(string name, string password)
{
```

LISTING 22.31   Continued

```
_serviceClient.ValidateUserAsync(name, password);
return null;
}
```

Note that these are asynchronous calls. To keep it simple (well, kind of), we don't modify the JavaScript method calls, so we simply return null to indicate that there was no error so far, and that the login dialog should be closed.

8. We still need two event handlers. The first one (for the method ValidateUser) is shown in Listing 22.32:

LISTING 22.32   ValidateUserCompleted Event Handler

```
void _serviceClient_ValidateUserCompleted(object sender,
  ValidateUserCompletedEventArgs e)
{
  UserInformation userInfo = e.Result;
  if (userInfo.PasswordOk)
  {
    LastVisitTextBlock.Text = "(Your last visit was: "
      + userInfo.LastVisit.Value.ToShortDateString()
      + " " + userInfo.LastVisit.Value.ToLongTimeString() + ")";
  }
  else
  {
    LastVisitTextBlock.Text = "";
    HtmlPage.Window.Alert("Invalid user/password combination");
    // Here you should probably stop the application!
  }
}
```

▶ The parameter e.Result is of type UserInformation. This is the *client-side proxy* for this server-side class. We have access to all the public members we marked with the DataMember attribute.

▶ This parameter also provides access to information about the service call: An Error property indicating whether something bad occurred during the call, a flag (Cancelled) showing whether the remote call has been cancelled for some reason, and a UserState property that holds any object you want to save between the moment you send the request and when the response arrives. You can set this object when you call the method on the service client, for example, ValidateUserAsync.

> ▶ If the password check fails, we display a JavaScript alert with the corresponding message. Otherwise, we set the `LastVisitTextBlock` according to the timestamp we got from the WCF service.

9. And finally, implement the second event handler as shown in Listing 22.33:

LISTING 22.33 `AddUserCompleted` Event Handler

```
void _serviceClient_AddUserCompleted(object sender,
  AddUserCompletedEventArgs e)
{
  if (e.Result != null)
  {
    HtmlPage.Window.Alert(e.Result);
  }
  else
  {
    LastVisitTextBlock.Text = "(This is your first visit)";
  }
}
```

The method `AddUser` on the server returns an error message (as a `string`) if an error occurred. In that case, we display the error in a JavaScript alert.

At this point, you can run the application and try the login functionality. You will notice a slight delay between the moment you click the Submit button and the application's reaction. This delay is bigger if you run the application from the web server (use the Publish functionality from Visual Studio to copy all the files there!). The call to a remote method lasts longer. On the other hand, we don't store any passwords on the client anymore.

Another neat feature of putting the user name and password check on the web server is that the functionality is now consistent on any computer in the world. Since the file is stored on the server, the date of last login will be saved independently of which computer is used to display the application.

> **WARNING**
>
> Sending passwords in clear text over the network is a bad idea! You should really encrypt the password before sending it. This is pretty advanced, so we won't demonstrate this, but Silverlight offers an interface to encryption methods. For more information, check this page: http://silverlightuk.blogspot.com/2008/06/silverlight-encryption-part-1.html.

More Connectivity

In this chapter, we saw multiple ways for a Silverlight application to connect to the web server it originates from. In the next chapter, we will see that the application can even connect to other web servers (in this case, the Flickr photo service).

Silverlight was really developed with connectivity in mind. In fact, what we saw here is only a part of what Silverlight can do. There are built-in classes to handle RSS and Atom feeds (such as those exposed by blog servers), and you can even use sockets. These topics are out of the scope of this book however, and you will find plenty of information about this on the Internet!

Summary

This chapter was really advanced and exciting. We opened the doors to the World Wide Web! Or almost: Our Silverlight applications can only connect back to the server-of-origin for the moment. In Chapter 23, we learn how to place requests to other servers and make our Silverlight applications even more connected.

Placing Cross-domain Requests and Handling Exceptions

Communicating with services is one of the major strengths of Silverlight, but it would be much less powerful if it was limited only to services located on the same server as the Silverlight application itself. Thankfully, other web services can also be called by Silverlight, but only if certain conditions are respected (for security reasons).

In this chapter we also talk about exceptions and error handling. This is an important part of programming: Good error handling makes an application more stable.

Placing Cross-domain Requests

In the previous chapters, we saw different ways for a Silverlight application to connect back to its server of origin. This can be handy if you don't want to load all the data for your application right when it is starting, for example, or if you have a database on the server and want to use a WCF service to place requests to it, or to get the latest information about a user account that might have been updated from another source, and so on. In short, communicating with the server it came from is important for a *rich interactive application*. But in this time of "software and services," there are all kinds of providers for various types of data on the Internet.

However, connecting to any web server other than the one it comes from is illegal for any application running in a web browser. Many information thieves try to forge a fake identity to trick you into entering secret data and then steal that data. Web browsers' makers decided to prevent this kind of forgery by forbidding any application running inside a web browser to connect to a third-party website. This is also why JavaScript cannot communicate with an `iframe` unless it originates from the same web server. Remember when we said that programming would be easier if humanity was honest?

Of course, Silverlight complies with this restriction. Thankfully, however, there is a way to stay legal and place requests to a third-party website anyway, but only if this site explicitly allows it.

TIP

To allow the request to go through, Silverlight checks the following:

▶ Is the *domain* the same? For example, *www.galasoft.ch* is **not the same as** *galasoft.ch*.

▶ Is the *protocol* the same? For example, *http* is **not the same as** *https* (secure HTTP).

▶ Is the *port* the same? (The port is a "gate" through which all requests and responses go.) For example, http://galasoft.ch:8080 is **not the same as** http://galasoft.ch (note that by default, all HTTP requests go through port 80, so http://galasoft.ch is equivalent to http://galasoft.ch:80).

If all three conditions are met, the request can go through.

Using the Flash Cross-domain Policy File

The problem of cross-domain communication is not new. Adobe Flash (which is probably the technology currently the closest to Silverlight) has the same issues. The good people at Adobe came up with a solution: Enable the publishers of a web service to place an XML file (named crossdomain.xml) on their web server that explicitly allows third-party client applications to access their service. Silverlight supports this file, so a Flash-enabled web service also works with Silverlight. Note however that Silverlight only sends cross-domain requests if the file crossdomain.xml allows access to the whole website.

A sample of a supported Flash cross-domain file is shown in Listing 23.1:

LISTING 23.1   File crossdomain.xml

```
<?xml version="1.0"?>
<!DOCTYPE cross-domain-policy SYSTEM
  "http://www.macromedia.com/xml/dtds/cross-domain-policy.dtd">
<cross-domain-policy>
  <allow-access-from domain="*"/>
</cross-domain-policy>
```

Simply place this XML markup in a file named crossdomain.xml and save it at the root of the web server.

Using the Silverlight Cross-domain Policy File

Because of some limitations of the Flash cross-domain policy file format, Silverlight also supports its own policy file, named clientaccesspolicy.xml. This file allows more specific settings; especially, it allows restricting only certain folders while allowing others.

Here is a sample in Listing 23.2:

LISTING 23.2   File clientaccesspolicy.xml, Sample 1

```
<?xml version="1.0" encoding="utf-8"?>
<access-policy>
  <cross-domain-access>
    <policy>
      <allow-from http-request-headers="*">
        <domain uri="*"/>
      </allow-from>
      <grant-to>
        <resource path="/myservice"
                   include-subpaths="true"/>
      </grant-to>
    </policy>
  </cross-domain-access>
</access-policy>
```

▶ This file allows access from any third-party application and any kind of HTTP headers.

▶ It provides access to all files located under the folder myservice and to subfolders.

Another example is shown in Listing 23.3:

LISTING 23.3   File clientaccesspolicy.xml, Sample 2

```
<?xml version="1.0" encoding="utf-8"?>
<access-policy>
  <cross-domain-access>
    <policy>
      <allow-from http-request-headers="SOAPAction,Content-Type">
        <domain uri="http://galasoft.ch"/>
        <domain uri="http://www.galasoft.ch"/>
        <domain uri="http://galasoft-lb.ch"/>
        <domain uri="http://www.galasoft-lb.ch"/>
      </allow-from>
      <grant-to>
        <resource path="/" include-subpaths="true"/>
      </grant-to>
```

LISTING 23.3   Continued

```
    </policy>
  </cross-domain-access>
</access-policy>
```

▶ This file forbids access to any application except those hosted on the four domains listed.

▶ Even for these four domains, it only allows access if the request's header contains the HTTP headers SOAPAction and/or Content-Type. Effectively, this allows an ASMX or WCF service client (such as the one created in Chapter 22, "Connecting to the Web") to contact the web server. SOAP is the default protocol used by such web services to communicate.

▶ It allows access to any file and any subfolder located on the web server (the path / is the web server's root).

In effect, this last client access policy file enables any Silverlight application located at the four domains listed to place calls to any SOAP or WCF service located on this web server.

Understanding the Restrictions

Silverlight may not send any request to just any URL. Some rules must be respected, as listed in this section.

Server of Origin

If the request is sent to the server of origin, the following restrictions apply:

▶ Only GET and POST requests are supported. GET requests are simple requests, for example, what you do when you simply type a URL in the web browser's location bar. POST requests are more complete and can contain complex content, such as files.

▶ The only codes supported are 200 (OK) and 404 (File not found).

▶ Most standard and custom headers are supported.

Cross-domain Requests

In addition to the restrictions mentioned for the server of origin, the following restrictions apply to cross-domain requests:

▶ HTTP is supported by the Silverlight and by the Flash cross-domain policy files.

▶ HTTPS is supported only by the Silverlight cross-domain policy file.

▶ The application may not add headers to the request. For POST requests, some headers might be enabled by the cross-domain policy file explicitly, but some others are always forbidden.

- The "path" part of the URL can only contain certain characters:

    - a-z, A-Z, 0-9.

    - The characters '/', '-', '_', '~', '=', ';'.

    - A period '.' is allowed, but a double period '..' is not. The double period allows navigating to a folder's parent, which could cause security issues.

> **TIP**
>
> The "path" part of a URL is located between the domain part and the query string part: http://www.galasoft.ch:8080/[PATH]?param=value#target
>
> For example, in the following fictive URL, the path is myfolder/myapplication.aspx: http://www.galasoft.ch/myfolder/myapplication.aspx?param=value

- The policy file is cached by the Silverlight application, so if you modify it, the changes apply only after the application is stopped and restarted.

- The Silverlight policy file is looked for first, and if it is missing, the Flash policy file is requested.

- The cross-domain policy file must be placed at the root of the web server, even if you try to access a URL located lower in the directory structure. For example, for a request sent to http://www.galasoft.ch:8080/myapplication/, the Silverlight application will look for the policy file at http://www.galasoft.ch:8080/clientaccesspolicy.xml.

If the service you try to access doesn't have a cross-domain policy file, you will need to call your own web server from the Silverlight application, and then place the remote call from the web application running on the server (for example, an ASP.NET application). The cross-domain restriction doesn't apply to ASP.NET running on the web server.

Karen Corby, program manager for Silverlight 2, has a nice series of three posts about the cross-domain policy file on her blog: http://scorbs.com/2008/04/05/silverlight-http-networking-stack-part-1-site-of-origin-communication.

Communicating with Third-Party Services

In Chapter 22, we saw how to use the `WebClient` class to place simple GET requests to your own web server. This class is the simplest way to send requests to the network. For more complex requests, the alternative is named `HttpWebRequest` (and its pendant `HttpWebResponse`). In this section, we see how to send a request to a Flickr service delivering a set of picture URLs based on a keyword search.

Accepting the Flickr Terms of Services

Before you start creating your own Flickr application, take a close look at Flickr's

> **NOTE**
>
> For all the operations related to Flickr, you need to register for a Yahoo account. Yahoo is the owner of the Flickr service.

terms of services (TOS). In this section, we use a noncommercial key. Its usage is restricted: www.flickr.com/services/api/tos.

Getting a Flickr API Key

Many services, such as Google Maps, Google Search, and in this case Flickr, use a unique key to identify the caller of their services. This ensures that certain conditions are met, for example, that a maximum number of requests per day are not exceeded. Getting a Flickr API key is straightforward:

1. Navigate to the URL www.flickr.com/services/api/misc.api_keys.html.

2. Click on the Apply for Your Key Online Now link.

3. In the next page, enter your details, and click on Apply.

4. Write down the key given to you. We will use it in our application.

A Note About Authentication

For some Flickr API methods, an authentication is needed. For example, if you provide a service allowing a user with a Flickr account to add descriptions to his own pictures, to modify pictures, and so on, the user needs to log in to the Flickr

> **TIP**
>
> Many methods are available in the Flickr API. They are all documented here: www.flickr.com/services/api/.

service. In that case, check the API Key Authentication Setup section in the Flickr API keys management page.

Preparing and Sending the Request

For the sake of the example, we use an `HttpWebRequest` (and its companion `HttpWebResponse`). We could perform the same action using the `WebClient`. As we said previously, that class, though easy to use, is powerful enough for many operations. Using `HttpWebRequest`, though not necessary in this particular case, introduces this more complex and powerful class in case you need it in a future scenario. Apply the changes described in this section to the Thumbnails application we edited last in Chapter 22.

> **TIP**
>
> Karen Corby shows how to make a POST request using the `HttpWebRequest` class in Silverlight. It's a must read: http://scorbs.com/2008/04/05/silverlight-http-networking-stack-part-1-site-of-origin-communication/.

1. Open the Thumbnails application in Visual Studio, and then open the file media.xml. Add the entry shown in Listing 23.4 within the `medias` tag. Our code will be able to handle multiple Flickr searches, so you can enter more than one such section in the XML file.

LISTING 23.4   `flickr-search` Entry

```
<flickr-search keywords="Perhentian,Diving"
                per-page="20"
                start-page="1"/>
```

2. Open the MediaInformationFile.cs file. Because of the nice encapsulation we provided, most of the changes occur in this file only. We need to update the UI only slightly to take advantage of the new functionality.

> **CAUTION**
>
> The Flickr terms of services require that no application display more than 30 pictures per page.

3. Add the two classes shown in Listing 23.5 for the events we declare later and then build the application:

LISTING 23.5   Two New Classes

```csharp
public class AnyProgressChangedEventArgs : EventArgs
{
  public string Message
  {
    get; set;
  }
}
public class NewMediaFoundEventArgs : EventArgs
{
  public MediaEx MediaInfo
  {
    get; set;
  }
}
```

4. On top of the class `MediaInformationFile`, add the constants shown in Listing 23.6:

LISTING 23.6   Two New Classes

```csharp
private const string FLICKR_API_KEY
  = "[ENTER YOUR API KEY HERE]";

private const string FLICKR_URI_BASE
  = "http://api.flickr.com/services/rest/"
  + "?method=flickr.photos.search"
  + "&api_key={0}&tags={1}&page={2}&per_page={3}"
  + "&format=json&tag_mode=all";
```

LISTING 23.6   Continued

```
private const string FLICKR_IMAGE_BASE
  = "http://farm{0}.static.flickr.com/{1}/{2}_{3}.jpg";


private const string FLICKR_PREFIX = "jsonFlickrApi";
```

Make sure that you replace the placeholder [ENTER YOUR API KEY HERE] with the key that you got from Flickr in the section Getting a Flickr API key earlier in the chapter.

5. Add two events and one helper method as shown in Listing 23.7. We need these events to notify the Page when a new image is loaded from Flickr. This code should be added to the MediaInformationFile class. Here too, you should be able to build the application. A warning tells you that the NewMediaFound event is not used, but we will take care of this later.

LISTING 23.7   Two Events and a Helper Method

```
public event EventHandler NewMediaFound;
public event EventHandler AnyProgressChanged;
private void OnAnyProgressChanged(string message)
{
  if (AnyProgressChanged != null)
  {
    AnyProgressChangedEventArgs args
      = new AnyProgressChangedEventArgs();
    args.Message = message;
    AnyProgressChanged(this, args);
  }
}
```

6. Declare a private attribute. We explain it later. You can build the application after adding a using directive.

```
private SynchronizationContext _context;
```

7. In the method client_OpenReadCompleted, add a call to a new method to start the Flickr search. Note that we only perform a search if someone subscribed to the NewMediaFound event—no need to start this operation if no one is interested in the result! Add the code in Listing 23.8 after the last line (OnMediaFileLoaded(output, lastError);).

LISTING 23.8   Checking if Someone Subscribed

```
if (NewMediaFound != null)
{
  SendFlickrRequests();
}
```

8. Still in the `MediaInformationFile` class, implement the method shown in Listing 23.9:

LISTING 23.9   SendFlickrRequests Method

```
1  private void SendFlickrRequests()
2  {
3    var flickrSearches
4      = from xmlSearch
5        in _document.Descendants("flickr-search")
6        select new
7        {
8          Keywords = xmlSearch.Attribute("keywords").Value,
9          PerPage
10           = Int32.Parse(xmlSearch.Attribute("per-page").Value),
11         StartPage
12           = Int32.Parse(xmlSearch.Attribute("start-page").Value)
13       };
14
15   _context = SynchronizationContext.Current;
16
17   foreach (var flickrSearch in flickrSearches)
18   {
19     OnAnyProgressChanged("Starting loading Flickr searches");
20     string uriString = string.Format(FLICKR_URI_BASE,
21       FLICKR_API_KEY,
22       flickrSearch.Keywords,
23       flickrSearch.StartPage,
24       flickrSearch.PerPage);
25
26     Uri uri = new Uri(uriString, UriKind.Absolute);
27     HttpWebRequest request
28       = WebRequest.Create(uri) as HttpWebRequest;
29     request.Method = "GET";
30     IAsyncResult result
31       = request.BeginGetResponse(
32         new AsyncCallback(ResponseCallback), request);
33   }
34 }
```

▶ Lines 3 to 13 create a new LINQ query against the XDocument that we loaded before. This time, we're looking for descendants named flickr-search. Note that if this section is missing from the XML file, the returned result will be empty, and no Flickr request will be sent.

▶ Because we don't have an object type for this particular query, and because we don't want to create one, we use an anonymous type. This is visible on line 3 (with the use of the keyword var) and on line 6 (we use the anonymous statement `select new` instead of `select new MediaEx` as we did before).

▶ On line 15, we save the current *threading context* to a private attribute that we declared earlier. We learn why we need this attribute a little later in this chapter.

▶ Lines 17 to 33 loop through the collection of Flickr searches. Note the use of the `var` keyword, because we use anonymous types.

▶ After notifying the user on line 19, we create a new string URL on lines 20 to 24. As we did before, we use the convenient method `string.Format` to help us. The URL contains information about the API key, which keywords should be used for searching, how many results per page should be displayed, and which page is wanted.

> **TIP**
>
> The page www.flickr.com/services/api/ flickr.photos.search.html describes the API method and all the possible variations. You can even use the so-called API explorer (the link is located at the bottom of the API documentation page) to try the URL by yourself.

▶ Lines 26 to 28 create a new `HttpWebRequest` instance and set its parameters. We use the GET method (this is, in fact, the default) because we just want to GET some information from the server, without modifying anything.

▶ Finally, lines 30 to 32 send the request asynchronously. Here too, Silverlight only supports asynchronous web requests. We provide a handler for the asynchronous callback (this handler is implemented in Listing 23.10), and we also pass the request itself as the second parameter of the `BeginGetResponse` method. This is a handy way to save any information that you will reuse later, when the response arrives. The framework passes this object back to you, so you don't need to save it locally for each request.

▶ Because of the location of this code in the `Completed` event handler, the Flickr search is started only after the Zip file is completely loaded. This is user friendly: The user can start using the application and watching the local media before the slower requests to Flickr are sent.

Handling the Response

After the request is sent, the user can start working with the local thumbnails and display them. This is the main advantage of an asynchronous web request: It doesn't block the user interface. When the response arrives, we can decode it and send new requests, this time for the images themselves.

Add a new method to the `MediaInformationFile` class as shown in Listing 23.10. This is the method that we use as our `AsyncCallback` in the preceding example.

LISTING 23.10   ResponseCallback Method

```
private void ResponseCallback(IAsyncResult result)
{
  HttpWebRequest request = result.AsyncState as HttpWebRequest;
  WebResponse response = request.EndGetResponse(result);
  _context.Post(ExtractResponse, response);
}
```

▶ The property result.AsyncState is the exact object that we passed as second parameter of the method BeginGetResponse in the preceding example.

▶ The WebResponse containing all the information sent by Flickr can be obtained by using EndGetResponse on the HttpWebRequest instance. Now we see why it was necessary to save the request!

▶ Finally, we use the SynchronizationContext that we saved before to call a method named ExtractResponse and pass it the response as a parameter.

Switching the Execution Context

This last part needs explaining. The issue here is that the HttpWebRequest is executed in a different *thread*, to avoid blocking the application's user interface. A thread is a little like a lightweight application running independently (more or less) from other threads. While the *background thread* in which the HttpWebRequest is sent is waiting for the response, all the other threads can continue to run normally.

Multithreading programming is probably one of the most complex tasks you can imagine. This is truly advanced, and we do not go any further into the details here. We just need to *switch the execution context* back to the main thread, and this is what this line does.

> **NOTE**
>
> We didn't need to switch the context when we worked with the WebClient class, because this class does it automatically.

Decoding the Response

We now implement the code decoding Flickr's response.

1. Declare the method shown in Listing 23.11. You should build the application now, because we added a lot of code before. Building allows you to check that you didn't make mistakes while typing.

LISTING 23.11   ExtractResponse Method

```
private void ExtractResponse(object state)
{
}
```

2. Notify the user of what we are doing and then get the Stream containing the information from Flickr (Listing 23.12). This code goes into the method `ExtractResponse` we just added. You can build the application now.

LISTING 23.12   Notifying the User and Getting the Stream

```
OnAnyProgressChanged("Flickr response received, decoding");
HttpWebResponse response = state as HttpWebResponse;
Stream flickrStream = response.GetResponseStream();

if (flickrStream == null)
{
  OnAnyProgressChanged("Error in Flickr Stream");
  return;
}
```

If anything goes wrong, the `Stream` will be null, and we stop here. But before we stop, we inform the user.

3. The next operations are critical too and could cause the application to crash. To avoid this, we enclose them in a `try…catch` block shown in Listing 23.13. Even if the Flickr search fails, the user can continue to work with the local media files. Enter this code at the end of the `ExtractResponse` method. Build the application again.

LISTING 23.13   try…catch Block

```
try
{
}
catch (Exception)
{
  OnAnyProgressChanged("Error with Flickr search");
}
```

Decoding a JSON String

Flickr can return a response in a number of formats. The default is an XML document that can be parsed using LINQ as we did previously for our own media information file. Another interesting format is JSON, the JavaScript Object Notation that we discussed before. We can get a JSON response from Flickr by setting the parameter `format=json` in the request URL (see Listing 23.6). JSON has the advantage of being compact and less *verbose* than XML (which means that it will be loaded faster from the Flickr server).

In addition to LINQ to XML (that we used in Chapter 22 and also earlier in this chapter), Silverlight also provides LINQ to JSON, that can be used to easily convert JSON strings into .NET objects. This is what we will use in this section.

The Flickr service returns a string with a special format, for example as shown in Listing 23.14:

LISTING 23.14   Flickr JSON Response

```
jsonFlickrApi({ "photos": { "page":1,
                            "pages":3702,
                            "perpage":10,
                            "total":"37012",
                            "photo":[{ "id":"2494494793",
                                       "owner":"11273400@N05",
                                       "secret":"9438aa56c1",
                                       "server":"3244",
                                       "farm":4,
                                       "title":"Bearded Collie",
                                       "ispublic":1,
                                       "isfriend":0,
                                       "isfamily":0 }]
                   },
              "stat":"ok" })
```

The photo attribute is an array of picture information (in the example shown here, there is only one picture). This is what we are interested in. Note also that Flickr encloses the JSON information inside a string saying jsonFlickrApi(). We need to trim this extra information from the string.

NOTE

Another way to handle this would have been to call the web browser's JavaScript framework, also able to convert a JSON string into a series of objects. However, calling the JavaScript interfaces is slower than using built-in .NET code.

In addition, Silverlight also has a class named DataContractJsonSerializer that can be used to encode/decode JSON strings. This class is complex, however, and we do not use it here.

1. Add a reference to the System.Json assembly in the Thumbnails project. To do this, right click on this project, choose Add Reference and select System.Json from the .NET tab.

2. Inside the try block in Listing 23.13, read the string returned by Flickr and use the Substring method to remove the extra information we mentioned in the beginning of this section (see Listing 23.15). The jsonFlickrApi prefix is stored in one of the constants we declared before: FLICKR_PREFIX.

LISTING 23.15   Reading the String

```
string jsonString;
using (StreamReader responseReader = new StreamReader(flickrStream))
{
```

LISTING 23.15   Continued

```
jsonString = responseReader.ReadToEnd();
// Remove prefix and parenthesis
jsonString = jsonString.Substring(FLICKR_PREFIX.Length);
jsonString = jsonString.Substring(1, jsonString.Length - 2);
}
```

3. Using the string we just trimmed, create a `StringReader` as in Listing 23.16. This class will be used to load the JSON string and to parse it using JSON. Add this code in the `try` block, after what we wrote in step 2.

LISTING 23.16   Creating a StringReader

```
using (StringReader stringReader = new StringReader(jsonString))
{
  // Decode string with JSON here
}
```

4. Replace the line saying `// Decode string with JSON here` with the code shown in Listing 23.17 and then build the application.

LISTING 23.17   Creating a StringReader

```
1  JsonObject jsonResponse = JsonObject.Load(stringReader) as JsonObject;
2
3  var photos = from photo in (JsonArray) jsonResponse["photos"]["photo"]
4               let castedPhoto = photo as JsonObject
5               select new
6               {
7                 Farm = castedPhoto["farm"],
8                 Server = (string) castedPhoto["server"],
9                 Id = (string) castedPhoto["id"],
10                Secret = (string) castedPhoto["secret"],
11                Title = (string) castedPhoto["title"]
12               };
13
14 // Loop through all photos here
```

▶ Line 1 creates a new `JsonObject`, with a syntax very similar to what we did with the `XDocument` class when we used LINQ to XML.

▶ Lines 3 to 12 look familiar: They show a LINQ request, again very similar to what we did before.

- ▶ Note the use of the `let` keyword on line 4. This creates a new variable inline in the LINQ request. This new variable contains the LINQ variable photo, casted to the type `JsonObject`.

- ▶ We select only certain properties from the JSON response. `Farm`, `Server`, `Id` and `Secret` are needed to build the picture's URL. As for `Title`, we will show this in the `MediaInfoDisplay` control.

Sending Requests for the Pictures

If we have results, we must loop through them and send an additional request for each picture. This time, we want to get the actual picture data, the bits and bytes. Like we did before when we used LINQ to XML, we can enumerate these pictures, with the code in Listing 23.18. Replace the line saying `// Loop through all photos here` with this code:

LISTING 23.18   Looping Through the Photos, Placing Requests

```
foreach (var photo in photos)
{
  string photoUriString = string.Format(FLICKR_IMAGE_BASE,
    photo.Farm,
    photo.Server,
    photo.Id,
    photo.Secret);

  Uri photoUri = new Uri(photoUriString, UriKind.Absolute);

  WebClient clientPhoto = new WebClient();
  clientPhoto.OpenReadCompleted
    += new OpenReadCompletedEventHandler(
      clientPhoto_OpenReadCompleted);
  clientPhoto.OpenReadAsync(photoUri, photo.Title);
}
```

- ▶ We build a new string URL using the photo's properties.

- ▶ Then we build a new `WebClient` and send the request after setting the event handler.

- ▶ Note that we saved the `title` of the picture in the user state (second parameter of `OpenReadAsync`).

> **TIP**
>
> The way to match a photo's information to the picture's URL is described here: www.flickr.com/services/api/misc.urls.html.

For every picture requested, we must handle the response. This is a new event handler (Listing 23.19) which must be placed into the MediaInformationFile class.

LISTING 23.19   clientPhoto_OpenReadCompleted Event Handler

```
void clientPhoto_OpenReadCompleted(object sender,
  OpenReadCompletedEventArgs e)
{
  try
  {
    string title = e.UserState.ToString();
    MediaEx mediaInfo = new MediaEx();
    mediaInfo.Description = title + " (Flickr search result)";
    mediaInfo.MediaSource = e.Result;
    NewMediaFoundEventArgs args = new NewMediaFoundEventArgs();
    args.MediaInfo = mediaInfo;
    NewMediaFound(this, args);
  }
  catch (Exception)
  {
    OnAnyProgressChanged("Error with Flickr image");
  }
}
```

▶ If the e.Result is null, this is an error, so we notify the user.

▶ Remember that we saved the picture's title as the e.UserState. We can get it back now, and just to be sure we call the ToString method on this object.

▶ We build a new MediaEx instance. The media stream is saved directly in this new instance's MediaSource, and we also set the Description according to the picture's title.

▶ Finally, we build a new NewMediaFoundEventArgs and raise the NewMediaFound event.

That's it, our requests are sent and the responses decoded. Build the application to make sure that everything is ok. Now we only need to update the user interface to handle the new events, and we're done!

Updating the UI

The user interface will display a status bar showing what happens with the Flickr requests. Since everything is asynchronous and the user can start working with the application while the requests are executing, it is important that he knows what is going on in the background.

The rest is just a matter of updating the collection of MediaEx elements with the new received pictures. Through the magic of data binding, the UI will automatically be updated when new pictures arrive. Follow the steps:

1. In the file Page.xaml, add a TextBlock to display status messages related to the Flickr search, as shown in Listing 23.20. You must add this TextBlock at the end of the LayoutRoot Grid, but before the Cache (so that the Cache remains in front of every other control in the Page).

LISTING 23.20   Status TextBlock

```
<TextBlock x:Name="LiveStatustextBlock"
           Grid.Row="2" Margin="0,0,10,10"
           HorizontalAlignment="Right"
           VerticalAlignment="Bottom" />
```

2. In Page.xaml.cs, add a private attribute:

```
private int _flickrIndex = 1;
```

3. Add two event handlers to the _mediaFile in Page_Loaded, before the call to the method LoadMediaFile (Listing 23.21).

LISTING 23.21   Registering Two Event Handlers

```
_mediaFile.AnyProgressChanged
  += new EventHandler(_mediaFile_AnyProgressChanged);
_mediaFile.NewMediaFound
  += new EventHandler(_mediaFile_NewMediaFound);
```

4. Implement the event handlers shown in Listing 23.22 in the Page class:

LISTING 23.22   Implementing Two Event Handlers

```
void _mediaFile_AnyProgressChanged(object sender, EventArgs e)
{
  AnyProgressChangedEventArgs args = e as AnyProgressChangedEventArgs;
  LiveStatustextBlock.Text = args.Message;
}
void _mediaFile_NewMediaFound(object sender, EventArgs e)
{
  NewMediaFoundEventArgs args = e as NewMediaFoundEventArgs;
  MediaExCollection itemsSource = ThumbnailsViewer.ItemsSource;
  itemsSource.Add(args.MediaInfo);
```

LISTING 23.22   Continued

```
LiveStatustextBlock.Text
  = string.Format("New Flickr picture found ({0})",
    _flickrIndex++);
}
```

▶ The first handler is called every time the `MediaInformationFile` class has something to communicate to the user. The corresponding message is displayed in the new status bar we just added.

▶ The second handler is called when a new picture is fully loaded from Flickr. Because of everything we put in place, displaying the picture is as easy as adding the `MediaInfo` property to the `MediaExCollection`. Through the magic of the `ObservableCollection` and of the `DataTemplate`, the visual is displayed automatically.

The application is ready for testing. Run it and have fun! See how the pictures are gradually and asynchronously added to the `ItemsControl` as they arrive. You can click every picture and see the animation we designed applied to it. Also, note how the picture's title is displayed by our `MediaInfoDisplay` control.

Placing POST Requests

When sending an HTTP request to any service (even something as simple as GETting a web page's content), you must specify the *method* of the request. Silverlight 2 supports only two methods: GET (used primarily to read information from the server) and POST (used primarily to write information to the server). A number of additional methods are available to HTTP clients (such as HEAD, PUT, DELETE, and so on), but Silverlight 2 doesn't support these yet.

Depending on the web service's implementation, it is possible to write information using a GET method, but it is not the recommended way to do things. POST requests, on the other hand, are handy, for example, to send a file to a web server. We all know the Browse button available in some web pages to upload pictures or videos, or in fact any other file. The web browser can attach this file to a POST request and send it to the web server. Of course, the web server must be able to understand and handle the file.

Tim Heuer, Silverlight Evangelist at Microsoft, has published a video demonstrating the use of Silverlight on select files (using the `OpenFileDialog`) and sending them to the web server using a POST command with the `WebClient` class. This video is informative and

> **NOTE**
>
> We mentioned already in Chapter 22 that Silverlight 2 allows placing even more complex requests. For example, you can open sockets, or use so-called *polling duplex* communication. In the space we have, we cannot talk much about such complex topics. If you need this in a project, make sure to dig into the documentation.

rather than creating a similar example, here is the link: http://silverlight.net/learn/learn-video.aspx?video=69793.

In this video, you see that the `WebClient` class, simple as it is, can also be used to write information to the web server.

Throwing and Catching Exceptions

Let's talk about something different now. In the course of this book, we have been mentioning exceptions and even handled some of them. In this section, we will talk more about this important aspect of programming, about throwing, catching and handling errors, and making your application more stable.

For example, the code taken from the `User` class created for the Thumbnails application is shown in Listing 23.23. It has a constructor parsing a line of text and extracting values:

LISTING 23.23   User Class Constructor

```
 1  public User(string line)
 2  {
 3    try
 4    {
 5      LastVisit = DateTime.Parse(line);
 6    }
 7    catch (ArgumentNullException)
 8    {
 9      LastVisit = null;
10    }
11    catch (FormatException)
12    {
13      LastVisit = null;
14    }
15  }
```

▶ Line 3 uses the keyword `try` to notify the compiler that the statements in the next block might throw exceptions, and that we want to `catch` some of them.

▶ Lines 7 to 10 define the behavior if an `ArgumentNullException` is thrown by the statement at line 5. In that case, we set the `LastVisit` property to `null`.

▶ On lines 11 to 14, we do the same thing, but this time only if the `FormatException` is thrown by the statement on line 5.

▶ All other exception types are not handled.

▶ If you want to do something with the exception being thrown (such as logging a message to a web service, for example), you should name the `Exception` parameter: `catch (ArgumentNullException ex)`. However, if you do not use the named parameter, you get a warning from the compiler. In that case, you should rather use `catch (ArgumentNullException)`.

This is important: If an exception is thrown by a method but is not handled anywhere in the code, your application will crash. A Silverlight application will become white and will not "move" anymore, not until it is restarted. This behavior should be avoided, and this is why it is important to handle exceptions.

> **CAUTION**
>
> You might think that the best way to avoid an application crash is to simply always catch all possible exceptions even if you do nothing about them. For example, we could handle all XAML errors. This would be a bad idea, however, because it would leave the application in an unknown state. Generally, it is bad practice to just catch any exception type without doing anything to handle them.

Bubbling Exceptions

If an exception occurs in a method and is not handled within, it *bubbles* to the method's caller. If the caller doesn't handle the exception, the exception, again, bubbles up to the caller's caller. Eventually, the exception arrives in the `Application` object where a last chance to handle it is given to the application's developer (as we see in Listing 23.24).

1. Create a Silverlight application and implement the following three methods in the `Page` class.

2. Make sure that you call the method `DoSomething` in the `Page` constructor, just after the call to `InitializeComponent`.

3. Place a breakpoint on the call to `DoSomething` and step in the code.

LISTING 23.24   Bubbling Exceptions

```
public void DoSomething()
{
  try
  {
    DoSomethingElse();
  }
  catch (ArgumentNullException ex)
  {
    HtmlPage.Window.Alert("Error with argument: " +
      ex.Message);
  }
  catch (FileNotFoundException)
  {
    // ...
```

LISTING 23.24   Continued

```
    }
}

public int DoSomethingElse()
{
    DoYetSomethingElse(null);
    return -3;
}

public bool DoYetSomethingElse(object anyParameter)
{
    if (anyParameter == null)
    {
        throw new ArgumentNullException("anyParameter ");
    }
    return true;
}
```

▶ This code, albeit silly, illustrates the point: Even though the exception is thrown in DoYetSomethingElse, it just bubbles through DoSomethingElse and is handled only in DoSomething.

▶ The exception is handled according to its type. In this case, the Alert is displayed by the HTML page because the exception thrown is of type ArgumentNullException and not FileNotFoundException, which is shown in Figure 23.1.

CAUTION

Don't forget polymorphism! If you create an exception type MyOwnFileNotFoundException deriving from FileNotFoundException, the second catch block will be executed if an exception of that custom type is thrown.

FIGURE 23.1   JavaScript alert displaying an ArgumentNullException

Re-throwing Exceptions

Sometimes, you want to do something about an exception, but you don't want to handle it completely. You may want to log a message or take an action, but still want to notify your caller that that particular exception is not properly handled yet. This can be done by re-throwing the exception.

In this case, the best practice is to simply call the statement throw.

1. For example, modify the method DoSomethingElse as in Listing 23.25.

LISTING 23.25   Re-throwing an Exception

```
public int DoSomethingElse()
{
  try
  {
    DoYetSomethingElse(null);
  }
  catch (ArgumentNullException ex)
  {
    HtmlPage.Window.Alert("Error in DoSomethingElse");
    throw;
  }
  return -3;
}
```

2. Run the code. Two alerts are displayed now.

"Packing" and Re-throwing Exceptions
In other cases, you want to catch an
exception, and then throw your own
exception type. This can be useful if you
want to add information about the error.
You should, however, always pass the
original exception in the new exception's
InnerException property. This way, the
real cause of the error is not lost.

> **CAUTION**
>
> You may have seen an application re-throw-
> ing an exception with throw ex instead of
> simply throw. In that case, however, the
> StackTrace property (we talk about that
> property in the section "Understanding an
> Exception's Properties" later in the chapter)
> is reset, and the previous information about
> the exception is lost. This is why you
> shouldn't do it.

For example, if the Silverlight application defines somewhere the custom exception
defined in Listing 23.26:

LISTING 23.26   Custom Exception

```
public class MyOwnFileNotFoundException : FileNotFoundException
{
  public DateTime TimeStamp
  {
    get; private set;
  }
  public MyOwnFileNotFoundException(string message,
    Exception innerEx, DateTime timestamp)
    : base(message, innerEx)
  {
    TimeStamp = timestamp;
  }
}
```

Then you can do what is shown in Listing 23.27:

LISTING 23.27   "Packing" and Re-throwing an Exception

```
catch (FileNotFoundException ex)
{
  MyOwnFileNotFoundException newEx
    = new MyOwnFileNotFoundException("Ooops", ex, DateTime.Now);
  throw newEx;
}
```

When a `MyOwnFileNotFoundException` instance is created, the `base` constructor is called (that's the `FileNotFoundException` constructor). Every `Exception` constructor can accept 0, 1, or 2 parameters. In this last case, the second parameter becomes the `InnerException` property.

Understanding an `Exception`'s Properties

An `Exception` instance (as well as any derived class) provides the following information about the error:

▶ `Data` is a collection of custom information. The user can add any custom information to this collection. This is a handy way to provide extra information about the error. It is recommended to fill this collection with enough information to identify the cause of the error. Don't forget that other developers might end up using your code, and need to understand what is happening!

▶ `HResult` is a protected property set automatically by the system. It uniquely identifies this exception type. `HResult` is a rather old way to identify an `Exception` type and is available for compatibility with older technologies such as the one known as COM.

▶ We talked about `InnerException` already and said that it contains a reference to the exception that caused the current one. The `InnerException` can contain another nested `InnerException` and so on. To get the original exception at the cause of it all, you can use the method `ex.GetBaseException()`. This method gets the InnerException's InnerException's InnerException's... until it reaches the root.

▶ `Message` contains a clear text information message about the error. For built-in exceptions, the text is provided in the system's language and culture (if available). Custom messages should also be provided in the system's language and culture.

▶ `StackTrace` shows through which methods the exception just bubbled. It helps identify the original root of the error.

Catching Unhandled Exceptions

We saw before that it is bad practice to just catch any exception type without handling them. However, unhandled exceptions will crash the application, and that can have nasty side effects. For example, imagine that your Silverlight client requests the web server to block a resource (for example, a database), but then the client application crashes. The web server will not be notified of this fact, and in effect, the resource will be blocked indefinitely.

> **NOTE**
>
> In practice, this would never happen because a good web application frees the resource after a *timeout*. It means that if the web client doesn't send any messages for a given period of time, the web application running on the server will consider the client "dead" and free the resource. This is not the cleanest behavior, however, and a client should always free the resources it uses.

Another reason to want to be notified of unhandled exceptions is for saving the application's state so that when the user refreshes the web page, he doesn't need to re-enter all the information entered before the error occurred. For instance, should our Thumbnails application crash, we could save the scroll offset of the ScrollViewer and what thumbnails are currently displayed, so that the user retrieves the same state after he refreshes the page.

Thankfully, there is a way to be notified of any unhandled exception, and to use this last chance to close existing resources before crashing. This is a *graceful crash*, or a controlled emergency landing if you like.

The key to catching unhandled exceptions is to handle the event UnhandledException in the App.xaml.cs file. This event is raised just before the application crashes. If you check the App class in an existing Silverlight application now, you see that this event is handled already, and a default implementation is provided. This implementation passes the error to the web browser's JavaScript engine.

By modifying this event handler with your own implementation, for example, to send a last message to the web server (like a bottle to the sea), and by closing local resources (such as isolated storage files, in case this is not done already), you have a chance to clean up before the crash.

Marking the Exception as Handled

The ApplicationUnhandledExceptionEventArgs parameter that you get in the UnhandledException event contains two public properties:

▶ ExceptionObject is the unhandled exception that is causing the crash. If you log information about the error to the web server, make sure to include enough information so that you can trace the error and correct it.

▶ The Handled flag (a Boolean) can be set to true. In that case, the exception is marked as handled, and the application does not crash.

This last statement should be taken with a grain of salt. In fact, marking an unhandled exception as handled can be dangerous, because you don't know for sure what the state of the application is at that stage. Trying to recover a crashing application at all costs is not a best practice. Sometimes it is better to crash gracefully—saving enough information to be able to restore the application's state easily, informing the web server if needed, displaying a friendly user message, and then just letting go.

Creating **Custom** Exceptions

We saw how to catch existing exception types. In some other cases you want to create your own exceptions and throw them. Let's review how to do that.

- ▶ Any custom exception should derive from the Exception class (or from one of the built-in classes deriving from this type).

- ▶ The basis Exception class provides three constructors:

  - ▶ Exception() creates a default exception.

  - ▶ Exception(string) creates an exception with an error message.

  - ▶ Exception(string, Exception) creates an exception with an error message and an inner exception.

- ▶ For each custom exception type, you should provide at least three constructors. This is to make sure that the basis Exception class is initialized with the correct parameters. For example in Listing 23.28:

LISTING 23.28   Custom Exception Constructor

```
public MyOwnFileNotFoundException(DateTime timestamp)
{
  TimeStamp = timestamp;
}
public MyOwnFileNotFoundException(string message,
  DateTime timestamp)
  : base(message)
{
  TimeStamp = timestamp;
}
public MyOwnFileNotFoundException(string message,
  Exception innerEx, DateTime timestamp)
  : base(message, innerEx)
{
  TimeStamp = timestamp;
}
```

- ▶ By convention, any custom Exception type must be suffixed with the word "Exception."

▶ Once the custom `Exception` type is defined, you (or your class library's users) can create a new instance, and throw it. Because any custom exception derives from the basis `Exception` class, the public property `StackTrace` and the protected property `HResult` are set automatically.

Handling Silverlight Errors in JavaScript

When you create a website (as we did in Chapter 14, "Letting .NET and JavaScript Talk," for our Thumbnails application) and add a link to a Silverlight application, an HTML test page is created. This page contains a JavaScript event handler (onSilverlightError) hooked to the onerror event of the Silverlight application. This function will be executed if an error occurs. It is even provided with a default implementation. However, note the following:

▶ This JavaScript function will not be executed if the `Handled` property of the `ApplicationUnhandledExceptionEventArgs` parameter is set to `true` in App.xaml.cs.

▶ In the JavaScript error handler, the parameter `args` contains additional information about the error: error code, error type, error message, line number, character position, and name of the method where the error occurred. For XAML errors, it also contains the name of the XAML file in which the parser found the error.

While you are free of course to choose your implementation, a recommended practice for handling errors in Silverlight could be

1. Delete the content of the `Application_UnhandledException` method in App.xaml.cs.

2. Instead, use this method to send a message to the web server if needed, to clean up, to save the application's state in the isolated storage and so on.

3. In the HTML page, use the `onSilverlightError` event handler to notify the user about the error. If you want, you can even reload the page programmatically, for example, with the code in Listing 23.29:

LISTING 23.29   Custom Exception Constructor

```
if (confirm("Do you want to reload?"))
{
  window.location.reload();
}
```

4. Then, in the `Application_Startup` event handler (in App.xaml.cs), read the application state from the isolated storage (if available) and restore it.

This strategy has a down side though: If the stored state caused the application to crash, restoring this same state will probably cause it to crash again. This is why you should try to make sure that the state information saved doesn't cause such a situation.

Summary

Our Thumbnails application is complete. We used this application to demonstrate many aspects of Silverlight, and it is pretty advanced now. You should spend some time reviewing the code, find ways to improve it, invent your own features. Even for unrelated applications, you should be able to find ideas and inspiration in this code base.

As for exceptions and error handling, it is a complex and important part of any application. By handling, but also throwing errors appropriately, you make an application more stable and reliable, and you also make it easier to find errors in your code.

23

Silverlight: Continuing the Journey

We will start this chapter with a few advanced topics that didn't really fit anywhere else. Then, we will conclude with material that should facilitate the continuation of your journey in Silverlight... because even though this book is coming to an end, this is only the beginning!

Updating a Service Reference

We saw in Chapter 22, "Connecting to the Web," how to make requests to a WCF service (and mentioned that it's similar to making requests to "classic" ASMX web services). Remember how we added a service reference to our Silverlight application? In this process, the Visual Studio environment creates a *proxy* class representing the server-side service on the client application.

Obviously, when you change something in the service class, you need to update the client-based reference. Or else how would the Silverlight application know about the changes? Visual Studio assists you in updating the reference; let's see how with the following steps:

1. Create a new Silverlight application, including a test website.

2. In the test website, add a new Silverlight-enabled WCF service (like we did in Chapter 22).

3. Modify the method DoWork's implementation as in Listing 24.1, then build the application:

LISTING 24.1   Modifying the DoWork Method

```
[OperationContract]
public string DoWork(string anyParameter)
{
  return anyParameter;
}
```

4. In the Silverlight application, add a service reference.

5. Use the service in the Silverlight application, again as we did in Chapter 22. For example, call the method DoWork in the Page constructor.

6. Modify the name of the WCF service's method DoWork in DoSomething.

7. Try to run your application in debug mode. After a few moments, you should get an error in the Reference.cs file saying "The requested page was not found". The file Reference.cs is generated by Visual Studio when you add a service reference. The error "requested page not found" is the same as the one returned by a web server when a file can't be found. Calling web services and WCF services happens over HTTP, and the same protocols and error codes are used. It simply means that the URI of the DoWork method doesn't exist anymore on the web server.

8. In Visual Studio, right-click on the service reference in the Silverlight application (in the Solution Explorer). Then from the context menu, select Update Service Reference (see Figure 24.1).

FIGURE 24.1   Update Service Reference

Visual Studio downloads the new service description and updates the proxy class. You need to update your client application now according to the new method signature, or the compilation will fail.

Killing a Process

We are only human... and so it happens that sometimes, we make errors in our code, and the application cannot recover. For example, if you create an infinite loop (such as a while loop for which the end condition is never met), the application will try to run as fast as possible, bringing your processor to run to almost 100% of its capacity.

In such a condition, the only way to recover is to "kill" the application. In this section, we see how to cause an infinite loop and then how to kill the Silverlight process in Windows with the following steps.

1. Create a new Silverlight application in Visual Studio.

2. Modify the code of the Page constructor as in Listing 24.2:

LISTING 24.2   Endless Loop

```
public Page()
{
  InitializeComponent();

  int index = 0;
  while (index == 0)
  {
    // Do something
  }
}
```

3. Run the code in normal mode, by pressing Ctrl+F5 in Visual Studio. Immediately, you will notice that your PC runs slower. Almost the whole processor time is used by your application, because the end condition is never met: index is never bigger than 0.

4. In Windows, right-click on the Windows Taskbar with your mouse and select Task Manager in the context menu.

5. In this application, select the Processes tab, shown in Figure 24.2.

6. Click on the CPU column. This shows the amount of processor time used by each process. Clicking on the column sorts it according to the CPU percentage. You should see the process iexplore.exe pretty much on top of this column. Even though it is your Silverlight application that is caught in an infinite loop, the application is hosted by Internet Explorer, so this process appears in the list.

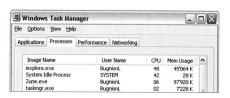

FIGURE 24.2   Windows Task Manager

> **NOTE**
>
> Depending on your PC's configuration, the CPU usage of iexplore.exe may vary. On a dual core PC, only one core will be used (this is why Figure 24.2 shows only 48% CPU for this process). On a single core machine, the number will be close to 100%, and the PC will be "sluggish."

7. Right-click on the iexplore.exe process and select End Process from the context menu. Notice that the instance of Internet Explorer disappears completely, and your PC recovers and runs normally again.

Killing the Process in Debug Mode

When you run the same code in debug mode (by pressing the F5 key in Visual Studio), you don't need to kill the process like we did before. Instead, you can simply stop the debugger in Studio with these steps:

1. Run the same code as before, by pressing the F5 key in Visual Studio.

2. Again, the PC will be slow because the Silverlight application uses all the CPU time.

3. In Studio, click on the Stop Debugging button shown in Figure 24.3. Alternatively you can press Shift+F5 or select Debug, Stop Debugging from the menu. Note that stopping an application being debugged can take a few moments.

FIGURE 24.3   Stop Debugging in Visual Studio

About Protecting Your Work

The question "How do I protect my work" is often asked on JavaScript or other web-related forums. The answer is always the same: "If you really want to protect your work, don't publish it." This may sound like a joke, but it's really not: To execute the code, the user has to download it to the web browser. From this moment on, it is available for the user to view.

▶ XAML and JS files are visible as clear text.

▶ Any image or video files are available "as-is," to be viewed in a picture editor or a video player, respectively.

▶ Compiled files (the DLLs in the ClientBin folder) are indeed compiled, but even DLLs can easily be decompiled, for example with the tool Reflector created by Lutz Roeder and currently managed by Red Gate.

> **NOTE**
>
> .NET code can be *obfuscated*, meaning that it will be "garbled" in a way that makes it more difficult to read. Obfuscation is not encryption, however, and it doesn't really protect your code. Free and commercial obfuscators are available on the market. Note, however, that XAML code cannot (to this date) be obfuscated, so the XAML code will remain readable anyway.

Protecting Your Work Anyway

So what can you do to protect your source code? In fact, the only totally foolproof measure is to keep the critical code on the web server. We saw that Silverlight applications can easily connect to the web server to call web services, WCF services, and so on.

Calling web services comes with a cost, however: It is much less responsive than doing calculations on the client. Each request/response sequence takes time. Additionally, the web server may be overloaded, or simply off the network for one reason or another.

As usual with engineering, deciding where to place which code is a matter of compromises. It is important to design your application with these considerations in mind, to create a flexible, safe, and reliable system.

Binding in Special Configurations

We talked about data binding in Silverlight in previous chapters. In this section, let's review a couple of special cases, and how to set bindings to handle these. Expression Blend is a great help when you must create complex bindings. In this section, we see how to use the tool's abilities. We also talk about advanced binding parameters.

Setting a Binding in Blend

We saw in Chapter 19, "Creating User Controls and Custom Controls," how to use Blend to deal with data sources. You can use a similar workflow to create data binding in an easy way with the following steps.

1. Create a new Silverlight application in Blend and name it DataBindingSilverlight.

2. Right-click on the Solution in the Project panel and choose Edit in Visual Studio.

3. In Studio, add a new class to the project and name it MediaInfo.

4. Implement the class as in Listing 24.3:

LISTING 24.3   MediaInfo Class

```
public class MediaInfo : INotifyPropertyChanged
{
  public event PropertyChangedEventHandler PropertyChanged;

  private void OnPropertyChanged(string propertyName)
  {
    if (PropertyChanged != null)
    {
      PropertyChanged(this,
        new PropertyChangedEventArgs(propertyName));
    }
  }

  private DateTime _timestamp = DateTime.Now;
  public DateTime Timestamp
  {
    get { return _timestamp; }
```

LISTING 24.3   Continued

```
    set
    {
      _timestamp = value;
      OnPropertyChanged("Timestamp");
    }
  }
}
```

5. Choose File, Save All from the menu. Then, go back into Expression Blend. Because you added a new class to the project, Blend asks you if you want to reload it. Accept and wait until the project is reloaded.

6. In Expression Blend, add a `TextBox` and a `TextBlock` to the main `Grid`.

7. Select the `TextBox` and click on the small square next to the `Text` property. Then select Data Binding.

8. In the Create Data Binding dialog, click on + CLR Object.

9. In the Add CLR Object Data Source, select the class `MediaInfo`. Enter a name for this data source, for example `MediaInfoSource`. Then press OK.

10. In the Create Data Binding dialog, select the `MediaInfo` data source. In the Fields panel, expand the MediaInfo and select the `Timestamp` property.

> **TIP**
>
> If you don't see a property when you do a data binding in Blend, try setting the Show combo box to All Properties. You might have to implement a converter though.

11. On the bottom of the Create Data Binding dialog, expand the Advanced Properties.

12. Set the Binding Direction to TwoWay and click Finish.

13. Repeat step 10 for the `TextBlock`. This time leave the Binding Direction set to OneWay.

14. Run the application and change the date in the `TextBox`. Then press the Tab key to remove the focus from the `TextBox` and check that the value of the `TextBlock` changes too.

The `Binding`'s `Path` property can be complex. Remember when we talked about animations, and we saw that identifying the `TargetProperty` of a `StoryBoard` was difficult sometimes. It is exactly the same for bindings. Thankfully, Blend assists you, and you can find a property "buried" deep inside a list of objects rather easily thanks to the Create Data Binding dialog.

Handling Validation Errors

Since bindings can also update the source object (in TwoWay mode), you need to make sure that the value entered can be converted. In the case of a `DateTime` class, for example, if the user enters an invalid string, the framework won't be able to create a `DateTime` instance with this value. The default behavior in this case is to just leave the source object untouched. This can be confusing, however, because the string in the `TextBox` will not be corrected, and the invalid value will still be displayed. You can test this in the application we created in the preceding section: Enter an invalid date string, for example 8/aa/2008 9:55:01 PM and press the Tab key. The `TextBox` keeps the invalid value, and the `TextBlock` remains unchanged.

To change this default behavior, you need to implement an event handler to the `TextBox`'s `BindingValidationError` event with the following steps. This event is available on every `FrameworkElement`.

1. Change back to Visual Studio and open the application DataBindingSilverlight's Page.xaml.

2. In the `TextBox` we added to the application, handle the `BindingValidationError` event:

   ```
   BindingValidationError="TextBox_BindingValidationError"
   ```

2. Implement the event handler in Page.xaml.cs as in Listing 24.4. This event handler will be called when a validation error appears, but also when it disappears, making it handy to restore the element to its original state.

LISTING 24.4   TextBox_BindingValidationError Error Handler

```
private void TextBox_BindingValidationError(object sender,
  ValidationErrorEventArgs e)
{
  if (e.Action == ValidationErrorEventAction.Added)
  {
    (sender as TextBox).Foreground = new SolidColorBrush(Colors.Red);
  }
  else
  {
    (sender as TextBox).Foreground = new SolidColorBrush(Colors.Black);
  }
}
```

4. If you run the application now, nothing happens. We still need to notify the `Binding` that the event `BindingValidationError` must be raised. Two additional properties must be set on the Binding in the `TextBox` (Listing 24.5):

LISTING 24.5   Validation Properties

```
Text="{Binding Mode=TwoWay, Path=Timestamp,
                Source={StaticResource MediaInfo},
                NotifyOnValidationError=True,
                ValidatesOnExceptions=True}"
```

This syntax is complex, but it is needed to be compatible with Windows Presentation Foundation where more advanced validation mechanisms are available.

Run the application and enter an invalid date in the TextBox. You see the text color turn to red. If later you place the cursor back in the TextBox and correct the value, the text goes back to black. You could also use this event handler to display a message to the user.

Binding Through a Converter, ConverterParameter, ConverterCulture

We already talked about value converters and how to implement one. We also mentioned shortly the ConverterParameter and ConverterCulture parameters. Let's see how to use them with the following steps:

1. In the Silverlight application we just created, add a new class in Visual Studio and name it DateTimeConverter.cs. The code is in Listing 24.6:

LISTING 24.6   DateTimeConverter Class

```
public class DateTimeConverter : IValueConverter
{
  public object Convert(object value, Type targetType,
    object parameter, System.Globalization.CultureInfo culture)
  {
    double parameterAsDouble = 0.0;
    if (parameter != null)
    {
      parameterAsDouble = Double.Parse(parameter.ToString());
    }

    DateTime valueAsDateTime
      = (DateTime)value + TimeSpan.FromDays((parameterAsDouble));
    return valueAsDateTime.ToString(culture);
  }
  public object ConvertBack(object value, Type targetType,
    object parameter, System.Globalization.CultureInfo culture)
  {
    string valueAsString = value.ToString();
    return DateTime.Parse(valueAsString, culture);
  }
}
```

2. Add a new namespace in the UserControl tag, pointing to the DataBindingSilverlight namespace in which we implemented the converter:

```
xmlns:src="clr-namespace:DataBindingSilverlight"
```

3. Add an instance of the Converter to the `UserControl` resources:

```
<src:DateTimeConverter x:Key="DateTimeConverter" />
```

4. Modify the `TextBlock`'s `Text` property's binding as in Listing 24.7:

LISTING 24.7   Modifying the `Binding`

```
Text="{Binding Mode=OneWay,
               Path=Timestamp,
               Source={StaticResource MediaInfo},
               Converter={StaticResource DateTimeConverter},
               ConverterParameter=2,
               ConverterCulture=fr-CH}"
```

Running this code displays a different date (two days later) in the `TextBlock` than in the `TextBox`. Additionally, the culture specified is used and the display looks different.

Binding to an Object Rather Than a Property

Sometimes it can be interesting to bind to an object directly rather than to a property of this object. There are two possibilities:

▶ Setting the `Source` of the `Binding` without setting the path. For example in Listing 24.8:

LISTING 24.8   Binding to an Object

```
<Rectangle Fill="{Binding Source={StaticResource MyBrush}}"
           Width="120"
           Height="240" />
```

▶ Setting the `Binding` to the `DataContext` directly. For example, if the `DataContext` of a Grid is set to a `SolidColorBrush`, you can do as in Listing 24.9:

LISTING 24.9   Binding to the `DataContext`

```
<Grid DataContext="{StaticResource MyBrush}">
  <Rectangle Fill="{Binding}"
             Width="120"
             Height="240" />
</Grid>
```

The {Binding} syntax is a bit weird, but remember that if the Source of the binding is not set explicitly, the DataContext is used. Since this object is inherited from parent to children, we can just set an "empty" binding.

This is particularly interesting for DataTemplates when you deal with an ItemsControl. Remember that the children of the ItemsControl are created dynamically, and that the DataContext of each is set to the data item that they represent. Knowing this, you can display a list of brushes using a Rectangle as DataTemplate, and set its Fill property to {Binding}.

Using the ASP.NET Controls Silverlight and MediaPlayer

When you run an ASP.NET website, you are used to dealing with ASPX pages and controls. With this method, you can build a web page by placing ASP.NET controls on the page and setting their parameters. For instance, you can drag and drop an ASP.NET control named DropDownList on the web page, set a few of its parameters as well as a list of items using a designer, and then run the application. In the ASPX page, the markup looks like Listing 24.10:

> **CAUTION**
>
> Do not mix the concepts: ASP.NET controls are rendered on the web server. What is sent to the web client is HTML markup (and possibly JavaScript, CSS, and so on). On the opposite, Silverlight code runs in the web browser. For ASP.NET, we talk of *thin clients* because the web client doesn't need much to be able to render the web page. For Silverlight, we talk of *rich clients* because they need more (the Silverlight plug-in), but they also can do more (.NET runs on the client).

LISTING 24.10   ASP.NET Control

```
<asp:DropDownList ID="DropDownList1" runat="server">
  <asp:ListItem Value="0">My value 0</asp:ListItem>
  <asp:ListItem Value="1">My value 1</asp:ListItem>
</asp:DropDownList>
```

The generated HTML markup that is sent to the web browser looks different, however, as in Listing 24.11:

LISTING 24.11   HTML Control

```
<select name="DropDownList1" id="Select1">
  <option value="0">My value 0</option>
  <option value="1">My value 1</option>
</select>
```

The ASP.NET engine translated the ASP.NET markup into HTML. ASP.NET pages can be created and programmed for example in Visual Web Developer Express Edition, available for free at www.microsoft.com/express/vwd.

Two ASP.NET controls are available for Silverlight. These controls will eventually render the HTML markup needed to run a Silverlight application into a web page. They are easy to use and make Silverlight even more accessible for ASP.NET developers.

Using the `Silverlight` **ASP.NET Control**

This ASP.NET control creates a Silverlight application according to its parameters. Let's see how with these steps:

1. Open the application SilverlightDraw that we created in Chapter 16, "Digging Deeper into Silverlight Elements," and modified in Chapter 18, "Data Binding and Using Data Controls."

2. Add a new website to it: Right-click on the Solution in the Solution Explorer and select Add, New Web Site from the context menu. Name the new website SilverlightDraw.Web and place it into the same folder as the file SilverlightDraw.sln and the folder SilverlightDraw containing the Silverlight application. This is not compulsory, but it makes things much easier to manage.

3. Right-click on the website and select Property Pages.

4. In the Silverlight Applications section, add a link to the SilverlightDraw application.

   Visual Studio creates two additional web pages for the website. One is an ASPX (dynamic page) named SilverlightDrawTestPage.aspx. The other is the static HTML page we already know.

5. Open the page SilverlightDrawTestPage.aspx and switch to Design mode with the buttons on the bottom-left corner.

   You see two controls: One is a `ScriptManager` control, represented as a rectangle with the name ScriptManager in bold. It is used to generate JavaScript code dynamically. The `Silverlight` and `MediaPlayer` ASP.NET controls use the `ScriptManager` control to include JavaScript code (such as the one contained in Silverlight.js). The other control is the `Silverlight` control, and takes the whole page's width.

6. Select the `Silverlight` control and press F4. This displays the Properties panel for this control.

7. Set the `Width` to 600px and the `Height` to 500px.

8. Switch to Source view. You should see the ASP.NET markup shown in Listing 24.12:

LISTING 24.12   Silverlight ASP.NET Control

```
<asp:Silverlight ID="Xaml1" runat="server"
  Source="~/ClientBin/SilverlightDraw.xap" MinimumVersion="2.0.30904.0"
  Width="600px" Height="500px" />
```

9. Right-click on the SilverlightDraw.Web website and select Set as StartUp Project. Right-click on SilverlightDrawTestPage.aspx and select Set as Start Page.

10. Run the application.

The SilverlightDraw application runs embedded inside the HTML page. The ASP.NET framework renders the HTML and JavaScript code needed to run Silverlight. Note that the `ScriptManager` control is not visible: it is a control running on the server only!

> **TIP**
>
> The `MinimumVersion` attribute defines what version of Silverlight is needed to run this application. If you set it to 3.0, for example, your users see a dialog asking them to upgrade.

Using the `MediaPlayer` ASP.NET Control

The `MediaPlayer` is a control deriving from the `Silverlight` ASP.NET control we just discussed. This control is specialized to play video and audio files. It is in fact similar to the output of the Expression Encoder application that we created in Chapter 12, "Encoding Videos with Expression Encoder." Follow the steps:

1. In Visual Studio, select File, Close Solution and then select File, New, Web Site.

2. In the New Web Site dialog, select ASP.NET Web Site. Enter a new name for your website, for example, TestMediaPlayer. Select a location and then click OK.

3. Right-click on the TestMediaPlayer project in the Solution Explorer and select New Folder. Name this folder MediaFiles.

4. Right-click on the new MediaFiles folder and select Add Existing Item.

5. Select a video file from your hard disk. It should be in WMV format. Remember that you can convert pretty much any video format to WMV using the application Expression Encoder that we studied in Chapter 12.

6. In Visual Studio, open the file Default.aspx and set the designer in Design mode.

7. In the toolbox, find the `ScriptManager` control (in the AJAX Extensions section). Drag and drop it from the Toolbox on the page. If you don't see the toolbox, you can open it by selecting View, Toolbox from the menu.

8. Still from the toolbox, select the `MediaPlayer` control from the Silverlight section. Drag and drop it right under the `ScriptManager` control that we added previously (see Figure 24.4).

9. Expand the MediaPlayer Tasks panel and set the properties. Alternatively, you can also set them in the Properties panel (but their name is a bit different):

   ▶ Click on the link Import Skin... and locate a Skin file. You can find Media Player Skins in the SDK folder located in C:\Program Files\Microsoft SDKs\Silverlight\v2.0\Libraries\Server\MediaPlayerSkins.

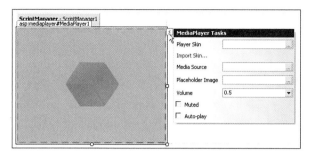

FIGURE 24.4   MediaPlayer in ASP.NET Design mode

> ▶ Set the Media Source (or the MediaSource property) to the video file that you
>   added just before in the MediaFiles folder.

> ▶ Set the other attributes as you want.

10. Resize the control to an appropriate size for your movie (or use the Height and Width
    properties).

11. Set the player's ID to VideoPlayer in the Properties panel. Note that the ID must be
    unique throughout the whole web page.

12. Run the application and see the results!

Programming the Control in JavaScript

As we already did, you can also write JavaScript code to handle events raised by the
control. For more information about the available events, check the reference documentation available at http://msdn.microsoft.com/en-us/library/system.web.ui.silverlightcon-
trols.mediaplayer(VS.95).aspx.

For example, you can force the video to play in a loop with these steps:

1. In Source view, add a JavaScript event handler in the head section of the ASPX page
   (Listing 24.13):

LISTING 24.13   VideoPlayer_Ended Event Handler

```
<script type="text/javascript">
  function VideoPlayer_Ended(sender, args)
  {
    sender.play();
  }
</script>
```

2. Add the OnClientMediaEnded attribute to the asp:MediaPlayer tag as in Listing 24.14,
   then run the application and start the movie. It will run in a loop.

LISTING 24.14   MediaPlayer ASP.NET Control with Event Handler

```
<asp:MediaPlayer ID="VideoPlayer" runat="server"
  Height="240px" Width="320px" MediaSkinSource="~/Expression.xaml"
  MediaSource="~/MediaFiles/mov1.wmv"
  OnClientMediaEnded="VideoPlayer_Ended">
</asp:MediaPlayer>
```

Creating a Chapters List

A nice functionality of the MediaPlayer ASP.NET control is the possibility to define chapters in your movie simply by adding markup into the MediaPlayer tag. For example in Listing 24.15:

LISTING 24.15   MediaPlayer ASP.NET Control with Chapters

```
<asp:MediaPlayer ID="VideoPlayer" runat="server"
  Height="240px" Width="320px" MediaSkinSource="~/Expression.xaml"
  MediaSource="~/MediaFiles/mov1.wmv"
  OnClientMediaEnded="VideoPlayer_Ended">
  <Chapters>
    <asp:MediaChapter Position="0" Title="Chapter 1"
      ThumbnailSource="~/MediaFiles/thumb1.png" />
    <asp:MediaChapter Position="2" Title="Chapter 2"
      ThumbnailSource="~/MediaFiles/thumb2.png" />
  </Chapters>
</asp:MediaPlayer>
```

You can also use the visual designer to do this, with the following steps:

1. In Design mode, select the MediaPlayer control.

2. In the Properties panel, find the property named Chapters.

3. Click on the "…" button, and then use the dialog to add chapters.

> **CAUTION**
>
> The Chapters dialog is displayed in the Silverlight video player only if you specify thumbnails for the various chapters.

Using this tool, you can add chapters with the same features as in Expression Encoder, such as a title and a thumbnail.

Handling an Expression Encoder Chapter File

Another way to create chapters is to use the XML file created by Expression Encoder. In Chapter 12, in the "Creating Chapters" section, we mentioned that you can export markers to an XML file. After you exported such a file, follow the steps:

1. Add the XML chapters file to your ASP.NET website.

2. Open the page Default.aspx containing the MediaPlayer control.

3. Make sure that the Design mode is selected.

4. Select the `MediaPlayer` control.

5. In the Properties panel, find the `MediaDefinition` property and set it to the location of the XML chapters file.

> **CAUTION**
>
> If the XML chapters file contains references to images, for the chapters' thumbnails, you need to make sure to include the pictures in the website too.

Creating Unit Tests for Silverlight

One popular new way of developing applications is called *Test Driven Development (TDD)*. Many discussions are ongoing in the .NET developer community as to what is the "purest" way of doing TDD and what is the best TDD framework, but fundamentally it comes down to this:

▶ For each functionality that you implement in your application, implement a test first.

▶ Implement the functionality until the test passes, but not more. If you feel that you need additional features in this functionality, it means new tests.

▶ Every time you modify your application, run all the tests again to make sure that you didn't break anything.

TDD gives a nice feeling of trust to the developers, because existing tests can be run again and again, and you can be sure that existing features still work, even though you add new features, refactor existing ones, and so on.

A test for a feature is named a *unit test*. It tests a unit of code. Typically, you create one test class per object being tested. Writing unit tests is difficult and requires honed developer skills. Put as much effort into your unit tests as you put into your code!

Silverlight comes with a *unit test framework* based on the one released by Microsoft for the full version of .NET (named MSUnit). In this section, we see how to install the unit test framework for Silverlight, and how to implement the `TryFindResource` functionality available in Windows Presentation Foundation.

> **TIP**
>
> To learn more about the Silverlight unit test framework, check this post: http://www.jeff. wilcox.name/2008/03/31/silverlight2-unit-testing.

Installing the Silverlight Unit Test Framework

The unit test framework is not part of the default Silverlight installation, and must be installed separately. Follow these steps:

1. Navigate to the page http://code.msdn.microsoft.com/silverlightut.

24

2. Follow the indications to download and install the test framework.

3. You should also install the Visual Studio project template and the class template. These two templates allow you to create new test projects and test classes with the Add New Project and Add New Item menus.

Creating a New Silverlight Test Application

Once the test framework is installed, we can use it to create a test application with the following steps:

1. Start in Visual Studio by creating a new Silverlight class library for our `TryFindResource` utility method. For this, in Visual Studio, choose File, New Project and select Silverlight Class Library from the Silverlight section.

2. Name the new project SilverlightUtility.

3. In the Solution Explorer, rename the Class1.cs to Extensions.cs. In the dialog asking whether you also want to rename the class, click Yes.

4. Modify the class declaration to make it static.

```
public static class Extensions
```

> **NOTE**
>
> Marking a class `static` means that no one can create a new instance of this class in code. The class contains static methods only. Later we see that this class will contain an *extension method* and understand what this means.

Now is the time to start writing tests. We write tests before we even write the first functionality. This is one important principle of TDD: Test first, implement later. Follow the steps:

1. Right-click on the Solution in the Solution Explorer and select Add, New Project from the context menu.

2. In the dialog, click on Visual C# and under My Templates, select the Silverlight Test Project.

3. Name this project SilverlightUtility.Test and click OK.

4. In the new test project, rename the file Test.cs to ExtensionsTest.cs. By convention, name each Test class according to the class you want to test, with the Test suffix.

Now we add a reference from the Test project to the class library with the following steps:

1. Right-click on the Test project and choose Add Reference. In the dialog, under the Projects tab, select the SilverlightUtility project.

2. Add a new Page to the test application by right-clicking on the Test project and choosing Add, New Item from the context menu. Select Silverlight User Control and name this new item TestControl.xaml.

We initialize the test class using a method named `TestInitialize` and marked with the special attribute `TestInitialize`. This notifies the test framework that the method must be executed first, before all the test methods. Note that the method may be named anything, only the attribute is important. Follow the steps:

1. In `ExtensionsTest`, add the attribute and method shown in Listing 24.16:

LISTING 24.16   Test Initialization Method

```
private FrameworkElement _element;

[TestInitialize]
public void TestInitialize()
{
  TestControl control = new TestControl();
  _element
    = control.FindName("LayoutRoot") as FrameworkElement;
}
```

2. Rename the `TestMethod` method to `TestTryFindResourceInLayoutRoot`.

3. Modify the `TestTryFindResourceInLayoutRoot` method as in Listing 24.17:

LISTING 24.17   TestTryFindResourceInLayoutRoot Method

```
[TestMethod]
public void TestTryFindResourceInLayoutRoot()
{
  SolidColorBrush brush
    = _element.TryFindResource("BrushInRoot") as SolidColorBrush;
  Assert.AreNotEqual<Brush>(null, brush);
  Assert.AreEqual(Colors.Red, brush.Color);
}
```

▶ As you understood already, all public methods marked with the `TestMethod` attribute will be executed to test the functionality.

▶ The `Assert` class is used to test the conditions. If a condition is not met, the test fails. It contains a number of static methods that can be used to create various conditions for the functionality.

▶ The first `Assert` checks that the object returned is not `null`.

▶ The second checks whether the `brush` is indeed red.

4. Make sure that the project SilverlightUtility.Test is set as Startup project (you can select this by right-clicking on the project and choosing Set as Startup Project) and run the application.

The application shouldn't even compile, because there is no method named
TryFindResource on the Grid control.

Creating the TryFindResource Extension Method

Let's imagine that you want to add functionality to a class, but you cannot modify this
class. For example, you want to add the functionality TryFindResource to every
FrameworkElement (as in WPF). In .NET 3.5 and Silverlight, you can do this with so-called
Extension Methods, with the following steps:

1. In the SilverlightUtility project, in the Extensions class, add the method shown in
   Listing 24.18:

LISTING 24.18   TryFindResource Method

```
public static object TryFindResource(this FrameworkElement element,
  object resourceKey)
{
  return null;
}
```

2. The first parameter of this method is a FrameworkElement marked with the keyword
   this. The compiler "adds" this method to any instance of the FrameworkElement
   class it finds in this application. The effect is just as if the method had been defined
   on the FrameworkElement class.

3. We add the TryFindResource method to the FrameworkElement class, because a look
   in the WPF documentation reveals that this is where the method is defined in the
   .NET framework. We want to be as compatible as we can.
   http://msdn.microsoft.com/en-
   us/library/system.windows.frameworkelement.tryfindresource.aspx.

4. The method's signature is also compatible with the one defined in the full .NET
   framework (apart from the this parameter, of course).

   If you compile the application now, you see that it builds. The extension method
   has been recognized and *extends* the FrameworkElement's functionality.

5. Set the project
   SilverlightUtility.Test to the
   StartUp project and run the application now (do not run it in the
   debugger, but with Ctrl+F5). You
   see the Silverlight unit test framework window, and your test should
   fail (see Figure 24.5).

FIGURE 24.5   Silverlight unit test failed

Making the Test Pass

In this section, we will implement the functionality so that the test passes and turns green. We know that when a `FrameworkElement` has a resource in its own `ResourceDictionary`, the method `TryFindResource` should return it. Let's implement this with the following steps:

1. Modify the method `TryFindResource` like Listing 24.19:

LISTING 24.19   Modified `TryFindResource` Method

```
public static object TryFindResource(this FrameworkElement element,
  object resourceKey)
{
  if (element.Resources != null
    && element.Resources.Contains(resourceKey))
  {
    return element.Resources[resourceKey];
  }
  return null;
}
```

2. Additionally, our test is looking for a red `SolidColorBrush`, so let's add it to the `Grid` `LayoutRoot` (Listing 24.20).

LISTING 24.20   Adding a `SolidColorBrush`

```
<Grid x:Name="LayoutRoot" Background="White">
  <Grid.Resources>
    <SolidColorBrush x:Key="BrushInRoot"
                     Color="Red" />
  </Grid.Resources>
</Grid>
```

3. Run the application again. This time, the test should be successful, as shown in Figure 24.6.

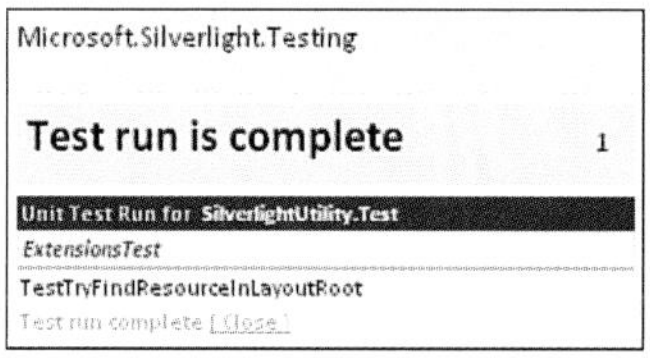

Microsoft.Silverlight.Testing

Test run is complete   1

Unit Test Run for **SilverlightUtility.Test**
ExtensionsTest
TestTryFindResourceInLayoutRoot
Test run complete [Close]

FIGURE 24.6   Successful unit test

Implementing Recursion

Anyone who used the method `TryFindResource` in WPF knows that this method "walks the tree." If the resource is not found on the element, the parent will be searched, then the parent's parent, until the `Application` object. Let's start by implementing the test for this with the following steps, and watch it fail:

1. Add two methods to the class `ExtensionsTest` in the project SilverlightUtility.Test, as in Listing 24.21:

LISTING 24.21   Two Methods

```
[TestMethod]
public void TestTryFindResourceInParent()
{
  SolidColorBrush brush
    = _element.TryFindResource("BrushInParent")
      as SolidColorBrush;
  Assert.AreNotEqual<Brush>(null, brush);
  Assert.AreEqual(brush.Color, Colors.Orange);
}

[TestMethod]
public void TestTryFindResourceInApplication()
{
  SolidColorBrush brush
    = _element.TryFindResource("BrushInApplication")
      as SolidColorBrush;
  Assert.AreNotEqual<Brush>(null, brush);
  Assert.AreEqual(brush.Color, Colors.Blue);
}
```

2. Just to be thorough, let's add a last test: Looking for a nonexistent resource. The method should return `null`. Add the test method shown in Listing 24.22:

LISTING 24.22   TestTryFindResourceNotFound Method

```
[TestMethod]
public void TestTryFindResourceNotFound()
{
  SolidColorBrush brush
    = _element.TryFindResource("BrushNonExisting")
      as SolidColorBrush;
  Assert.AreEqual<Brush>(null, brush);
}
```

3. Run the application. The tests fail. However, the first test is still okay.

4. In TestControl.xaml, add the resources to the main `UserControl` as shown in Listing 24.23:

LISTING 24.23   A New `SolidColorBrush`

```
<UserControl.Resources>
  <SolidColorBrush x:Key="BrushInParent"
                   Color="Orange" />
</UserControl.Resources>
```

5. Then, add the following Brush to App.xaml (Listing 24.24):

LISTING 24.24   Brush in App.xaml

```
<Application.Resources>
  <SolidColorBrush x:Key="BrushInApplication"
                   Color="Blue" />
</Application.Resources>
```

6. Modify the method `TryFindResource` in the class Extensions (in the project SilverlightUtility) as shown in Listing 24.25:

LISTING 24.25   Modified Method `TryFindResource`

```
public static object TryFindResource(this FrameworkElement element,
  object resourceKey)
{
  if (element.Resources != null
    && element.Resources.Contains(resourceKey))
  {
    return element.Resources[resourceKey];
  }
  if (element.Parent != null
    && element.Parent is FrameworkElement)
  {
    FrameworkElement parent = element.Parent as FrameworkElement;
    return parent.TryFindResource(resourceKey);
  }
  else
  {
    return Application.Current.TryFindResource(resourceKey);
  }
}
```

Notice how we use *recursion*: We call the same method on the parent as the one we're in already.

7. Notice how the last `else` block in
Listing 24.25 calls the method
`TryFindResource` on
`Application`.`Current`. However,
`Application`.`Current` is not a
`FrameworkElement`, so this extension method doesn't exist for that
object type. To be able to compile,
we must add an *overload* of the

> **CAUTION**
>
> Recursion is powerful, but it's also slower
> than other programming techniques, and it
> can lead to a crash if you don't have a fool-
> proof "stop" condition. In this case, it's okay
> because we're sure that the parent will be
> `null` sometimes.

`TryFindResource` extension method, this time on the `Application` class. Add Listing
24.26 in the `Extension` class, under the existing `TryFindResource` method. Since the
methods' signatures (the number and type of parameters) are different, you can
overload one method with the other. The Silverlight framework will select the
correct method based on the type and number of parameters when you call it.

LISTING 24.26   Method `TryFindResource` Overloaded for the Application Class

```
public static object TryFindResource(this Application application,
  object resourceKey)
{
  if (application.Resources != null
    && application.Resources.Contains(resourceKey))
  {
    return application.Resources[resourceKey];
  }
  return null;
}
```

8. Run the application again. All the
tests should be green.

Even though we modified the method
`TryFindResource` to add functionality,
the first test still passes, so we're sure
that we didn't break anything. This
feeling of security is the main advantage
of TDD.

> **TIP**
>
> We could have solved the problem differently,
> but the full .NET also defines a method
> named `TryFindResource` on the
> `FrameworkElement` class and another one on
> the `Application` class. This way, we
> increased the compatibility of our Silverlight
> application with the full .NET framework.

Learning More About Unit Test

This section is by no means a complete reference about unit tests. Other attributes can be
used to define expected behavior. For instance, the `ExpectedException` attribute can decorate a method to notify the test framework that the test method should throw an exception (you can even specify the `Exception`'s type). This can be useful to make sure that
underlying code throws the correct error if something wrong happens.

For more information about Silverlight unit testing, check Jeff Wilcox's blog mentioned in the beginning of this section. Other bloggers write often about unit tests in general and you can find much information about this programming technique on the Internet.

Reusing Microsoft Unit Tests

Microsoft is also using unit tests intensively on Silverlight and other projects. For example, all the Silverlight controls are intensively unit tested before they are released. Together with the source code, Microsoft is also publishing the unit tests that they are using on some components. This is a great way to learn how to write unit tests, how the controls are working, and also to extend and reuse the code when you extend the controls for your own use.

At the time of writing, the controls' source code for the final version of Silverlight has not been released yet, but stay posted on MSDN and www.microsoft.com for announcements.

Making or Buying XAML Resources

Throughout this book, you saw how Silverlight enables a better workflow between developers and designers. The key to this collaboration is the XAML language, used as a bridge between both worlds.

When you develop a Silverlight (or Windows Presentation Foundation) application, you often need XAML resources. For example, you might need a special template for a button, or a fancy looking icon, or a nice brush with a highlight, and so on. Silverlight is new—very new—and XAML is still relatively young, even in computer years. In time, you will be able to find more and more XAML resources online, just like you can download today millions of raster icons and other graphical assets.

In the mean time, one possibility is of course to use Expression Blend to create this resource yourself. There are a few other possibilities that we will mention here.

Using Expression Design

One obvious choice to create XAML resources is Expression Design. A member of the Expression Suite (like Blend and Encoder), Design can be downloaded on the Expression website. Expression Design can only be purchased together with the rest of the Expression Studio. At the time of writing, the whole Expression Studio (including Blend, Encoder, Design, Web, and Media) costs $699.

Expression Design is a good editor for assets. In addition to exporting to XAML, it also allows exporting to other graphic formats. It also imports Adobe Illustrator files.

Describing Expression Design more is outside the scope of this book, but thankfully good, simple tutorials are available online. The best place to start is a hands-on lab created by one of Microsoft's WPF evangelists Karsten Januszewski (see Figure 24.7). This lab

FIGURE 24.7   Expression Design/Blend hands-on lab

guides you in learning to use Expression Design to create an XAML icon, and then to integrate it into a Windows Presentation Foundation application. It is available at http://wpf.netfx3.com/files/folders/labs/entry9074.aspx. Even though this document is for WPF, you can use this knowledge for Silverlight applications too.

CAUTION

The integration of Expression Design with Blend is not as good as you might want. In fact, there is no "round-trip" between both applications. You can create a resource in Design, export it to XAML, import it in Blend, and integrate it in your Silverlight application. There is currently no way, however, to "load" an existing XAML resource in Expression Design, modify it, and reload it into Blend.

The current version of Expression Design is slightly different from the older version used in this tutorial, but the actions are similar.

Finding XAML Resources Online

Instead of making the resources yourself, you can also find some that others did for you. Here are a few options:

Silverlight Controls Skins

For Silverlight controls, we already mentioned Corrina Barber's blog and especially her "Controls Skins" posts. Using these skins is easy with the following steps:

1. Create a new Silverlight application and add a button in the Grid LayoutRoot.

2. Navigate to Corrina's blog and find the skin you want to use: http://blogs.msdn.com/corrinab.

3. Download the skin's Zip file (for example, the "bubbly" skin from http://blogs.msdn.com/corrinab/archive/2008/07/20/8757236.aspx).

4. Extract the files from the Zip file to a temporary folder and open the Solution file in Visual Studio.

5. In Page.xaml, copy the three brushes `BaseColorBrush`, `HoverBrush`, and `HyperlinkBrush` from the `UserControl.Resources` to your own page's resources. Alternatively, you can copy these brushes to the file App.xaml and place them in the `Application`'s resources.

6. Copy the `ButtonStyle` style from Corrina's Page.xaml to your own page's (or application's) resources.

7. Finally, set the `vsm` prefix on the UserControl tag (in Page.xaml) or on the Application tag (in App.xaml).

   ```
   xmlns:vsm="clr-namespace:System.Windows;assembly=System.Windows"
   ```

8. Set the Style on your button as in Listing 24.27:

LISTING 24.27   Using the Bubbly Style

```
<Button Width="80" Height="40"
        Content="Click me"
        Style="{StaticResource ButtonStyle}"/>
```

Here, too, it is certain that other designers will publish their own skins on the Web. Stay tuned to Silverlight-related blogs!

XAMLArchive.com

You can find free XAML resources online! One example is the XAML Archive website (http://www.xamlarchive.com). This website is still relatively new but should grow with time and add new XAML or Expression Design resources.

Purchasing XAML Templates

Another approach to this problem is to buy XAML templates. At the time of writing, one website is already active in the field of Windows Presentation Foundation (but not Silverlight yet): http://www.xamltemplates.net.

Keeping an eye on this website is probably a good idea. It's possible to adapt WPF templates to Silverlight without too many headaches. Additionally, it's probable that Silverlight support will be added sooner or later.

Converting Files to XAML

Other UI technologies have been around for a long time, and tons of resources are already available for these older frameworks. If a technology uses resources in vector format (as opposed to raster format like bitmaps), it is often possible to convert the vector-based resources from one format to another.

Adobe Illustrator and Flash

Mike Swanson (a Microsoft employee who published these tools on his free time) created two useful converters for existing Adobe-based designs:

▶ Adobe Illustrator to XAML converter—This Adobe Illustrator plug-in allows exporting an existing Adobe Illustrator design to Silverlight XAML (www.mikeswanson.com/xamlexport).

▶ Adobe Flash to XAML converter—This standalone tool can convert an Adobe Flash SWF file's frame into a corresponding XAML file. As usual, this XAML file can then be imported into Expression Blend and integrated into a Silverlight application (www.mikeswanson.com/swf2xaml).

These two free tools still have limitations and will probably be improved in time, so stay tuned! Mike also has a nice list of XAML-related tools on his blog: http://blogs.msdn.com/mswanson/articles/WPFToolsAndControls.aspx.

Another Impressive Flash Versus Silverlight Resource

Slightly out of the scope of this section, but really worth mentioning, a very impressive resource is found on the Shine Draw website at www.shinedraw.com.

This site compares Flash effects and Silverlight effects, and you can download the effect's implementation. You can visually compare the effect in Flash and in Silverlight and you can even vote on which implementation you find better. It's a very interesting way to help people with good Flash knowledge to transition to Silverlight, and a very good way for beginners in Silverlight to know about the graphical abilities of that technology compared to the well known Flash framework.

Microsoft Visio

Another impressive converter is the Microsoft Visio to XAML converter created by Saveen Reddy and available on CodePlex: ww.codeplex.com/VisioExportToXAML.

Like all projects on CodePlex, this is an open source application, and you can contribute to it if you want. If you find any bugs or have enhancement wishes, don't hesitate to collaborate.

Scalable Vector Graphics SVG

Scalable Vector Graphics SVG is another vector-based technology and is in many ways an ancestor of XAML. It is also XML-based and various web browser plug-ins allow this technology to be integrated into web pages.

There are a couple of SVG to XAML converters, one example being the project initiated by Thierry Bouquain on CodePlex: www.codeplex.com/XamlTune.

Using Third-Party Controls and Libraries

In addition to the external resources we talked about in this section, there are a few providers of third-party controls for Silverlight. It's difficult to mention one at the risk of forgetting another. Probably the most well-known providers of third-party Silverlight controls are

- ▶ Infragistics—www.infragistics.com
- ▶ SoftwareFX—www.softwarefx.com
- ▶ Xceed—http://xceed.com
- ▶ Telerik—www.telerik.com
- ▶ agTweener—An animation library in open source www.codeplex.com/agTweener

As usual in software engineering, the decision to "make or buy" depends on many factors: Time to market, total project cost, the developer's (or designer's) abilities, desire to learn, and so on.

Reading Silverlight-Related Blogs

There are many Silverlight-related blogs online, and a list would probably quickly become obsolete. A great starting point is Dave Campbell's Silverlight Cream. Dave (a fellow Client Application Development expert in the Microsoft Most Valuable Professional program) puts a lot of effort and enthusiasm into this periodic summary of the planet Silverlight (www.silverlightcream.com).

Two must-read blogs are without a doubt those written by Adam Kinney and Tim Heuer. These two Developer Evangelists at Microsoft have rich content and make it a pleasure to learn and improve your Silverlight knowledge.

- http://timheuer.com/blog
- http://adamkinney.com

And of course, if you want to stay tuned with news about this book, download related material or simply contact the author for more information, check http://blog.galasoft.ch

Summary

This chapter wrapped up our journey through Silverlight. I hope that reading this book was fun. I am sure it was also hard sometimes. More than anything else, I wanted to show how interesting and how fun it is to develop Silverlight applications. I hope I brought you, my readers, to a point where you are able to program applications using the industry's best practices, and to continue learning on your own. Even for experienced client application developers, I dare to believe that this book brought a better understanding of what happens "under the cover" and probably taught a few new things (or in any case helped recap and consolidate what you already knew).

Silverlight is evolving fast, and new resources appear every week. Thankfully, you will also find many additional ways to learn and become a better Silverlight developer. It's a never ending journey, and it just started. Honestly, there are some concepts that I only understood after years of programming (and don't repeat this, but there are some concepts that I still didn't completely understand yet). This is an amazing profession/hobby, because it is one where we never stop learning. You can never say that you master software engineering. Learning is as much part of the job as programming (and by the way, every software firm should make continuous education one of its priorities, but it's another story!). Reading this book was a great move, but it's only the beginning of your journey in Silverlight. Check the Internet, read blogs, read more books, and more importantly, develop, develop, develop. And by all means, have fun while you code. Happy coding!

Numerics

A

How can we make this index more useful? Email us at indexes@samspublishing.com

How can we make this index more useful? Email us at indexes@samspublishing.com

M

ToString, 271, 447-448

ValidateUser, 277, 493-495

Methods AddUser listing (14.18), 276

Methods Equals and GetHashCode listing (14.15), 274

Methods GetUser listing (14.20), 278

Methods LoadUsers listing (14.16), 275

Methods SaveUsers listing (14.17), 276

Methods ValidateUser listing (14.19), 277

MFC (Microsoft Foundation Classes), 155

Microsoft Silverlight Streaming servers, publishing on, 250-252

Microsoft Visio, converters, 552

mixing colors, 67-69

Modified method TryFindResource listing (24.25), 547

Modified test div element listing (21.24), 455

Modified TryFindResource method listing (24.19), 545

modifying paths with splines, 93

Modifying the Binding listing (24.7), 535

Modifying the DoWork method listing (24.1), 528

multiple JavaScript event handlers, registering, 440-441

multiple users, handling, 274-277

MultiScaleImage control, deep zooming, 339

multithreading programming, 509

MyDate class, 446

N

namespaces, 23, 176

changing, 430-431

defining, 24-25

UserControl, adding, 397

using directive, 176-177

navigating property paths, 51-52

.NET, 154

code, obfuscation, 530

deprecated functionality, 154

events

catching, 285-287

HTML elements, attaching to, 454-457

JavaScript, handling in, 263-267

HTML pages, accessing, 443-445

JavaScript

calling methods from, 267-269

data exchange, 445-452

interoperability, 261-269, 289

methods, calling from JavaScript, 269

objects, 180

Silverlight applications, registering with, 262-263

System.Windows.Browser namespace, availability, 262

RegisterScriptableObject method, 262-263

ScriptableMember attribute, 261-262

types, 163

converting to other types, 165

floating point types, 164-165

integer types, 163

versions, 154

New button listing (14.5), 264

New event handler handleCounterTicked listing (21.17), 449

New event handler HtmlButton_Click listing (21.27), 456

new keyword (JavaScript), 132

New method ToString listing (21.16), 449

New SizeSlider listing (18.4), 366

New SolidColorBrush listing (24.23), 547

nonsquare shapes, clipping paths, 94-95

notifications, binding errors, 367-368

Notifying the user and getting the stream listing (23.12), 510

null value (JavaScript), 135

O

obfuscation, .NET code, 530

Object class, 292

P-Q

passing
    parameters, 470
    standard data formats, 448-449
Passing initialization parameters in JavaScript listing (21.21), 453
passwords, storing on web clients, 270
Path Markup Syntax, 95
paths
    clipping paths, 94-95
    creating, 92
    in XAML, 95
    modifying with splines, 93
    shapes, combining, 93-94
Paths control, 387
pausing videos, 82-83
Pen tool, 92, 426
Pencil tool, 92
photographs, sending for requests, 513-514
placing POST requests, 516-517
playing videos, 82-83
polymorphism, 32, 166, 180
pop-up controls, 310-311
POST requests, placing, 516-517
predefined color listing, 68
presenting
    data, ItemsControl, 335-337
    media, 324
    text, 317-319
preventing HTML page access, 445
Preview tab UserControl, 399
primitives, 387
priorities, property setters, 349-350
processes, killing, 528-530
profiles (Expression Encoder), 227-228
programming, multithreading programming, 509
progressive downloads, 240
project files, 58
Project panel (Expression Blend), 58-59
projects
    classes, moving, 430
    creating, 56
    web site projects, debugging, 463

properties, 178-179
    Application object, 435
    attached properties, 305-307
    attaching, 26
    CustomTimestamp, 446
    DataContex, setting, 370-371
    DependencyProperties, 393-396
        adding to, 408-410
        LongDescription DP, 409
        MediaInfo DP, 410
        registration, 394
        SelectedItem DependencyProperty, 395-396
        ShortDescription DP, 408
    DescriptionPanelPart, 411-412
    Exception instance, 521
    ItemsSource, adding, 393-396
    OpacityMask, 90, 92
    resetting to default value, 64
    setting in XAML, 30-31
    stretch, 83
    User class, 270
    UserControl, 98-101
    VideoBrush, 84-85
Properties panel (Expression Blend), 60
Property CustomTimestamp listing (21.12), 446
Property in Application object listing (20.10), 435
property paths, navigating, 51-52
property setters, 348-350
protecting source code, 530
prototype property (JavaScript), 132
proxies, client-side, 496
public .NET members, creating scriptable public members, 261-262
Publish Web Site dialog, 457
publishing
    on Microsoft Silverlight Streaming servers, 250-252
    videos on website, 240-241
    websites with Visual Studio, 457-458

How can we make this index more useful? Email us at indexes@samspublishing.com

R

RadialGradientBrush, 63

RadioButton control, 320

raising events, 187

    CounterTicked event, 264-265

    SelectionChanged event, 403-405

raster graphics, 72

re-throwing exceptions, 519-521

Re-throwing an exception listing (23.25), 520

reading

    XML files. LINQ, 473-476

    Zip files, 483-485

Reading the string listing (23.15), 511

Rectangle control, 387

recursion, implementing unit testing, 545-548

redefining equality operators, 272

Redefining the equality operators listing (14.14), 272

refactoring, 432-434

referenced assemblies, 176

References folder, 429

reflection

    adding to videos, 104

    creating under thumbnails, 102-104

registering multiple JavaScript event handlers, 440-441

Registering and unregistering event handler to a Silverlight element listing (21.4), 441

Registering one event handler listing (21.1), 440

Registering two event handlers listing (21.3), 441

Registering two event handlers listing (23.21), 515

RegisterScriptableObject method (.NET), 262-263

registering

    DependencyProperties, 394

    .NET objects with Silverlight applications, 262-263

Release version

    creating, 458-459

    Debugged version, comparing, 458

RenderTransform property, 37-39

RepeatButtons control, 319-320

    disabling, 423

    event handlers, 423

    styling, 427-428

    templates

        binding, 427

        creating, 425-428

    testing, 427

    transitions, changing, 426-427

requests

    cross-domain requests, placing, 499-503

    Flickr

        preparing for, 504-508

        sending to, 504-508

    pictures, sending for, 513-514

    POST requests, placing, 516-517

    security checks, 500

    sending, 471-472

    triggering, 477

    WCF, sending to, 488-497

requirements for Silverlight, 11, 16-17

resetting Blend properties to default value, 64

ResourceDictionaries, 343-344

resources

    App.xaml file, storing in, 347-348

    Blend expression, moving in, 354

    brushes, storing in, 345

    code-behind, using in, 345

    data objects, creating in, 365-366

    Silverlight-related blogs, 553

    storing, 343-344

    Style class, 348

        creating, 348-349

        creating in Expression Blend, 350-351

        editing in Expression Blend, 351-352

        priority system, 349-350

        using, 349

    XAML

        creating and purchasing, 549-552

        defining in, 344

        online resources, 550-551

        using in, 345-347

How can we make this index more useful? Email us at indexes@samspublishing.com